Juvenile Delinquency in
Literature

Thomas West Gregory

University of Richmond

Longman

New York & London

Longman English and Humanities Series
Series Editor: Lee A. Jacobus, University of Connecticut, Storrs

For François Truffaut,
who spent part of his youth
in a reformatory

Juvenile Delinquency in Literature

Longman Inc., New York
Associated companies, branches, and representatives
throughout the world.

Developmental Editor: Gordon T. R. Anderson
Editorial and Design Supervisor: Judith Hirsch
Interior Design: Pencils Portfolio, Inc.
Cover Design: Dan Serrano
Cover Illustration: Pencil drawing by Thomas West Gregory
Manufacturing and Production Supervisor: Robin B. Besofsky
Composition: A&S Graphics, Inc.
Printing and Binding: Fairfield Graphics

Manufactured in the United States of America

9 8 7 6 5 4 3 2 1
Library of Congress Cataloging in Publication Data
Main entry under title:

Juvenile delinquency in literature.

 (Longman English and humanities series)
 Bibliography: p.
  1. Juvenile delinquency—Fiction. 2. Short
stories, American. 3. Short stories, English.
I. Gregory, Thomas West. II. Series.
PZ1.J84 [PS648.J87]   813'.0108   79-26833
ISBN 0-582-28163-6

Acknowledgments

"Concerning Hooligans" by Clarence Rook. From *Working-Class Stories of the 1890's* edited by P. J. Keating. Copyright © 1971 by Routledge & Kegan Paul Ltd. Reprinted by permission of Routledge & Kegan Paul Ltd.

"Hoods I Have Known" by Sondra Spatt Olsen. Copyright © 1956 by Street and Smith. Originally appeared in *Mademoiselle*. Reprinted by permission of Sondra Spatt Olsen.

"Everything Under the Sun" by James Purdy. *Children is All,* Copyright © 1959 by James Purdy. Reprinted by permission of New Directions.

"The Absences" by Zulfikar Ghose. Copyright © 1968 by Zulfikar Ghose. First published by Macmillan & Co. Ltd., London in *Winter's Tales 14* edited by Kevin Crossley-Holland. Reprinted by permission of the author.

"The Little Girl" by Grace Paley. From *Enormous Changes at the Last Minute* by Grace Paley. Copyright © 1974 by Grace Paley. Reprinted with the permission of Farrar, Straus, and Giroux, Inc.

"Bleat Blodgette" by John Phillips. Copyright © 1968 by John Phillips. Originally appeared in *The Paris Review*. Reprinted by permission of John P. Marquand, Jr. a.k.a. John Phillips.

"A South Summer Idyll" by Terry Southern. Published in *Red-Dirt Marijuana and Other Tastes* by Terry Southern published by New American Library. Copyright © 1957 by Terry Southern. Reprinted by permission of Sterling Lord Agency, Inc.

"The Death of Horatio Alger" by LeRoi Jones (Imamu Amiri Baraka). From *Tales* by LeRoi Jones (Imamu Amiri Baraka). Copyright © 1963, 1964, 1965, 1967 by LeRoi Jones. Reprinted by permission of Grove Press, Inc. and Sterling Lord Agency.

"Boys and Girls" by James T. Farrell. Reprinted from *A Dangerous Woman and Other Stories* by James T. Farrell by permission of the publisher, Vanguard Press, Inc. Copyright © 1957 by James T. Farrell.

"The Truck" by Michael Rumaker. Published in *Exit 3 and Other Stories* in 1966 by Penquin Books. Reprinted by permission of Harold Ober Associates Incorporated. Copyright © Michael Rumaker, 1966.

"The Hillies" by John Updike. Copyright © 1969 by John Updike. Reprinted from *Museums and Women and Other Stories* by John Updike, by permission of Alfred A. Knopf, Inc. Originally appeared in *The New Yorker*.

"Red-Dirt Marijuana" by Terry Southern. Published in *Red-Dirt Marijuana and Other Tastes* by Terry Southern in 1967 published by New American Library. Copyright © 1967 by Terry Southern. Reprinted by permission of Sterling Lord Agency, Inc.

"Hector Rodriguez" by Jeremy Larner. From *The Addict in the Street* by Jeremy Larner. Reprinted by permission of Grove Press, Inc. Copyright © 1954 by Grove Press, Inc.

Contents

Introduction

Fiction writers attempt to dramatize life. This is not the intention of behavioral scientists, who report their observations more directly as statistics, definitions, and case studies. Nonetheless, since the turn of the century, writers of fiction have used the discoveries and methods of the behavioral sciences to analyze human actions, and a growing number of sociologists and psychologists have discovered the merits of using literature to help explain their disciplines. This anthology has been designed to illustrate the theories of delinquent behavior set forth in textbooks.

In order to group the stories effectively, I conducted an extensive survey of textbooks on juvenile delinquency and found that their authors used numerous classification systems and typologies to define their subject. The more widely accepted classifications are based on how often delinquent behavior is displayed, with what degree of commitment the delinquent breaks the law, the offender's personal characteristics, and the kind of offense the juvenile commits. Because the classifications rely on similar data, it is hardly surprising that many of them overlap.

Of the different classifications, delinquent behavior is most frequently categorized by kinds of offenses, probably because this category is easily understood by professionals and lay persons. This book uses primarily an offense classification. Part 1, "Causes of Delinquency," considers various conditions that give rise to delinquent behavior. The second part, "Minor Offenses," examines the more common statute offenses, such as truancy, incorrigibility, running away from home, and fistfighting. The next part, "Victimless Offenses," confronts the widespread problems of alcoholism, drug abuse, and sexual misconduct. Part 4, "Property Offenses," includes shoplifting, vandalism, car theft, and robbery—the most-written-about delinquencies; and "Personal Offenses" explores the stark world of rape, assault and degrees of attempted and accomplished homicide. The final part, "Treatment of Offenders," considers several modes of rehabilitation for delinquents and reflects on how infrequently they accomplish their aim.

Generally speaking, juvenile delinquency laws dictate that certain behaviors of children make them responsible to a juvenile court rather than an adult court. Juvenile delinquency is a relatively new legal term that describes a centuries-old phenomenon. In 1945 the federal government, every state government, the District of Columbia, and Puerto Rico defined juvenile delinquency in pertinent laws that resulted in fifty-three definitions. For some time, however, common law and statutory rule have asserted that children under seven years of age, because of their immaturity, are incapable by legal definition of committing a crime and therefore cannot be prosecuted. Children between the ages of seven and fourteen are also presumed to be incapable of a criminal act unless the court can prove in criminal proceedings that these children have the maturity to commit a crime with criminal intent. In most instances, then, antisocial acts committed by youngsters between the ages of seven and eighteen are defined by law as delinquencies to be adjudicated in courts specifically designed for youthful offenders.

The stories of delinquency in this book portray male and female offenders, various ethnic groups, different geographical locations, and diverse social strata. They form a comprehensive, composite portrait of delinquency from the turn of the century to the present, with an emphasis on delinquency since World War II. As a collection, the stories reflect a wide range of writing styles, schools of literature, and methods of characterization. Nevertheless, two basic schools of writing dominate: realism and naturalism. Realistic fiction attempts to accurately render daily living. As the label implies, specific actions, observable causes and effects, the close at hand, and present time are major concerns of realistic writers. They attempt in their imitation of life to model it after the subject as closely as possible. Ethics is a primary concern; a character's conduct is carefully recorded—as in "A Criminal's Christmas," which records in minute detail the youthful offender's theft of six dollars and the agonizing guilt he feels.

Naturalistic fiction emphasizes a mechanistic world of nature and society that victimizes humanity through heredity and environment, both of which control the destiny of humans but are often not understood by them. Strongly evident in naturalist writings are the influences of Darwin, Freud, Marx, Newton, Comte, Taine, and Zola, to name the most important. Naturalists are like realists in their careful observations of people and their surroundings, but naturalists organize their material differently. They structure their observations of life to reveal how the laws of nature and the forces of society determine human actions. For example, "A Bottle of Milk for Mother" is more a dramatization of Bruno Lefty Bicek's destruction by the conditions of his neighborhood than it is a story about the death of a wino. Realists and naturalists find themselves on common ground when their attentions focus on the nature, functions, and effects of the society in which their characters live. A comparison of "A Criminal's Christmas" and "A Bottle of Milk for Mother" demonstrates the basic difference between realistic and naturalistic fiction: the former is a faithful report of the offender's actions, whereas the latter emphasizes the causes of the actions.

Before the turn of the century, with Victorian censorship on the wane, writers began to explore a number of disturbing social issues, and juvenile delinquency was one of them. Explaining and informing these interests were the emerging disciplines of sociology and psychology. In the 1890s slum life became a special interest of fiction writers, who explained it from the rational, more objective viewpoint of the behavioral sciences. The slums of New York, Chicago, San Francisco, London, and other major cities were discovered by ministers, philanthropists, socialists, journalists, educators, and writers, who often moved into slums to help the needy and describe their plight to a more affluent society that might offer some aid. Clarence Rook's "Concerning Hooligans"—written in 1899 and in some respects more a social indictment than a tightly constructed short story—clearly illustrates the sociological interest in delinquency in the East End slum of London. On this side of the Atlantic, Theodore Dreiser, Stephen Crane, and many other writers investigated in unflinching detail slum life and its effects on youngsters.

Though occasional novels and short stories of juvenile delinquency appeared during the first two decades of this century, it was not until the late 1920s and early '30s that a significant number were published, and these were concerned mainly with the sociological and psychological dimensions of delinquent behavior. Writers' sympathies were generally with delinquents, who were usually viewed as victims of society rather than as willful violators of its rules. Incorrigible or pathological delinquents rarely appeared in literature before 1930.

The proletarian literature of the 1930s, written primarily about the industrial and rural working classes, often portrayed those in authority as adversaries of the people they controlled; and writers depicted the conditions and behavior of the proletariat as the result of adverse socioeconomic predicaments imposed by those in power. During the Great Depression, authors considered much, if not most, delinquent behavior as the logical consequence of young people overwhelmed by adverse social conditons.

Soon after World War II, analyses of the mind below the level of consciousness became popular. Sociological conditions believed to cause delinquency were perused with the diligence of a scientist examining a slide under a microscope. Almost all the writing on juvenile delinquency from the Second World War to the present has stressed violence, sex, alcohol, drug abuse, and bizarre patterns of conduct.

During the early 1950s the failure of home life became a concern for writers. Young slum dwellers were typically described as living in squalor without moral instruction, and with parents who seemed little concerned about or callously ignored the behavior of their children. The delinquents' enemies were the police, social workers, and teachers; if they were not actually enemies, certainly they were not to be listened to or emulated. The few adults admired by delinquents were usually successful criminals living in the neighborhood who, by ostentatiously displaying their gaudy clothes and cars, gained the adulation of the young. By the late 1950s writers turned their attentions to the home life of delinquents living in middle- and upper-class sections of cities and suburbs. Authors criticized parents who were preoccupied with making money, social connections, and a good impression on others—and in the process neglected their children or tried to substitute material gifts for parental attention. The delinquencies of affluent youngsters, often caused by boredom or thrill-seeking, were seen to be as destructive as those committed by the less privileged. Writers rejected the belief that financial prosperity would prevent juvenile delinquency, and delinquency was no longer considered the exclusive affliction of the poor.

Rarely were stories written about delinquent girls before the 1950s, and when they were, the behavior was hardly that of chronic delin-quency. Girls' delinquency seemed only to consist of a peccadillo or two. This changed radically in the late 1950s with portrayals of the behavior of girls occasionally surpassing that of boys in its brutality.

By the late 1950s the strong influence of naturalism had waned sig-nificantly, although it was still in evidence; what supplanted naturalism, for the most part, was the strident, often hysterical literature of the "beat generation" with its existential philosophy of pessimism, nihilism, and re-bellion. In opposition to the naturalists, existentialists held that people were not victimized by the laws of nature and society but were free and responsible for their actions. Yet, ironically, this freedom and responsibil-ity—with the difficult decisions they required of people—caused a great deal of anguish and dread. As a consequence, much of the delinquency of the early 1960s was a frenetic delinquency of despair and sensual escape. From that time to the present, the existential view of humanity has changed to include much of what is absurd, grotesque, and macabre.

PART 1 _____

_____ Causes of Delinquency

What causes juvenile delinquency? A large body of writing by both behavioral scientists and creative writers focuses on this question. Though numerous theories have been proposed, to date, no single theory explains the causes of delinquent behavior to everyone's satisfaction. Nevertheless, experts agree that a complex interrelationship of many factors gives rise to this antisocial behavior.

Generally speaking, causal theories are grouped as physiological, psychological, or sociological. Physiological theories may seem naive or occasionally ludicrous, but they deserve consideration because many people still believe them. At one time it was widely supposed that patterns of behavior were directly related to physical characteristics and body types; thus, if we could learn how these physical traits influenced behavior, we could predict how individuals would act. Today, the educated are unwilling to believe that guilt or innocence can be established by studying physical build or the way people's skulls are formed. And such things as a malfunctioning endocrine system, epilepsy, inherited traits from a "bad family," feeblemindedness, chromosomal abnormalities, and the like are also discredited as single causes for delinquent behavior—though they may be contributing factors.

With the development of psychology and sociology, personality disorders and unfavorable environmental conditions have been advanced as primary causes of juvenile delinquency. Youngsters are likely to engage in aberrant behavior if they have lost faith in themselves, if their achievements go unrecognized, or if they have no positive sense of identity. A healthy, supportive family environment is a good defense against delinquency because it is within the home that

1

many destructive instincts are conditioned into socially acceptable conduct. Economic determinism, which dictates an unequal distribution and consumption of goods, has often been cited as a cause of delinquency because it creates economic systems in which many people are poor. Those in need are inclined to use any means to fulfill their wants and needs, even if it involves breaking the law. Adolescents who are, for one reason or another, outcasts from middle-class society, school organizations, or athletic teams frequently band together to form their own subcultures, which have specified entrance requirements, codes of ethics, hierarchies of goals, and meaningful totems. One of the best examples of a unified subculture is the gang, which often compensates for low self-esteem by striking back at society with malicious, destructive behavior.

In addition to family, community, and church, the school plays an important role in socializing children. Most contemporary schools are purveyors of middle-class values, and the majority of those who teach in them come from middle-class backgrounds. Students who have the support of their families and community, who have been reared in the language and culture of middle-class society, who have healthy minds in healthy bodies—in short, students who fit within the modern school system—are likely to do well and profit from their schooling. Those who are not so lucky—who are intellectually, socially, emotionally, or economically deprived—have a difficult time meeting the expectations of the middle-class culture of their schools, even though bilingual-bicultural programs, vocational-technical training, special counseling services, and job-placement assistance have been designed for them in many schools.

Without exception, every story in this book could have been included in this part, for each in its distinctive way explores elements that cause delinquent behavior. The four stories that are included here give as broad a chronological, sociological, and geographical overview of delinquency as possible. They cover the period from the turn of the century to the present, and societies ranging from the slums of London to the middle-class neighborhoods of Pittsburgh and Brooklyn. "Concerning Hooligans" is the lead story for a number of reasons: it is the earliest written of the collection and vividly describes lower-class London in 1899 and how it molds the character of young Alf. Much of the story explores the strong influence of worldly Patrick Hooligan on the lives of his young protégés, and this theme of an older criminal shaping the lives of young admirers is significant in many stories of delinquency. His "exuberance of lawlessness," his "skill and strength," and his being "a leader among men" are Hooligan's qualities that draw the admiration if not the adulation of juveniles in his neighborhood. As a teacher he excels in training his disciples not only in the particulars of lying, stealing, conning, and passing counterfeit currency but also in his predatory philosophy of life—which sustains his pupils in their precarious, lower-class environment. Young Alf's neighborhood, Lambeth Walk, is in many respects—especially in its lack of opportunity for the young—similar to the Polish section in "A Bottle of Milk for Mother." Slum life, no matter where or when it exists, seems much the same; perhaps the outcome of deprivations in slum stories is best summed up in the observation that the youngsters "start with a grievance against society, and are determined to get their own back." And most stories of slum life examine in detail just how delinquents go about getting what they think is justly owed them. The subculture dialect of Lambeth Walk, in addition to supplying local color to the story, is important in the way it labels—in fact, brands—the narrator as the product of a disreputable society.

Delinquency is not restricted to slums, as some believe. In "Paul's Case," Paul lives in a middle-class neighborhood of law-abiding citizens who appear relatively content. His home affords him the creature comforts he can reasonably expect—though they are not the luxuries his agitated imagination desires—and he works as an usher at Carnegie Hall only because his father thinks "a boy ought to be earning a little." The culture of Paul's neighborhood emphasizes a philosophy of no-nonsense and hard work, saving money, deferring some of today's pleasures for future gains, grades in school, and admiration for those who have the energy and talent to be upwardly mobile, perhaps even into the society of "iron kings" and "magnates" of large steel corporations. Though Paul is not in want, his surroundings seem exceedingly common to him. His dissatisfaction is rooted in his disturbed psychological condition. The "hysterical brilliance" and the abnormally large pupils of his eyes, "as though he were addicted to belladonna," are outward symptoms of Paul's emotional distress. Though his teachers hold him in low regard, they have trouble articulating what has led to his suspension. As his drawing master sees it: " 'There is something wrong about the fellow.' "

"Hoods I Have Known" is one of the few humorous stories written about delinquency. Though it is lightheartedly told, the story is an indictment of schools that segregate pupils by social class in the classroom. The seventh-grade class of P.S. 333 in Brooklyn is divided into two worlds: the front half consists of those students who read books, answer questions eagerly, and agree "with the teacher on all points"; the back half is there "only by the grace of the truant officer" and is populated by boys with "aggressive-looking sideburns and great masses of curly black or blond hair." The activities of the latter group include slouching, muttering, destroying books, and occasional fighting, all of which are met with the teacher's "silent or you-don't-exist treatment" because she is unprepared or unwilling to deal with the situation. The low social status of the back of the room is defined by its distance from the teacher, by the way she ignores it, and by her belief that "the worst punishment anyone can inflict on a clean, well-brought-up little girl" is to consign her to the back of the class with the hoods.

Many stories of delinquency examine the effects on youngsters of homes broken by divorce or death. Too often, children are not given the attention they need when they live with a single parent. Some children are taken in by relatives or adopted by strangers who attempt to be surrogate parents but do not succeed. Some are left to shift for themselves, as is the case in "Everything Under the Sun." Though Cade is fifteen and living with Jesse, who is five years older, the relationship is a far cry from the kind Cade would have if his parents were alive; in fact, in the power struggle that develops between Jesse and Cade, it is Cade's precocious desire to smoke, drink, loaf, and chase women that prevails over Jesse's more mature judgment. This story, like a number of its kind, illustrates how young people without families enter into relationships intended in some way to be substitutes for the families they have lost.

CONCERNING HOOLIGANS

Clarence Rook

There was, but a few years ago, a man called Patrick Hooligan, who walked to and fro among his fellow-men, robbing them and occasionally bashing them. This much is certain. His existence in the flesh is a fact as well established as the existence of Buddha or of Mahomet. But with the life of Patrick Hooligan, as with the lives of Buddha and of Mahomet, legend has been at work, and probably many of the exploits associated with his name spring from the imagination of disciples. It is at least certain that he was born, that he lived in Irish Court, that he was employed as a chucker-out at various resorts in the neighborhood. His regular business, as young Alf puts it, was "giving mugs and other barmy sots the push out of pubs when their old swank got a bit too thick." Moreover, he could do more than his share of tea-leafing, which denotes the picking up of unconsidered trifles, being handy with his fingers, and a good man all round. Finally, one day he had a difference with a constable, put his light out, and threw the body into a dust-cart. He was lagged, and given a lifer. But he had not been in gaol long before he had to go into hospital, where he died.

There is little that is remarkable in this career. But the man must have had a forceful personality, a picturesqueness, a fascination, which elevated him into a type. It was doubtless the combination of skill and strength, a certain exuberance of lawlessness, an utter absence of scruple in his dealings, which marked him out as a leader among men. Anyhow, though his individuality may be obscured by legend, he lived, and died, and left a great tradition behind him. He established a cult.

The value of a cult is best estimated by its effect upon its adherents, and as Patrick Hooligan is beyond the reach of cross-examination, I propose to devote a few words to showing what manner of men his followers are, the men who call themselves by his name, and do their best to pass the torch of his tradition undimmed to the nippers who are coming on.

I should perhaps not speak of them as men, for the typical Hooligan is a boy who, growing up in the area bounded by the Albert Embankment, the Lambeth Road, the Kennington Road, and the streets about the Oval, takes to tea-leafing as a Grimsby lad takes to the sea. If his taste runs to street-fighting there is hope for him, and for the community. He will probably enlist, and, having helped to push the merits of gin and Christianity in the dark places of the earth, die in the skin of a hero. You may see in Lambeth Walk a good many soldiers who have come back from looking over the edge of the world to see the place they were born

in, to smell the fried fish and the second-hand shoe-leather, and to pul-
sate once more to the throb of a piano-organ. On the other hand, if his
fingers be lithe and sensitive, if he have a turn for mechanics, he will slip
naturally into the picking of pockets and the rifling of other people's
houses.

The home of the Hooligan is, as I have implied, within a stone's-throw
of Lambeth Walk. Law breakers exist in other quarters of London: Drury
Lane will furnish forth a small army of pickpockets, Soho breeds para-
sites, and the basher of toffs flourishes in the Kingsland Road. But in and
about Lambeth Walk we have a colony, compact and easily handled, of
sturdy young villains, who start with a grievance against society, and are
determined to get their own back. That is their own phrase, their own
view. Life has little to give them but what they take. Honest work, if it can
be obtained, will bring in but a few shillings a week; and what is that
compared to the glorious possibility of nicking a red 'un?

Small and compact, the colony is easily organized; and here, as in all
turbulent communities, such as an English public school, the leader gains
his place by sheer force of personality. The boy who has kicked in a door
can crow over the boy who has merely smashed a window. If you have
knocked out your adversary at the little boxing place off the Walk, you
will have proved that your friendship is desirable. If it becomes known—
and it speedily becomes known to all but the police—that you have
drugged a toff and run through his pockets, or, better still, have cracked a
crib on your own and planted the stuff, then you are at once surrounded
by sycophants. Your position is assured, and you have but to pick and
choose those that shall work with you. Your leadership will be recognized, and every morning boys, with both eyes skinned for strolling splits,
will seek you out and ask for orders for the day. In time, if you stick to
work and escape the cops, you may become possessed of a coffee-house
or a sweetstuff shop, and run a profitable business as a fence. Moreover,
your juniors knowing your past experience, will purchase your advice—
paying for counsel's opinion—when they seek an entrance to a desirable
house in the suburbs, and cannot decide between the fan-light and the
kitchen window. So you shall live and die respected by all men in Lambeth Walk.

— The average Hooligan is not an ignorant, hulking ruffian, beetle-
browed and bullet-headed. He is a product of the Board School, writes a
fair hand, and is quick at arithmetic. His type of face approaches nearer
the rat than the bull-dog; he is nervous, highly strung, almost neurotic.
He is by no means a drunkard; but a very small quantity of liquor causes
him to run amuck, when he is not pleasant to meet. Undersized as a rule,
he is sinewy, swift and untiring. For pocket-picking and burglary the
featherweight is at an advantage. He has usually done a bit of fighting

with the gloves, for in Lambeth boxing is one of the most popular forms of sport. But he is better with the raws, and is very bad to tackle in a street row, where there are no rules to observe. Then he will show you some tricks that will astonish you. No scruples of conscience will make him hesitate to butt you in the stomach with his head, and pitch you backwards by catching you round the calves with his arm. His skill, born of constant practice, in scrapping and hurricane fighting, brings him an occasional job in the bashing line. You have an enemy, we will say, whom you wish to mark, but, for one reason or another, you do not wish to appear in the matter. Young Alf will take on the job. Indicate to him your enemy; hand him five shillings (he will ask a sovereign, but will take five shillings), and he will make all the necessary arrangements. One night your enemy will find himself lying dazed on the pavement in a quiet corner, with a confused remembrance of a trip and a crash, and a mad whirl of fists and boots. You need have small fear that the job will be bungled. But it is a matter of complaint among the boys of the Walk, that if they do a bit of bashing for a toff and get caught, the toff seldom has the magnanimity to give them a lift when they come out of gaol.

The Hooligan is by no means deficient in courage. He is always ready to fight, though he does not fight fair. It must, indeed, require a certain amount of courage to earn your living by taking thngs that do not belong to you, with the whole of society, backed by the police force, against you. The burglar who breaks into your house and steals your goods is a rep-rehensible person; but he undoubtedly possesses that two-o'clock-in-the-morning courage which is the rarest variety. To get into a stranger's house in the dead of night, listening every instant for the least sound that denotes detection, knowing all the time that you are risking your liberty for the next five years or so—this, I am sure, requires more nerve than most men can boast of. Young Alf has nearly all the vices; but he has plenty of pluck. And as I shall have very little to disclose that is to his credit, I must tell of one instance in which his conduct was admirable. One afternoon we were at the Elephant and Castle, when suddenly a pair of runaway horses, with a Pickford van behind them, came pound-ing into the traffic at the crossing. There was shouting, screaming and a scurrying to clear the way, and then I saw young Alf standing alone, tense and waiting, in the middle of the road. It was a perilous thing to do, but he did it. He was used to horses, and though they dragged him for twenty yards and more, he hung on, and brought them up. A sympa-thetic and admiring crowd gathered, and young Alf was not a little em-barrassed at the attention he commanded.

"The firm oughter reckernize it," said a man in an apron, looking round for approval. "There's a matter of two 'underd pound's worth of prop'ty that boy's reskid."

We murmured assent.

"I don't want no fuss," said young Alf, glancing quickly around him.

Just then a man ran up, panting, and put his hand over the harness. Then he picked up the reins, and, hoisting himself by the step, peered into his van.

"You're in luck today, mister," said a boy.

The man passed the back of his hand across a damp forehead, and sent a dazed look through the crowd.

"One of them blarsted whistles started 'em," he said.

"That's the boy what stopped 'em," said a woman with a basket pointing a finger at young Alf.

"That's awright," muttered young Alf. "You shut yer face."

"Give the gentleman your name," persisted the woman with the basket, "and if everybody 'ad their rights—"

"Now then," said a friendly policeman, with a hand on young Alf's shoulder, "you give him your name and address. You want a job, you know. You bin out of work too long."

Young Alf's brain must have worked very quickly for the next three seconds, and he took the right course. He told the truth. It required an effort. But, as the policeman seemed to know the truth, it would have been silly to tell a lie.

The next day young Alf had the offer of employment, if he would call at headquarters. For a day or two he hesitated. Then he decided that it was not good enough. And that night he went to another kip. By this time he might have been driving a Pickford van. But he never applied for the job.

Regular employment, at a fixed wage, does not attract the boy who is bred within sound of the hawkers in the Walk. It does not give him the necessary margin of leisure, and the necessary margin of chance gains. Many of them hang on to the edge of legitimate commerce as you may see them adhering to the tail-boards of vans; and a van-boy has many opportunities of seeing the world. The selling of newspapers is a favourite occupation. Every Lambeth boy can produce a profession in answer to magisterial interrogation. If you ask young Alf—very suddenly—what his business is, he will reply that he is a horse-plaiter. With time for reflection he may give quite a different answer, according to the circumstances of the case, for he has done many things; watch-making, domestic service, and the care of horses in a travelling circus have stored his mind with experience and given his fingers deftness.

Young Alf is now eighteen years of age, and stands 5 feet 7 inches. He is light, active and muscular. Stripped for fighting he is a picture. His ordinary attire consists of a dark-brown suit, mellowed by wear, and a cloth cap. Around his neck is a neatly knotted neckerchief, dark blue, with white spots, which does duty for collar as well as tie. His face is by no means brutal; it is intelligent, and gives evidence of a highly strung nature. The eyes are his most remarkable feature. They seem to look all round his head, like the eyes of a bird; when he is angry they gleam with a fury that is almost demoniacal. He is not prone to smiles or laughter, but he is in no sense melancholic. The solemnity of his face is due rather, as I should conclude, to the concentration of his intellect on the practical problems that continually present themselves for solution. Under the influence of any strong emotion, he puffs out the lower part of his cheeks. This expresses even amusement, if he is very much amused. In his manner of speech he exhibits curious variations. Sometimes he will talk for ten minutes together, with no more trace of accent or slang than disfigure the speech of the ordinary Londoner of the wage-earning class. Then, on a sudden, he will become almost unintelligible to one unfamiliar with the Walk and its ways. He swears infrequently, and drinks scarcely at all. When he does, he lights a fire in the middle of the floor and tries to burn the house down. His health is perfect, and he has never had a day's illness since he had the measles. He has perfect confidence in his own ability to look after himself, and take what he wants, so long as he has elbow-room and ten seconds' start of the cop. His fleetness of foot has earned him the nickname of "The Deer" in the Walk. On the whole, few boys are better equipped by nature for a life on the crooked, and young Alf has sedulously cultivated his natural gifts.

PAUL'S CASE
A STUDY IN TEMPERAMENT
Willa Cather

It was Paul's afternoon to appear before the faculty of the Pittsburgh High School to account for his various misdemeanours. He had been suspended a week ago, and his father had called at the Principal's office and confessed his perplexity about his son. Paul entered the faculty room suave and smiling. His clothes were a trifle outgrown and the tan velvet on the collar of his open overcoat was frayed and worn; but for all that there was something of the dandy about him, and he wore an opal pin in his neatly knotted black four-in-hand, and a red carnation in his buttonhole. This latter adornment the faculty somehow felt was not properly significant of the contrite spirit befitting a boy under the ban of suspension.

Paul was tall for his age and very thin, with high, cramped shoulders and a narrow chest. His eyes were remarkable for a certain hysterical brilliancy and he continually used them in a conscious, theatrical sort of way, peculiarly offensive in a boy. The pupils were abnormally large, as though he were addicted to belladonna, but there was a glassy glitter about them which that drug does not produce.

When questioned by the Principal as to why he was there, Paul stated, politely enough, that he wanted to come back to school. This was a lie, but Paul was quite accustomed to lying; found it, indeed, indispensable for overcoming friction. His teachers were asked to state their respective charges against him, which they did with such a rancour and aggrievedness as evinced that this was not a usual case. Disorder and impertinence were among the offences named, yet each of his instructors felt that it was scarcely possible to put into words the real cause of the trouble, which lay in a sort of hysterically defiant manner of the boy's; in the contempt which they all knew he felt for them, and which he seemingly made not the least effort to conceal. Once, when he had been making a synopsis of a paragraph at the blackboard, his English teacher had stepped to his side and attempted to guide his hand. Paul had started back with a shudder and thrust his hands violently behind him. The astonished woman could scarcely have been more hurt and embarrassed had he struck at her. The insult was so involuntary and definitely personal as to be unforgettable. In one way and another, he had made all his teachers, men and women alike, conscious of the same feeling of physical aversion. In one class he habitually sat with his hand shading his eyes; in another he always looked out of the window during the recitation; in another he made a running commentary on the lecture, with humorous intention.

His teachers felt this afternoon that his whole attitude was symbolized by his shrug and his flippantly red carnation flower, and they fell upon him without mercy, his English teacher leading the pack. He stood through it smiling, his pale lips parted over his white teeth. (His lips were continually twitching, and he had a habit of raising his eyebrows that was contemptuous and irritating to the last degree.) Older boys than Paul had broken down and shed tears under the baptism of fire, but his set smile did not once desert him, and his only sign of discomfort was the nervous trembling of the fingers that toyed with the buttons of his overcoat, and an occasional jerking of the other hand that held his hat. Paul was always smiling, always glancing about him, seeming to feel that people might be watching him and trying to detect something. This conscious expression, since it was as far as possible from boyish mirthfulness, was usually attributed to insolence or "smartness."

As the inquisition proceeded, one of his instructors repeated an impertinent remark of the boy's, and the Principal asked him whether he thought that a courteous speech to have made a woman. Paul shrugged his shoulders slightly and his eyebrows twitched.

"I don't know," he replied. "I didn't mean to be polite or impolite, either. I guess it's a sort of way I have of saying things regardless."

The Principal, who was a sympathetic man, asked him whether he didn't think that a way it would be well to get rid of. Paul grinned and said he guessed so. When he was told that he could go, he bowed gracefully and went out. His bow was but a repetition of the scandalous red carnation.

His teachers were in despair, and his drawing master voiced the feeling of them all when he declared there was something about the boy which none of them understood. He added: "I don't really believe that smile of his comes altogether from insolence; there's something sort of haunted about it. The boy is not strong, for one thing. I happen to know that he was born in Colorado, only a few months before his mother died out there of a long illness. There is something wrong about the fellow."

The drawing master had come to realize that, in looking at Paul, one saw only his white teeth and the forced animation of his eyes. One warm afternoon the boy had gone to sleep at his drawing-board, and his master had noted with amazement what a white, blue-veined face it was; drawn and wrinkled like an old man's about the eyes, the lips twitching even in his sleep, and stiff with a nervous tension that drew them back from his teeth.

His teachers left the building dissatisfied and unhappy; humiliated to have felt so vindictive toward a mere boy, to have uttered this feeling in

cutting terms, and to have set each other on, as it were, in the grewsome
game of intemperate reproach. Some of them remembered having seen
a miserable street cat set at bay by a ring of tormentors.

As for Paul, he ran down the hill whistling the Soldiers' Chorus from
Faust looking wildly behind him now and then to see whether some of
his teachers were not there to writhe under his light-heartedness. As it
was now late in the afternoon and Paul was on duty that evening as
usher at Carnegie Hall, he decided that he would not go home to supper.
When he reached the concert hall the doors were not yet open and, as it
was chilly outside, he decided to go up into the picture gallery—always
deserted at this hour—where there were some of Raffelli's gay studies of
Paris streets and an airy blue Venetian scene or two that always exhilarated him. He was delighted to find no one in the gallery but the old
guard, who sat in one corner, a newspaper on his knee, a black patch
over one eye and the other closed. Paul possessed himself of the place
and walked confidently up and down, whistling under his breath. After a
while he sat down before a blue Rico and lost himself. When he
bethought him to look at his watch, it was after seven o'clock, and he
rose with a start and ran downstairs, making a face at Augustus, peering
out from the cast-room, and an evil gesture at the Venus of Milo as he
passed her on the stairway.

When Paul reached the ushers' dressing-room half-a-dozen boys were
there already, and he began excitedly to tumble into his uniform. It was
one of the few that at all approached fitting, and Paul thought it very
becoming—though he knew that the tight, straight coat accentuated his
narrow chest, about which he was exceedingly sensitive. He was always
considerably excited while he dressed, twanging all over to the tuning of
the strings and the preliminary flourishes of the horns in the music-room;
but to-night he seemed quite beside himself, and he teased and plagued
the boys until, telling him that he was crazy, they put him down on the
floor and sat on him.

Somewhat calmed by his suppression, Paul dashed out to the front of
the house to seat the early comers. He was a model usher; gracious and
smiling he ran up and down the aisles; nothing was too much trouble for
him; he carried messages and brought programmes as though it were his
greatest pleasure in life, and all the people in his section thought him a
charming boy, feeling that he remembered and admired them. As the
house filled, he grew more and more vivacious and animated, and the
colour came to his cheeks and lips. It was very much as though this were
a great reception and Paul were the host. Just as the musicians came out
to take their places, his English teacher arrived with checks for the seats
which a prominent manufacturer had taken for the season. She betrayed
some embarrassment when she handed Paul the tickets, and a *hauteur*

which subsequently made her feel very foolish. Paul was startled for a moment, and had the feeling of wanting to put her out; what business had she here among all these fine people and gay colours? He looked her over and decided that she was not appropriately dressed and must be a fool to sit downstairs in such togs. The tickets had probably been sent her out of kindness, he reflected as he put down a seat for her, and she had about as much right to sit there as he had.

When the symphony began Paul sank into one of the rear seats with a long sigh of relief, and lost himself as he had done before the Rico. It was not that symphonies, as such, meant anything in particular to Paul, but the first sigh of the instruments seemed to free some hilarious and potent spirit within him; something that struggled there like the Genius in the bottle found by the Arab fisherman. He felt a sudden zest of life; the lights danced before his eyes and the concert hall blazed into unimaginable splendour. When the soprano soloist came on, Paul forgot even the nastiness of his teacher's being there and gave himself up to the peculiar stimulus such personages always had for him. The soloist chanced to be a German woman, by no means in her first youth, and the mother of many children; but she wore an elaborate gown and a tiara, and above all she had that indefinable air of achievement, that world-shine upon her, which, in Paul's eyes, made her a veritable queen of Romance.

After a concert was over Paul was always irritable and wretched until he got to sleep, and to-night he was even more than usually restless. He had the feeling of not being able to let down, of its being impossible to give up this delicious excitement which was the only thing that could be called living at all. During the last number he withdrew and, after hastily changing his clothes in the dressing-room, slipped out to the side door where the soprano's carriage stood. Here he began pacing rapidly up and down the walk, waiting to see her come out.

Over yonder the Schenley, in its vacant stretch, loomed big and square through the fine rain, the windows of its twelve stories glowing like those of a lighted card-board house under a Christmas tree. All the actors and singers of the better class stayed there when they were in the city, and a number of the big manufacturers of the place lived there in the winter. Paul had often hung about the hotel, watching the people go in and out, longing to enter and leave school-masters and dull care behind him forever.

At last the singer came out, accompanied by the conductor, who helped her into her carriage and closed the door with a cordial *auf wiederschen* which set Paul to wondering whether she were not an old sweetheart of his. Paul followed the carriage over to the hotel, walking so rapidly as not to be far from the entrance when the singer alighted and disappeared behind the swinging glass doors that were opened by a negro in a tall hat and a long coat. In the moment that the door was ajar it seemed to Paul that he, too, entered. He seemed to feel himself go after her up the steps, into the warm, lighted building, into an exotic, a tropical world of shiny, glistening surfaces and basking ease. He reflected upon the mysterious dishes that were brought into the dining-room, the green bottles in buckets of ice, as he had seen them in the supper party pictures of the *Sunday World* supplement. A quick gust of wind brought the rain down with sudden vehemence, and Paul was startled to find that he was still outside in the slush of the gravel driveway; that his boots were letting in the water and his scanty overcoat was clinging wet about him; that the lights in front of the concert hall were out, and that the rain was driving in sheets between him and the orange glow of the windows above him. There it was, what he wanted—tangibly before him, like the fairy world of a Christmas pantomime, but mocking spirits stood guard at the doors, and, as the rain beat in his face, Paul wondered whether he were destined always to shiver in the black night outside, looking up at it.

He turned and walked reluctantly toward the car tracks. The end had to come sometime; his father in his night-clothes at the top of the stairs, explanations that did not explain, hastily improvised fictions that were forever tripping him up, his upstairs room and its horrible yellow wallpaper, the creaking bureau with the greasy plush collar-box, and over his painted wooden bed the pictures of George Washington and John Calvin, and the framed motto, "Feed my Lambs," which had been worked in red worsted by his mother.

Half an hour later, Paul alighted from his car and went slowly down one of the side streets off the main thoroughfare. It was a highly respectable street, where all the houses were exactly alike, and where business men of moderate means begot and reared large families of children, all of whom went to Sabbath-school and learned the shorter catechism, and were interested in arithmetic; all of whom were as exactly alike as their homes, and of a piece with the monotony in which they lived. Paul never went up Cordelia Street without a shudder of loathing. His home was next to the house of the Cumberland minister. He approached it to-night with the nerveless sense of defeat, the hopeless feeling of sinking back forever into ugliness and commonness that he had always had when he came home. The moment he turned into Cordelia Street he felt the waters close above his head. After each of these orgies of living, he experienced all the physical depression which follows a debauch; the loathing of respectable beds, of common food, of a house penetrated by kitchen odours; a shuddering repulsion for the flavourless, colourless mass of every-day existence; a morbid desire for cool things and soft lights and fresh flowers.

The nearer he approached the house, the more absolutely unequal Paul felt to the sight of it all; his ugly sleeping chamber; the cold bathroom with the grimy zinc tub, the cracked mirror, the dripping spiggots; his father, at the top of the stairs, his hairy legs sticking out from his night-shirt, his feet thrust into carpet slippers. He was so much later than usual that there would certainly be inquiries and reproaches. Paul stopped short before the door. He felt that he could not be accosted by his father to-night; that he could not toss again on that miserable bed. He would not go in. He would tell his father that he had no car fare, and it was raining so hard he had gone home with one of the boys and stayed all night.

Meanwhile, he was wet and cold. He went around to the back of the house and tried one of the basement windows, found it open, raised it cautiously, and scrambled down the cellar wall to the floor. There he stood, holding his breath, terrified by the noise he had made, but the floor above him was silent, and there was no creak on the stairs. He found a soap-box, and carried it over to the soft ring of light that streamed from the furnace door, and sat down. He was horribly afraid of rats, so he did not try to sleep, but sat looking distrustfully at the dark, still terrified lest he might have awakened his father. In such reactions, after one of the experiences which made days and nights out of the dreary blanks of the calendar, when his senses were deadened, Paul's head was always singularly clear. Suppose his father had heard him getting in at the window and had come down and shot him for a burglar? Then, again, suppose his father had come down, pistol in hand, and he had cried out in time to save himself, and his father had been horrified to think how nearly he had killed him? Then, again, suppose a day should come when his father would remember that night, and wish there had been no warning cry to stay his hand? With this last supposition Paul entertained himself until daybreak.

The following Sunday was fine; the sodden November chill was broken by the last flash of autumnal summer. In the morning Paul had to go to church and Sabbath school, as always. On seasonable Sunday afternoons the burghers of Cordelia Street always sat out on their front "stoops," and talked to their neighbours on the next stoop, or called to those across the street in neighbourly fashion. The men usually sat on gay cushions placed upon the steps that led down to the sidewalk, while the women, in their Sunday "waists," sat in rockers on the cramped porches, pretending to be greatly at their ease. The children played in the streets; there were so many of them that the place resembled the recreation grounds of a kindergarten. The men on the steps—all in their shirt sleeves, their vests unbuttoned—sat with their legs well apart, their stomachs comfortably protruding, and talked of the prices of things, or told anecdotes of the sagacity of their various chiefs and overlords. They occasionally looked over the multitude of squabbling children, listened affectionately to their high-pitched, nasal voices, smiling to see their own proclivities reproduced in their offspring, and interspersed their legends of the iron kings with remarks about their sons' progress at school, their grades in arithmetic, and the amounts they had saved in their toy banks.

On this last Sunday of November, Paul sat all the afternoon on the lowest step of his "stoop," staring into the street, while his sisters, in their rockers, were talking to the minister's daughters next door about how many shirt-waists they had made in the last week, and how many waffles some one had eaten at the last church supper. When the weather was warm, and his father was in a particularly jovial frame of mind, the girls made lemonade, which was always brought out in a red-glass pitcher, ornamented with forget-me-nots in blue enamel. This the girls thought very fine, and the neighbours always joked about the suspicious colour of the pitcher.

To-day Paul's father sat on the top step, talking to a young man who shifted a restless baby from knee to knee. He happened to be the young man who was daily held up to Paul as a model, and after whom it was his father's dearest hope that he would pattern. This young man was of a ruddy complexion, with a compressed, red mouth, and faded, near-sighted eyes, over which he wore thick spectacles, with gold bows that curved about his ears. He was clerk to one of the magnates of a great steel corporation, and was looked upon in Cordelia Street as a young man with a future. There was a story that, some five years ago—he was now barely twenty-six—he had been a trifle dissipated but in order to curb his appetites and save the loss of time and strength that a sowing of wild oats might have entailed, he had taken his chief's advice, oft reiterated to his employees, and at twenty-one had married the first woman whom he could persuade to share his fortunes. She happened to be an angular school-mistress, much older than he, who also wore thick glasses, and who had now borne him four children, all near-sighted, like herself.

The young man was relating how his chief, now cruising in the Mediterranean, kept in touch with all the details of the business, arranging his office hours on his yacht just as though he were at home, and "knocking off work enough to keep two stenographers busy." His father told, in turn, the plan his corporation was considering, of putting in an electric railway plant at Cairo. Paul snapped his teeth; he had an awful apprehension that they might spoil it all before he got there. Yet he rather liked to hear these legends of the iron kings, that were told and retold on Sundays and holidays; these stories of palaces in Venice, yachts on the Mediterranean, and high play at Monte Carlo appealed to his fancy, and he was interested in the triumphs of these cash boys who had become famous, though he had no mind for the cash-boy stage.

After supper was over, and he had helped to dry the dishes, Paul nervously asked his father whether he could go to George's to get some help in his geometry, and still more nervously asked for car fare. This latter request he had to repeat, as his father, on principle, did not like to hear requests for money, whether much or little. He asked Paul whether he could not go to some boy who lived nearer, and told him that he ought not to leave his school work until Sunday; but he gave him the dime. He was not a poor man, but he had a worthy ambition to come up in the world. His only reason for allowing Paul to usher was, that he thought a boy ought to be earning a little.

Paul bounded upstairs, scrubbed the greasy odour of the dish-water from his hands with the ill-smelling soap he hated, and then shook over his fingers a few drops of violet water from the bottle he kept hidden in his drawer. He left the house with his geometry conspicuously under his arm, and the moment he got out of Cordelia Street and boarded a downtown car, he shook off the lethargy of two deadening days, and began to live again.

The leading juvenile of the permanent stock company which played at one of the downtown theatres was an acquaintance of Paul's, and the boy had been invited to drop in at the Sunday-night rehearsals whenever he could. For more than a year Paul had spent every available moment loitering about Charley Edwards's dressing-room. He had won a place among Edwards's following not only because the young actor, who could not afford to employ a dresser, often found him useful, but because he recognized in Paul something akin to what churchmen term "vocation."

It was at the theatre and at Carnegie Hall that Paul really lived; the rest was but a sleep and a forgetting. This was Paul's fairy tale, and it had for him all the allurement of a secret love. The moment he inhaled the gassy, painty, dusty odour behind the scenes, he breathed like a prisoner set free, and felt within him the possibility of doing or saying splendid, brilliant, poetic things. The moment the cracked orchestra beat out the overture from *Martha*, or jerked at the serenade from *Rigoletto*, all stupid and ugly things slid from him, and his senses were deliciously, yet delicately fired.

Perhaps it was because, in Paul's world, the natural nearly always wore the guise of ugliness, that a certain element of artificiality seemed to him necessary in beauty. Perhaps it was because his experience of life elsewhere was so full of Sabbath-school picnics, petty economics, wholesome advice as to how to succeed in life, and the unescapable odours of cooking, that he found this existence so alluring, these smartly-clad men and women so attractive, that he was so moved by these starry apple orchards that bloomed perennially under the lime-light.

It would be difficult to put it strongly enough how convincingly the stage entrance of that theatre was for Paul the actual portal of Romance. Certainly none of the company ever suspected it, least of all Charley Edwards. It was very like the old stories that used to float about London of fabulously rich Jews, who had subterranean halls there, with palms, and fountains, and soft lamps and richly apparelled women who never saw the disenchanting light of London day. So, in the midst of that smoke-palled city, enamoured of figures and grimy toil, Paul had his secret temple, his wishing carpet, his bit of blue-and-white Mediterranean shore bathed in perpetual sunshine.

Several of Paul's teachers had a theory that his imagination had been perverted by garish fiction, but the truth was that he scarcely ever read at all. The books at home were not such as would either tempt or corrupt a youthful mind, and as for reading the novels that some of his friends urged upon him—well, he got what he wanted much more quickly from music; any sort of music, from an orchestra to a barrel organ. He needed only the spark, the indescribable thrill that made his imagination master of his senses, and he could make plots and pictures enough of his own. It was equally true that he was not stage struck—not, at any rate, in the usual acceptation of that expression. He had no desire to become an actor, any more than he had to become a musician. He felt no necessity to do any of these things; what he wanted was to see, to be in the atmosphere, float on the wave of it, to be carried out, blue league after blue league, away from everything.

After a night behind the scenes, Paul found the school-room more than ever repulsive; the bare floors and naked walls; the prosy men who never wore frock coats, or violets in their buttonholes; the women with their dull gowns, shrill voices, and pitiful seriousness about prepositions that govern the dative. He could not bear to have the other pupils think, for a moment, that he took these people seriously; he must convey to them that he considered it all trivial, and was there only by way of a jest, anyway. He had autographed pictures of all the members of the stock company which he showed his classmates, telling them the most incredible stories of his familiarity with these people, of his acquaintance with the soloists who came to Carnegie Hall, his suppers with them and the flowers he sent them. When these stories lost their effect, and his audience grew listless, he became desperate and would bid all the boys good-bye, announcing that he was going to travel for a while; going to Naples, to Venice, to Egypt. Then, next Monday, he would slip back, conscious and nervously smiling; his sister was ill, and he should have to defer his voyage until spring.

Matters went steadily worse with Paul at school. In the itch to let his instructors know how heartily he despised them and their homilies, and how thoroughly he was appreciated elsewhere, he mentioned once or twice that he had no time to fool with theorems; adding—with a twitch of the eyebrows and a touch of that nervous bravado which so perplexed them—that he was helping the people down at the stock company; they were old friends of his.

The upshot of the matter was that the Principal went to Paul's father, and Paul was taken out of school and put to work. The manager at Carnegie Hall was told to get another usher in his stead; the door-keeper at the theatre was warned not to admit him to the house; and Charley Edwards remorsefully promised the boy's father not to see him again.

The members of the stock company were vastly amused when some of Paul's stories reached them—especially the women. They were hard-working women, most of them supporting indigent husbands or brothers, and they laughed rather bitterly at having stirred the boy to such fervid and florid inventions. They agreed with the faculty and with his father that Paul's was a bad case.

The east-bound train was ploughing through a January snow-storm; the dull dawn was beginning to show grey when the engine whistled a mile out of Newark. Paul started up from the seat where he had lain curled in uneasy slumber, rubbed the breath-misted window glass with his hand, and peered out. The snow was whirling in curling eddies above the white bottom lands, and the drifts lay already deep in the fields and along the fences, while here and there the long dead grass and dried weed stalks protruded black above it. Lights shone from the scattered houses, and a gang of labourers who stood beside the track waved their lanterns.

Paul had slept very little, and he felt grimy and uncomfortable. He had made the all-night journey in a day coach, partly because he was ashamed, dressed as he was, to go into a Pullman, and partly because he was afraid of being seen there by some Pittsburgh business man, who might have noticed him in Denny & Carson's office. When the whistle awoke him, he clutched quickly at his breast pocket, glancing about him with an uncertain smile. But the little, clay-bespattered Italians were still sleeping, the slatternly women across the aisle were in open-mouthed oblivion, and even the crumby, crying babies were for the nonce stilled. Paul settled back to struggle with his impatience as best he could.

When he arrived at the Jersey City station, he hurried through his breakfast, manifestly ill at ease and keeping a sharp eye about him. After he reached the Twenty-third Street station, he consulted a cabman, and had himself driven to a men's furnishing establishment that was just opening for the day. He spent upward of two hours there, buying with endless reconsidering and great care. His new street suit he put on in the fitting-room; the frock coat and dress clothes he had bundled into the cab with his linen. Then he drove to a hatter's and a shoe house. His next errand was at Tiffany's, where he selected his silver and a new scarf-pin. He would not wait to have his silver marked, he said. Lastly, he stopped at a trunk shop on Broadway, and had his purchases packed into various travelling bags.

It was a little after one o'clock when he drove up to the Waldorf, and after settling with the cabman, went into the office. He registered from Washington; said his mother and father had been abroad, and that he had come down to await the arrival of their steamer. He told his story plausibly and had no trouble, since he volunteered to pay for them in advance, in engaging his rooms; a sleeping-room, sitting-room and bath.

Not once, but a hundred times Paul had planned this entry into New York. He had gone over every detail of it with Charley Edwards, and in his scrap book at home there were pages of description about New York hotels, cut from the Sunday papers. When he was shown to his sitting-room on the eighth floor, he saw at a glance that everything was as it should be; there was but one detail in his mental picture that the place did not realize, so he rang for the bell boy and sent him down for flowers. He moved about nervously until the boy returned, putting away his new linen and fingering it delightedly as he did so. When the flowers came, he put them hastily into water, and then tumbled into a hot bath. Presently he came out of his white bath-room, resplendent in his new silk under-wear, and playing with the tassels of his red robe. The snow was whirling so fiercely outside his windows that he could scarcely see across the street, but within the air was deliciously soft and fragrant. He put the violets and jonquils on the taboret beside the couch, and threw himself down, with a long sigh, covering himself with a Roman blanket. He was thoroughly tired; he had been in such haste, he had stood up to such a strain, covered so much ground in the last twenty-four hours, that he wanted to think how it had all come about. Lulled by the sound of the wind, the warm air, and the cool fragrance of the flowers, he sank into deep, drowsy retrospection.

It had been wonderfully simple; when they had shut him out of the theatre and concert hall, when they had taken away his bone, the whole thing was virtually determined. The rest was a mere matter of opportu-nity. The only thing that at all surprised him was his own courage—for he realized well enough that he had always been tormented by fear, a sort of apprehensive dread that, of late years, as the meshes of the lies he had told closed about him, had been pulling the muscles of his body tighter and tighter. Until now, he could not remember the time when he had not been dreading something. Even when he was a little boy, it was always there—behind him, or before, or on either side. There had always been the shadowed corner, the dark place into which he dared not look, but from which something seemed always to be watching him—and Paul had done things that were not pretty to watch, he knew.

But now he had a curious sense of relief, as though he had at last thrown down the gauntlet to the thing in the corner.

Yet it was but a day since he had been sulking in the traces; but yesterday afternoon that he had been sent to he bank with Denny & Carson's deposit, as usual—but this time he was instructed to leave the book to be balanced. There was above two thousand dollars in checks, and nearly a thousand in the bank notes which he had taken from the book and quietly transferred to his pocket. At the bank he had made out a new deposit slip. His nerves had been steady enough to permit of his returning to the office, where he had finished his work and asked for a full day's holiday to-morrow, Saturday, giving a perfectly reasonable pretext. The bank book, he knew, would not be returned before Monday or Tuesday, and his father would be out of town for the next week. From the time he slipped the bank notes into his pocket until he boarded the night train for New York, he had not known a moment's hesitation. It was not the first time Paul had steered through treacherous waters.

How astonishingly easy it had all been; here he was, the thing done; and this time there would be no awakening, no figure at the top of the stairs. He watched the snow flakes whirling by his window until he fell asleep.

When he awoke, it was three o'clock in the afternoon. He bounded up with a start; half of one of his precious days gone already! He spent more than an hour in dressing, watching every stage of his toilet carefully in the mirror. Everything was quite perfect; he was exactly the kind of boy he had always wanted to be.

When he went downstairs, Paul took a carriage and drove up Fifth Avenue toward the Park. The snow had somewhat abated; carriages and tradesmen's wagons were hurrying soundlessly to and fro in the winter twilight, boys in woollen mufflers were shovelling off the doorsteps; the avenue stages made fine spots of colour against the white street. Here and there on the corners were stands, with whole flower gardens blooming under glass cases, against the sides of which the snow flakes stuck and melted; violets, roses, carnations, lilies of the valley—somehow vastly more lovely and alluring that they blossomed thus unnaturally in the snow. The Park itself was a wonderful stage winterpiece.

When he returned, the pause of the twilight had ceased, and the tune of the streets had changed. The snow was falling faster, lights streamed from the hotels that reared their dozen stories fearlessly up into the storm, defying the raging Atlantic winds. A long, black stream of carriages poured down the avenue, intersected here and there by other streams, tending horizontally. There were a score of cabs about the entrance of his hotel, and his driver had to wait. Boys in livery were running in and out of the awning stretched across the sidewalk, up and down the red velvet carpet laid from the door to the street. Above, about, within it all was the rumble and roar, the hurry and toss of thousands of human beings as hot for pleasure as himself, and on every side of him towered the glaring affirmation of the omnipotence of wealth.

The boy set his teeth and drew his shoulders together in a spasm of realization; the plot of all dramas, the text of all romances, the nerve-stuff of all sensations was whirling about him like the snow flakes. He burnt like a faggot in a tempest.

When Paul went down to dinner, the music of the orchestra came floating up the elevator shaft to greet him. His head whirled as he stepped into the thronged corridor, and he sank back into one of the chairs against the wall to get his breath. The lights, the chatter, the per-fumes, the bewildering medley of colour—he had, for a moment, the feeling of not being able to stand it. But only for a moment; these were his own people, he told himself. He went slowly about the corridors, through the writing-rooms, smoking-rooms, reception-rooms, as though he were exploring the chambers of an enchanted palace, built and peo-pled for him alone.

When he reached the dining-room he sat down at a table near a win-dow. The flowers, the white linen, the many-coloured wine glasses, the gay toilettes of the women, the low popping of corks, the undulating repetitions of the *Blue Danube* from the orchestra, all flooded Paul's dream with bewildering radiance. When the roseate tinge of his cham-pagne was added—that cold, precious, bubbling stuff that creamed and foamed in his glass—Paul wondered that there were honest men in the world at all. This was what all the world was fighting for, he reflected; this was what all the struggle was about. He doubted the reality of his past. Had he ever known a place called Cordelia Street, a place where fag-ged-looking businessmen got on the early car; mere rivets in a machine they seemed to Paul,—sickening men, with combings of children's hair always hanging to their coats, and the smell of cooking in their clothes. Cordelia Street—Ah! that belonged to another time and country; had he not always been thus, had he not sat here night after night, from as far back as he could remember, looking pensively over just such shimmering textures, and slowly twirling the stem of a glass like this one between his thumb and middle finger? He rather thought he had.

He was not in the least abashed or lonely. He had no especial desire to meet or to know any of these people; all he demanded was the right to look on and conjecture, to watch the pageant. The mere stage properties were all he contended for. Nor was he lonely later in the evening, in his loge at the Metropolitan. He was now entirely rid of his nervous misgivings, of his forced aggressiveness, of the imperative desire to show himself different from his surroundings. He felt now that his surroundings explained him. Nobody questioned the purple; he had only to wear it passively. He had only to glance down at his attire to reassure himself that here it would be impossible for anyone to humiliate him.

He found it hard to leave his beautiful sitting-room to go to bed that night, and sat long watching the raging storm from his turret window. When he went to sleep it was with the lights turned on in his bedroom; partly because of his old timidity, and partly so that, if he should wake in the night, there would be no wretched moment of doubt, no horrible suspicion of yellow wall-paper, or of Washington and Calvin above his bed.

Sunday morning the city was practically snow-bound. Paul breakfasted late, and in the afternoon he fell in with a wild San Francisco boy, a freshman at Yale, who said he had run down for a "little flyer" over Sunday. The young man offered to show Paul the night side of the town, and the two boys went out together after dinner, not returning to the hotel until seven o'clock the next morning. They had started out in the confiding warmth of a champagne friendship, but their parting in the elevator was singularly cool. The freshman pulled himself together to make his train, and Paul went to bed. He awoke at two o'clock in the afternoon, very thirsty and dizzy, and rang for ice-water, coffee, and the Pittsburgh papers.

On the part of the hotel management, Paul excited no suspicion. There was this to be said for him, that he wore his spoils with dignity and in no way made himself conspicuous. Even under the glow of his wine he was never boisterous, though he found the stuff like a magician's wand for wonder-building. His chief greediness lay in his ears and eyes, and his excesses were not offensive ones. His dearest pleasures were the grey winter twilights in his sitting-room; his quiet enjoyment of his flowers, his clothes, his wide divan, his cigarette and his sense of power. He could not remember a time when he had felt so at peace with himself. The mere release from the necessity of petty lying, lying every day and every day, restored his self-respect. He had never lied for pleasure, even at school; but to be noticed and admired, to assert his difference from other Cordelia Street boys; and he felt a good deal more manly, more honest, even, now that he had no need for boastful pretensions, now that he could, as his actor friends used to say, "dress the part." It was charac-

teristic that remorse did not occur to him. His golden days went by without a shadow, and he made each as perfect as he could.

On the eighth day after his arrival in New York, he found the whole
affair exploited in the Pittsburgh papers, exploited with a wealth of detail
which indicated that local news of a sensational nature was at a low ebb.
The firm of Denny & Carson announced that the boy's father had re-
funded the full amount of the theft, and that they had no intention of
prosecuting. The Cumberland minister had been interviewed, and expressed his hope of yet reclaiming the motherless lad, and his Sabbath-
school teacher declared that she would spare no effort to that end. The
rumour had reached Pittsburgh that the boy had been seen in a New
York hotel, and his father had gone East to find him and bring him
home.

Paul had just come in to dress for dinner; he sank into a chair, weak to
the knees, and clasped his head in his hands. It was to be worse than jail,
even; the tepid waters of Cordelia Street were to close over him finally
and forever. The grey monotony stretched before him in hopeless, un-
relieved years; Sabbath-school, Young People's Meeting, the yellow-
papered room, the damp dish-towels; it all rushed back upon him with a
sickening vividness. He had the old feeling that the orchestra had suddenly stopped, the sinking sensation that the play was over. The sweat
broke out on his face, and he sprang to his feet, looked about him with
his white, conscious smile, and winked at himself in the mirror. With
something of the old childish belief in miracles with which he had so
often gone to class, all his lessons unlearned, Paul dressed and dashed
whistling down the corridor to the elevator.

He had no sooner entered the dining-room and caught the measure of
the music than his remembrance was lightened by his old elastic power of
claiming the moment, mounting with it, and finding it all sufficient. The
glare and glitter about him, the mere scenic accessories had again, and
for the last time, their old potency. He would show himself that he was
game, he would finish the thing splendidly. He doubted, more than ever,
the existence of Cordelia Street, and for the first time he drank his wine
recklessly. Was he not, after all, one of those fortunate beings born to the
purple, was he not still himself and in his own place? He drummed a
nervous accompaniment to the Pagliacci music and looked about him,
telling himself over and over that it had paid.

He reflected drowsily, to the swell of the music and the chill sweetness
of his wine, that he might have done it more wisely. He might have
caught an outbound steamer and been well out of their clutches before
now. But the other side of the world had seemed too far away and too
uncertain then; he could not have waited for it; his need had been too
sharp. If he had to choose over again, he would do the same thing to-

morrow. He looked affectionately about the dining-room, now gilded with a soft mist. Ah, it had paid indeed!

Paul was awakened next morning by a painful throbbing in his head and feet. He had thrown himself across the bed without undressing, and had slept with his shoes on. His limbs and hands were lead heavy, and his tongue and throat were parched and burnt. There came upon him one of those fateful attacks of clear-headedness that never occurred except when he was physically exhausted and his nerves hung loose. He lay still and closed his eyes and let the tide of things wash over him.

His father was in New York; "stopping at some joint or other," he told himself. The memory of successive summers on the front stoop fell upon him like a weight of black water. He had not a hundred dollars left; and he knew now, more than ever, that money was everything, the wall that stood between all he loathed and all he wanted. The thing was winding itself up; he had thought of that on his first glorious day in New York, and had even provided a way to snap the thread. It lay on his dressing-table now; he had got it out last night when he came blindly up from dinner, but the shiny metal hurt his eyes, and he disliked the looks of it.

He rose and moved about with a painful effort, succumbing now and again to attacks of nausea. It was the old depression exaggerated; all the world had become Cordelia Street. Yet somehow he was not afraid of anything, was absolutely calm; perhaps because he had looked into the dark corner at last and knew. It was bad enough, what he saw there, but somehow not so bad as his long fear of it had been. He saw everything clearly now. He had a feeling that he had made the best of it, that he had lived the sort of life he was meant to live, and for half an hour he sat staring at the revolver. But he told himself that was not the way, so he went downstairs and took a cab to the ferry.

When Paul arrived at Newark, he got off the train and took another cab, directing the driver to follow the Pennsylvania tracks out of the town. The snow lay heavy on the roadways and had drifted deep in the open fields. Only here and there the dead grass or dried weed stalks projected, singularly black, above it. Once well into the country, Paul dismissed the carriage and walked, floundering along the tracks, his mind a medley of irrelevant things. He seemed to hold in his brain an actual picture of everything he had seen that morning. He remembered every feature of both his drivers, of the toothless old woman from whom he had bought the red flowers in his coat, the agent from whom he had got his ticket, and all of his fellow-passengers on the ferry. His mind, unable to cope with vital matters near at hand, worked feverishly and deftly at sorting and grouping these images. They made for him a part of the ugliness of the world, of the ache in his head, and the bitter burning on his tongue. He stooped and put a handful of snow into his mouth as he walked, but that, too, seemed hot. When he reached a little hillside, where the tracks ran through a cut some twenty feet below him, he stopped and sat down.

The carnations in his coat were drooping with the cold, he noticed; their red glory all over. It occurred to him that all the flowers he had seen in the glass cases that first night must have gone the same way, long before this. It was only one splendid breath they had, in spite of their brave mockery at the winter outside the glass; and it was a losing game in the end, it seemed, this revolt against the homilies by which the world is run. Paul took one of the blossoms carefully from his coat and scooped a little hole in the snow, where he covered it up. Then he dozed a while, from his weak condition, seemingly insensible to the cold.

The sound of an approaching train awoke him, and he started to his feet, remembering only his resolution, and afraid lest he should be too late. He stood watching the approaching locomotive, his teeth chattering, his lips drawn away from them in a frightened smile; once or twice he glanced nervously sidewise, as though he were being watched. When the right moment came, he jumped. As he fell, the folly of his haste occurred to him with merciless clearness, the vastness of what he had left undone. There flashed through his brain, clearer than ever before, the blue of Adriatic water, the yellow of Algerian sands.

He felt something strike his chest, and that his body was being thrown swiftly through the air, on and on, immeasurably far and fast, while his limbs were gently relaxed. Then, because the picture making mechanism was crushed, the disturbing visions flashed into black, and Paul dropped back into the immense design of things.

HOODS I HAVE KNOWN

Sondra Spatt Olsen

Whenever I reminisce about old beaux, I begin with poor Larry Dinhofer, who sat behind me in the eighth grade and asked me to the P.S.
333 prom because I asked him to my graduation party. From gratitude
for that first invitation, Larry's mother bought me a monstrous bottle of
Sweet Primrose toilet water, which I have kept to this day. The primroses
or whatever they were have become so fermented through the years that
I now use it for rubbing alcohol and think "Dinhofer" whenever I have
an ache in my back. But strictly speaking, although memorable, Larry
was not my first but only my first respectable beau. Before Larry I had an
unrespectable romance, long suppressed, a seventh-grade affair with the
dirty, untrustworthy Danny Tooey, who was a hood.

Perhaps I should explain about hoods. Hoods in Brooklyn are boys
who go to school only by the grace of the truant officer, "hood" being
short for "hoodlum." "Juvenile delinquent" is a much longer word and
not half as piquant. Our seventh-grade hoods were comparatively unag-
gressive. They never did much but loaf at the back of the class and throw
spitballs at each other, sometimes at the teacher. They wore dungarees
or chartreuse pants with pistol pockets in imitation of the Avenue E Boys,
who were model hoods and real court cases. Our hoods, although harmless, grew aggressive-looking sideburns and great masses of curly black or
blond hair. All of them shaved. Danny Tooey was the biggest, tallest,
hairiest of the lot and the one who had been left back most often. He was
fifteen.

When Danny was first left back into our class, we ignored each other.
Our social milieux, even in school, were different. I sat in the front of the
room, covered my books, raised my hand in answer to all questions and
agreed with the teacher on all points. I had already set my eye on the
General Excellence Award at graduation. Danny, as I have already
pointed out, never did anything in school except pledge allegiance to the
flag, proving that hoods were untrustworthy but not unpatriotic.

Danny did not cover books; he destroyed them. Miss Malcolm thought
well-bound books in hoody hands a waste, so Danny scattered the leaves
of his worn-out volumes like nuts in May, sometimes maliciously, more
often from the sort of pure disinterest playboys show when they run their
Jaguars off cliffs in the movies. No one had ever called upon Danny to
read from these books, you see. It was *l'acte gratuit*.

When I fell into disgrace, Danny was the first hood whose friendship I
won. I was in with the leader of the gang, so to speak. I had been the

Winged Messenger of the seventh grade and scurried around corridors clutching notes from Miss Malcolm with the expression postmen have when they meet up with the sleet or snow or fog people have been telling them about. I took my messenger position seriously, even though the notes, whenever I paused to open them, revealed nothing more serious than a date for tea or a lift to the beauty parlor. One day Miss Malcolm decided to affix a postscript to a note that she'd dispatched with me and came around a corner unexpectedly, giving both of us a shock.

"Since you have proved yourself a criminal, I'm going to treat you that way," she announced pontifically before the class, and made me clean out my desk and remove my books and self to the back of the room.

As a criminal, I found myself in a peculiar position. It had only been a note asking for more toilet supplies for the teachers' rest room, and hardly worth the drastic punishment, I felt. It was a mundane confidence I'd broken, though Miss Malcolm had mysteriously underlined "toilet supplies" for some reason I could not fathom. Nevertheless, I was disgraced, not only with the teacher but with all my friends. From that day on Miss Malcolm would not call on me in class, even though I was the only one who knew the three most important Atlantic fishing ports and waved my arm wildly like a drowning Atlantic fisherman. She instructed the class to ignore me too. My friends from the front of the room, oh, perfidy, had been waiting all these years, I found, praying that I would fall from grace. They simply would not turn their heads or accept my notes.

Instead of being crushed by my fate I was confident and not at all apologetic. After all, I was the star pupil. And what would Miss Malcolm do without me when we reached the difficult Middle Atlantic States? As for my friends, "those schmoey kids" as I called them, my contempt for them was boundless. I vowed if I ever achieved my pure state again I'd make them suffer.

Miss Malcolm seated Danny and me in a double seat, thinking, dear woman, that close contact with a hood was the worst punishment anyone could inflict on a clean, well-brought-up little girl. She expected me to cry and beg to be let back, at least to the class middle. That was because Miss Malcolm herself was afraid of that hairy creature who slouched into class with disquieting tread and rumbled unintelligible answers deep in his throat. "Urghs" was Danny's favorite comment, and it frightened Miss Malcolm.

When I arrived at the last seat, last row, Danny didn't know quite what to think. I was obviously a pseudo hood and not destined to stay very long. Danny didn't rumble anything at me but regarded me mildly, even amusedly, that first afternoon. "You staying here, little girl?" he asked sarcastically as I piled my books in the desk. His tone implied that I didn't look dangerous enough to merit such a position. I don't think Danny fully realized the moral turpitude of note-reading.

No, I didn't think I was going to stay with Danny long either, at first. But days went by, and Miss Malcolm's gaze never glided past the dividing line—Raymond de Fato, who occasionally threw a spitball but wore a tie. I began to grow more and more uncomfortable. The classroom was long and crowded. Because of scufflings and murmurings around me I couldn't hear anything that was going on past Raymond; Raymond wouldn't tell me, and even if I did hear no one would call on me. But I could not go to Miss Malcolm begging to be let back. I was proud.

I began to bring *Jane Eyre* to school and spent the whole day reading ferociously. But even that splendid book couldn't make up for the fact that I was missing the Middle Atlantic States. Nor did snubbing Miss Malcolm every day in front of the coatroom bring the desired satisfaction. I couldn't complain at home because my mother thought I should beg for mercy. She said I was "a stubborn fool" and "just like your father." I was an outcast and everybody knew it.

I would have been completely miserable if Danny hadn't decided to take me into his group.

Danny began making the first overtures by looking on with me as I read *Jane Eyre*. Of course I was surprised. Until then it had been mere peaceful coexistence. I didn't even know Danny could read. He'd just sat for days looking at me sardonically from under his tousle of black curls. Occasionally he had cocked an eyebrow at me and his entire broad and grimy brow had moved.

"Dat looks like a good book," he said to me one day, looking interested, and I immediately lent him my four-color pencil to doodle with. From then on we were friends. Even the good girls in my class didn't read Brontë because they couldn't understand words like "choler" and "lineaments." Such praise from a hood made me glow with pleasure.

Our friendship was sealed next day, when we had an examination. Danny gave me his rabbit foot for keeps. It was for luck, he explained, and you could write the answers on a little piece of paper in the claw.

"Are you sure you don't want it?" I remember asking diffidently. "You probably need it more than I do."

"Oh, I can copy off you—dat's all right," he said.

I really didn't want that rabbit foot. A crib sheet was a little too far out on the road to dishonesty for a former star pupil, and I knew my New England products backward and forward anyway. Still, I accepted the foot for luck and as a token. I still remember the softness of it, and the little sharpnesses that were the nails.

The next thing Danny did was introduce me to the boys. This was difficult, but he managed to get them to ask me to lend them pencils. They were the shiest hoods imaginable. There were really ten of us in the back, but I only got to know five: Danny, Harry la Marca, Alan Brodnik, Ronny Abry and Jo-Jo Begoyne.

These were the Destry Road Boys. Because of his age, ability and the fact that he had been approached by the Avenue E Boys for possible merger, Danny was definitely the leader. He ruled with an iron hand. Once Harry and Jo-Jo had a fight in the back of the room, and they might have ripped each other to pieces if Danny hadn't broken it up. They moved silently, slowly, crouching a little by the door to the gym. "You never seen a shiv fight before?" Danny asked when he saw my wonder afterward, and he showed me the knives, six inches long.

"Dose guys are gonna get into real trouble one day—dey're only tirteen—dey don't have any sense," he said. During the fight Miss Malcolm had gone on with the class in the front of the room as though nothing was happening. After twenty years of dealing with crime Miss Malcolm had found her method—the silent or you-don't-exist treatment.

The boys got a great deal of pleasure out of telling me about shiv fights and how the Avenue E Boys got away with robbing a candy store. The Destry Road Boys had never gotten away with anything because they had never pulled anything, except turning in false alarms, which any five-year-old can do. They were a small-time bunch and they knew it. Our neighborhood, Newton Park, was just too quiet and genteel to start any trouble, and there wasn't any point going over to Avenue E to find some because Danny wouldn't let them. "You want to get your heads knocked off?" he asked. Danny was the most cautious, perhaps because he was the only gang leader I've ever known. He'd been around and he knew that it was safest to do nothing and if anybody asked you anything to just mumble along.

I found that I too could expound to the boys on topics they hadn't heard before, usually last month's lessons. I think I may have been more interesting than Miss Malcolm, because when I told them about Cortes in Mexico and killing the great chief Montezuma, their eyes gleamed and they clasped imaginary sword handles. Alan Brodnik expressed a desire to make a poniard or a rapier in shop that week. "Swords, dat's all you guys need," Danny said in disgust, but I could see that he was interested too.

"Why didn't dey make a deal wit Montezuma and get a percentage?" he asked me once when I got involved with the more intricate dealings. "A percentage is better. Dopey Spaniards." I could see that Danny had everything all figured out.

I had been sitting in the back of the room for a week and a half when I began to notice a perceptible change in Danny. He began to wear white polo shirts instead of his old saggy yellow one and smelled faintly of Ivory soap. His face was clean and his hair was somehow higher, pulled together into a compact pompadour. Danny even turned his club jacket inside out so that the plain black showed instead of the worn fuchsia silk with its huge black "Destry Boys" lettering. " 'Stoo flashy," Danny said, and that afternoon, after lunch, all the boys had their jackets turned around too.

Soon, whenever Danny and I read together because of Danny's pageless volumes, his fingers curled around my white-clean covers were white-clean too. The fingers also turned the pages exactly right, which proved that Danny could actually read as fast as I did. I began to think that Danny wasn't really a hood, or was just pretending, or that being a hood wasn't so bad at all if only the teacher would notice you. If we listened very carefully, Danny and I, we could hear Miss Malcolm's voice reading *Evangeline* far off, and once, when we got to the part that goes

Black were her eyes as the berry that grows on the thorn by the
  wayside—
Black, yet how softly they gleamed beneath the brown shade of her
  tresses!
Sweet was her breath as the breath of kine that feed in the mead-
  ows . . .

Danny bent over and whispered. "She looks like you."

Since I was definitely blond and blue-eyed, and since Danny had never whispered before in his life, I began to think something was wrong. Or, if Danny was becoming poetic, something might be right. But anyway—something. Yes, I thought rather priggishly, Danny has probably never sat next to a good poetry-reading little girl in his life; my presence has probably opened the door to a whole new world of clean-smelling respectability.

It occurred to me that I might tame Danny and turn him into a star pupil, thus killing two birds with one stone and getting me a seat in Respectability too. Why, I could probably persuade Danny to take elocution lessons. Then he could learn to pronounce "th" and other things and Miss Malcolm would understand him. I had a little difficulty myself sometimes. And if I could convince his mother to get him some crisp white shirts and a tie. . . . Maybe my mother would iron them for him if Mrs. Tooey was busy.

Ronny, Harry, Alan and Jo-Jo, although they showed no immediate signs of conversion, might still follow their leader out of hood-hood and I would have a whole gang to my credit. I could learn to iron shirts myself. Soon I would walk down Destry Road to be pointed at and stared at by the citizenry. "There's the girl who saves hoods," ladies would say as they waited on line by the fruit counter at Willy's. "Can you come and talk to my boy after school?" "Dere's dat dame." The Avenue E Boys would scowl and lurk behind the gum machine in front of Harry's. "She's the one who's been takin' our best material. Why, Danny Tooey, he could've been the best hood in Brooklyn, he's studyin' for the ministry."

Yes, I would save Danny. I determined to bring my *Believe-It-Or-Not* Ripley book to school immediately so Danny could begin assimilating the mass of interesting facts so necessary to star pupils. We would sit in the first row, side by side.

Alas. While I had been making plans for reformation, I had overlooked the real reason for Danny's behavior, which was, of course, sex. Danny Tooey wanted me to be more than just a friend. On Friday morning, May 11, Danny asked me to go to the movies with him the next evening, May 12. Not in the afternoon. In the evening. It was a sword-fighting picture, he said, and I would like it. I was shocked. Respectable seventh-grade girls, especially me, didn't wear lipstick or go out with boys; eighth-grade girls could wear lipstick and go out, if they didn't make too much fuss about it. But no decent girl ever went anywhere, morning or evening, with a hood.

Oh, yes, there were a few. But they were scrawny and inky-haired and went to P.S. 293 and only appeared hanging around outside by the homogenized-bagel man at three o'clock. They weren't decent either. Because when the boys didn't show up, they would flirt with the homogenized-bagel man, and when he wasn't there they would go to Harry's and stand in front of the gum machine. And they would make remarks like "Look who's here," whenever someone passed. The Avenue E Dolls, an auxiliary of the Boys, set the fashion in this case, and any girl hood who didn't have long black hair had to grow it or dye it quick, or run the risk of not being à la mode hood. A la mode hood also meant doe eyes, ultrabright lipstick, gold bangle earrings, cheap, tight skirts and the black and white uniform: black bra and white sweater or white bra and black sweater. And no slip. These girls didn't need to wear bras and I did. Only I didn't, and always felt self-conscious when I passed Harry's Candy Store in my light lawn dresses.

No, I couldn't possibly go out with Danny. I might convert him, but I couldn't go out with him. He probably would want me to kiss him in the movies. I knew what went on in the Destry Theatre; I went every Saturday night with my mother and father; I knew. Those hoods. Surely Danny with all his hoodish savoir-faire knew that a girl in a pinafore dress, long blond braids and well-fed expression was highly inappropriate for the leader of a gang. It was just the lure of the unknown, and was, of course, impossible.

I told Danny politely that I appreciated the thought but didn't think my mother would let me go out since I was only eleven years old. I had skipped several grades, I explained. Danny was very understanding about it and said I certainly looked older. At the end of the day I gave him my *Believe-It-Or-Not* Ripley book for keeps, saying that my mother had refused permission at lunchtime but that this was for him, blushing all the while, I suppose. Danny was very embarrassed. He didn't blush, at first only mumbled "Urghs," but later came over to me at the coatroom and said: "Tanks. I don't know how to make just retribution." He was sweet about the whole thing.

Actually, I hadn't told my mother about Danny's invitation at all. I doubted whether she'd think the connection savory. But I thought about this, my almost first date, all the way home from school and all weekend. In fact, I couldn't stop thinking about it. No sooner would I settle down with my favorite book than the name Tooey would intrude itself into my mental stream. I felt the irresistible urge to write Danny Tooey, Danny or just plain D. T. on all my clean book covers. Finally, in desperation, I wrote Yeoot Ynnad very small in the top of my stationery box. Such a thing had never happened to me before.

I decided to look up similar occurrences in my library, my highest source of wisdom. But mine proved an unprecedented occurrence. Heathcliff had been bad and Cathy had decided to be his girl friend, but he hadn't reformed and they had both died. That was the best I could find. But still . . . Jane Eyre wouldn't marry Mr. Rochester when he was already married to Bertha, so it didn't seem right for me to go out with Danny while he was still a hood. But after he reformed . . . it would probably take till eighth grade and then we could go out legitimately. Girls in the eighth grade not only went out, they could kiss too.

My mother noticed my mood of sorrowful melancholy, interspersed with come-hither glances and a slight puckering motion of the lips, and wrongly attributed my strange behavior to worry about the Middle Atlantic States. She instructed me to sue for Miss Malcolm's favor immediately or she would come up to school herself. Poor Mamma. How was she to know? After all, I had been a terrible bookworm, and I was only eleven years old.

When I went to the movies Saturday night with my parents I tried to reconstruct Danny's features. All that hair made it difficult; it was all I could reconstruct. Underneath Danny was handsome, I decided, and the features of the man on the screen melted, dimmed and turned Tooey-esque in the darkness. What if it had not been my father sitting next to me, wheezing slightly from the air conditioning? What if it had been . . . To this day I can give no accurate description of Danny. The years have blurred even that blurry face. No matter how handsome and hairy and suave the fifteen-year-old Danny may have been, I hardly think he could have looked as I still picture him today—the precise image of Clark Gable.

Coming out of the Destry after the show, I managed to walk into an embarrassing situation. There stood Alan Brodnik, leaning against the fire hydrant, his arms round a girl. Alan looked at me appealingly and removed his arms. I made no comment, walked by without turning my head. My heart was sad though, oh, sad. For what if it had been Yeoot Ynnad?

When I arrived at school Monday morning I found our back-seat idyl broken. No longer could we peruse the same book like lion and lamb. Danny and I breathed hard and stared in whatever direction was opposite; we both mumbled. At last I had enough courage to ask Danny if he had learned anything interesting from the *Believe-It-Or-Not* Ripley book. He only looked at me vaguely and mumbled "Urghs." He had retrogressed.

Danny continued shy all day and did not speak to me. But he gave long, piteous glances and drew girls' heads in ink on the backs of his hands. This was terrible. I decided to follow Danny after school and make him talk to me. It was only to find out something of his home life for future reform, I told myself. When three o'clock and Danny and Harry, Jo-Jo, Alan and Ronny broke upon the homogenized-bagel man, I was there too.

The boys looked at me curiously. All the other little girls were retreating away from school as fast as they could go, backs straight and heads held high. Was it true? Was it true? Jo-Jo winked at Harry. Danny said nothing but asked me if I wanted salt on my bagel. No, don't buy me bagels, don't, I felt like crying out. I don't *want* to be your girl friend. I just want to find out about your home life. However, I took one with salt.

Danny seemed relaxed and at ease now. He spoke animatedly, even vivaciously, and I could catch nearly every word he was saying. He took my arm and headed me, yes, toward Harry's Candy Store. The boys followed. I would not go to Harry's Candy Store, I told myself firmly, I would not under any conditions go to Harry's Candy Store. . . .

On the way to the candy store, Danny told me about his job as utility man, whatever that was, on a small fishing boat out of Sheepshead Bay. The boat and Danny left every day at three in the morning and didn't return till eight-thirty, just in time to drop Danny off for school. "Dat's why I'm so sleepy in da mornings," Danny explains.

When he was sixteen, next year, he wouldn't have to come to school any more and could be a full-time fisherman. How exciting, I thought, thinking of *Captains Courageous*, but then I remembered. If Danny left school, he'd never reach eighth grade, and what would happen to his "th's" and his white shirts and . . . our date for the movies. Even if he became a fisherman—? what if there were a fish famine or something? Without me Danny would have to go back to being a hood. I would not let that happen. I would persuade Danny not to leave school. I would go with him to Harry's Candy Store every day and stand around with him near the gum machine.

When we reached Harry's, there were no girls from 293 around, thank goodness. Danny did nothing worse than hitch himself up on the wooden rack that held the newspapers and let his feet dangle on the New York *Post*. He'd been working since he was ten, he said, and it was all right. Except when the weather was bad and he didn't get paid. Or just got paid in fish. His Aunt Bella didn't like fish he added a little glumly; she hated fish.

Aunt Bella's strong aversion to fish was all I ever found out about Danny Tooey's home life. "Look who's here," Danny said next, and when I looked, there stood Miss Malcolm.

"I want to talk to you, dear," she said.

Miss Malcolm and I walked home together. We had a long, intimate conversation on the way, though I couldn't imagine why. I still hadn't apologized, and I certainly wasn't going to. I suppose Miss Malcolm had come out of school at three and seen her ex-star pupil in informal conversation with a recognized hood. Poor Miss Malcolm. She thought she'd been responsible for starting me on a life of crime.

"You don't know it, dear, but I've been watching you," she said. I clutched my stationery box, but she only took my arm as we crossed the street as though I was her little girl.

"I've noticed how unhappy you've been at the back of the room. You've just been moping around and moping around, haven't you?"

I made no reply. I wondered what Miss Malcolm wanted me to do for not telling my mother about Harry's Candy Store. Yes, blackmail was on my mind. I had the makings of a first-class hood.

"You've been unhappy because you've wanted to come up to me and apologize for reading my note, haven't you?"

We were nearing my home. I thought about walking Miss Malcolm right past it and right on down to Sheepshead Bay. We could go down to the pier and watch the fishing boats come in. My Lord, I really was a fiendish child, now that I think of it.

"But you've been afraid. You've been afraid I was going to say something unkind, weren't you?"

She patted me kindly on the arm. I thought of how I had walked past her every morning on my way to the coatroom, my head held high.

"But you know, I wouldn't have said anything unkind. Because I like you, dear. I think you're my best pupil."

I still didn't say anything. I was her best pupil. I wondered what Miss

Malcolm was planning to study next. It must be something harder than
the Middle Atlantic, because three people had raised their hands that day
and she didn't need me.

"And because I know you've wanted to apologize for a long time,
tomorrow morning I am going to let you come back to the first seat, first
row."

I couldn't stop the pleasure that I felt.

I didn't know why I had been reinstated but I was glad. Justice, as I
had always maintained, does triumph. And oh, what I would do to all
those schmoey kids. I was a nasty-good little girl.

Miss Malcolm came inside the house to meet my mother and we all
had tea. I didn't mind taking the enemy inside. Danny would approve, I
was sure. And from my influential position, what couldn't I do for my
friends. Soon I would convince Miss Malcolm of Danny's merits—and
then . . .

"Do you think seventh-grade girls are too young to go out?" I remember asking Miss Malcolm as Mamma poured tea.

Alas, again. All my plans were in vain. The end of the affair came next
day.

As Miss Malcolm announced the happy news and I carried my books
away from our scarred double seat to my honored one, Danny stared at
me sullenly without saying a word. He didn't say good-by, but on my last
trip to the front of the room he piled his *Believe-It-Or-Not* Ripley book on
top of my grammar and the stationery box with the secret Yeoot Ynnad.
He looked at me as though from across a million rows of double seats.
Then he turned back to carving his name on the desk.

Hurt and bewildered, I couldn't understand Danny's heartlessness.
I followed him out of the school building at three, lingered shyly by
the homogenized-bagel man, but he just walked away. His back was
slouched and his hair was no longer kempt. He was whistling.

After this I never went near Danny or any of the other boys again. And
when Larry Dinhofer asked me for a date to the senior prom I pretended
that he was the first. But I always kept track of the Destry Road Boys,
secretly, ashamedly. I felt a strong sense of communion with them and
liked to think that my short stay had done them all good. Alan and
Ronny and Harry went on to high school with me, but were put in special
RX classes where they could sit around all day and throw spitballs without
being disturbed by anyone. They just had a happy, lazy time. Occasionally I'd glimpse them having refreshments in front of the school. It was a
different, nonhomogenized-bagel man, but the same boys all right. When
I passed they would stare but never make any sign of recognition.

Although none of the Destry Boys ever made Honor Society or anything like that, they never got any more delinquent than they were. As it turned out, only one boy from P.S. 333 ever ended up in jail, and that was Larry Dinhofer. He robbed a liquor store, and he had always worn white cuffs and sat in the first row, and no one I know has ever found a logical explanation. So Larry does belong among the hoods I've known after all. Alan Brodnik, bless him, was the only Destry Boy whose degenerate career I followed after high school. I've lost touch with him since, but the last I heard he'd turned up at Brooklyn College carrying *Tropic of Capricorn* and wearing a neat black goatee and a red velvet cummerbund. I never could quite understand that one either.

As for Danny, I never saw him after graduation. In fact, I don't think he stayed around that long but left after his sixteenth birthday sometime in March. I believe he gave the Destry Road Boys to Jo-Jo because he was the smartest. By that time my wounded feelings had healed, since I'd decided what had motivated him. It was all due to Danny's pure moral philosophy or something, I deduced, that was stronger than mere romance. Hoods didn't do anything but pledge allegiance to the flag. Star pupils sat in the first row. We just couldn't be friends. It was against all established codes, and Danny supported codes. I had to admire that.

Someone I know says she thinks she saw someone who looked like Danny in a summer theatre production in Woodstock last year. She said that he was still big and had a lot of hair but that he spoke English perfectly. She said he was sweet and looked like Marlon Brando. Despite what my friend says, I don't like to think Danny became an actor. I don't like to think that at all. It makes me sad and a little embarrassed, for that would mean after all my seventh-grade heartbreak and eleven-year-old plans somebody else had reformed Danny after all. I'd rather have him be a fisherman. I'd rather have him be a hood.

EVERYTHING UNDER THE SUN
James Purdy

"I don't like to make things hard for you," Jesse said to Cade, "but when you act like this I don't know what's going to happen. You don't like nothing I do for you anyhow."

The two boys, Jesse and Cade, shared a room over the south end of State Street. Jesse had a job, but Cade, who was fifteen, seldom could find work. They were both down to their last few dollars.

"I told you a man was coming up here to offer me a job," Cade said.

"You can't wait for a man to come offering you a job," Jesse said. He laughed. "What kind of a man would that be anyhow."

Cade laughed too because he knew Jesse did not believe anything he said.

"This man did promise me," Cade explained, and Jesse snorted.

"Don't pick your nose like that," Jesse said to Cade. "What if the man seen you picking."

Cade said the man wouldn't care.

"What does this man do?" Jesse wondered.

"He said he had a nice line of goods I could sell for him and make good money," Cade replied.

"Good money selling," Jesse laughed. "My advice to you is go out and look for a job, any job, and not wait for no old man to come to teach you to sell."

"Well nobody else wants to hire me due to my face," Cade said.

"What's wrong with your face?" Jesse wanted to know. "Outside of you picking your nose all the time, you have as good a face as anybody's."

"I can't look people in the eye is what," Cade told him.

Jesse got up and walked around the small room.

"Like I told you," Jesse began the same speech he always gave when Cade was out of work, "I would do anything for you on account of your brother. He saved my life in the goddam army and I ain't never going to forget that."

Cade made his little expression of boredom which was to pinch the bridge of his nose.

"But you got to work sometimes!" Jesse exploded. "I don't get enough for two!"

Cade grimaced, and did not let go the bridge of his nose because he knew this irritated Jesse almost as much as his picking did, but Jesse could not criticize him for just holding his nose, and that made him all the angrier.

"And you stay out of them arcades too!" Jesse said to Cade. "Spending the money looking at them pictures," Jesse began. "For the love of. . . ." Suddenly Jesse stopped short.

"For the love of what?" Cade jumped him. He knew the reason that Jesse did not finish the sentence with a swear word was he went now to the Jesus Saves Mission every night, and since he had got religion he had quit being quite so friendly to Cade as before, cooler and more distant, and he talked, like today, about how good work is for everybody.

"That old man at the trucking office should have never told you you had a low IQ," Jesse returned to this difficulty of Cade's finding work.

But this remark did not touch Cade today.

"Jesse," Cade said, "I don't care about it."

"You don't care!" Jesse flared up.

"That's right," Cade said, and he got up and took out a piece of cigarette from his pants cuff, and lit a match to the stub. "I don't believe in IQ's," Cade said.

"Did you get that butt off the street?" Jesse wanted to know, his protective manner making his voice soft again.

"I ain't answering that question," Cade told him.

"Cade, why don't you be nice to me like you used to be," Jesse said.

"Why don't I be nice to you!" Cade exclaimed with savagery.

Suddenly frightened, Jesse said, "Now simmer down." He was always afraid when Cade suddenly acted too excited.

"You leave me alone," Cade said. "I ain't interferin' with your life and don't you interfere with mine. The little life I have, that is." He grunted.

"I owe something to you and that's why I can't just let you be any old way you feel like being," Jesse said.

"You don't owe me a thing," Cade told him.

"I know who I owe and who I don't," Jesse replied.

"You always say you owe me on account of my brother saved your life just before he got hisself blowed up."

"Cade, you be careful!" Jesse warned, and his head twitched as he spoke.

"I'm glad he's gone," Cade said, but without the emotion he usually expressed when he spoke of his brother. He had talked against his brother so long in times past in order to get Jesse riled up that it had lost nearly all meaning for both of them. "Yes, sir, I don't care!" Cade repeated.

Jesse moved his lips silently and Cade knew he was praying for help.

Jesse opened his eyes wide then and looking straight at Cade, twisted his lips, trying not to let the swear words come out, and said: "All right, Cade," after a long struggle.

"And if religion is going to make you close with your money," Cade began looking at Jesse's mouth, "close and *mean*, too, then I can clear out of here. I don't need you, Jesse."

"What put the idea into your head religion made me close with my money?" Jesse said, and he turned very pale.

"You need me here, but you don't want to pay what it takes to keep me," Cade said.

Jesse trembling walked over to Cade very close and stared at him.

Cade watched him, ready.

Jesse said, "You can stay here as long as you ever want to. And no questions asked." Having said this, Jesse turned away, a glassy look on his face, and stared at the cracked calcimine of their wall.

"On account of my old brother I can stay!" Cade yelled.

"All right then!" Jesse shouted back, but fear on his face. Then softening with a strange weakness he said, "No, Cade, that's not it either," and he went over and put his arm on Cade's shoulder.

"Don't touch me," Cade said. "I don't want none of that *brother* love. Keep your distance."

"You behave," Jesse said, struggling with his emotion.

"Ever since you give up women and drinking you been picking on me," Cade said. "I do the best I can."

Cade waited for Jesse to say something.

"And you think picking on me all the time makes you get a star in heaven, I suppose," Cade said weakly.

Jesse, who was not listening, walked the length of the cramped little room. Because of the heat of the night and the heat of the discussion, he took off his shirt. On his chest was tattooed a crouched black panther, and on his right arm above his elbow a large unfolding flower.

"I did want to do right by you, but maybe we *had* better part," Jesse said, crossing his arms across his chest. He spoke like a man in his sleep, but immediately he had spoken, a scared look passed over his face.

Cade suddenly went white. He moved over to the window.

"I can't do no more for you!" Jesse cried, alarmed but helpless at his own emotion. "It ain't in me to do no more for you! Can't you see that, Cade. Only so much, no more!"

When there was no answer from Cade, Jesse said, "Do you hear what I say?"

Cade did not speak.

"Fact is," Jesse began again, as though explaining now to himself, "I don't seem to care about nothing. I just want somehow to sit and not move or do nothing. I don't know what it is."

"You never did give a straw if I lived or died, Jesse," Cade said, and he just managed to control his angry tears.

Jesse was silent, as on the evenings when alone in the dark, while Cade was out looking for a job, he had tried to figure out what he should do in his trouble.

"*Fact* is," Cade now whirled from the window, his eyes brimming with tears, "it's all the other way around. I don't need you except for money, but you need me *to tell you who you are!*"

"What?" Jesse said, thunderstruck.

"You know goddam well *what*," Cade said, and he wiped the tears off his face with his fist. "On account of you don't know who you are, that's why."

"You little crumb," Jesse began, and he moved threateningly, but then half remembering his nights at the Mission, he walked around the room, muttering.

"Where are my cigarettes?" Jesse said suddenly. "Did you take them?"

"I thought you swore off when you got religion," Cade said.

"Yeah," Jesse said in the tone of voice more like his old self, and he went up to Cade, who was smoking another butt.

"Give me your smoke," he said to Cade.

Cade passed it to him, staring.

"I don't think you heard what I said about leaving," Cade told Jesse.

"I heard you," Jesse said.

"Well, I'm going to leave you, Jesse. God damn you."

Jesse just nodded from where he now sat on a crate they used as a chair. He groaned a little like the smoke was disagreeable for him.

"Like I say, Jesse," and Cade's face was dry of tears now. "It may be hard for me to earn money, but I know who I am. I may be dumb, but I'm *all together!*"

"Cade," Jesse said sucking on the cigarette furiously. "I didn't mean for you to go. After all, there is a lot between us."

Jesse's fingers moved nervously over the last tiny fragment of the cigarette.

"Do you have any more smokes in your pants cuff or anywhere?" Jesse asked, as though he were the younger and the weaker of the two now.

"I have, but I don't think I should give any to a religious man," Cade replied.

Jesse tightened his mouth.

Cade handed him another of the butts.

"What are you going to offer me, if I do decide to stay," Cade said suddenly. "On account of this time I'm not going to stay if you don't give me an offer!"

Jesse stood up suddenly, dropping his cigarette, the smoke coming out of his mouth as though he had all gone to smoke inside himself.

"What am I going to offer you?" Jesse said like a man in a dream. "What?" he said sleepily.

Then waving his arms, Jesse cried, "All right! Get out!"

And suddenly letting go at last he struck Cade across the mouth, bringing some blood. "Now you git," he said. "Git out."

Jesse panted, walking around the room. "You been bleedin' me white for a year. That's the reason I'm the way I am. I'm bled white."

Cade went mechanically to the bureau, took out a shirt, a pair of shorts, a toothbrush, his straight razor, and a small red box. He put these in a small bag such as an athlete might carry to his gym. He walked over to the door and went out.

Below, on the sidewalk, directly under the room where he and Jesse had lived together a year, Cade stood waiting for the streetcar. He knew Jesse was looking down on him. He did not have to wait long.

"Cade," Jesse's voice came from the window. "You get back here, Cade, goddam you." Jesse hearing the first of his profanity let loose at last, swore a lot more then, as though he had found his mind again in swearing.

A streetcar stopped at that moment.

"Don't get on that car, Cade," Jesse cried. "Goddam it."

Cade affected impatience.

"You wait now, goddam you," Jesse said putting on his rose-colored shirt.

"Cade," Jesse began when he was on the street beside his friend. "Let's go somewhere and talk this over. . . . See how I am," he pointed to his trembling arm.

"There ain't nowhere to go since you give up drinking," Cade told him.

Jesse took Cade's bag for him.

"Well if it makes you unhappy, I'll drink with you," Jesse said.

"I don't mind being unhappy," Cade said. "It's *you* that minds, Jesse."

"I want you to forgive me, Cade," Jesse said, putting his hand on Cade's arm.

Cade allowed Jesse's arm to rest there.

"Well, Jesse," Cade said coldly.

"You see," Jesse began, pulling Cade gently along with him as they walked toward a tavern. "You see, I don't know what it is, Cade, but you know everything."

Cade watched him.

They went into the tavern and although they usually sat at the bar, today they chose a table. They ordered beer.

"You see, Cade, I've lied to you, I think, and you're right. Of course your brother did save my life, but you saved it again. I mean you saved it more. You saved me," and he stretched out his trembling arm at Cade.

Jesse seeing the impassive look on Cade's face stopped and then going on as though he did not care whether anybody heard him or not, he said: "You're all I've got, Cade."

Cade was going to say *all right now* but Jesse went on speaking frantically and fluently as he had never spoken before. "You know ever since the war, I've been like I am. . . . And Cade, I need you that's why . . . I know you don't need me," he nodded like an old man now. "But I don't care now. I ain't proud no more about it."

Jesse stopped talking and a globule of spit rested thickly on his mouth.

"I'm cured of being proud, Cade."

"Well, all right then," Cade finally said, folding his arms and compressing his mouth.

"All right?" Jesse said, a silly look on his face, which had turned very young again.

"But you leave me alone now if I stay," Cade said.

"I will," Jesse said, perhaps not quite sure what it was Cade meant. "You can do anything you want, Cade. All I need is to know you won't really run out. No matter what I might some day say or do, you stay, Cade!"

"Then I don't want to hear no more about me getting just any old job," Cade said, drinking a swallow of beer.

"All right," Jesse said. "All right, all right."

"And you quit going to that old Mission and listening to that religious talk."

Jesse nodded.

"I ain't living with no old religious fanatic," Cade said.

Jesse nodded again.

"And there ain't no reason we should give up drinking and all the rest of it at night."

Jesse agreed.

"Or women," Cade said, and he fumbled now with the button of his shirt. It was such a very hot night his hand almost unconsciously pushed back the last button which had held his shirt together, exposing the section of his chest on which rested the tattooed drawing of a crouched black panther, the identical of Jesse's.

"And I don't want to hear no more about me going to work at all for a while," Cade was emphatic.

"All right, then, Cade," Jesse grinned, beginning to giggle and laugh now.

"Well I should say *all right*," Cade replied, and he smiled briefly, as he accepted Jesse's hand which Jesse proferred him then by standing up.

PART 2 _____

_____ Minor Offenses

Truancy, running away from home, a prank against one's school, irresponsibly shooting a gun, and fistfighting are behaviors that most of us were guilty of at one time or another as youngsters. When these derelictions are detected—and frequently they are not—adults react differently toward them: some are ignored, some laughed at, some reprimanded by parents, and some brought to the notice of a juvenile court. By and large, the reactions of adults to youngsters' minor delinquencies are not in proportion to the seriousness of the offenses.

In order to establish how serious an offense is, a few basic issues have to be considered. It is important to know how frequently the offense has been committed. An occasional truancy from school might go unnoticed or be judged an understandable lapse in behavior. If it is a chronic transgression, however, truancy is viewed by adults as serious and is dealt with more harshly. It is necessary to determine how serious the offense is in the eyes of the community. A spur-of-the-moment fistfight in which a nose is bloodied or an eye blackened might well be viewed as an instructive learning experience for young combatants. Yet, if a stronger juvenile maliciously injures his victim, it will be considered a serious breach. Some forms of delinquency arouse more alarm than others. There is little doubt that a minor who threatens another with a loaded gun will find himself in serious trouble, whereas an adolescent who tries to intimidate one of his peers by shouting threats will not. And, of course, the personality of the juvenile must be taken into account; if he is emotionally disturbed, his actions will be judged in the light of his psychological condition. Generally speaking, minor offenses occur infrequently, are not deemed serious by adults, are forms of behavior that do not

gravely injure property or persons, and do not result from a psycho-
logically disturbed personality.

Much short fiction has been written about the minor offenses of
young people. In these stories adult reactions to the offenses are
usually expressed in clichés like "Well, kids will be kids." When parents are concerned, it is more a matter of worrying over the safety of
their children than about what they have done. Authorities, too, show ·
basically the same leniency as parents—in fact, authorities often are
more understanding and less harsh in their punishment than parents.
Not infrequently, the stories have a humorous flavor that is reminiscent of *The Adventures of Tom Sawyer*.

Cutting school has been a venerated tradition among students
since the invention of the classroom, and many stories describing this
pastime are narrated in a humorous or mock-serious fashion from the
viewpoint of truants. On their return to the classroom the absentees
invariably regale their classmates with exaggerated accounts of their
adventures. "The Absences" gives a fresh view of a truancy story, for
it is narrated by a tolerant teacher who understands his students' desire to be away from school every now and then. Much of the humor
is found in the contrived excuses his students dream up: it is ludicrous how suddenly they are incapacitated by illness or personal
disaster on the afternoon of some hotly contested sports event. And
the reader chuckles at the naiveté of students who think their teacher
truly believes their transparent fibs—not realizing that such tales have
been used before, more than likely by the teacher himself. Almost all
stories about truancy depict it as a not altogether bad thing and rep-
rehensible only when students are absent for excessively long
periods or get involved in more serious delinquent behavior.

The literature on running away from home has changed considerably over the past eighty years. Around the turn of the century many
youngsters, almost always males, would suddenly leave home without notice to make their way in the world. The runaway frequently
signed on board a ship as a common seaman, worked as a farmhand
or cowboy, clerked in a store, or was apprenticed in a trade. Most
families would philosophically conclude—often with a sense of relief—that it was inevitable their child should leave. During the 1920s,
'30s, and '40s running away was less condoned by parents and the
law. It was not unusual for runaways to be brought home forcibly by
the police. Most often, because of the hardships they encountered,
runaways returned on their own to the protective arms of their parents, and much was learned by both children and parents from the
experience. Stories from the mid-1960s to the present dramatize a
different running away. In these, the runaways are extremely dissatis-

fied with their family, or school, or friends, or the world in general. Their primary reason for leaving home is their belief, often unfounded, that their parents fail to understand them.

"The Little Girl" could well be a sensational report taken from a national newspaper during the 1960s and '70s. Most of the stories written before that time depicted runaways as experiencing trying ordeals but rarely being brutalized. Those who did not return home or returned after a long absence were able to find a job, a sympathetic ear, a substitute family, or some other form of security.

Stories about pranks played by youngsters on their teachers, adults, and peers are as varied as the personalities of the children who perpetrate them. Some are merely childish, others stretch the imagination with their inventiveness, and others overshoot their mark and land pranksters in more trouble than they had bargained for. Many accounts are narrated from the point of view of delinquents whose mounting anticipation as they plan some mischief adds to the humor. Generally, children's pranks are motivated by boredom or the desire to get even with someone who has injured or insulted them. Bleat Blodgette's revenge on his prep school is predictable when one considers the indignities it has made him suffer; surely any boy with spirit would react in some way to the humiliation of having his hair shorn like a sheep or having his ear wrenched and his shins kicked by a teacher—but Bleat's revenge oversteps what propriety will allow and he is expelled. Bleat's only defense for desecrating the school chapel is a weak " 'I just went crazy.' " In most instances pranksters do not understand their own actions. With this in mind, one might ask if Bleat's punishment is in proportion to his crime. In almost all stories about pranks, punishments are either too lenient or too severe.

It has often been observed that the delinquencies of city children are more frequently detected and more harshly punished than those of rural children. In "A South Summer Idyll," there is little doubt that if Big Lawrence and Howard lived in a city, they would find themselves before a judge for shooting a gun at a cat, the glass signal disks on a railroad tower, and the side of a passing freight train. At home in the countryside around Dallas, however, they enjoy their derelictions with apparent impunity.

Fistfight stories are popular among readers. Typically they delineate the conflicts between twelve- to fifteen-year-old boys usually precipitated by a misunderstood statement or action. Once the emotions are ignited and the fists start flying, there is little chance of the fighters stopping quickly. Inevitably onlookers get caught up in the excitement of the action and goad the combatants on until both drop from exhaustion or one is beaten. In the process of the fight the combatants learn much about their strengths and weaknesses and the results of impulsively giving in to their anger. "The Death of Horatio Alger" is one of the best stories of this kind, especially in the way it captures the vitriolic rage of Mickey as he finds himself being badly beaten by his opponent: "I could have murdered God, in that simple practical way we kick dogs off the bottom step." Another kind of fist-fight story considers older adolescents, usually between the ages of fifteen and eighteen, purposefully involved in a fight—often with knives, chains, or other paraphernalia—in order to decide the leadership of a gang. These conflicts do not result from impulsive actions or misunderstandings; on the contrary, they are premeditated and often planned well in advance, especially when gang leadership is being sought. During such contests the supporters of the fighters lend any manner of encouragement, short of becoming involved themselves.

THE ABSENCES
Zulfikar Ghose

I keep the register fastidiously neatly. A rectangular box for each day, with a dotted line running down its middle so that a boy can be marked present or absent for each of the morning and afternoon sessions, daily receives the kind of careful attention which I give to paring my fingernails. I use a red biro—a most serviceable BiC, the extraordinarily cheap price of which so amazes me that I sometimes wonder why the manufacturers do not export it to Japan—to mark a boy present, making a deft diagonal stroke across the one half of the box, from the bottom left hand corner to the top right hand corner in the mornings and from the top left hand corner of the second half of the box to the bottom right hand corner in the afternoons. I check in the boys present first, leaving blank spaces for the absentees; then, putting the biro away in my desk, I take out my fountain-pen—a modest Parker "17"—wipe the nib on the edge of a piece of blotting paper, and, with a steady hand, inscribe a nought in the relevant box of an absentee. My manner is perhaps a trifle ceremonious (though certainly *not* pedantic), but I believe in a methodical execution of duty. I do things scrupulously; otherwise, I ask myself, why attempt a task at all? A philosophical justification is important in an age which doubts, nay, scorns the old veritities of religious belief. Each one of us has to construct his own order. If I have any reason to think that my hand will shake when putting in the diagonal stroke to mark a boy present, I use a ruler, and sometimes indulge myself to the extent of congratulating myself on my presence of mind.

Sometimes a pattern emerges in the register. I can account, for example, for Walker's frequent absences in the afternoons this summer term. I know that he suffered from asthma in his first year and had his appendix removed, but his recent absences can be related to the sporting calendar. I have teased him on this score. Once, during the lunch break, he came to me and complained of a stomach ache. I looked at him sternly and his face, exposed to my silent scrutiny, reddened a little.

"Yes, Walker," I said with excessive sympathy in my voice, "you look pale, you're obviously ill."

He lowered his eyes. Perhaps he was overwhelmed, perhaps ashamed. Putting a hand to his forehead, I went on, "I believe you have a temperature. You must go home at once."

He made to walk away, thanking me in a whisper to demonstrate how weak he was, and I said, calling after him, "Walker." And paused as I caught his eyes which had been anxious to steal away.

"Sir?" He spoke the word as though I were a priest come to his bed-side.

"I hope, Walker," I said as if I were remarking on the weather, "the Wimbledon final this year will not be disappointing."

The solemnity of expression, which he had so studiously maintained, collapsed, but I walked away, leaving his own conscience to confront his blushing smile.

I have, however, not wished to be the rain to Walker's sunny sporting afternoons when, I have no doubt, he takes his illness as far as the school gates, runs home, which is empty because both his parents work, switch-es on the television and sinks into a comfortable sofa. For a good sport-ing contest can sometimes be more instructive than what Walker, with his mind at Wembley or at Lord's, is likely to obtain from a member of my profession on the same afternoon.

Bowen's illnesses, which have inflicted him suddenly at eleven o'clock on certain Tuesday mornings, I consider more serious, for his obvious intention has been to miss Technical Drawing. The pain which he feels on such mornings in his chest is very real and once, having been sent home on Tuesday morning, he was away for a fortnight. I met his par-ents, who came to discuss their son with me—to talk over their "prob-lem" child, as they were so anxious to call him in a mood of parental self-martyrdom. They had taken him to a chest specialist, although they knew that the boy was as aware as they, the doctor and myself that the pain, though he experienced it as a very real one, was in fact imaginary. Modern children, it seems, have intuitively anticipated modern psycholo-gy. How interesting, I reflected, this paradox of an imagined reality, the unreality of which one knew and yet was convinced that it was real! Could not one suffer (I elaborated the paradox to myself) the reverse of Bowen's condition and believe that one was in perfect health when, say, one's lungs were rotted with thirty years of tobacco? And perhaps also believe that one had been living with a certain pain all one's life and did not know of it.

Such thinking was too advanced for me to mention to Bowen's par-ents, but it did occur to me that the ability to appreciate a bodily condi-tion from the point of view of pure thought which so loved to manipulate paradox would be a decided advantage were I ever to be struck by an incurable illness.

The problem with soft-fleshed, almost girlish Bowen remains a psycho-logical one which he and the Technical Drawing teacher will have to resolve. I can only, in certain informal moments when I can avoid re-sembling a psychiatrist, talk to Bowen and try to eliminate his fear of Mr. Congdon, a lean, hollow-faced man who, as he walks, gives the impres-sion of having measured his relationship to the earth with a set-square.

The register, then, provides me with evidence of the boys' idiosyncrasies, their fears and the state of their health. The summer term invariably separates the studious from the pleasure-seekers.

A day after the fishing season commenced this term, I noticed that Williams, Lamb and Knight were away. The three of them sit in a corner at the back of the class and I viewed with suspicion their corporate absence. Their absence continued to the fourth day in succession. It is normal to fill in a form on the third day of a boy's absence so that an inspector may visit his home to discover the reason for his being away. It is my habit to ignore this practice because, one, I am determined not to give employment to petty bureaucracy and, two, I like my boys to trust me enough to make their own decisions by consulting only the strict notion of responsibility and duty which I have endeavoured to inculcate upon their minds. I know that they sometimes do not reciprocate this trust, but I do not feel betrayed. I have pointed out to them and will repeatedly do so, despite their affectionate irritation when they snigger and say to one another " 'Ere 'e goes agine," that all decisions are moral decisions. On the occasion, however, of the combined absence of Williams, Lamb and Knight it was obvious even to Paynter (to whose atrocious essay on *The Uselessness of Stamp Collecting* I had given a generous delta plus) that the three were out fishing, I was obliged to fill in the form.

The next morning, Williams and Lamb were standing outside my door, looking—the word is apt despite the surname of the latter—sheepish. The good weather of the previous three days had tanned their faces and before I could ask them a question, Lamb said, "We bin fishin', sir."

I was satisfied with his truthfulness and restrained myself from pursuing orthodox punitive action against which my principal objection is that it is boring. But where was Knight?

Williams pulled out a piece of paper from his pocket. It was a tiny piece of paper from a note-book the size bus conductors carry in their breast pockets. It had been ripped out so carelessly that the irregularity of the tear described a wedge deep enough to have gone past the margin.

"Thass from Joe's mum," Williams said, giving me the note.

There was no date, none of the embellishments of formality. Scrawled in a round hand in a blue biro, which it had obviously been necessary to press hard into the paper, were the words, "Dear Sir, Please fogive Joe's migrain and absents. Mrs. Knight."

I knew it to be genuine. At least the spelling was authentic, and, backward though Williams and Lamb were in the subject I taught them, I had taken pains to make it clear to them that assonance and rhyme were no guarantee of a similarity of spelling.

Why, I wondered, did Knight suffer from migraine? It distressed me to reflect that an aspect of the character of one of my pupils was obscure to me. I had always assumed him to be a robust, healthy boy. He was the tallest in the class and so endowed with athletic ability as to be regarded with respectful esteem by senior boys while the juniors admired him to the point of adulation. They all called him Bomber Joe. I had once seen him play in a soccer match when he was in his second year and was not yet thirteen. The school team was a goal down and the match had progressed well into the second half; desperately though they tried, the forwards could not score. Then Knight came up from centre-half to take a corner kick. He walked to the corner flag slowly, thoughtfully. He placed the ball down firmly, then walked back a few paces. He looked at the players who had crowded in front of the goal-mouth. He looked up at the sky and then stared at the ball. One, two, three strides and he kicked the ball. I was standing behind the goal and saw the ball first soar into the air, then swerve above the heads of the players and dip into the far corner of the net. Knight had used the wind as an ally.

The class had become noisy while I tried to recall what I could of Knight in an attempt at enlightenment, for I understood migraine to be a nervous illness and I hoped that my analysis of Knight's behaviour, habits and eccentricities would give me some direction.

"I suggest you contain your gossip for a few minutes," I called to the class.

"Sir," said shrill-voiced Yeo Wren (some parents!) whom the boys had nicknamed Piss-pot from his first day at the school, "Sir," he said, looking very innocent so that I anticipated his cheek, "would you like a pregnant silence?"

There was a roar of laughter.

"Very funny, Wren," I said, "I shall die laughing."

Quickly came the answer, "I hope you do, sir."

I was lost for a rejoinder—in a Secondary Modern school you have to be quicker than in the House of Commons—and the class laughed and banged upon the desks. I rose, stared silently at the class until the noise died down and the boys, sixty maliciously merry eyes, awaited my next move.

"I do not know what this jubilation is all about," I said, ponderously choosing my words, but quickly enough to prevent someone taking the chance to cry out, "Didn't your muvver tell yer, sir?" and went on, "but allow me, Wren, to point out that you cannot win a cheap laugh at the expense of the English language. The word 'pregnant' "—I pronounced the two syllables distinctly, giving equal stress to each—"means teeming with ideas, imaginative, inventive and fruitful in results,' and that being so, I think we can state with absolute certainty that there is no danger of you ever being pregnant. So, shut up."

There was a snigger, a giggle or two and, in the silence which followed, I observed one boy discreetly turn the pages of a dictionary and, finding the exact words which I had quoted, show them to his friend in astonishment.

Knight had never used in an innocuous context words which many boys considered naughty, words which were certain to embarrass the teacher. Intellectually, Knight was a little naive and he did not share the habit of the other boys to turn the most ordinary phrase, like "stick it in," into a sexual pun. Reading *Oliver Twist,* he alone had not at first seen why Dickens's frequent references to Charley Bates as Master Bates were such a tedious joke.

Perhaps this lack of imagination and intelligence—which incidentally explained why he was instinctively so good at soccer and hopeless at cricket—indicated a reason for Knight's nervous condition. I wondered what sorts of situations could occur in his life with which he could not intellectually cope and to which his only reaction would be one of mental disorder. My guessing was futile, for my knowledge of him, which I had considered to be adequate, was now proved to be hopelessly incomplete. His absences stared at me from the register.

One morning, when I had neatly imprinted another nought to record his absence, my eyes seemed to lose focus, and the oval shapes of the absences I had recorded became distorted and enlarged; Knight's absences multiplied, became a whole score of absences. The faces of many of my friends, whom I had not seen for several years, appeared through the noughts and vanished again. I had never attempted to explain *their* absences. In some cases, their exclusion from my existence had a simple reason, like working in a distant country, and in some other cases I preferred to be without their presence.

Absence, it occurred to me, was a state one continually sought from someone or other and sometimes from oneself: but always with a psychological or emotional reason. Man has devised a multiplicity of reasons to be absent. To be busy, to be not available on the telephone, to be not at home, to want to get away, to need a holiday—the phraseology of absence was considerable. From what, though, this compulsion to be away? From the awfulness of being present? Or, simply, from the burden of being?

I expelled this sudden intrusion of a metaphysical paradox from my mind and again considered Knight's absences which I had still not succeeded in explaining. I had consulted the file with the Headmaster containing information about the boys' families; but there had been nothing there to indicate that Knight came from a problem family, one, say, where the parents were divorced. Such knowledge is often illuminating as, indeed, is the medical history of the boys. Once I silenced a boy for a

week by saying in front of the class, "Did you not suffer from piles, Finn,
I'd have you bend over and give you three strokes of my cane." No, as
far as I could ascertain, Knight came from a normal family. He was, as I
have said, healthy, athletic. He ate well and at milk time always had an
extra milk if there were any left over. I had seen him munch apples
during the morning breaks. I had once caught him climbing over the
fence at the end of the sports ground into a private garden in order to
help himself to a pear. Whether observing the rules of discipline or breaking them, he was the average, normal boy.

Having failed to explain his absences, I decided finally to send an inspector to his house again; and, not without anxiety, I awaited his report.
I stopped speculating; indeed, for a day, stopped thinking of Knight. The
day's teaching passed without incident, though Wren again tried to trip
me with another sexual riddle.

"What's a period, sir?" he piped, the freckly-faced idiot.

"A period, Wren, is a full stop."

"Bugger me," he muttered and his companion, who was attempting to
compose a piece on *The Selfishness Encouraged by Sport* (I set them
subjects which direct them to the truth), said to him, "Belt up, Piss-pot!"
But I was not supposed to have heard either remark.

The next day, the inspector's report lay on my desk. I put it aside to
mark the register first. I called out the names and was greeted with either
"Yes, sir" or "Present, sir." Wren tried to make the former sound like
"Sex, sir," and raised a laugh, so that I had to pause, stare at him and
say, "Are you in any doubt, Wren?" I noted the absences, and then read
the report on Knight, which was as follows:

> Mother states child has been poorly with migraine attacks, which
> resumed on Tuesday 10th. Further states she feels the boy has
> some tension over his mongol sister and this causes the migraine.
> Will NOT visit the doctor and hasn't seen him for over a year. The
> parents will try and persuade him to go. Personal feeling—mother is
> covering up for him.

I am continually being given evidence that God is a phoney justicer, a
hypocrite without a conscience, a dispenser of inclemency, who is so
execrably conceited about his own damned perfection as to *want* to
create worsening degrees of imperfection in man. That is why I do things
scrupulously, construct my own ordered world.

Knight was fourteen now and probably had only recently realised what
responsibility his sister's mental deformity threw on him. I questioned
Williams indirectly, obliquely, so that he would not sense that he was
telling on Knight.

" 'E takes 'er on walks, sir. In the park. She goes like this, guh-guh-guh."

Elbows sticking out and hands shaking limply, he described a generalised gesture of idiocy.

"She's batty, sir."

He giggled rather than laughed.

And Knight was probably already having to fight against the laughter of others. She would be there every morning at breakfast, spilling the milk out of the cereal bowl, holding the spoon awkwardly. There would always be something to tidy or to mop up, for disorder and filth attended mental deficiency.

I would not again pursue his absences. If he returned and drove a pen-knife into his desk or spilled ink over his work or aimed a pellet at someone's ear or chewed gum during a lesson or talked without permission or was involved in a fight during break or neglected to do his homework, I would not try to teach him the irrelevant catechism of discipline. The vandalism of despair is not for my censure.

THE LITTLE GIRL

Grace Paley

Carter stop by the café early. I just done waxing. He said, I believe I'm
having company later on. Let me use your place, Charlie, hear?

I told him, Door is open, go ahead. Man coming for the meter (why I
took the lock off). I told him Angie my lodger *could* be home but he
strung out most the time. He don't even know when someone practicing
the horn in the next room. Carter, you got hours and hours. There ain't
no wine there, nothing like it. He said he had some other stuff would
keep him on top. That was a joke. Thank you, brother, he said. I told
him I believe I *have* tried anything, but to this day, I like whiskey. If you
have whiskey, you drunk, but if you pump up with drugs, you just crazy.
Yeah, hear that man, he said. Then his eyeballs start walking away.

He went right to the park. Park is full of little soft yellow-haired baby
chicks. They ain't but babies. They far from home, and you better believe it, they love them big black cats walking around before lunchtime,
jutting their apparatus. They think they gonna leap off that to heaven.
Maybe so.

Nowadays, the spades around here got it set out for them. When I was
young, I put that kettle to cook. I stirred it and stirred it. And these dudes
just sucking off the gravy.

Next thing: Carter rested himself on the bench. He look this way and
that. His pants is tight. His head making pictures. Along comes this child.
She just straggling along. Got her big canvas pocketbook and she looking
around. Carter hollers out. Hey, sit down, he says. By me, here, you
pretty thing. She look sideways. Sits. On the edge.

Where you from, baby? he ask her. Hey, relax, you with friends.

Oh, thank you. Oh, the Midwest, she says. Near Chicago. She want to
look good. She ain't from maybe eight hundred miles.

You left home for a visit, you little dandylion you, your boy friend let
you just go?

Oh no, she says. Getting talky. I just left and for good. My mother
don't let me do a thing. I got to do the breakfast dishes when I get home
from school and clean and do my two brothers' room and they don't
have to do nothing. And I got to be home in my room by 10 p.m.
weekdays and 12 p.m. just when the fun starts Saturday and nothing is
going on in that town. Nothing! It's dead, a sleeping hollow. *And the
prejudice, whew!* She blushes up a little, she don't want to hurt his feelings. It's terrible and then they caught me out with a little bit of a roach I
got off of some fellow from New York who was passing through and I

couldn't get out at all then for a week. They was watching me and watching. They're disgusting and they're so ignorant!

My! Carter says. I don't know how you kids today stand it. The world is changing, that's a fact, and the old folks ain't heard the news. He ruffle with her hair and he lay his cheek on her hair a minute. Testing. And he puts the tip of his tongue along the tip of her ear. He's a fine-looking man, you know, a nice color, medium, not too light. Only thing wrong with him is some blood line in his eye.

I don't know when I seen a prettier chick, he says. Just what we call fattening the pussy. Which wouldn't use up no time he could see. She look at him right away. Oh Lord, I been trudging around. I am tired. Yawns.

He says, I got a nice place, you could just relax and rest and decide what to do next. Take a shower. Whatever you like. Anyways you do is O.K. My, you are sweet. You better'n Miss America. How old you say you was?

Eighteen, she jump right in.

He look at her satisfied, but that was a lie and Carter knew it, I believe. That the Number One I hold against him. Because, why her? Them little girls just flock, they do. A grown man got to use his sense.

Next thing: They set out for my apartment, which is six, seven blocks downtown. Stop for a pizza. 'Mm this is good, she says (she is so simple). She says, They don't make 'em this way back home.

They proceed. I seen Carter courting before. Canvas pocketbook across his shoulder. They holding hands maybe and hand-swinging.

Open the front door of 149, but when they through struggling up them four flights, she got to be disappointed, you know my place, nothing there. I got my cot. There's a table. There two chairs. Blanket on the bed. And a pillow. And a old greasy pillow slip. I'm too old now to give up my grizzily greasy head, but I sure wish I was a young buck, I would let my Afro flare out.

She got to be disappointed.

Wait a minute, he says, goes into the kitchen and brings back ice water, a box of pretzels. Oh, thank you, she says. Just what I wanted. Then he says, Rest yourself, darling and she lie down. Down, right in her coffin.

You like to smoke? Ain't that peaceful, he says. Oh, it is, she says. It sure is peaceful. People don't know.

Then they finish up. Just adrifting in agreement, and he says, You like to ball? She says, Man! Do I! Then he put up her dress and take down her panties and tickle her here and there, nibbling away. He says, You like that, baby? Man! I sure do, she says. A colored boy done that to me once back home, it sure feels good.

Right then he get off his clothes. Gonna tend to business. Now, the bad thing there is, the way Carter told it, and I know it so, those little girls come around looking for what they used to, hot dog. And what they get is knockwurst. You know we are like that. Matter of fact, Carter did force her. Had to. She starting to holler, Ow, it hurts, you killing me, it hurts. But Carter told me, it was her asked for it. Tried to get away, but he had been stiff as stone since morning when he stop by the store. He wasn't *about* to let her run.

Did you hit her? I said. Now Carter, I ain't gonna tell anyone. But I got to know.

I might of hauled off and let her have it once or twice. Stupid little cunt asked for it, didn't she? She was so little, there wasn't enough meat on her thigh bone to feed a sick dog. She could of wriggled by the scoop in my armpit if I had let her. Our black women ain't a bit like that, I told you Charlie. They cook it up, they eat the mess they made. They proud.

I didn't let that ride too long. Carter's head moves quick, but he don't dust me. I ask him, How come when they passing the plate and you *is* presented with the choice, you say like the prettiest dude, A little of that white stuff, please, man?

I don't! He hollered like I had chopped his neck. And I won't! He grab my shirt front. It was a dirty old work shirt and it tore to bits in his hand. He got solemn. Shit! You right! They are poison! They killing me! That diet gonna send me upstate for nothin but *bone* diet and I got piles as is.

Joking by the side of the grave trench. That's why I used to like him. He wasn't usual. That's why I like to pass time with Carter in the park in the early evening.

Be cool, I said.

Right on, he said.

He told me he just done shooting them little cottonhead darkies into her when Mangie Angie Emporiore lean on the doorway. Girl lying on my bloody cot pulling up a sheet, crying, bleeding out between her legs. Carter had tore her up some. You know, Charlie, he said, I ain't one of your little Jewboy buddies with half of it cut off. Angie peering and peering. Carter stood up out of his working position. He took a quick look at Angie, heisted his pants and split. He told me, Man, I couldn't stay there, that dumb cunt sniffling and that blood spreading out around her, she didn't get up to protect herself, she was disgusting, and that low white bug, your friend, crawled in from under the kitchen sink. Now on, you don't live with no white junkie, hear me Charlie, they can't use it.

Where you going now Carter? I ask him. To the pigs, he says and jabs his elbow downtown. I hear they looking for me.

That exactly what he done, and he never seen free daylight since.

Not too long that same day they came by for me. They know where I

am. At the station they said, You sleep somewhere else tonight and tomorrow night. Your place padlocked. You wouldn't want to see it, Charlie. You in the clear. We know your whereabouts to the minute. Sergeant
could see I didn't know nothing. Didn't want to tell me neither. I'll explain it. They had put out a warrant for Angel. Didn't want me speaking
to him. Telling him anything.

Hector the beat cop over here can't keep nothing to himself. They are
like that. Spanish people. Chatter chatter. What he said: You move,
Charlie. You don't want to see that place again. Bed smashed in. That
little girl broken up in the bottom of the airshaft on top of the garbage
and busted glass. She just tossed out that toilet window wide awake alive.
They know that. Death occur on ground contact.

The next day I learned worse. Hector found me outside the store. My
buffer swiped. Couldn't work. He said, Every bone between her knee
and her rib cage broken, splintered. She been brutally assaulted with a
blunt instrument or a fist before death.

Worse than that, on her leg high up, inside, she been bitten like a
animal bit her and bit her and tore her little meat she had on her. I said,
All right, Hector. Shut up. Don't speak.

They put her picture in the paper every day for five days, and when
her mother and daddy came on the fifth day, they said, The name of our
child is Juniper. She is fourteen years old. She been a little rebellious but
the kids today all like that.

Then court. I had a small job to say, Yes, it was my place. Yes, I told
Carter he could use it. Yes, Angie was my roommate and sometimes he
lay around there for days. He owed me two months' rent. That the
reason I didn't put him out.

In court Carter said, Yes, I did force her, but he said he didn't do
nothing else.

Angie said, I did smack her when I seen what she done, but I never bit
her, your honor, I ain't no animal, that black hippie must of.

Nobody said—they couldn't drag out of anyone—they lacking the evidence who it was picked her up like she was nothing, a bag of busted
bones, and dumped her out the fifth-floor window.

But wasn't it a shame, them two studs. Why they take it out on her?
After so many fluffy little chicks. They could of played her easy. Why
Carter seen it many times hisself. She could of stayed the summer. We
just like the UN. Every state in the union stop by. She would of got her
higher education right on the fifth-floor front. September, her mama and
daddy would come for her and they whip her bottom, we know that. We
been in this world long enough. We seen lots of the little girls. They go
home, then after a while they get to be grown womens, they integrating

the swimming pool and picketing the supermarket, they blink their eyes and shut their mouth and grin.

But that was my room and my bed, so I don't forget it. I don't stop thinking. That child. . . . That child. . . . And it come to me yesterday, I lay down after work: Maybe it wasn't no one. Maybe she pull herself the way she was, crumpled, to that open window. She was tore up, she must of thought she was gutted inside her skin. She must of been in a horror what she got to remember—what her folks would see. Her life look to be disgusting like a squashed fish, so what she did: she made up some power somehow and raise herself up that windowsill and hook herself onto it and then what I see, she just topple herself out. That what I think right now.

That is what happened.

BLEAT BLODGETTE

John Phillips (John P. Marquand, Jr.)

His mother's face had not always looked so round. He could remember it pale and maidenly, when the cheekbones showed and when it was soft but not fleshy and relatively unpolluted by woe. Mrs. Blodgette wasn't forty yet. Nothing made her face so luminous as tears could, and she must have been only discovering that this was so. She seemed to make a cosmetic asset of it: no rouge or powder flawed her cheeks, to be caked and corrugated by her tears. The spring twilight gave his mother's moist skin a near Rubenesque luster, he believed, being strangely moved by colors at this his most formative age. Colors had on him the power of staying his instincts. It was only when he thought he couldn't stand another word she said that he'd hit her across the mouth. He was callow and high-strung; she ought to have known she was putting him under a great strain.

"My poor boy," she'd been weeping. "It doesn't matter about me, but when he turns his back on his two sons, then I say it is his black blood coming out. He's done it before. I knew this would happen."

"It's not, Mah."

"My poor boy, what are you going to do?"

"It's not black blood."

"My poor darling."

And for this, for this Mrs. Blodgette had come from Eighty-second Street to the western Massachusetts village where her son had almost completed the expensive secondary education his great-aunt was providing him. As it were from Ghent to Aix, she'd sped here by taxicab and Pullman car and, sparing herself in her desperate haste none of the inconveniences of travel in that year 1940, had changed at Springfield to a Greyhound bus—bringing news of Papa. She also brought for reading on the train a contemporaneous book of child psychology, *As the Twig Is Bent*. Though an erratic reader, she plainly had given it considerable attention. He noticed almost as soon as he saw her that the jacket was torn and there were smudges of ink where she'd marked certain pages.

He met her on the steps of Headmaster's House, that reception place of parents, and saw how her face was radiant with emergency. "What's the matter, Mah?" — "Poor Steven!" She tried to clasp him in her short arms when *As the Twig Is Bent* flopped open on the bricks and the torn halves of the jacket were swept off in the May breeze. He had to chase over the lawn to retrieve them. "How come you read this junk?" he

asked her, although the reason was on her face. "Something's happened. Your mother must be the one who tells you," she said.

Supper was over at the school and during the short interim before
Evening Prayer, shirt-sleeved boys were all round outdoors chasing tennis balls and playing nigger baby. His mother was nervous and frumpy in
her brown dress. She was the same height as her son. Even some severely astigmatic schoolmate pausing in his play and squinting through
the growing dusk might at once perceive their kinship. They can see us,
he realized, with an excruciation strong and cruel, beyond the categories
of every book of juvenile psychology. He took his little mother, shoved
her, all but hurled her through the screen door. "Oh, Steven!" He tumbled after her into Headmaster's Parlor and the door sprang shut against
his heel.

"Here's your book," he said. "Why do you have to read that junk?"

His mother put the book on the table, where it rested among the cups
and sandwiches. Wednesday afternoons Mrs. Kew, the Headmaster's
wife, served tea to Faculty Wives, but by this hour the room was abandoned. Entirely to themselves, mother and son, they had the vase of
tulips, the chipped white and green crockery, the knives and spoons, the
curtains of smelly yellow muslin, and the considerable length of the
leather sofa on which they sat at distant ends. He thought of what to say
to make up for shoving her through the door. From now on he would
call her mama as politely as could be; no more talking to her like some
slob.

She told him, "Something has happened. You will have to be brave."

"About my father," he said.

"I know you're going to be a brave boy."

"It's some lady."

"No *lady*." His mother had the little handkerchief in her hand ready
for when they would need it.

"He got married."

"Poor darling, how do I explain? You must be brave. Naturally it's not
our affair. I was so afraid you'd see it in the newspapers, because this is a
married woman."

"The hell with the newspapers. Everybody has the right to live their
own life, I guess."

The mother smote the sofa with her handkerchief. "All his life Papa
has only thought about one person and that person is himself!"

She would not stop talking. He only stood there beside the window as
far from her as he could decently be. Outdoors on the lawns the boys ran
free, throwing tennis balls that soared up, and up in the evening sky.
They shouted while his mother talked, and then he heard the chapel bell
tolling down an end to the day's frivolity. The boys gathered up their

coats and began trudging off to Evening Prayer, while tightening their neckties, and the sun cast pale crepuscular colors on their shirts. He felt an impulse of love for his fellows, those other creatures of this hothouse who might some day have to fight the world. Their turn would come, they'd see their family names debauched in newspapers. One boy, last winter, had his father fall drunk out of a hotel room he was hiring with a showgirl. A father squashed like an old tomato on the sidewalk, and this boy learned about it in the morning paper they showed him at breakfast.

"In Catholic countries," his mother explained, "the conventions are different from ours. Divorce is an unusual thing. The Europeans have customs . . . marriage customs . . . that may seem hypocritical to you and me."

"Mah." He winced for her; he'd lived in France, he'd written a term paper about Henry the Eighth. "Mah, do you think I'm a child?" His excruciation for her was worse than last year, on the occasion of his sixteenth birthday, when she traveled up to the school convinced it was *her Duty*—his father having abdicated his—to explain to him how babies are made.

"She is a rich woman from New Mexico married to an Austrian nobleman. There isn't the *possibility* of a divorce," his mother was saying. "She's Baroness Stoeffenblus and she is not a lady, Steven. She's not Austrian either."

"I still bet she's French." He could see the fleeting wraith of this baroness. A creature of fantastic allure, a courtesan; she had diamonds and a beauty spot and a towering wig. She was Ethel Merman, Madame Du Barry, whom he saw on his father's lap, kissing his father, tickling his chin, patting the bald spot on his head. Sugar Daddy. He saw a big photograph of them on the front page of the New York *Journal-American*, and a scarlet headline and columns of soul-baring print.

"She isn't French," his mother corrected him, very shrill, "Papa's Baroness is nothing but the daughter of a cop-per min-er." Her voice quailed on the syllables and broke, and he couldn't stand to hear her. "A rich vulgar woman who married a fortune hunter for his name . . . poor Steven . . . poor children . . ." She got going again on the black Blodgette blood.

He would bring her to her senses. "Mah, that's crazy!" He would shake her if she made him do it.

"You are my brave boy."

"Now cut it out, Mah."

"You are so brave. Now I can tell Aunt Norah and Little Howard that you were so brave when I told you."

He would ask her a question, calm her, divert her. Quickly ask any old question. "Mah, how do you say that name Stoffus?"

Toward the window and the setting sun, his mother turned her round, uncomprehending face. "Stoeffenblus?" she asked, and began by syllables. "Stuff—n—" she said. "Stuff—" The rose-red light glistening on her moist face gave it almost a Rubens color that made him forget what was happening. If only she had sat completely still in that light and not, mistaking his pain for helplessness, darted on over at him almost jubilantly on her tiny ballerina's feet.

"My poor boy." She came at him as if the tears were of joy, and flung out her arms almost triumphantly to receive him. "My brave boy."

His fist flew up high like one of the tennis balls. He sighted for her open mouth and hit it, he would never be sure how hard. She recoiled but she didn't fall. The backs of his fingers felt wet and tingled from the touch of her teeth, and he believed she was crying something at him that he couldn't hear. He was too surprised to move, and for the first time in his life a vice of pain clamped round his chest.

"Can I interest anyone in Evening Prayer?"

Dr. Kew, Emmanuel's Headmaster, poked head and shoulders through the screen door. It may have been that when he asked his question he was attempting a quip of his, giving the old "Tennis anyone?" an ecclesiastical twist. The Reverend Dr. Kew, not heavily endowed with tact, was all the same a kindly man. He passed the academic year in daily contact with traumata and still he was no voyeur or glutton; he would never have intruded on this ugly scene except that the chapel bell was tolling, bringing out his shepherd's instincts. "Last call for prayers," Dr. Kew called in to the Blodgettes cheerfully, exactly as he would to any other son and mother who seemed to have forgotten the hour. "Last call for chapel."

"Oh thank God," Mrs. Blodgette sighed, "Dr. Kew, it's you."

The Headmaster stepped into his Parlor, a well-shouldered, fine-eyed man, trim, vigorously middle-aged, his gray forelock subtly tousled as if to say that he had been a boy himself and that if he'd grown up to be an ordained minister, it was because he loved boys and was interested in their problems. It was a standing joke in school that Dr. Kew could have doubled for Spencer Tracy any day as Father Flannigan in Boys Town. A two-fisted man of God, Dr. Kew arrived on the untidy scene clasping the Book of Common Prayer against a distinctly Anglican surplice. "Mrs. Blodgette, good evening. Good evening, Blodgette. You didn't hear the bell?" he said. "Something the matter with your hand?"

"Good evening, sir." Blodgette had his offending fist behind his back.

"Oh, Dr. Kew, thank God you came," Mrs. Blodgette said.

"Well now," the Headmaster began. "Can't be as bad as that now, can it?" He had only a minute of his time to soothe this nerve-racked mother. In these circumstances, as dispensation, he excused Blodgette from Evening Prayer, and left them.

Wrung with penance, the boy stayed with his mother, to be squeezed, kissed, copiously forgiven, and forgiving in his turn. In a dismal bathroom they washed their faces on Mrs. Kew's guest towels. When it was time to go, his mother reached out to kiss him through the open door of the taxicab. "I forgot my *As the Twig Is Bent!*" she said, and he had to run back to the parlor and fetch the book. For that she kissed him several times. The last thing she said before he shut the taxi door was that she felt much better, "much much better."

Twenty-four hours passed, and then when the gloaming came again, with the shouts and the tennis balls flying outdoors, Blodgette was summoned to Headmaster's Study. In this barnlike room which gave off Headmaster's Parlor, the Head Man was waiting there in his vestments. "Well now, Steve, I'm afraid I have sad tidings."

"Yes, sir."

He wasn't going to ask if his mother had swallowed a bunch of sleeping pills. Or had she by chance defenestrated? He understood at once that his mother was dead. He saw a vision of the New York *Journal-American* that announced her red-headlined death, so hard and bright he had to blink.

"This afternoon I had a telephone conversation with Mrs. . . ." the Headmaster searched for the name. "Mrs. Safford."

"Yes, sir. She's my great-aunt."

"Well now, your aunt is good and mad at you. Steve." Dr. Kew was being kindly, and yet even after six years' acquaintance, it was embarrassing to have the Head Man call you by the diminutive of your Christian name. "Can you think why?" he asked.

"My aunt's always mad about something."

"Well now, your mother has had some sort of attack, I gather."

"A nervous attack."

"The doctor has sent her to bed. Complete rest and quiet."

"Then it's nothing, sir. Our family lives on nerves."

"That's a might funny thing for a fellow to say about his family, Steve."

"It's a mighty funny family, sir."

"Well now," said the Headmaster, low in his throat, that mildly gruff and yet to many endearing "well now" which a generation of Emmanuel graduates had come to mimic, with nostalgia. "Mrs. Safford—your aunt believes there is a connection between your mother's visit yesterday and her . . . and what happened to her when she got home." Dr. Kew tilted his face upward, his voice rose heavenward: "Far be it from me to inquire what happened with Mother in the parlor last evening. There are terrible powers dwelling inside us. Which one of us does not crave forgiveness for these terrible powers which visit us from the dark sides of our souls, Steve, and make us wretched and afraid?"

"Well, we already forgave each other, sir."

"That's fine, that's very good," said Dr. Kew, who had been drumming his fingers quite a bit on the cover of his prayer book. "Well now, but that was before Mother had this . . . bad turn, should I say? I wonder about now, this minute. I wonder if *right now* you are enjoying full forgiveness?"

"I don't suppose I am, sir."

" 'The Lord is my shepherd.' " Facing the ceiling, the Headmaster uttered some of the Twenty-third Psalm. He said, "To me these are the most beautiful words ever written. They tell us what forgiveness means . . . 'Thy Rod and Thy Staff they comfort me.' " He examined the boy. "Are you embarrassed by that? I'm not.

"His Divine Providence will absolve you. Give you clean hands and a pure heart. But you must seek it."

"Yes."

"Be a man. Manful."

"Yes."

"Seek and be manful."

"Yes."

Blodgette was excused tonight from Study Hour. He was to stay in chapel after Evening Prayer and offer his solitary conscience to the Lord, stay until the floodgates opened and bathed him in forgiveness. He might stay all night, for he had the Headmaster's permission.

Emmanuel Academy's chapel was an architectural anomaly thrust up from the center of a sedulously Georgian campus that was a particular pride of old Emmanuelers.

A Yankee cynosure, a panoramic symmetry of bricks and white columns which, erected as it was foursquare upon Hamilton's Federalist terrain, would have delighted even the eccentric Thomas Jefferson, a rhapsodic alumnus, Torbert Case, '96, had written in a fund-raising brochure. *Delighted too are Emmanuel's sons whose generosity (all the more remarkable in this age of fiscal chaos and decadent government!) has traditionally maintained the high order of both buildings and grounds. Our task is a self-perpetuating one, and one which today more than ever, to employ a phrase, costs money!*

The chapel, though, had been erected in a less chaotic age, the aftermath of the war with Spain. Considerable of the brutality and bombast associated with the battleship *Maine* was captured in its lines, and the building expense had been borne alone by three rich alumni in honor of a departed classmate. The architect, like many Emmanuel graduates, had attended Harvard at least long enough to join a final club, and he must have fallen in the Victorian-Gothic spell of Memorial Hall—that flabbergasting monument to the quantity of Harvard men exterminated in the War of Secession. And evidently this architect had been as well a man of eclectic taste; the chapel had diminutive flying buttresses on two of its sides and it was a hybrid phantasy: round and square, flat and thin, and amalgamating brick, slate, stucco, porphyry, oak, copper, stained glass and mullion among its ingredients. Set above the entrance was a hatchment of Vermont marble. It announced the name and dates of the prominent Emmanueler to whose memory, as though some insidious alternative to God, this presumptuous fane was built. And here lay a duplicity scalding to the conscience of Steven Safford Blodgette, '40, having been baptized in infancy an Episcopalian Christian of terrifying faith.

Three years ago last February, having come to the Years of Discretion and having the full Instruction of his church, Blodgette received the Laying on of Hands—in this chapel—from Diocesan Bishop Walsh, a graduate of Emmanuel who was by no coincidence Honorary Chairman of the Academy's Board of Trustees.

His Confirmation, he fully understood, was the clear consequence of unnatural, inward events that had happened before Christmas vacation. As usual, when he had to go home to Eighty-second Street, the prospect had brought on such fits of brooding as theologians have named *Tristitia*. He thought of being back with the aged maids, his great-aunt and mother and little brother in French velvet knickerbockers, all the descendant Saffords fulfilling their destiny like spirits stifled in an attic. He saw their grotesque significance, the ashen curse upon his stock, his *morbus originis*; from this he had a sense of Original Sin more harrowing than the manly notion that Dr. Kew had in mind in weekly Christian Studies class when he read to his students excerpts from Cardinal Newman's *Apologia*. Blodgette was fourteen years old when he experienced that first early terror of being a rabbit cast down kicking in the glacial night. All Hell was a frozen land from which he begged to be redeemed.

The time came when Blodgette took his place in a rank of kneeling boys. He feared his soul would die before he felt on his head the Bishop's hand as the Bishop passed from head to head bowed along the altar rail. In swirling raiment the Bishop hovered over him and in trembling baritone inflected the mounting phrases of the liturgy, in half-song, "Defend, O Lord, this thy CHILD with thy heavenly GRACE . . ."

and on to the next boy. Blodgette's scalp thrilled. Fearfully he touched the spot where Bishop Walsh's hand had lain. His hair was warm; he could tell that a miraculous deliverance had been granted him.

Afterward, it was easier to go home and almost painless to rejoin the family circle. He grew unconscionably jealous of his redemption. He was afraid of doubts which threatened it, and horribly afraid of the contempt he felt for the Higgs Memorial Chapel as a monument to Mammon and degrading to the Lord.

His scorn was centered on the marble hatchment. On it was cut out a fat cross that got encrusted with bird droppings in the spring. Below the carved cross the words *In Honored Memory of Thy Faithful Servant* were followed by the name and dates of the honored Higgs. To hear Blodgette decry the inscription as a sacrilege, his friends were amazed. "It's the *plaque* that's in honor of the guy," they would remonstrate. "You wack, that's different from the chapel." "It is, like hell," Blodgette would say. He was a crackpot on this subject. One day he made so bold to bring it up in the Headmaster's Christian Studies class.

They were discussing sanctity; Dr. Kew was asking for definitions of the word. "Sir!" Blodgette raised his hand, was recognized, and his tongue ran off with his inchoate thought. "Sanctity isn't putting up a chapel or something holy like that when it's supposed to be for God and then go dedicate it to a graduate of the school, sir. Just because he used to be a fat-cat millionaire. Sanctity means it's supposed to be for God! I mean, don't you see what I mean?"

"Well now," said Dr. Kew, the benign Spencer Tracy smiling on the clear young faces. "Blodgette raises an interesting point." He liked a boy who had the grit to speak out what was on his mind so long as it wasn't just smart aleck. The Head Man paused to examine the faces of Blodgette's classmates. In the averted eyes and hand-clutched mouths before him was evidence of laughter, and the Head Man played upon it. "Well now." He cocked his face to the ceiling, showed a nice sense of timing. "I'd better put it this way—It *may be* our friend raises an interesting point . . . but Blodgette gets so all-fired passionate when he talks that I'll be double-all-day darned if I can catch a word he says!"

There was a cachinnation in the class, of sheep calls and mirthful voices ragging. "Bleat!" "Tell about the chapel, Bleat." "Bleat, Bleat, he can't be beat!" The Headmaster easily ignored the breach of discipline.

"It's not funny!" The boy was incensed. "I'm not a smart aleck, sir. I mean it."

They laughed as the shepherds laughed at the boy who cried wolf so much. In the wheels within wheels of schoolboy life, each presumed to know the other's fears and foibles better than he knew his own. Bleat

Blodgette had never been serious in his life. If their disbelief was cruel, Bleat had himself to blame.

He had chosen to be a clown from his first weeks at Emmanuel, a new boy entering the bottom class. He was small, *imberbe*, odd of face, unshorn, looking for all the world like a Bedlington terrier.

Vindictive Mr. Frapp, who taught elementary French, could not forgive the preposterous boy his fortuitous knowledge of the language. This master once caught his overqualified pupil drowsing in the classroom. *"Qu'est-ce que vous avez, Blodgette?"* Today's lesson was the idiomatic uses of *avoir*. *"Vous AVEZ sommeil?"* Mr. Frapp commenced to enunciate for the class. *"Oui, Monsieur Blodgette A sommeil . . . Monsieur Blodgette A mal à la tête, peut-être? . . . Comme il A des cheveux affreux! Il A besoin de se faire couper les cheveux. Nous AVONS tous honte de Monsieur Blodgette. J'AI horreur de Monsieur Blodgette!"* Mr. Frapp stamped his feet; his pupils were a dull bunch and his fey sally was wasted on them. In Blodgette, however, he had a whipping post for the vexations of twenty-five years of teaching school, for his thwarted scholarship and unacclaimed translations of Pierre Louÿs. "I give you fair warning. If you have not been to the barber by tomorrow—tomorrow, is that clear? I shall with my own razor personally shave your head until it glows in the light of the moon. *Sek ek.*" Mr. Frapp ended with his horrid laugh.

Blodgette came to class the next day shorn in the village barber's fruitbowl cut like the tonsure of a novice monk. Where the ringlet curls dangled over his ears yesterday, his scalp shone a fishy white.

"Blodgette, let's have a look at you." The stridulous tone of his voice warned that Mr. Frapp was succumbing to a hysterical quirk. Boys sensed the black anthology of this master's temper. A slight person with an aesthete's moustache, his seizures gave him a rude strength as he pitched boys across doorsills, and kicked their shins.

Blodgette stepped in the front of the room, and Mr. Frapp snatched an ear that winged from his shaved scalp. "Ow, sir."

"Turn."

"Sir, cut that out. Sir, please."

"*Sek ek.* So we can have a look at you. Turn."

Blodgette was twisted full circle on the pivot of his ear so all could see the barber's work.

"*Sek ek.* We have a cropped sheep with us."

"You better quit that, sir."

"A cropped sheep, *ek.*"

"Sir, I said quit that," Blodgette heard the roots of his ear crunching;

his shoes were sliding and the floor spun. He saw chairfeet, boysfeet, chalkdust, schoolbooks whirling down on the floor, and down there he saw a delicate foot in a womanish shoe that tapered to a vicious point on an oxblood toe. He stamped on Mr. Frapp's foot, hard on top of the metatarsal arch. The ear-crunching stopped; he saw Mr. Frapp's eyes bug out and mouth open as wide as it would go. "I didn't want to hurt you, sir: You were rooking my ear."

"Hurt?" The master seized Blodgette by the collar and abandoned himself to batter the boy's shin with his pointed shoe toe. Blodgette kicked back and an all-out kicking fight was on.

From their seats the pupils watched, entranced to see one of their own, hardly more than a decade on this earth, giving as good as he got from the freakish adult. Ever after, for year upon year of their excited discussions, the skirmish was known as The French Shin Fight.

When the class was dismissed, they gathered round in the corridor, laughing and laughing for him. It was then that someone named him "Bleat"—for his sheep's look. He had them; he would ever be secure in his name and fame, and the new power of being the hero fool. The French Shin Fight, in which his righteous anger had exploded into slapstick, taught him who Bleat was and how to be Bleat. He could always get them to laugh.

Christian Studies class ended and they clustered in the corridor, making an audience for the hero fool. "Tell us about the chapel." "Yeah, tell us the history." "Tell about Jeff Higgs." "Tell us, tell us." How was he to let them down? Bleat stepped a distance apart and made a face for them, striking a grandiose pose, and gave them the declamation that by now they knew almost as well as the joker.

"Jefferson Kemp Higgs," he started to declaim the history, "one of Emmanuel's early sons—" No sooner were the first words off his tongue than they were a silent audience stifling the merriment he'd provoked only by making the face. Each time he started they took it for granted their clown would be funnier than ever. To see him puff his cheeks and sniff through his big haughty nose was enough to send one or two of the fainter-minded into premature convulsions, dropping their books on the floor.

In the library once, while hunting for some reference book, Bleat had come upon an obscure shelf marked "Publications by Graduates," and tucked away among other unsuspected lucubrations on yachting, rock gardening, dog obedience, contract bridge, was a little volume (privately printed) entitled Emmanuel Academy—A History. The author, Torbert Case, '96, was a past president of the Alumni Society and the same rhapsodic alumnus who had written some remarkable fund-raising

brochures. Mostly Mr. Case's volume described the Academy's origins
and the dour, supralapsarian career of the Scottish clergyman Josiah
Birch who was its founder; but near the end was an account, possibly the
only one extant, of the Higgs Memorial Chapel. Bleat had committed this
to memory.

*"Jefferson Kemp Higgs, one of Emmanuel's early sons, belonged to
that proud and public-spirited bank of financiers who, ill content to rest
idle while the nation's honor was outraged by the bestial treatment of our
defenceless neighbors in Cuba by a foreign despot, raised in concert their
influential voices which finally impressed upon the Pontian conscience of
President McKinley that it was our duty to extirpate, once and for all
time, the decadent Spaniard from our Hemisphere!"*

"Hooray," they chorused for him. "Hooray for our Hemisphere!"

*"On the eighteenth of February, 1898, the USS Maine was treacher-
ously sunk, and what followed, as every Emmanueler knows, is a new
chapter of our American History!"*

"You tell us, Bleatster!"

*"Jefferson Higgs, most understandably, took a fatherly interest in the
infant republic and himself acquired lands in Cuba which were planted to
sugar cane!"* Bleat had got it down so that he could take in a breath and
declaim a paragraph of Mr. Case in a single exhalation. He could rock
back on his heels and expel the prose from his lungs. *"On returning from
Havana in 1901 Jefferson Higgs fell ill. At 'Satisfaction,' his summer
'chateau' on the rock-bound coast of Bar Harbour, Jefferson Higgs died,
unfortunately, of amoebic dysentery, caught while eating shellfish in the
land he had—fate's pawn—befriended. A loss mourned not only by his
Emmanuel brothers but by his country as well. . . .* How do you like
that?" He'd perfected, as well, the knack of shutting it off, of collapsing
the entire pose when he chose to interject opinions of his own. "Here's
this fat-cat millionaire who helps start up a stupid war. Then they go build
the son of a bitch a *chapel*."

When he allowed his resentment to flare too high, he dismayed his
audience. Only mention "millionaire" and their faces warned: *that's
meatball talk.* Millionaire was a thorny word in their ears, a sensitive ab-
straction. New Deal stuff, like socialistic talk about the Great Unwashed,
meatball talk. It could actually be an insult to somebody's father.

"Okay, you don't agree." Bleat read their faces. This year he was
cultivating a rude gift for irony. "They build a chapel that's supposed to
be to the greater glory of God. Then they go dedicate it to this fat-cat
millionaire-politician war-starter. Okay, so you don't mind that? I do. I
think it stinks."

Somebody said, "You're talking like a meatball."

In a cold pause he stared the critic down. The boy withdrew and another and another, while Bleat kept silent and waited to win his game of cat and mouse. When his audience had almost dissipated itself, he had only to clap his hands and they ran back laughing.

"*Consider!*" he declaimed. "*Consider the Higgs Memorial Chapel as it stands today!*"

He made the face, he struck the pose. Through the window he pointed an indignant finger at the offensive steeple and that was that. He had them like trained seals. He relished the clown's power but a contempt came with it, for their letting it be so easy. "Tell us about the chapel." "Tell us about the aglopogic blooms!"

Tell us. He never let them down.

"*Consider the Higgs Memorial Chapel, as it stands today, in its classical, yet not pretentious contours, a form majestic as it is modest, which might be described by the classicist's phrase, 'multum in parvo!' *" He brandished his arms to the rhythms of Torbert Case, '96. "*Its colored glass and mullionwork, both, are equally 'first rate,' while travelers have compared its stone buttresses to the very best Gothic of Cologne and Chartres, while he is a rare visitor who fails to agree that its steeple, reaching Godwards in a matutinal sky, is one of the most majestic in western Massachusetts!*

"*Noteworthy too are the ivies and bosky shrubs which embrace and enhance the chapel walls. These are the pride of Grounds Superintendent Stanislaus Kloczec and his staff of good gardeners. It is no small tribute to 'Stan' that the proudly apogeotropic blooms of his laurel bushes have won more than one award from the Springfield County Chapter of the Garden Club of America, a botanical paean by which the memory of Jefferson Kemp Higgs is, truly, 'done proud.' *"

"Yay, Jeff Higgs!"

"Here's looking up your old apogologopical bloom!"

Gradually, to see his audience teary-eyed and applauding, dropping their books all over the place, he came to be embarrassed by them.

He wearied of the Jefferson Higgs thing and soon he stopped doing it. That was four years ago and the stunt was forgotten now among all the other stunts he had done for them since.

This evening the Hero Fool slouched toward Evening Prayer bowed down with his sins. Passing into the shadow of the Higgs Memorial Chapel made him shudder.

Be a man, Dr. Kew said. *Manful. . . . Keep faith with thy God. Honor thy father and thy mother. Lord have mercy upon us, and incline our hearts to keep this law.*

It's telling lies to be honest—that's all. I will kneel down in there and I'm going to lie. Does that bring forgiveness? I slugged my mother and I wished she was dead.

Up in the steeple the cast-iron bell banged the harder the closer he came. He was near enough to see the memorial plaque and the fat cross with the bird turds that one time, oh funny, he called the Guano Memorial Plaque. The steeple bell stopped and from the inside came the noise of Mr. Tryle, Organist-Choirmaster, blasting away on the hundred-thousand-dollar memorial organ.

Listen to the man take something fantastic by Haydn and turn it into so much loud wind and honking you can't stand it. The most tremendous music and he rooks it. Keep faith with thy God all the same.

Bleat reached the chapel steps in a drove of schoolmates, and here he carefully fell behind. They went up the steps tucking shirttails in, cramming tennis balls in jacket pockets, chattering till they reached the open doors on top. "Shh—quiet." They walked into the dark. Bleat stopped on the bottom step, afraid to follow. They'd had a dry spring. The air was warm and clear, not a cloud in the May sky. On the chapel wall the ivy looked crisp and the lawns were unseasonably brown. It was a fact that the celebrated laurel bushes were late with their apogeotropic bloom, as Grounds Superintendent Kloczec was only too aware. Every evening as soon as the sun had sunk behind the chapel, Stan Kloczec would rush to its eastern side a battery of hoses and lawn sprinklers. Pinwheels of water hissed and splattered over the parched turf and garden beds, wetting down the fertilizers of bone meal and cow manure. A mizzle of spray hung in the air and sometimes, past the shadow line of the steeple, miniature rainbows were formed by the sun. Squinting, Bleat tried to find a rainbow in the vapor. Stan Kloczec blocked his view: the Academy's ageless Pole, ruthlessly supervising a couple of his grandsons.

The young Kloczecs stood more than six feet tall, yet they hadn't the brawn of their progenitor, who was built low to the ground and like the bell in the steeple, dense and cumbrous. Stan's face was swarthy, theirs milky and soft. The first one spaded manure out of the wheelbarrow and the other tamped the fertilizer around the bush roots, while the grandfather gave them orders in a basso old-country dialect. No one talked back to Stan; the trees themselves, the grasses, the shrubs, owed him obeisance and it was among the Grounds Superintendent's prerogatives to choose his ground-keeping staff from the line of his Polish-American descendants. Bleat saw him as one of Millet's peasants, an insuperable grubber in the earth, hectoring his two weakling epigones who couldn't do anything right. Old Kloczec scowled. A bumblebee settled on the brim of his baseball umpire's cap. That cap: it was as if he were never without the grimy black thing resting high on the crown of his cueball head, so no one could say for sure that Stan was totally bald. Stan took the bee and carefully squeezed its life out between his splayed fingers that had been smashed in fuse boxes, gears, buzz saws, and had survived like garden hose.

There was a lull in the organ music and Bleat heard the grandsons singing at their work. They sang no old Polish folk song, but a "Your Lucky Strike Hit Parade" selection, "Three little fishies in a itty bitty poo and they thwam and they thwam wight ovah the dam." Two voices rose in chorus, "Dink boom sittum down in wattum-*choo!*" It vexed the old man, he broke into English: "Sdupid, you do that noise beside *church!* You some sdupid—" He had a grandson by the collar and was boxing his ears in the old country fashion. Fighting free, the grandson tripped over the hose and upset the sprinkler. The device lay on its side, half its rotating arms caught in the sod so that the water pressure was increased through its unhampered openings. It struggled throbbing in the grass like a weird marine creature, squirting to considerable heights the water which fell in lashes to the ground. One of these convulsions splattered from shoulders to skirts the vestments of Dr. Kew, just as he was entering the vestry door on the side of the chapel.

"Sdupid, whadmadda wi' you?" Stan Kloczec, mortified, excoriated his grandson.

The Headmaster stepped nimbly through the door, then he thought to ease the Koczecs' pain with a quip: "Well now, I expect *that* is as close as we Episcos come to total immersion!" Chuckling, he was about to shut the vestry door, when he saw the boy. "You're coming in, Steve," Dr. Kew called. "You're not forgetting your promise?" Once again the organ was blasting away, and he had to raise his voice, though not harshly: he hated to see a tormented face—and on a boy.

"Nosir." Bleat shook his head. He ran up the chapel steps as the organ reached a climactic blast and was the last one in.

The chapel's transept, the oaken choir stalls and the pews, and all the white faces which filled them, were romantically dappled in colored sunbeams falling through the stained Italianate windows. There were candles on the altar, and lights the shape of candles burning yellow on the stone walls, and a bronze lamp hung by a long chain from the ceiling of the nave. The interior was warm and dry from the spring weather. Throughout the basilica the atmosphere varied with the season like the hayloft of an old wood barn.

Frankincense and myrrh. Who could say what the words meant exactly? Different-smelling kinds of stuff they used to burn in churches or old Pharaohs' tombs. If you ever got deep inside a tomb of the Pharaohs, you'd probably smell all kinds of smells in there. Like a regular Chinese restaurant. Smells so stocky that if they got way up your nose it was hell to get them out. These ideas came to him literally by way of his nose, when in the first moments of kneeling in his pew in the true schoolboy ritual—an arm draped on back of the pew ahead and eyes buried in the elbow's blue-flannel crook—he essayed a rapid prayer, a casual salutation of his God; but it was hard to keep his mind on it when he was so conscious of his classmates squeezed in on him right and left, their salutations done, and wondering what was taking him so long with his. He realized through his nostrils tilted down that his neighbor's sneakers were awfully smelly.

"Jesus, Goodwiller," he whispered. "Peeyewee. You can't wear sneakers in chapel."

"Shhh."

"What a stink, Goodwiller."

"Quiet, you whack."

"Wear sneakers in chapel."

"Shhh. Quiet."

They whispered in the terminal hush before the Head Man entered from the vestry and took his place before the altar.

"O worship the Lord in the beauty of holiness . . . let the whole earth stand in awe of Him." Dr. Kew's voice rose fantastic from the nave.

The pews and the prayer stools creaked and scraped under the thumping of about seven hundred knees when Student Body knelt down simultaneously with Faculty and Faculty Wives. Their various voices, the girlish high, the faltering, the virile profundo, were joined in the common susurruss of the Confession:

". . . We have offended against thy holy laws.

"We have left undone those things which we ought to have done. And we have done those things which we ought not to have done.

"And there is no health in us."

No words wrung him like these. First, a flash of horrow struck him down to his old perdition and back near to the doomsday suffocation of before. Strange and fast as it had come, the horror receded and released him, so he was aware of himself as himself once again and kneeling in the accepted pose, eyes pressed behind the elbow of his flannel First Classman's blazer. It was impossible to seek the Lord without appearing to do so. Still all his self-consciousness could not quite stifle his rejoicing. (*I know that my redeemer liveth.*) His obedient lips moved in the incantation that made the chapel rumble with Student Body and Faculty and Wives beseeching the most meaningful Father to restore the penitent, that hereafter they might live a godly, righteous, and sober life. The Confession drew him down in the mighty oceans with Noah, and when it finished his spirit burst up rejoicing on the sunny beaches. Amen. Bleat unblinded his eyes and propped his chin on the ridge of the forward pew, where he could look over the crook of his arm and contemplate the minister.

"The almighty and merciful Lord grant you absolution and remission of all your sins . . ." The daytime Dr. Kew, the classroom Christian, was incapable of this. In the evening he had on his robes and appeared here where his very presence was transformed by the chanted glories which arose from him, a draped figure part-hidden in a stall several paces from the altar. Bleat strained his eyes to be sure it truly was the same Head Man.

"LET US PRAY."

At once the stones and timbers reverberated under the Lord's Prayer. The acoustics were so comforting that Bleat forgot to pray, and only listened to the blessed roll and soughing of those words, which took effect on him in a new rush of sentiment for his comrades he saw now, heads buried in their arms, as he looked over the sleeve of his blazer. They too had on, a good many of them, their blue blazers that were the emblems of their station, worn with pride; stitched to the breast pockets just over their hearts the E and the green and white crest of Emmanuel which none but athletes might wear. A glimpse of his own blazer—a coagulum of egg yolk on the sleeve, left from a recent breakfast—gave him satisfaction. He wore the blazer and the E because he indeed was coxswain on the first Emmanuel crews. It had taken five years; going out shivering on the lake each year when the crocus bloomed and the tree buds were barely formed, he coxed and learned the high-minded sport of rowing: from the cumbrous beginners' barge and the intermediate wherries until, this spring at last, he coxed the swift black Pocock shells that were the Academy's pride, worth thousands of alumni dollars. He learned to take a racing shell over bending streams and wind-chopped reservoirs, and risk impalement, in early March for instance, on a chunk of unmelted ice—a peril which Mr. Claud by quaint conceit (a Homeric soul dies hard) would name Aeolia's Floating Isle. A submerged elm at the dam end of the lake was Scylla, and Charybdis a shelf of limestone jutting out from the old quarry. Mr. Claud's oarsmen were the valorous Achaeans. And Mr. Claud would be their Agamemnon, the imperious Classics Master even before he was the stoic Coach of Crew, a disconsolate ex-English hero who in a distant time had rowed at Henley, a scholar-soldier of the Georgian stripe, who had a ferocious nose, limped romantically for having lost four toes at Gallipoli, played the oboe, mourned the ancient verities, made his creased bleak face a battlefield of perpetual disappointment. And Bleat perforce revered him. As though their two strange natures and two ferocious noses formed a bond, Mr. Claud had broken precedent and made Bleat all but openly his pet. On seeing his runt of a cox, one hundred twelve pounds of guile hectoring a crew of blistered muscle-bulging drudges, the coach's face had now and then smiled. Wily Odysseus, Mr. Claud had said. Odysseus sacker of cities. Resourceful Odysseus, stalwart Odysseus. Out on the lake, snug in the helm of a Pocock, in a seat of illimitable power, he faced down his oarsman. *Chock chock, chock-a-chock*; he hit the wooden grips of the steering guys against the brass-plated gunnels and beat out the stroke for them, and *"in out,* hin-hout," he yelled at them too. "You're late number six! . . . I want to move this boat . . . move it," he yelled in the little megaphone strapped to his head. Anything he told them to do they did, like apes or galley slaves; for six afternoons out of seven now as the spring grew greener he was their commander. "Hin-hout," he yelled in his megaphone and the shell shot forward. A pretty sight to see them bending to their oars and cleaving the wine-dark waters.

"O Lord, open thou our lips."

The congregation rose up for the *Gloria Patri*, then settled down in a creaking of pews. Dr. Kew read the lesson from the Gospel according to St. John and gave it his hieratic all, as though the verses were still in Latin. Bleat took to scratching the egg yolk off his sleeve, and fell back into his nostalgias. A refrain golden, clear and slender as a cornet call strengthened this sweet mood: a song like the evening sunbeams came from the choir stalls where a lonely mouth, one of the little first sopranos, sang, "LORD now let-test THOU thy serVANT depart in peace— *deepaht een pea-ees-ss*—ac-CORD-ing to thy word."

Bleat smiled into the sweet sound; the *Nunc Dimittis* was sealing off in distant, mindlost pleasures, and the spell of it lasted him through the austerities of the Creed and Collects. The hymn this evening was "Awake, my soul, stretch every nerve"—a rouser, but even so, and all blanketed in lusty voices, he didn't listen. The service ended very fast. He must not have heard Dr. Kew pronounce the last Amen. Everybody was going; they were ploughing over his legs, crowding past him in their haste to leave the pew. "Hey, take it easy, Goodwiller."

The chapel doors were thrown wide, the organ boomed and blasted, the debouchment was under way, in groups of Wives preceding Faculty preceding Student Body, one after the other following down the stone aisles and out of doors. Bleat with his dreamer's smile sat and watched them go. He slid his languid weight to the outer edge and corner of the empty pew and sat limp, hands crossed on his lap, soundless, gone past so much as breathing, in a state of suspended animation. He might have been invisible or at least transparent, because the Chapel Boy didn't see him.

The Chapel Boy had an ectoplasmic quality: a timid lad several years Bleat's junior, named Payler, T., pale and stark as bone, who went about his sexton's chores, putting hymnals and prayer stools in place, and polishing the altar, tending the candles, scraping drippings from the altar, putting God's house to bed all in a form of devout regret, even as if, much against his will, Payler, T., had the bounden duty every day and twice the Sabbath to put to bed God. And the boy scarcely made a noise in his work, only occasionally the rebel sneeze—Yahker-*chew*—of one who is congenitally mortified by hay fever. Yahker-*chew*. The sneezes caromed off the stones and vaults and poor Payler, T., would cringe. Scared of his own sneezes! Bleat felt an affectionate contempt. Well, what do you expect? He's Chapel Boy.

The job was a reward for piety. The Headmaster awarded it each year to a new communicant.

Yahker-*chew*, Payler, T., was at the organ, dusting off the keyboard, and probably it was the impetus of his sneezing that released one of the stops. There was a sudden squawk, a belch of wind from the pipes, and the sounds must have unnerved Payler, T., who hurried down the aisle. The lights went off in the transept; a scuffle of shoeleather on the steps and the big doors clapped shut. Bleat was enclosed in the Jefferson Kemp Higgs chapel.

I slugged my mother when I wished she was dead, he remembered very slowly. Red headlines in the middle of the air: Boy's Blow Breaks Mother's Heart, Berserk Mom Died. She daid.

He recited the Lord's Prayer and listened to it echo back phrase by phrase, anything to keep back his fear. He sang, "Lord, now lettest thou thy ser-vant dee-paht een pea-ace." He sang a clear Amen up to the darkened windows, but when the echo died, his misery was greater. He felt start the same imaginary chest pain he had when he hit her yesterday.

Now I am scared, he said, and fell to his knees. . . . We have done those things which we ought not to have done and there is no health in us. . . . Once more with his head in the crook of his arm and blinding himself in the blue flannel, he waited for divine forgiveness. When it came he would know it at once, he was quite sure: first a vibration of the scalp and down his spine a joyous current and he would be purged in the spirit and the flesh as when Bishop Walsh's hand lay upon his head. Nothing happened except his shivers got worse and he turned hot and cold. . . . Almighty and most merciful Father, we have erred and strayed from thy ways like lost sheep. . . . All he felt was the systole and diastole of his fright mounting on each breath, and he wondered if he were going to die there. But nothing happened. So he got up and left the pew.

Going down quickly in the shadows and the dusty smells, he got to the main aisle where he nearly bolted for the door. When he saw the altar, though, and the cone of electric light falling across it from the ceiling, and saw the burnished porphyry, the cloth of linen, the cross of bronze, the candelabra, the white candles the Chapel Boy had lovingly snuffed out, and, lastly, when rising in back (backing the full tableau of holies which Payler, T., was warder of) the tall altarpiece confronted him, Bleat stood still. The last was a painting in triptych form, richly gilt and ostentatious, imported from Italy by Jefferson Kemp Higgs' classmates; he knew this fact because Dr. Kew once emphasized to him the left panel, which showed his name saint being stoned in a fairly shameless imitation of Fra Angelico's style. Strangely, it was not the stoning of Stephen but the big center panel that lured him toward the altar. The light fell full on this panel and made its bright areas shine with a special radiance out of the growing night. From the top a cluster of white angel-heralds hung, their trumpets aimed down at a band of panoplied knights on snowy mounts which in turn were suspended over the head of an elongated man in black robes and whose pale hand was up in benediction. Who they all were, what exactly they were doing, he'd never asked; he made for them on slowly dragging feet and not once took his eyes off them but followed his own eyes. The vaguely Byzantine figure in the black robe of course made him think of Bishop Walsh when he hovered over his head in swirling raiment, chanting, "Defend, O Lord, this thy child. . . ." About ten feet from the altar he reached the wooden rail and tried to find the exact spot he'd bowed before the bishop. At the altar rail he fell on his knees, this time banging them quite painfully on the stones, so impatient he was to relearn and recover mysteries.

He was praying harder than he knew. He held his back rigid and knelt now erect from the waist in the most militant supplication. Shoulders back, chest out, neck and head strained upward, his body was a lightning rod to catch the sweet flashes from on high. . . . God and Father, I have done things I ought not to have done, and there is no health in us or me. Excuse me. . . . He prayed open-eyed, boring in his elbows on the railing, keeping stiff his arms and wrists and fingertips to the point of his chin like Dr. Kew. . . . Excuse me, Lord; the Lord forgive the thing I did— Father, forgive me. Bishop Walsh, forgive me. Give me peace. . . . His knees on the stone floor were sore, so were his elbows on the rail, the tendons of his hands were starting to ache; the rigors of kneeling disturbed his prayer. It seemed in the shadows that faces were mocking him. He was as craven and dishonored as the meanest of his Puritan forefathers ever to have been put on the pillory. An ancestor of his, some one of those grisly Pilgrims and Huguenots, must have known the chagrin of being collared and manacled to the post: the town booby. His eyes devised a different triptych wherein the man in black robes was not Bishop Walsh anymore but this penitent ancestor whose glowing white head and hands stuck through the holes of the pillory. The right arm stuck out all the way from the shoulder, enabling the hand to salute him.

"No—" He shook his head furiously, he forced himself to pray aloud. "Our Father—" but he heard a high sniggering burst from his throat; an ugly shrill little hee-hee-hee laugh which he confessed to be a quirk of his blood. It sounded as bad, as mean, as his brother at home laughing on a

Sunday morning, when little Buddy stood in the kitchen saying dirty limericks to Aunt Norah's aggrieved, nun-pure, hairpin-spewing biddies coming back from Mass. "God forgive me," he muttered and waited, but there was no comfort, no peace; he braced his body on the altar rail. This time he covered his eyes with his hands and sealed off the outer distractions and apparitions, tight inside his hands, where the black was thick as cat's fur. Loathing what he had done, dreading what he might become, he drove knuckles and fingerbones into the bone of his forehead even as if trying to hold his cranium intact. . . . There is no health, no help in us. Lord, where is this health? Is it You? . . . Oppressive, ever answerless, his question perished in the blackness where he discerned here and there a patch or whorl or lesser blackness where, conceivably, a match had flickered once in the eitons and alautons of time before the Creation and the Flood. By pushing, he soon discovered, the heels of his thumbs against his eyes he could explode the black and induce sensations of being inside a furnace of cold orange fire terrible enough to turn the soul to stone. When he relaxed the pressure on his eyes, all subsided into blackness. Several such extrasensory leaps and he was beside himself with terror . . . log dog bog she daid begon mom no nodog. In his final silent gibbering he struggled, although by now his thoughts had marched down to the ends of the earth.

Mark him well as he leaves off praying for good. In one athletic surge he rises and hurdles the altar rail. The nave is lighted from above, so that the same cones of light that fall over the altar, whitening the faces painted on the triptych, catch his skin too. Everywhere but here the chapel is dark; the stained Italian windows have turned so black you can't tell them from the stone walls. Not a shadow remains; only the dark, cavernous as the great fish's belly where Jonah went to repine; but out of it in this gymnastic instant Bleat leaps into the light.

He lands hard, his shoe heels smacking on the stones. So unaccountable a feat surprises him perhaps. (He could have reached the altar by walking through the opening in the rail, like anybody else.)

As he lands crouched, he freezes, knees bent and arms out. You might suppose from this posture that the boy is going to leap again or kneel again, while in fact he is merely contemplating the triptych from close up. His eyes rotate between the two panels whence both his martyred saint and his phantasmal black-gowned Pilgrim ancestor lower down at him. From their spectral gaze he draws a sort of deicidal energy—or apparently so, for now he laughs and smartly claps his hands, driving echoes through the chapel. As if an uproarious joke were detonated between him and the gods beyond, he laughs and claps, laughs and claps until the ribald mood has passed and then his nerves fail. Just the scuff of shoe-leather, the glimpse of his white face contorted in the light, the whirl of flannel shoulders before he escapes in the dark. He bolts up the aisle, his fingers slapping on the pew tops to guide him. High and low the vaults and stones echo back the clatter of his shoes, the slamming of his body against the doors. A fierce claustrophobia would seem to drive him, since he batters the iron doors with his mighty-atom weight for some bruising moments until he remembers to turn the handle.

Outside, drawing in deep breaths, he steals down the chapel steps under the black sky and deep night. He lifts his head to sniff the night air. At the same time he rubs the shoulder that hurts him and he touches his fingers to the lump that's rising on his forehead.

The night is by far more pungent than sticky smells of frankincense and myrrh. He is already down the steps and stealing away from the chapel. The moon is up; it is like a cake of white soap and gives him a hard light to move through like a rodent, furtively. He sniffs the air, testing it for gases. Now he halts and he lifts his eyes to the firmament. He looks up and he sees the stars, poisoned stars. On this balmy night the heavens envelope him in an arctic black, as if he were still praying with his hands on his eyes, and the white nebulae, the frozen suns and firmaments disdain him. Maybe it is to rebuke them, make them hear his wrath, that he cracks his hands together. The noise is nothing to what he could make inside the chapel; no echoes from the vaults of sky, but a moment's crepitating of hands, a small impertinence that faints into stillness and the chirping of tree toads in the hemlocks along the lake a mile off. Close by he hears the hiss and splatter of lawn sprinklers on the grass.

He steps from the gravel onto the slippery lawn. Step by step as he moves, the varied odors of the night congeal to a single smell whose source is in the bushes. He feels an icy lick across his cheek, and another. The water hisses in his ear. The lawn sprinklers, their cold whirligigs shooting through the moonbeams, intrigue him so that he nearly forgets he's in their range and he ducks ineptly, trips on the hose, and lands all fours on the soggy greensward. A loop of hose has snared his foot; no sooner he gets up than it brings him down. Laughing, talking to himself, trouser knees and blazer sleeves soaked through, Bleat sits at the edge of the laurel bed, where the manure smells the rankest, and tries to disengage his foot.

There is a coating of manure on the hose, some of it wipes off on his fingers and he moans, "Aw, come on!" When he is on his feet he finds the water has soaked through his trouser seat. Half-hidden by a laurel bush the wheelbarrow rests with a mound of cow manure into which is plunged a spade. No escaping its reek: Bleat's nostrils take him to the wheelbarrow whose moist contents in the moonlight take on a phosphorescent patina, a glow which to his intense eyes suggests the triptych standing in there on the altar. The moistly shining laurel blooms and rhododendron clusters scratching his cheek, he breaks off two or three and pokes the stems in the manure to garnish the load. The effect would seem to provoke him, for he is able to laugh once more and smack his hands together. *Crack-crack.* One reprise of fury, a final spurt of adrenalin is enough to break the last of the Episcopalian sanctions laid upon his soul.

Bleat hauls the wheelbarrow out of the shrubbery and onto the gravel path. He finds the cart compact in his grasp, solid and powerful; and himself exultantly in control of something warlike, he pretends, a battering ram or a tank. A Nazi panzer tank, he thinks, like in the newsreels. "Wah-ROOM," he makes it a tank with sound effects, and the garden spade sticking out like a machine gun. "A-tat-tat-tat-tat, bah-ROOM." Between these soul-destroying sounds and his laughing, the night is not so still. The axle creaks when he pivots the wheelbarrow on the gravel and aims it at the chapel. The loose wooden sides are rattling. Two or three strong steps to get momentum and he is borne on behind the heavy load so inexorably that he almost crashes it into the chapel steps. Again he pivots and starts to haul the wheel backward, the metal rim scraping the brownstone as it mounts. This would be hard going by daylight, but here, where the steeple blocks off the stars, there is no knowing how he will manage to feel his way. Will the panic come? A bad moment when the spade falls out and clanks on the paving, but he retrieves and plunges it back in the load. And his courage holds; he makes it to the top of the steps.

The school has gone to bed. He can see the yellow light bulbs burning in the long linoleum corridors that echoed with his name. Bleat, they shouted. Bad boy. Funny boy. Bleat. Now he only hears the lawn sprinklers hissing and the clee-peep song of tree toads near the lake. Bad boy, funny boy; he pauses to rest and load and test his courage, and from the summit of the chapel steps looks down in castigation at the blackened windows of the classrooms and dormitories where The French Shin Fight happened, where Bleat won his name.

He jerks the wheelbarrow. The axle creaks again as he turns the load around and heads it through the wide flung door at the chapel's mouth. His actions are well past the most ludicrous extreme, and still his nerves hold strong when the transept receives him into its maw.

Dimly seen by the lamp which hangs from the nave are the white candles Payler, T., blew out, and the white faces on the triptych. They are throwing stones at Stephen and the Pilgrim forebear is crouching in the stock. The floor stones rumble under the wheelbarrow. Bleat blunders down the aisle behind the load, pulled on after the frantic stench and weight of it, and hard down to the shimmering altar. Holy of holies.

He gets there, sets down the cart, takes the spade, and he falls to his work with a will.

"*Whadmadda wi' you, sdupid?*"

The question bursts directly in back of him, rising from the floor stones and caroming through the vaults and timbers of the ceiling. Not a voice, it seemed, but a noise, some infernal foghorn able to articulate words. Bleat heard it as though it came out of a tube, a winding long-clogged drain set into the floor and descending downwards through layers of ooze and algae to a chthonian larynx.

"Whadyou do wi' my wheebarra, sdupid?" demanded Grounds Superintendent Koczec.

"What does it look like I'm doing with it?" Bleat's response was spontaneous, mindless, and his gaze upon the altar. Between this and the wheelbarrow he made his stand, tossing on another spadeful of the stuff. He checked his arms and for an instant frowned at the spade, as if he'd quite forgotten that the thing was in his hands.

"You some fresh kid!" The words came from behind him in a hot breath, wafting into the heady night blends of garlic and perspiration. "Whadyou do make big shdpile insita *church?*"

Bleat turned and confronted inches from his nose a prognathous jaw, a broad Polish face above a barrel body. The honest gardener had on his head a baseball umpire's cap.

Bleat's hands were trembling, he could scarcely speak and he had at any cost to contrive the gay façade. He set the spade back carefully in the wheelbarrow, and sought some new diversion, one more stall for time. "Hey, Stan, where's the ball game? Hey, don't you know better than wear a hat in church?"

There came a glottal burst of Polish, and Bleat saw stars and yelled in pain. For a while the Grounds Superintendent was boxing his ears.

"You come. You and me go talk to Hetmasda!" And it ended there, with the Grounds Superintendent leading him by the scruff of his blazer, away to a fool's doom.

Late the next morning, alone in the white, sun-drenched infirmary, he emerged from sedation. The school physician noted contusions of the right upper humerus and clavicle, left and right tibiac, and the left kneecap. The patient complained that he still smelled "an awful smell everywhere." The doctor ordered X-rays of the head that had battered against the chapel door, and from these he diagnosed a concussion from a trauma sustained in the ethmoid region of the skull, with concomitant pressure upon the olfactory nerve. This opinion was to receive due attention. *A trauma to the olfactory nerve.* It was a physiological fact: so much for the addled nostrils that could not tell cow manure from "frankincense and myrrh," and so much for the less than ingenious attempt at exculpation ("I just went crazy, sir") which met with some mild chuckling when the Headmaster quoted it at Faculty Meeting only that night.

Two nights and a day young Apollyon lay in the bed, heavy-lidded from the injections which Mrs. Glappis, the Registered Nurse, kept sticking in his buttocks. She was a chubby, turkey-complected woman with a seraph's disposition. Certain favored boys could without qualm and to her face call her by the faintly insidious nickname of Mother Glap. This was the gently billowing nurse who through the years had given him enemas and nasal sprays, cared for his chicken pox and pinkeye, who had laughed with him at a hundred jokes. There was no question in his mind that she was on his side no matter what, and he loved her for such innocence of spirit and simplicity of mind. "Good Mother Glap." He lolled and babbled in the bedsheets, seeing her come at him again bearing the napkin-covered tray on which the hypodermic needle glistened like a scepter. His bed was beside an easy window, and as Nurse Glappis approached in the sunshine, the crisp starched little hospital cap on her snowy head reflected an aureole of mercy so powerful that he seemed to bask in it. "Good Mother Glap," he laughed. "Are you going to stick me with more truth serum?"

Nurse Glappis failed to laugh, failed to crack a smile, but put the tray on the bed table with a ghostly chill and a whiff of denatured alcohol. "You've played your last joke," was all she said. "Onto your stomach now and down with those pajamas." He felt the goose pimples go up his back and then her icicle fingers upon his skin and the cold swab of rubbing alcohol, but coldest of all the needle.

Nobody else would talk to him either, not his fellow patients in the ward, not the charwoman swabbing down the floor with germicides. As he lay in this state of hebetude and the hypodermics wore off and the pressure lifted from his olfactory nerve, eventually he understood that he was getting the silent treatment. On the Headmaster's orders.

"Apollyonism"—this word the Headmaster chose. A word worthy of Cardinal Newman; and taken to mean that Beelzebub had entered into Blodgette and bound over the boy's spirit to a black ordinance—made him indeed "a brother to dragons and a companion to owls."

"When he looked for good, then evil came unto him; when he waited for light, there came darkness." What other explanation was there? Was there an alternative to expulsion?

"There is no alternative," Dr. Kew answered himself.

"Nosir."

"You have made me sick at heart."

"Yesir."

The Head Man stood at the foot of Bleat's bed wearing in this parting moment an aspect very different from his usual. The Spencer Tracy in him, the bluff two-fisted Christian, had given way to the heathen Rhadamanthus who spoke his judgment in thunder. "To expel you is the severest punishment we can give. In your case—you were soon to graduate from this school and I can't believe it was your own will that determined your actions—this punishment may seem cruel. I can't do more in the temporal sphere for this sick soul of yours than banish it from the scene of . . . its collapse. It is not for me to grant the remission you will require so desperately. You must find it for yourself . . . and the Lord will help you."

"Will he though, will he? I don't mean to be fresh, sir." Bleat faltered. In the hypodermic's desperate aftermath, everything he said was wrong.

"It is not for me to divine His ways," said Dr. Kew. "But I'll venture to say that without Him . . . lacking His grace . . . your evil will smite hard for the rest of your days."

"Yesir."

"And you will fear for your immortal soul."

"Yesir," he only said, and from then on he did as he was told. No time for his trunk; they would pack it and send it in due course. He turned in his books, drew seven dollars, travel allowance, packed his suitcase, shut himself in his room. His release from the infirmary had been timed for the lunch hour when he would have no contact with his schoolmates gathered in the dining hall downstairs. He heard the clatter of crockery and the rumor of voices through the floor, as he sat on his bed and waited for Mr. Claud, the master Dr. Kew had thoughtfully assigned to take him home. At the sound of footsteps in the corridor, Bleat hurried to the door with his suitcase.

"Payler," he said, "I'm sorry about that."

It was merely Payler, T., the melancholy Chapel Boy. "I had to see you. I skipped lunch," he told Bleat in an angry whisper, a wild face. "If they catch me talking to you, I could get booted out too, don't forget." It was a martyr's warning, intended to rub in this extra salt of shame. "Why did you do it? I don't see how anybody could do a thing that dirty." Tears welled in Payler's eyes; he dabbed at them with a blue woolen necktie. "You should have seen what it looked like in the daytime."

"I said I was sorry. I didn't do it against you personally, Payler."

"It took a whole day to clean up. Nobody ever did a thing so dirty, I bet—not in the whole history of Church!"

"Thanks for the kind words, Payler, boy." Bleat would have liked to shrug them off, but they were the last spoken to him at Emmanuel and quite impossible to forget.

During the slow excruciating train ride to New York, he tried to talk to Mr. Claud. Mr. Claud, the doleful classicist and Coach of Crew, had been his favorite hero after all, without whose guidance he could not have won the white E on the brave green shield on the breast of his blue blazer; all of that polluted now, ruined, finished, never to be worn again. Bleat asked him, "Sir, will it blow over, do you think?"

The ferocious-nosed ex-English hero gazed at the floor of the day coach, his huge oarsman's hands clutched round the knee of the leg of the foot that was wounded at Gallipoli, and said what he could to solace his lost coxswain who sat on the seat beside him: "It may seen cold comfort to you now, but I suggest that in twenty years practically everyone will have forgotten." Because almost that many years ago, shortly after the Great War, when Mr. Claud first came to this country, the Rector Peabody had given him a position as a teacher of Greek at Groton School. An unutterably malicious desecration was done to the Groton Chapel, a calculated affront to the Rector—"an outside job," as they say, that had been carefully planned by a group of brummagem young Harvard students who must have borne an inexplicably cruel grudge against their old school, Groton. Ah, the scandal was furious and the social opprobrium so great that one of the young men had offered to release his fiancée from their engagement. "A shocking affair." Mr. Claud gave something like a reminiscent sigh. "Yet hardly anybody remembers it." A sigh again. "Certain of the details—which assuredly I shall not dwell upon—were similar to what you were possessed to do to the Higgs Chapel. Pity. I needn't say how distressed I am. Pity. Dreadful to have happened to one's cox!"

Through these Anglicisms, under the play-up and play-the-game pitch of the British accent, Bleat heard a note of compassion. He didn't really trust it, because in his next breath the classicist got archly Homeric and pontifical. "Pity that the gods chose to conspire against you," Mr. Claud said, and he quoted a self-conscious line: "Those whom the gods seek to destroy they first make—" he observed a heavy caesura—"Steven Blodgette."

Mr. Claud's bon mot stayed with Bleat, saying itself over in his mind for the entire train ride. When he got to his great-aunt's house at Eighty-second Street and touched his finger to the doorbell, he was still listening to it.

Then it was inevitably his mother in a dun-colored negligee who opened the door, huddling and peeking from behind it, to avoid being seen from the street. Awkwardly enough her first glimpse was of Mr. Claud, a strange man standing right there on the doorstep, and she recoiled from him as if from a rapist. As soon as she saw her son, she burst into tears.

"Oh, Steven," his mother cried. "Are you all right, darling?"

That was the end of his formal education.

A SOUTH SUMMER IDYLL

Terry Southern

A summer Saturday in Dallas and the boy Howard sat out on the back steps, knees up, propping in between an old singleload twelve-gauge shotgun. While he steadied and squeezed the butt in one hand, the other, with studied unbroken slowness, wrapped a long piece of friction tape around and around the stock—for beginning at the toe of the butt and stretching up about five inches was a thin dry crack in the old wood.

His mother came out, down off the back porch carrying an enameled basin heaped with twists of wet, wrung clothes.

"You wantta be careful with that old gun," she said, making a slight frown.

A squat woman and dark-haired, almost Eastern in the intensity she tried to bear on situations, her face was perhaps too open, eyes too widely spaced, and the effect was ever what she calculated. She would not suspect, however, that within the block only a few could take her seriously.

Her boy Howard did, of course, though if others were present, he might be embarrassed or a little irritated.

"Aw now you're kiddin'," he said, wanting mainly to reassure her about the gun.

She had just given him a dollar for the weekend, and before dark he would have spent over half of it. Sitting now on the back steps, he could reckon exactly how it would go. And with her standing there talking, he was aware too that except for the show she had no idea at all how he would spend the money.

At the kitchen table his father treated it lightly. "Where you *goin'* boy? Shootin'?"

"Aw just fool aroun'," said Howard, looking away, eating slowly at a piece of bread, buttered and covered with sugar.

"Who, you and Lawrence? What're y'all goin' *after?*"

"Aw I dunno," said Howard. "Just fool aroun', I guess."

"Where're you and Lawrence *goin'*, Howie?" asked his mother, back at the sink again.

"Aw out aroun' Hampton Airport, I guess," he said.

"You wantta be careful out there at Hampton," said his mother, "with the planes comin' in and all."

Howard tried to laugh, even to catch his father's eye. "They ain't any *planes* there now," he said, sheepish at having to be impatient with her. "They closed it down, didn't you know that?"

"I don't want you goin' up in that trainer-plane either," his mother went on as unhearing, almost closed-eyed, packing faded, dripless lumps of cloth in the basin.

"Aw now you're kiddin'," said Howard. "It don't cost but three dollars for fifteen minutes. Not likely I *will,* is it?"

At the table, though, his father spoke about the gun, the danger, abstractly, as if he himself had never fired it. And yet, when he saw the box of shells on the table, he opened it and shook two or three out, holding them loosely, so as to appear casual, familiar, he who had not held a gun in thirty years.

"Look like good 'uns," he said finally. "What'd they cost?"

Howard reached Big Lawrence's house by way of the alley. Stepping through an open place in the fence two houses before and cutting across the back yards, he could hear Lawrence on at the house and he saw his shadow dark there behind a window screen.

"Ka-pow! Ka-pow! Ka-pow!" was what Lawrence said. It was a small room.

Big Lawrence sat out on the edge of the bed, and all down around his feet the scattered white patches lay, fallen each as the poison cactus-bloom, every other center oil-dark, he cleaning his rifle, a 30-30 Savage.

Across one end of the bed, flat on his stomach looking at an old comic book, was Crazy Ralph Newgate, while Tommy Sellers sat on the floor, back flat to the wall. Tommy Sellers had a baseball and glove in his lap, and every so often he would flip the baseball up and it would twirl over his fingers like an electric top.

As Howard came in and sat down on the arm of a heavy-stuffed, mis-shapen chair, Lawrence looked up, laughing. Most of the time Lawrence's laugh was coarse and, in a way, sort of bitter.

"Well, goddam if it ain't old Howard!" he said, perhaps remembering a western movie they had seen a night before.

Somewhere, next door, a radio was playing loud, Saturday morning cowboy music from Station WRR in downtown Dallas.

Big Lawrence put the bolt back in, slapping it. "You ready?" he asked Howard, and Howard nodded. But before he could get up, Lawrence had turned around on the bed and leaned hard across Ralph Newgate's legs, sighting the rifle out over the back yard. There across the yard, out about three feet from the back fence, so crouched half-sitting that the feet were drawn way under, was a cat—a black cat—rounded small and un-blinking in the high morning sun.

Big Lawrence squeezed one out on the empty chamber. *"Ka-pow!"* he said and brought the gun down, laughing.

On the floor, next to the wall, the baseball spun twisting across Tommy Sellers' knuckles like a trained rat.

"Goddam! Right in the eye!" said Lawrence. He raised up and with some shells from his shirt pocket loaded the rifle; then he quickly threw out the shells, working the bolt in a jerky eccentric motion. One of the shells, as they flew all over the bed, went across the comic book Ralph Newgate was holding and hit the bridge of his nose. The other three boys laughed, but Crazy Ralph muttered something, rubbing his nose, and flipped the shell back over into the rest next to Lawrence's leg, as he might have playing marbles—and Big Lawrence flinched.

"You crazy bastard!" said Lawrence. "What if it'd hit the cap!" and he picked up the shell and threw it as hard as he could against the wall behind Ralph Newgate's head, making him duck. They left the shell where it fell on the floor behind the bed. Ralph didn't speak but just kept turning the pages of the comic book, while Lawrence sat there for about a minute looking at the book that was held in front of Ralph Newgate's eyes.

Lawrence reloaded the gun and drew another bead out the window. The black cat was still sitting there, head on toward the muzzle, when Lawrence moved the safety with his thumb, and next door someone turned the radio up a little more.

In the small room the explosion was loud.

The comic book jumped in Crazy Ralph's hand as if jerked by a wire. "Goddam*mit!*" he said, but he didn't look around, just shifted a little, as in settling to the book again.

The cat hardly moved. It seemed only to have been pushed back toward the fence some, still sitting there, head down, feet drawn under, staring at the screen.

But in the screen now, next to a hole made in opening the screen from the outside, was another, perfectly round, flanged out instead of in, worn suddenly by the passing of the bullet, all bright silver at the edge.

Big Lawrence and Howard walked a dirt road along one side of Hampton Airport. It was a hot, dry day.

"What's a box of shells like that cost?" Lawrence asked, and when Howard told, Lawrence said, "*Sure,* but for how many shells?"

At crossroads, the corner of a field, a place where on some Sundays certain people who made model airplanes came to try them, they found, all taped together, five or six shiny old dry-cell batteries as might be used for starting just such small engines. Howard pulled these batteries apart while they walked on, slower now beneath the terrible sun, and when Lawrence wanted to see if he could hit one in the air with the shotgun, they agreed to trade off, three rifle cartridges for one shotgun shell.

Howard pitched one of the batteries up, but Lawrence wasn't ready. "Wait'll I say '*Pull,*' " he told Howard.

He stood to one side then, holding the shotgun down as he might have seen done in a newsreel about skeet-shooting.

"Okay, now *pull!*"

Lawrence missed the first one, said that Howard was throwing too hard.

Howard tossed another, gently, lobbing it into the sun, glinting end over gleaming end, a small meteor in slow motion, suddenly jumping with the explosion, this same silver thing, as caught up in a hot-air jet, but with the explosion, coughing out its black insides.

"Got the sonofabitch," said Big Lawrence. "Dead bird goddammit!"

Howard laughed. "I reckon it is," he said softly.

Once across the field, away from the airport, they turned up the railroad track. And now they walked very slowly, straight into the sun, burning, mirrored a high blinding silver in the rails that lay for five miles unbending, flat against the shapeless waste, ascending, stretching ablaze to the sun itself—so that seen from afar, as quite small, they could have appeared as children, to walk unending between these two columns of dancing light.

With the rifle they took some long shots at the dead-glass disks on a signal tower far up the track, but nothing happened. When they were closer, though, one of the signals suddenly swung up wildly alight. A burning color. Lawrence was about to take a shot at it when they heard the train behind them.

They slid down an embankment, through the bullnettle and bluebonnets, to walk a path along the bottom. When the freight train reached them, however, they turned to watch it go by, and at one of the boxcars, Big Lawrence, holding the rifle against his hip, pumped three or four rounds into the side of it. Under the noise of the train the muted shots had no connection with the bursting way the dark wood on the boxcar door tore off angling and splintered out all pine white.

As they walked on, Howard said, "Don't reckon anybody was in *it,* do you?" Then he and Lawrence laughed.

They struck the creek hollow and followed it in file, Lawrence ahead, stepping around tall slaky rocks that pitched up abruptly from the hot shale. Heat came out of this dry stone, sharp as acid, wavering up in black lines. Then at a bend before them was the water hole, small now and stagnant, and they turned off to climb the bank in order to reach it from the side. Howard was in front now; as they came over the rise, he saw the rabbit first—standing between two oak stumps ten feet away, standing up like a kangaroo, ears winced back, looking away toward the railroad track. Then Lawrence saw it too and tried to motion Howard off with one hand, bringing his rifle up quickly with the other.

The sound came as one, but within one spurting circle of explosion, the two explosions were distinct.

On their side the half face of the rabbit twitched twice back and down even before it hit him, then he jumped straight up in a double flip five

times the height he had stood and landed across one of the old burned
out stumps like a roll of wet paper.

"*Goddam!*" said Lawrence, frowning. He walked slowly toward the
stumps, then looked at Howard before he picked up the rabbit. "Goddammit!" he said.

One side of the rabbit, from the stomach down, looked as though it
had been pushed through a meat grinder. "You must be crazy," Lawrence said. "Why didn't you let me get him, goddammit? I could have
gotten him in the head." He dropped the rabbit across the stump again
and stood looking at it.

Howard picked up the rabbit, studied it. "Sure tore hell out of it, didn't
it?" he said.

Lawrence spat and turned away. Howard watched him for a minute
walking down toward the water hole, then he put the rabbit back on the
stump and followed.

They leaned the guns against the dead-grassed ground that rose at
their backs and sat down. Howard got out the cigarettes and offered
them, so that Lawrence took one first, and then Howard. And Howard
struck the match.

"Got the car tonight?" he asked, holding out the light.

Big Lawrence didn't answer at once for drawing on the cigarette.
"Sure," he said then, admitting, "but I've got a date." In this sun the
flame of the match was colorless, only chemical, without heat.

"Where you goin'?" Howard asked. "To the show?"

"I dunno," said Lawrence, watching the smoke. "Maybe I will."

The water hole was small, less than ten feet across, overhung only by a
dwarfed sand-willow on the other bank, so that all around the dead burning ground was flushed with the sun, while one half of the hole itself cast
back the scene in distortion.

Over and on the water, though, in and through the shadow that fell
half across them, played wasps and water-spiders, dragonflies, snake-
doctors, and a thousand gray gnats. A hornet, deep-ribbed, whirring
golden bright as a spinning dollar, hung in a hummingbird twist just on
the water surface in the deepest shadow of the tree, and Howard threw a
rock at it.

Then an extraordinary thing happened. The hornet, rising frantically
up through the willow branches, twisted once and came down out of the
tree in a wild whining loop, and lit exactly on the back of Howard's shirt
collar, and then very deliberately, as Lawrence saw, crawled inside.

"Hold still," said Lawrence, taking a handful of the shirt at the back
and the hornet with it, holding it.

Howard had his throat arched out, the back of his neck all scrutched
away from the shirt collar. "Did you get it?" he kept asking.

"Hold still, goddammit," said Lawrence, laughing, watching Howard's face from the side, finally closing his hand on the shirt, making the hornet crackle as hard and dry as an old matchbox when he clenched his fist.

And then Lawrence had it out, in his hand, and they were both bent over in looking. It was dead now, wadded and broken, and in the shade of his hand the gold of the hornet had become as ugly-colored as the phosphorus dial at noon. It was the stinger, sticking out like a wire hair, taut in an electric quaver, that still lived.

"Look at that goddam thing," said Lawrence of the stinger, and made as if to touch it with his finger.

"Be careful, you'll get stung," said Howard.

"*Look* at it," said Lawrence, intent.

"They all do that," Howard said.

"Sure, but not like that." Lawrence touched it with his finger, but nothing happened.

"Maybe we can get it to sting something," said Howard, and he tried to catch a doodlebug crawling on a bluebonnet that grew alone between them, but missed it. So Lawrence bent the flower itself over, to get the stinger to penetrate the stem at the bottom.

"It'll kill it," he said; "it's acid."

Lawrence held the tail of the hornet tight between his thumb and finger, squeezing to get more of the stinger out, until it came out too far and stopped moving—and Lawrence, squeezing, slowly emptied the body of its white filling. Some of it went on his finger. Lawrence smelled it, then he let Howard smell it before he wiped his finger on the grass.

They lit another cigarette. Big Lawrence threw the match in the water, and a minute after it had floated out, took up the 30-30, drew a bead, and clipped it just below the burnt head. "*Why?*" he asked Howard, handing him the rifle. "Are you going to the show tonight?"

"I might," Howard said.

"No, but have you got a date?"

"I guess I could get one," said Howard, working the bolt.

"I've gone out with Helen Ward," said Lawrence.

Howard sighted along the rifle.

"You know her *sister?*" Lawrence asked.

"Who, Louise?"

"Sure, maybe we could get 'em drunk."

Howard held his breath, steadying the rifle. Then he took a shot. "Sure I know her," he said.

They shot water targets, mostly with the rifle, Howard using the shots Lawrence owed him. Once, however, after he dug an old condensed-milk can out of the bank and sat it on the water, Lawrence took up the shotgun and held the muzzle about a foot from the can.

"H-bomb," he said, pulling the trigger.

They sat there for an hour, talking a little and smoking, shooting at crawfish and dragonflies or underwater rocks that shone through the flat yellow or, more often, dull dead brown. Then they decided to go back to the house and drink some beer.

Near the stumps Howard crossed over and picked up the rabbit, Lawrence watching him. "What're you going to do with the damn thing?" Lawrence asked.

"Aw I dunno," said Howard. "Might as well take it along."

Lawrence watched while Howard held it by the ears and kicked at a piece of newspaper, twisted dry and dirty, yellow in the grass. He got the paper, shook it out straight, and he wrapped it around the rabbit.

They started across the field, Lawrence not talking for a while. Then he stopped to light a cigarette. "I know what," he said, cradling the 30-30 to one arm; "we can cook it."

Howard didn't answer right off, but once, as they walked back toward the stumps, he looked at the sun. "I wonder what time it is anyhow," he said.

Using Howard's knife, Big Lawrence, once it was decided, sat on one of the stumps to skin the rabbit while Howard went pushing around through the Johnson grass, folding aside with his feet, peering and picking, bundling back, to build the fire.

At the stumps, Lawrence cursed the knife, tried the other blade, and sawed at the rabbit's neck, twisting it in his hand.

"Wouldn't cut hot niggerpiss," he said, but somehow he managed to get the head off and to turn the skin back on itself at the neck, so that he pulled it down like a glove reversed on an unborn hand, it glistened so.

He had to stop with the skin halfway down to cut off the front feet, and in doing this, hacking once straight on from the point of the blade, the blade suddenly folded back against his finger. He opened the knife slowly, saying nothing, but he sucked at the finger and squeezed it between two others until, through all this heavy red of rabbit, sticking, covering his whole hand now, he could almost see, but never quite, where in one spot on his smallest finger he himself, up through the blood of the rabbit, was bleeding too.

He went down to the pool to clean his hands, but he finished skinning the rabbit first.

When he got back, Howard was down, ready to light the fire. "Are we goin' to the show or not?" Lawrence said.

"I don't care," said Howard, staring up at him. "Do you want to?"

"Well, we better get back if we're goin'."

Howard got the old newspaper from where he had put it to burn and wrapped it around the rabbit again, and he put this inside his shirt. He folded the skin square and put it in his pocket.

Lawrence had the rabbit's head. He tried to get the eyes to stay open, but only the white showed when he sat it on the stump. He took a brick from the windbreak Howard had built for the fire and put this on the stump too, behind the head, and then started across the field. When they were a little way out, they took shots at the head, and finally Lawrence used the last of the shells he had coming to go up close and shoot the head, brick, and even part of the stump away with the old twelve-gauge.

Before they reached Rosemont Street, they could hear Tommy Sellers cursing and Crazy Ralph Newgate farther away yelling, *"All the way! All the way!"* and as they turned in, Tommy Sellers was there, coming toward them, walking up the middle of the street swinging his glove by one finger.

Howard pulled the wad of newspaper out of his shirt and held it up to show, and Tommy Sellers stopped and kicked around at some dead grass piled in the gutter. *"Okay, all the way!"* Ralph Newgate was yelling halfway down the block, and Tommy Sellers found the ball with his foot. Then, bending over, in a low twisting windup from the gutter, never once looking where, he threw it—the ball that lifted like a shot to hang sailing for an instant in a wide-climbing arc.

Big Lawrence brought the rifle off his shoulder. *"Ka-pow!"* and the barrel point wavered, sighting up the lazy wake of the ball. "Dead son-ofabitch bird," he said.

Tommy Sellers was standing close, hands on his hips, not seeing down there an eighth of a mile where Ralph Newgate, with his eyes high, nervously tapping the glove palm, was trying to pick the bouncing throw off the headlight of a parked car.

"God it stinks," said Lawrence, making a face when Howard opened the newspaper. The paper now was like a half-dried cloth, stiff, or sticking in places and coming to pieces. Almost at once a fly was crawling over the chewed-up part of the rabbit.

"You know what it's like?" said Lawrence—*"goddam rotten after-birth!"* and he spat, seeming to retch a little.

"What is it?" asked Tommy Sellers, looking close at the rabbit, then up, away, not caring in dancing out to take the wild looping throw from Ralph Newgate.

They walked on. Howard wrapped the newspaper around the rabbit again and put it in his shirt.

"It's already beginning to rot," said Big Lawrence.

"Aw you're crazy," Howard said.

"Crazy!" repeated Lawrence. "You're the one who's crazy. What'll you do, eat it?" He laughed, angrily, spitting again.

They were walking in the street in front of Lawrence's house now. Tommy Sellers and Ralph Newgate were at the curb, throwing their gloves up through the branches of a cedar tree where the ball was caught.

There were some people standing around the steps at Lawrence's front porch. One was a youngish woman wearing an apron over her dress, and a little girl was holding on to the dress with both hands, pressing her face into the apron, swinging herself slowly back and forth, so that the woman stood as braced, her feet slightly apart. She stroked the child's head with one hand, and in the other she was holding the cat.

They watched Howard and Lawrence in the street in front of the house. Once the woman moved her head and spoke to the fat man standing on the porch who frowned without looking at her.

Howard didn't turn in with Lawrence. "See you at the show," he said.

As he walked on, the fall of their voices died past him. "How'd it happen, son?" he heard Lawrence's dad ask.

He turned off on a vacant lot that cut through toward his house. Half-way across, he pulled out the paper and opened it. He studied it, brought it up to his face, and smelled it.

"That rake'll reach!" Crazy Ralph was yelling way behind him. *"That rake'll reach!"*

THE DEATH OF HORATIO ALGER

LeRoi Jones (Imamu Amiri Baraka)

The cold red building burned my eyes. The bricks hung together, like the city, the nation, under the dubious cement of rationalism and need. A need so controlled, it only erupted out of the used-car lots, or sat parked, Saturdays, in front of our orange house, for Orlando, or Algernon, or Danny, or J.D. to polish. There was silence, or summers, noise. But this was a few days after Christmas, and the ice melted from the roofs and the almost frozen water knocked lethargically against windows, tar roofs and slow dogs moping through the yards. The building was Central Avenue School. And its tired red sat on the corner of Central Avenue and Dey (pronounced *die* by the natives, *day* by the teachers or any non-resident whites) Street. Then, on Dey, halfway up the block, the playground took over. A tarred-over yard, though once there had been gravel, surrounded by cement and a wire metal fence.

The snow was dirty as it sat dull and melting near the Greek restaurants, and the dimly lit "grocey" stores of the Negroes. The rich boys had metal wagons, the poor rode in. The poor made up games, the rich played them. The poor won the games, or as an emergency measure, the fights. No one thought of the snow except Mr. Feld, the playground director, who was in charge of it, or Miss Martin, the husky gym teacher Matthew Stodges had pushed into the cloakroom, who had no chains on her car. Grey slush ran over the curbs, and our dogs drank it out of boredom, shaking their heads and snorting.

I had said something about J.D.'s father, as to who he was, or had he ever been. And J., usually a confederate, and private strong arm, broke bad because Augie, Norman, and white Johnny were there, and laughed, misunderstanding simple "dozens" with ugly insult, in that curious scholarship the white man affects when he suspects a stronger link than sociology, or the tired cultural lies of Harcourt, Brace sixth-grade histories. And under their naïveté he grabbed my shirt and pushed me in the snow. I got up, brushing dead ice from my ears, and he pushed me down again, this time dumping a couple pounds of cold dirty slush down my neck, calmly hysterical at his act.

J. moved away and stood on an icy garbage hamper, sullenly throwing wet snow at the trucks on Central Avenue. I pushed myself into a sitting position, shaking my head. Tears full in my eyes, and the cold slicing minutes from my life. I wasn't making a sound. I wasn't thinking any thought I could make someone else understand. Just the rush of young fear and anger and disgust. I could have murdered God, in that simple practical way we kick dogs off the bottom step.

Augie (my best white friend), fat Norman, whose hook shots usually hit the rim, and were good for easy tip-ins by our big men, and useless white Johnny who had some weird disease that made him stare, even in the middle of a game, he'd freeze, and sometimes line drives almost knocked his head off while he shuddered slightly, cracking and recracking his huge knuckles. They were howling and hopping, they thought it was so funny that J. and I had come to blows. And especially, I guess, that I had got my lumps. "Hey, wiseass, somebody's gonna break your nose!" fat Norman would say over and over whenever I did something to him. Hold his pants when he tried his jump shot; spike him sliding into home (he was a lousy catcher); talk about his brother who hung out under the El and got naked in alleyways.

(The clucks of Autumn could have, right at that moment, easily seduced me. Away, and into school. To masquerade as a half-rich nigra with shiny feet. Back through the clean station, and up the street. Stopping to talk on the way. One beer gets you drunk and you stand in an empty corridor, lined with Italian paintings, talking about the glamours of sodomy.)

Rise and Slay.

I hurt so bad, and inside without bleeding I realized the filthy grey scratches my blood would carry to my heart. John walked off staring, and Augie and Norman disappeared, so easily there in the snow. And J.D. too, my first love, drifted against the easy sky. Weeping at what he'd done. No one there but me. THE SHORT SKINNY BOY WITH THE BUBBLE EYES.

Could leap up and slay them. Could hammer my fist and misery through their faces. Could strangle and bake them in the crude jungle of my feeling. Could stuff them in the sewie hole with the collected garbage of children's guilt. Could elevate them into heroic images of my own despair. A righteous messenger from the wrong side of the tracks. Gym teachers, cut-throats, aging pickets, ease by in the cold. The same lyric chart, exchange of particulars, that held me in my minutes, the time "Brownie" rammed the glass door down and ate up my suit. Even my mother, in a desperate fit of rhythm, was not equal to the task. Which was simple economics. I.e., a white man's dog cannot bite your son if he has been taught that something very ugly will happen to him if he does. He might pace stupidly in his ugly fur, but he will never never bite.

But what really stays to be found completely out, except stupid enterprises like art? The word on the page, the paint on the canvas (Marzette dragging in used-up canvases to revive their hopeless correspondence with the times), stone clinging to air, as if it were real. Or something a Deacon would admit was beautiful. The conscience rules against ideas. The point was to be where you wanted to, and do what you wanted to.

After all is "said and done," what is left but those sheepish constructions. "I've got to go to the toilet" is no less pressing than the Puritans taking off for Massachusetts, and dragging their devils with them. (There is in those parts, even now, the peculiar smell of roasted sex organs. And when a good New Englander leaves his house in the earnestly moral sub-towns to go into the smoking hells of soon to be destroyed Yankee Gomorrahs, you watch him pull very firmly at his tie, or strapping on very tightly his evil watch.) The penitence there. The masochism. So complete and conscious a phenomenon. Like a standard of beauty; for instance, the bespectacled, soft-breasted, gently pigeon-toed maidens of America. Neither rich nor poor, with intelligent smiles and straight lovely noses. No one would think of them as beautiful but these mysterious scions of the Puritans. They value health and devotion, and their good women, the lefty power of all our nation, are unpresuming subtle beauties, who could even live with poets (if they are from the right stock), if pushed to that. But mostly they are where they should be, reading good books and opening windows to air out their bedrooms. And it is a useful memory here, because such things as these were the vague images that had even so early, helped shape me. Light freckles, sandy hair, narrow clean bodies. Though none lived where I lived then. And I don't remember a direct look at them even, with clear knowledge of my desire, until one afternoon I gave a speech at East Orange High, as sports editor of our high school paper, which should have been printed in Italian, and I saw there, in the auditorium, young American girls, for the first time. And have loved them as flesh things emanating from real life, that is, in contrast to my own, a scraping and floating through the last three red and blue stripes of the flag, that settles the hash of the lower middle class. So that even sprawled there in the snow, with my blood and pompous isolation, I vaguely knew of a glamorous world and was mistaken into thinking it could be gotten from books. Negroes and Italians beat and shaped me, and my allegiance is there. But the triumph of romanticism was parquet floors, yellow dresses, gardens and sandy hair. I must have felt the loss and could not rise against a cardboard world of dark hair and linoleum. Reality was something I was convinced I could not have.

And thus to be flogged or put to the rack. For all our secret energies. The first leap over the barrier: when the victim finds he can no longer stomach his own "group." Politics whinnies, but is still correct, and asleep in a windy barn. The beautiful statue of victory, whose arms were called duty. And they curdle in her snatch thrust there by angry minorities, along with their own consciences. Poets climb, briefly, off their motorcycles, to find out who owns their words. We are named by all the things we will never understand. Whether we can fight or not, or even at the moment of our hugest triumph we stare off into space remembering the snow melting in our cuts, and all the pimps of reason who've ever conquered us. It is the harshest form of love.

I could not see when I "chased" Norman and Augie. Chased in quotes because, they really did not have to run. They could have turned, and myth aside, calmly whipped my ass. But they ran, laughing and keeping warm. And J.D. kicked snow from around a fire hydrant flatly into the gutter. Smiling and broken, with his head hung just slanted towards the yellow dog ice running down a hole. I took six or seven long running steps and tripped. I couldn't have been less interested, but the whole project had gotten out of hand. I was crying, and my hands were freezing, and the two white boys leaned against the pointed metal fence and laughed and slapped their knees. I threw snow stupidly in their direction. It fell short and was not even noticed as it dropped.

(All of it rings in your ears for a long time. But the payback . . . in simple terms against such actual sin as supposing quite confidently that the big sweating purple whore staring from her peed up hall very casually at your whipping has *never* been loved . . . is hard. We used to say.)

Then I pushed to my knees and could only see J. leaning there against the hydrant looking just over my head. I called to him, for help really. But the words rang full of dead venom. I screamed his mother a purple nigger with alligator titties. His father a bilious white man with sores on his jowls. I was screaming for help in my hatred and loss, and only the hatred would show. And he came over shouting for me to shut up. Shut Up skinny bastard. I'll break your ass if you don't. Norman had both hands on his stomach, his laugh was getting so violent, and he danced awkwardly toward us howling to agitate J. to beat me some more. But J. whirled on him perfectly and rapped him hard under his second chin. Norman was going to say, "Hey me-an," in that hated twist of our speech, and J. hit him again, between his shoulder and chest, and almost dropped him to his knees. Augie cooled his howl to a giggle of concern and backed up until Norman turned and they both went shouting up the street.

I got to my feet, wiping my freezing hands on my jacket. J. was looking at me hard, like country boys do, when their language, or the new tone they need to take on once they come to this cold climate (1940's New Jersey) fails, and they are left with only the old Southern tongue, which cruel farts like me used to deride their lack of interest in America. I turned to walk away. Both my eyes were nothing but water, though it held at their rims, stoically refusing to blink and thus begin to sob uncontrollably. And to keep from breaking down I wheeled and hid the weeping by screaming at that boy. You nigger without a father. You eat your mother's pussy. And he wheeled me around and started to hit me again.

Someone called my house and my mother and father and grandmother and sister were strung along Dey Street, in some odd order. (They couldn't have come out of the house "together.") And I was conscious first of my father saying, "Go on Mickey, hit him. Fight back." And for a few seconds, under the weight of that plea for my dignity, I tried. I feinted and danced, but I couldn't even roll up my fists. The whole street was blurred and hot as my eyes. I swung and swung, but J.D. bashed me when he wanted to.

My mother stopped the fight finally, shuddering at the thing she'd made. "His hands are frozen, Michael. His hands are frozen." And my father looks at me even now, wondering if they'll ever thaw.

PART 3 _____

Victimless Offenses

Victimless offenses result when persons procure certain unlawful goods or services of their own free will; nevertheless, they occasionally discover through alcoholism, drug addiction, venereal disease, or the like that they are indirectly victimized by their actions. For the most part, victimless offenses are difficult for legal authorities to detect because there is seldom a victim, in the traditional sense, to lodge a complaint, and the activities related to these offenses are clandestine. One of the main questions that arises is, What laws can be passed to protect people against themselves without violating their constitutional rights? The Eighteenth Amendment to the U.S. Constitution, ratified in 1919, which prohibited the consumption of alcoholic beverages, is a good example of legal authority overstepping itself. By and large, laws pertaining to victimless offenses are aimed at regulating moral behavior or preventing people from doing harm to themselves.

The most frequently written about victimless offenses are sexual delinquency and alcohol and drug abuse, which are primarily motivated by curiosity and excitement seeking. With the sexual revolution of the 1960s and '70s, adolescents began to experiment more freely with sex than they had previously. Even though the revolution may not have been accepted by many parents, teachers, and other adults, they had to tacitly acknowledge its existence; and often, by failing for one reason or another to talk with their children about sex, adults implicitly condoned many of the practices and attitudes they found objectionable. Nonetheless, when detected, some sexual delinquency (e.g., group sex) causes immediate parental and legal censure.

"Boys and Girls" is a disturbing account of gang sex in which young Studs Lonigan experiences a sad rite of passage. As in similar stories, excited anticipation deteriorates into conscious-stricken remorse. Studs' determination not to succumb to such temptations in the future does not help him; he is caught up in the peer pressure of his gang and forced to go through with his sexual initiation or lose face—something he does not dare risk. Even though Studs' motivation for his actions seems apparent, the reader might very well ask, What really is it that makes Iris behave as she does? Is it simply a matter of her enjoying "power" over the boys together with feeling "important"? Seldom in stories such as "Boys and Girls" are the actions and thoughts and feelings of young women considered in any detail; these are stories about young men. Occasionally youngsters who have participated in gang sex are detected by parents or legal authorities. When this happens, parents impose harsh restrictions and punishments—but do their best to keep the offense from being made public. On the other hand, when sexual delinquents are apprehended by the law, the community often learns of their activities and the youngsters are severely ostracized.

As children grow up, their experiences as consumers of alcoholic beverages are different. Some come from families in which it is the custom to have wine or beer with meals. In other families alcoholic beverages are not allowed until children reach an age set by law or an earlier age set by the family, at which time they are allowed to drink within the home. Some families are total abstainers and others heavy drinkers—each in some way affects the attitudes of their children toward drinking. Many adults seem concerned with their children's drinking only when it results in drunkenness, a drunk-driving arrest, an auto accident, or obvious signs of alcoholism.

Almost all stories about juvenile drinking depict it as an illicit affair of those who have neither the approval of their families nor the sanction of the law. Typically the participants come together to drink whatever can be stolen from the family liquor cabinet, purchased with a falsified identification card, or supplied by an older friend who is of legal age. The secret, conspiratorial gathering of adolescents in "The Truck" realistically captures the camaraderie and language of young drinkers and the effects of the low-grade alcoholic beverages they often drink: drunkenness, sickness, and an unfortunate encounter with the law that is likely to land some of the boys in a reformatory. Many stories about juvenile drinking focus less on drinking as an activity and more on the serious delinquencies that result from it.

Stories about the perils of juvenile drinking became rather old-fashioned with the advent of widespread drug use during the 1960s and '70s. The use of drugs has become a national concern and a preoccupation among writers who believe that describing the psychedelic experiences of drug users is more interesting than relating the happenings that result from drunkenness. Stories written about drugs include all socioeconomic strata and all kinds of drugs, though the emphasis is on the use of marijuana, heroin, and hallucinogens by lower-class youngsters.

"The Hillies" rejects the popular notion that narcotics are used almost exclusively by the poor. When the prim, puritan town of Tarbox discovers it is host to a large population of drug users—"less exotic than hippies" and many "the offspring of prominent citizens"—it must acknowledge that the problem is very much a product of the community itself. And it is not a simple problem to be solved with a single solution, for the drug culture is stratified (the "grassies," "pillies," etc.) with each group representing a distinct philosophy and reason for using its chosen drug.

The safe rural landscape of "Red-Dirt Marijuana" is very different from the threatening ghetto in "Hector Rodriguez." Harold's casual smoking of marihuana—perhaps to heighten the luxury of fishing on a summer afternoon—seems relatively harmless; it has none of the self-destructive intensity of Hector's addiction which is caused by the many irresistible temptations of his environment. In stories of rural delinquency, offenders are seldom apprehended or harshly punished. There is little doubt about what would happen to these boys if they were caught with a pillow case one third filled with "gage" marihuana: Harold would be reprimanded by his father; Hector would be sentenced to a reform school.

Hector starts using marijuana and heroin when he is eleven years old. His reportorial account documents how his casual experimentation results in his becoming a confirmed heroin addict by the age of fifteen. Like so many youngsters depicted in similar stories, Hector's primary motive for trying drugs is curiosity. The account of his grim life as an addict supplies more than enough reason for his decision to commit himself to a rehabilitation clinic several months after his sixteenth birthday. Few stories about drug addicts end as happily as this one.

The delinquents depicted in the stories of this section are affected by their own weaknesses and misjudgments, but are seldom directly preyed upon by others. Offenders more likely than not suffer from their actions in a number of ways: depression, a sense of guilt, an alcoholic hangover, drug addiction, loss of self-esteem, anxiety. These are difficult conditions for juveniles to cope with, but most are temporary and are later ruefully reflected upon as necessary for growing up.

BOYS AND GIRLS

James T. Farrell

Iris sat listening to the guys tell dirty stories. She looked innocent, and her face was a small and pretty oval incarnating purity and virginity. She told some good stories herself, and the guys laughed raucously. She always got excited thinking of boys, because she knew she had a power over them, and that she could get them all pop-eyed any time she wanted to. And she liked to sit as she was now, tantalizing them, having them look at her a long time, before she let them start the fireworks. She thought that this was a very funny thing to do, and it made her feel very important.

She rose and circled the room, walking as she imagined Theda Bara would if Theda Bara were in a room full of heroes. She kept telling them not to get sore eyes, because she didn't like to be the cause of anybody becoming a four-eyes. She stopped before Mush Joss and told him that she wasn't poison ivory. Then she sat down again on the flower-designed rug and told Red to tell them all some more dirty jokes. Red said that she was a dirty enough joke, and they laughed, and then he told some jokes. She sang "Rings on My Fingers" and "My Lulu." She told Jerry Rooney and Hugh Nolan, one of Jim Nolan's younger brothers, that they were both pretty young and they would have to be careful not to get cross-eyed. She sat sighing and thinking that she would start the parade soon. She felt good and thought that it was awful nice for boys and girls to play with each other.

Studs sat pop-eyed like the rest of the bunch. He talked as if all this were ordinary, and he knew what doing it was like. He sat looking holes through Iris, excited, afraid. After a pun of Red's, Jerry rolled on the floor, laughing like he had the St. Vitus's dance, and the guys kidded him about being a punk. They were going to take his britches off, but Iris wouldn't have it. She took Jerry into her mother's bedroom and told the guys to shake dice for their turns. As the door closed on them, Red said: "And a little child will lead them."

Everybody laughed. As they shook dice for turns, there was a lot of rough stuff and kidding. Studs won first crack.

He sat while Red told another dirty joke. At last he would do it. He told himself that this was luck. But he was afraid and upset. He remembered once in the eighth grade during Holy Week, Sister Battling Bertha had said that it was the sins of the flesh that God used as a test to see whether or not you were worthy of going to Heaven. Studs wondered, and he suddenly thought that he was paying too little attention to religion and his soul. Sometimes, after he committed a sin, he was afraid of death, and now he feared he had already committed a mortal sin by wanting to do it with Iris and listening to jokes, and he was about to commit an even more grievous mortal sin. He was awfully afraid, all right, and he guessed he must be a sinful guy or something. His conscience told him it was not right, but there he was, wanting to do it anyway. And how could he back out? Maybe he'd be good and careful the next time and not let himself get into the occasion of sin. But how could Studs Lonigan show a yellow streak now? If he did, he'd make himself into a laughingstock, with everybody giving him the merry ha-ha. And that was no way for a tough guy to act. Not by a damn sight. And he was losing his breath, just like he was yellow and trying to sneak out of a fight.

He had to go through with it, but still he wished he had made some excuse before coming up. He wished he were somewhere else. He determined he would be different in the future. He would receive the sacraments and pray regularly, and be forgiven, and try to win grace enough so that he could lead a better life. He would go to confession next Saturday night, and he'd try to be really and truly sorry for his sins. He promised Our Lord and the Blessed Virgin that he would never do it again. He found himself suddenly imagining what Hell was like, and it made him sweat with fear. It was hotter than a Gary steel mill, and there were all the souls in it, burning in fires, their suffering faces looking worse than if they had been mashed by a motor truck. And then he laughed and forgot about Hell because of a joke Red told them.

He talked with the guys to get his conscience off his mind, and he told them that it would be *Ummmmm* and sweet, and that if that punk Jerry didn't hurry up, he'd be losing some buttons. He talked and suddenly, for no reason at all, death seemed to walk through him like a skeleton, and he got awfully afraid again, and he wished that he wasn't there.

He knew he was starting to lose his nerve and getting leery about the idea of it, and the idea of letting a girl see him. He talked so they wouldn't suspect how he felt, and he wished it was over and it was tomorrow and he was somewhere else. He wondered too how he could stall and get some other guy to go in first. He wondered what would happen if her old lady came home. He thought of Lucy, Lucy sitting in a tree, swinging her legs, the wind on them both, and she seemed to him cool like that wind, and he was all hot and miserable, and he wished that he were cool and with Lucy. She'd hate him if she should ever find out, and he'd never be able to make it up with her.

Jerry came out, his face coloring, and Iris told them he wasn't very much of a man, and they kidded him, telling him to get strong on egg malted milks and to grow hair on his chest. Paulie Haggerty got Iris by him and tried to grab her, but she walked away. He crabbed so that

Weary Reilly told him not to be a dynamiter. Red told her to get back to business.

"Who's first?" she asked.

Studs got red, but he didn't try to get out of it. He couldn't talk, so he just got up and walked to the door, feeling like a condemned man.

Studs came out disappointed, sunk. It wasn't so much. It was nothing like he thought it would be. And it all ended in a bigger hurry than he thought it would. It wasn't any more fun than lots of things. He told them that she was waiting for the next guy. They asked him how it was, and he said it was *Ummmmmm*. He said it because that was the way it was supposed to be.

Davey Cohen went in and found Iris lying on the bed. When he entered, she insisted that she wouldn't let him touch her. He got hot and very sore, but she didn't care. She called him bowlegged, and he called her a bitch. He stood trying to think of worse things to call her, and he was as hot as a steam roller. She told him to get out. If he didn't, she would get Weary Reilly and the guys to sock him, and they would, because if they didn't, she would call off the party.

"You goddamn bitch. I ought to sock your teeth!" he said.

"Runt! Jus' try it! Jus' try it! Jus' try it, that's all! Jus' try it!"

He left the room. When the guys asked him what was wrong, he didn't answer and walked out of the apartment. Iris came out, proud, saying she didn't like him, and Weary agreed with her.

"Next?" she asked.

Paulie Haggerty was Johnny-on-the-spot and as flushed as a beet. She told him to hurry because she had a day's work ahead of her.

"No need to hurry. I can keep you busy for a long time, a long time," Paulie leered.

They told him not to get caught trying it. Studs told Paulie he wasn't such a good working man as he thought, and they laughed.

"Paulie, don't do nothing I wouldn't do," Red called at him.

"Leave it to your Uncle Dudley. *Ummmmm!*" Paulie exclaimed, following Iris out of the parlor.

Waiting, they gassed and shot craps for pennies. Weary was impatient and kept wanting them all to get a move on. He and Tommy Doyle talked tough to each other, and the guys hoped a fight would start, but they were disappointed. Mush Joss won a nickel and boasted that it was his first crap game.

"How was it, Studs?" asked Jerry.

"Ummmmmmmmmmm!" Studs exclaimed.

They boasted about what they would do, and bragged of what they had already done with girls. Hugh Nolan tried to talk of his experiences, but they told him to shut up because he was only a punk. One by one they went in and came out, *Ummmmmmmm*ing. The guys who had had their turns kept urging the others, so that there could be a second round. Hugh Nolan was next to last. When his turn came, Weary couldn't wait any longer and went in. Hugh crabbed, but Weary told him to shut up. Hugh did.

They waited while Weary was in there, hoping that they could get in again. But Weary never seemed to come out and nobody wanted to bang on the door, because Weary was tough. Even Studs, who had licked him, didn't want to interrupt.

After the gang shag, Iris would have Weary up every time she could because she said Weary was nicer than anybody else. So Weary would go up to see her. Until one day, while he was there, the bell rang. He didn't hear it. The bell rang again. Iris's mother found her key in her pocketbook and entered. She was fat and middle-aged, a lump of indistinguishable female flesh. Moving around, she found her daughter in bed with Weary. She screamed and fell into a mock faint. The faint was a failure. If she remained down on the floor, the villain might escape. She got to her feet while Weary was quickly dressing.

"You cur!" the mother screamed in a high-pitched voice.

Weary scowled.

"Who are you? What's your name? What right have you in my house? Ruining my daughter! My poor innocent little girl. What'll her father say? I'll put you in the reform school. If her father caught you, he'd kill you. Killing is too good for a dirty little sonofabitch like you. You little cur! My God! My little girl! Ruined! Disgraced! What'll the neighbors say? You ruined Iris. You pig! And you, you, Iris, you filthy little whore! You're no daughter of mine! Did he make you do it? The cur! You whore! Help! Oh God! God! I'll call the police and put you behind bars. My poor little girl!"

Iris hid her head under the sheets and cried like a small, frightened child.

"What's your name?" the mother demanded of Weary.

"None of your goddamn business."

"You cur! I'll put you behind bars. I'll put you in the reform school! I'll have you hung! Tell me your name! Dog! Beast!"

Iris peered out from the sheets and, red-eyed, she begged her mother to stop.

"Shut up, you slut!" her mother cried. She clutched Weary, shook him, and spat in his face. "Tell me your name!"

"Take your hands off me, you old bitch!" Weary sullenly commanded.

His command quelled the mother. He started to leave. She told him to stop. He turned to stick his tongue out at her. He leered, thumbed his nose. She asked Iris who he was, but the girl refused to answer. She cried tragically. Weary left. The mother fainted.

Weary walked out the front entrance and lit a cigarette. He met the guys from the gang at Fifty-eighth and Prairie. Davey was around trying to explain how he didn't care about what Iris had done to him that time, and, anyway, he was blowing town and going on the bum. Weary interrupted him and told them what had happened at Iris's. They nearly laughed their guts out, it was so funny. And they admired Weary. It was damn funny. Only now they wouldn't be able to go up there any more. Red said, what if they couldn't? The world was full of young bitches like Iris.

THE TRUCK

Michael Rumaker

Wally lifted the canvas flap and looked out the back end of the truck across the vacant lot toward 26th Street. It was getting dark. The street lights hadn't been turned on yet and he squinted his eyes, leaning far out over the tailgate to get a better look.

"Man, ain't he coming yet?" said Muskrat. Muskrat was hunched up in a corner of the truck, his baseball cap pushed back on his head. On two board seats held up by cinderblocks sat Gyp the Greek and Little Joe, and Hector and Lipper. They were playing poker for pennies.

"He ain't gonna come back," said The Greek, raking in a pot with one big hairy paw. "He'll take the money and skidaddle."

"That's how much you know," said Wally. "I see him coming now."

"You better look again," said Little Joe. "Hard to tell a smoke in this light."

"It's Rosemary all right," said Wally, lifting the flap again and looking out.

A tall, lean Negro was walking slowly across the lot toward the truck, a bulging brown paper bag held in one arm.

"Manochrist! Open that canvas wide," Muskrat said. "It stinks like sneaker crud in here."

"Ain't nobody wearing sneakers in here," said Little Joe, flipping a fresh hand around the board, supported on the knees of the players. "Excepting you."

"Hmmm, now ain't that a fact. Well, well."

"Shut up and do something useful," said The Greek. "Light us the lantern. I can't see the cards in front of my face."

"As if it being light made any difference," Lipper giggled.

The Greek reached over and gave Lipper a stiff rabbit punch on the arm.

"Shut up," he said. "You're jealous 'cause I don't go behind the billboards with you anymore."

"Ah, come off it," said Lipper, rubbing his sore arm. "You know I don't go behind the billboards anymore."

"Yeah, yeah," grunted The Greek. "You're one of the gang now. We know all about it."

"Come on, you guys," snapped Wally. "Stop the messing around. You wanta knock the truck off the blocks or something?"

"He started it."

"The hell I did!" The Greek said, rising from his seat and causing the truck to lurch to one side.

"Don't jiggle around, you guys, I said. You wanta knock the truck over?" Wally leaned down and pushed The Greek into his seat.

"Okay, okay. Just tell him to be careful."

"Man, let there be light!" shouted Muskrat. He swung a lantern up on a hook in the slatted ceiling of the truck. The flame spit weakly a few times, then leaped and held, burning with a steady, yellow glare.

"Isschibibblioo—eck! eck!" came from the outer side of the canvas flap.

"It's Rosemary," said Hector.

"That fruity shine's nuts. Don't pay attention to him," The Greek said.

"He gets the wine, don't he?" said Wally. "That's more'n you do."

"Yeah, but has he got it?"

A thin black face, sweaty and glistening in the lamplight, poked through the canvas flap.

"Tootie-potootie-skitzafrooti! I heard what you said, Gyp lover."

"Get outa here, you black pussy."

"Raggle-taggle ookliai—Dreadful—Dreadful."

"Man, drop that African nigger talk," said Muskrat. "Whyn't you talk like an American nigger? You get the wine?"

"Kiss and tell," said Rosemary, shyly.

"Drag him in here," said The Greek. "Let's depants him and see what it is."

"Isschibibblioo—eck! eck!" piped Rosemary, thrusting the bag into Wally's hands. "I'm virgin timber-imber."

"You're nuts, if you ask me," said The Greek.

"Who's asking?" snapped Rosemary. "Waa-waa. Can I come in?"

"It's too crowded," said The Greek.

"Yummie!"

"Get outa here. I don't want no black hands pawing me."

"Let Rosemary alone," said Wally, unscrewing the lid from a bottle.

"Yeah, you guys, Wally's gotta crush on Rosemary," said Lipper.

"Just let him alone," said Wally. He tilted the bottle to his lips and swallowed.

"What else you expect since he don't go behind the billboards with you anymore?" said The Greek. "You're jealous, Lipper."

"Can that stuff, will you?"

"Man, what the hell kinda poison is this?" said Muskrat, choking and gagging as he pushed the bottle at The Greek.

"Port, honey. Port's all I could get with what you gave me. I tried hard, baby, I really did. I look into that man's big blue eyes and I say, 'Honey, you sure we can't fix up something between what I got here and what you got there—I mean, to make up the difference, honey,' I says. But he's so crazy dumb he don't dig me at all. So I had to settle for port.''

"Man, you need a castiron stomach to pipe it. I'd like to puke.''

"Can I come in?" said Rosemary.

"Jump up," said Wally. "You'll have to sit on the tailgate though.''

"And hold open the flap," said Muskrat. "It stinks in here.''

Wally took Rosemary's hand and helped him to climb up. Rosemary sat down very quietly on the edge of the tailgate, crossing his long, thin legs and taking from his pocket a mashed rose. He sniffed at it and looked from face to face.

"Rosi-osi-prettiosi," he said, and waved the rose in front of him. "Stinking air's bad for the lungs.''

"If you don't like it, get out," said The Greek. "Whyn'ahell don't one of us hurry up and get to be twenty-one, so we don't have to put up with this smoked fairy?''

"Gyp don't like me," said Rosemary. "He's such a man I make him doubt him.''

"Go on, Gyp, and play cards," said Wally. "Don't try starting anything.'' He took a long swallow from the bottle and passed it around again.

Rosemary dropped the rose into his shirtfront and took a liqueur flask from his hip pocket. A smell like sweet apples filled the truck. Rosemary sipped a little now and then from the flask.

"Drink some of this rotgut, Rosemary," Wally said. "And throw away that holy water.''

"Afrateesiackalo—no—no," said Rosemary, taking another little sip of liqueur.

"For Christssake, Rosemary," said Muskrat. "You sound like you just got off the boat. Where'd you pick up that African lingo?''

"It ain't African. It's that bebop junk he picks up at the Dance Spot,'' said The Greek, not looking up from his cards.

"Nigger, nigger, on the wall," said Rosemary. "An' I can go pee in a white john anytime I please.''

"If you got the nickel," said Muskrat.

"I got the nickel-lickel-o," said Rosemary. He smacked his lips after another small sip.

"I know where you get them nickels," said The Greek, tossing another penny into the pot. "I seen you hanging around inside that subway head in Philly.''

"Have you got a nickel?" said Rosemary.

"Never you mind," said The Greek. "I know where you get your nickels.''

"Penny-enny-enny, Gyp lover.''

"Black fairy bastard!"

"Sticks and stones, Gyp lover."

They killed the first bottle and Wally opened the second, swallowed some and passed it around. It was getting dark outside. A streetlamp burned on each of the two corners of the lot. A couple of moths flapped around the lantern. The Greek slapped at a mosquito, then shuffled the cards, halving the deck, the cards making a ripping noise between his thumbs. He cut the deck himself and started spinning the cards around the board.

"No more for me," said Litte Joe. "Let's do something else."

"What the hell, after I get them dealt and all that. What's the matter? You guys sore 'cause I'm taking all your money?"

"I'm tired of cards."

"Me, too," said Hector.

"G'wan," said The Greek, gathering the cards together and inspecting each of the hands he had dealt. "You're both sore 'cause I took all your money."

"Can it," said Hector. He took a cigaret butt from behind his ear and lit it, then leaned back and eyed The Greek.

"Whatta you mean 'can it'?" The Greek said, twisting his mouth to one side and staring at Hector, tough-like.

"Just what I said."

"Lay off, Gyp," Wally said. "You're always trying to start trouble."

"*Me* start trouble?" said The Greek, raising his voice. "*They're* the soreheads!"

"Man, can't we have peace in this frigging truck for one night?" said Muskrat. "Sometimes I wisht I *was* back in Jamesburg the way you guys yackety-yackety-yack like a bunch of crabbing women. Take a swig of the bottle, Gyp, and button up."

"Everybody's always yapping at me!" shouted The Greek. "Nobody tells me what to do!"

He lifted an empty wine bottle over his head, striking the lantern and shattering it. Everybody ducked, each throwing his hands over his head. The truck was in darkness. For a moment there was silence. You could hear The Greek breathing heavily and then the truck began to lurch from side to side as though The Greek was rocking himself back and forth, from wall to wall, in the darkness. The old truck springs creaked and ground noisily on the cinderblocks.

"Man, you'll turn us over you don't quit that," said Muskrat.

Rosemary giggled and slid off the tailgate to the ground.

"Let me outa here!" said Lipper, pushing his way to the canvas flap. "The Greek's rammy again."

Wally leaped to the ground and held the flap open. Lipper climbed out and the rest followed. They stood around the tailgate looking into the dark, still-rocking truck.

"You think he'll throw a fit?" said Muskrat.

"I don't give a damn," said Wally. "He's always lousing things up. Come on outa there, Gyp!"

There was no answer. The truck swayed violently now, then tipped to one side, balanced precariously for an instant on two wheel-less hubs. Each boy held his breath. The truck crashed down, righting itself. The creaking stopped, the truck resting quietly on the cinderblocks.

"Come the hell out of there, Gyp!" said Wally.

They heard The Greek stumbling around inside the truck. He fell heavily and lay still for a moment, cursing and muttering to himself. Then he started crawling to the rear of the truck where he flung half his body over the tailgate and vomited. The boys jumped back.

"Jesus Christ! On that teeny bit of wine," said Hector. "The strong man, yeah."

Wally and Muskrat took hold of The Greek under the armpits and hauled him down to the ground.

"Man, I don't feel like dragging this bulk up to 33rd Street."

"Nuts, let him lay there till he sobers up," said Little Joe. "Less us go sneak in on the second show up the 'Vic.'"

"It ain't right to let him lay here like this," said Wally. "S'posing a cop comes along?"

"That's his toughluck," said Hector.

"What dear, true, everlasting friends," said Rosemary, mincing out of the shadows. "Hmph! I'll cart him home myself."

Rosemary leaned down and pulled The Greek up into a sitting position, then pulled out a handkerchief and wiped The Greek's sweaty face. The Greek moaned and his head fell back, his mouth flapping open. A trickle of saliva ran down his chin.

"Excuse me, baby," said Rosemary, and he began slapping The Greek hard on either cheek until The Greek's head rocked back and forth.

"Careful, man. You'll turn him over," snickered Muskrat.

"I'm okay, I'm okay," mumbled The Greek.

Rosemary wiped the spit from The Greek's chin and helped him to his feet.

"Lean, baby, lean," said Rosemary, throwing The Greek's arm around his neck to prop him.

The two started walking away across the lot, The Greek hanging onto Rosemary and Rosemary with one arm slung around The Greek's middle, holding him up.

"S'long," Wally called. But Rosemary didn't answer. He was talking all the time to The Greek and The Greek was grunting and saying, "I'm okay, I'm okay."

Lipper cupped his hands to his mouth and shouted, "Some Greek he-man, yeah! Put the baby to bed, Rosemary."

"Watch he don't burp on you!" shouted Little Joe, and turning to the others said, "Can you imagine? Just on that little stinking bit of wine?"

"That was mighty white of Rosemary," said Muskrat. "You guys oughta be ashamed of yourself." He flopped on the ground near the truck. "Christ, what a stink that guy left," he said, covering his nose with his hand. He crawled farther away and lay flat on his back, pulling his baseball cap over his face.

"Man, that wine sure knocks me for a dingdong."

"I didn't ever like The Greek," said Hector.

"Nor me," said Lipper. "He won't ever lay off to me about them billboards. Hell, I was only a little kid then. I don't see what he's gotta keep bringing it up like it's still happening or something."

"To hell with The Greek," said Little Joe. "Less us go sneak in on the second show up at the 'Vic.' We ain't done that in a helluva long time."

"What's on?" said Wally.

"Hell, I don't know. Whatsat matter? Less go."

"Oh, what the hell," said Wally. "The wine's out. You coming, Muskrat?"

"Man, I'm so bushed I feel like sleeping till doomsday. That old Polack and his grocery orders runs my poor little tail to a frazzle."

He crossed his arms over his chest and stretched out his legs, yawning beneath his baseball cap.

"The hell you say," said Wally. "Come on, you guys."

They all jumped on Muskrat, each grabbing a leg or an arm, and started carrying him over the lot toward 26th Street.

"Man, I'm telling you, this is a sin. This is one tired boy you're carrying off." He wriggled and tried to get free. "Rape! Rape!" he hollered.

They carried him for a couple of blocks, then set him on his feet. He slouched along behind them, his hands stuffed deep in his pockets and his cap pulled low over his eyes, grumbling to himself.

"Man, I gets fighty when I'm drinking."

"Yeah, yeah. We know all about it," said Wally.

"I sure hope it's a good picture," said Little Joe. "I sure hope it's got some beautiful women in it."

"Man, don't sit next to me if you're gonna start playing with yourself again," Muskrat said.

"Go to hell."

"You wait'll you get home this time," grumbled Muskrat. "Man, that's the trouble with us. All we got's Rosemary. I might just as well be back in Jamesburg as be here, irregardless of how much tail walks the street. I sure wisht I had three bucks. I sure wisht I did. I'd treat myself to something nice. I seen this little old brown girl in a pretty blue dress the other night. On Federal Street it was. And she had a flower in her hair and as she's coming up the street I can smell her perfume coming at me, and as she passes she says, without even looking my way, she says, 'Three bucks.' 'Three bucks,' she says, 'cause you know, she ain't no charity whore like Rosemary. Then she goes pretends to look at the junk in the five-and-dime window, kinda waiting to see what I'd do, you know. But all I could do was stand and look at her, 'cause, man, I sure in hell didn't have no three bucks. So she waits and watches me outa the corner of her eye, and when she sees me hesitating, she sorta sniffs at me and kicks up her pumps and walks off. Made me madder'n hell. If I only had them three bucks."

"Whyn't you save up on what the old Polack pays you?" said Wally.

"He barely *pays* me more'n three bucks a week and between that and what I can lift from the ole lady's purse, it hardly stretches to keep my poor ole tail and soul together. And you know it's harder'n hell for me to save. I'm so generous, you know."

"To your own gut," said Wally. "Muskrat, if you want something bad enough you'll go through hell and high water to get it."

"Hmph! Hmph!" snorted Muskrat, tugging at the peak of his baseball cap. "Now just listen to Parson Wallace, fellas. Just give a listen."

A policeman stepped out of an alley, stretching out his arms and blocking their way.

"Where you boys going?"

"What's that to you?" said Wally.

"Don't get wise with me, kid, or I'll—" He patted the long nightstick hanging at his belt.

"We ain't done nothing," said Wally, thrusting his hands on his hips and staring the policeman in the eye.

"Man, we're just out for a little evening stroll," said Muskrat.

"Keep quiet," said Wally.

"I ast you where you was going." The policeman unsnapped the nightstick from his belt and held it clenched at his side.

"We're out walking," said Wally.

"Oh, out walking, huh? Where?"

"None of your goddamned business."

The policeman lifted the stick high, threatening to strike.

"Don't get funny, kid. So Christ help me, I'll split your skull wide open."

Wally spit a lunger into the gutter and wiped his mouth slowly with the back of his hand.

"It's awful late for you boys to be out. Looks kinda funny."

"Man, this ain't Russia, you know," said Muskrat.

"Don't get sassy with me, kid, I'm telling you. You know damned well there's a nine o'clock curfew. Any kid out later than nine gets stopped, see?"

"We ain't up to nothing either, see?" Wally said.

"Yeah? Where'd you get the booze? The smell of the whole pack of you is enough to knock me over. There's not a one of you of age."

"My old man treated us to a little wine," said Wally. "It's my birthday."

"That's an old hooch story. Tell me another. Tell me who your old man is."

"Why do you pester him that way on his birthday?" said Muskrat, stepping up close to the policeman. "We're all witnesses—It's his birthday, like he says, and his old man breaks out a bottle for once. So it's an event, but, man, that don't give you no reason for trying to lock us up."

"What's your name, shorty? You'd make a damned good lawyer."

"Look, Muskrat, I told you to keep outa this, didn't I?"

"So, big boy, you wanta be the mouthpiece, eh? Just tell me where you're headed, that's all. Maybe you're going up the 'Vic' movies, eh? Maybe you're the guys that raped that girl in the men's toilet the other night."

"I ain't never raped nobody," said Muskrat, gloomily.

"Or maybe you belong to the milkbottle gang. Or maybe you're the guys that started the fire in the high school cellar. Or turned the car over on Federal Street last Friday night. How do I know? I gotta check, see? Gotta find out your names and addresses and where you're going. 'Cause it's after nine o'clock, see?"

"Man, you mean you ain't caught all them criminals yet?" said Muskrat. "Some police force, I'll say. Why, it's dangerous to walk the streets with a police force slow as that."

"Yeah, mister, you got it all right," said Wally. "You're on the job for once. And right now we're gonna catch a bus to Trenton."

"Well, well. And whata you gonna do there?" said the policeman, fingering his nightstick. "See the governor maybe?"

"Naw, to hell with the governor. Things are kinda dull in Camden. Not much left to do. So we're gonna hop the bus and go up and rob and rape old lady Roebling, see? You want an in?"

"Comedian, eh?" The policeman whacked Wally across the face with his stick. "Funny guy."

"Man, you sonofabitchin cop, you can't do that!" Muskrat squatted low in a football position and charged into the policeman, hitting him just below the knees. The policeman let out a yell and fell over backwards, his nightstick flying out of his hand and clattering away over the pavement.

"Haul ass!" shouted Muskrat, spinning around and shooing his arms at the others. He grabbed hold of Wally. The boys turned on their heels and started to run up the dark street. Behind came the shrill whistle of the policeman.

"Don't stop till you get to the lot!" panted Wally, turning to glance back as they raced around a corner. "Ole cop's still flat on his back!"

"I shoulda cut his windpipe," said Muskrat. "Just listen to him toot." He glanced over at Wally, who was running beside Lipper.

"Did he hurt you?"

"Like to broke my nose," said Wally. "I'll be all right."

They crossed 26th Street and as they were running over the lot, Little Joe tripped and sprawled flat on his face. Wally caught Muskrat by the arm and pulled him back to where Little Joe had fallen. They took hold of him and dragged him over to the truck. Hector and Lipper were already inside. Lipper was holding open the canvas flap and jumping up and down with excitement.

"Hurry up, you guys, hurry up!" he called in a hoarse whisper.

Wally and Muskrat boosted Little Joe up into the truck and they piled in after.

"Watch out for the broken glass, you guys," said Wally.

"Man, damn that Greek. I feel it crunching under foot," said Muskrat, all out of breath. "I sure wish we had a light so I could see where I'm stepping."

"No lights," said Wally.

They became silent, listening, all of them sweating and breathing hard from the run.

"You okay, Little Joe?" Wally said.

"I'm okay. Hell, I shoudn'ta tripped over my own feet like that. You guys mighta got caught."

"That cop's probably still flat on his ass," sneered Muskrat.

Wally went to the canvas flap, opened it cautiously and peered out.

"You know, that cop had shins like iron bars," said Muskrat. "I never come across a set o' bones like that in all my life. My shoulder's still aching."

"Don't talk so loud," whispered Wally.

"Why, man? What's you see?" said Muskrat, lowering his voice.

"There's a car coming slow down 26th Street."

"Hell, that ain't nothing. Plenty cars come down 26th Street."

"What'll we do?" said Little Joe.

"Yeah, what if it is the cops?" said Hector.

"We can't do nothing but sit here and keep quiet," said Wally. "Don't nobody light any cigarets or anything. I'm going to hold the flap open and keep a lookout."

"Man, I ain't *got* any cigarets to light," said Muskrat. "Hell, boys, ain't this just like a movie?"

"Don't talk so loud," said Wally.

"I only wisht you hadn't mentioned cigarets, that's all," whispered Muskrat. "Makes me hungry for one."

The truck grew quiet. Wally watched as the automobile cruised down 26th Street. It made a U-turn at the corner and came back again, a brilliant spotlight, hitched to the side of the car, moving slowly back and forth across the empty lot.

"It's them," said Wally. "They didn't waste much time."

"Manoman, and me still out on good behavior," said Muskrat. "Dear, sweet Jamesburg, here I come again," he sighed.

A sniffling noise came from somewhere in the darkness of the truck. The truck trembled a little, creaking lightly on the springs.

"Who's that?" said Wally.

"I wanta get outa here," said Lipper in a choking voice. "I don't wanta go to Jamesburg."

"Nobody's going to Jamesburg," said Wally. "Cut out that crying."

"I wanta get outa here," repeated Lipper, shaking the truck with his sobs.

"Man, stop that blubbering," whispered Muskrat. "If anybody goes to Jamesburg it'll be *me*. Who knocked that cop on his ass, anyway?"

"You did," cried Lipper. "I seen you do it, Muskrat."

"Well, just don't you squeal," said Muskrat. He reached out for Lipper, but Lipper crawled away into a corner, pressing himself up tight in it.

"Stop moving around, you guys," said Wally. "And quit the talking."

"Yeah, and who's got a record a mile long?" whispered Muskrat angrily. "You think you got something to cry about. . . . Ah shit!" He laughed softly. "Hey, Wally, you know, this'll be my third time up? Back home for me, boys. I'll be seeing you all in a couple of years."

The car had turned around, the spotlight still playing over the lot. The car stopped and the light made a fast sweep over the flat ground in the direction of the truck, picked it out and rested there. A thin bar of light cut in through the chink in the canvas where Wally was looking out. It threw a faint illumination into the truck so that the boys could see each other's faces, pale and tense. Wally closed the chink and sank down on the floor.

"Goddamn it," he said.

"I wanta get outa here," said Lipper, and started to cry again.

"Are they coming?" said Hector.

"They got us spotted."

"You think maybe I shouldn'ta tackled that cop, Wally?"

"Hell, no!"

"I wanta get outa here," said Lipper.

"Goddamn you, Lipper . . ."

"Shutup," Wally said. He kneeled up and pulled open the flap a little. The same bar of light shot in through the chink. He looked out and saw the flashlights playing over the lot and moving in the direction of the truck. He pulled the flap to.

"They're coming," he said. "Just sit tight and act casual."

"You think that cop'll remember us?" whispered Hector.

"He'd have to be blind if he don't," said Wally.

"Let me outa here!" cried Lipper, leaping up and stumbling toward the rear of the truck.

"Get back here, you crazy sonuvabitch," said Wally. He grabbed Lipper around the knees and dragged him into his lap, keeping a tight hold on him.

"If you run out they'll shoot you."

"I don't wanta go to Jamesburg," sobbed Lipper, struggling to get free of Wally.

"Man, Jamesburg ain't so bad," said Muskrat. "You oughtn't to talk that way. I been there. I know— But, you know, I sure wish I could pull stunts like the one that cop told us happened up at the 'Vic's' craphouse. They don't seem to catch them guys."

"Listen!" said Hector.

From outside came the sound of footsteps moving closer to the truck. There were low voices, but the boys couldn't make out what was being said. They sat waiting, hardly moving, trying to catch the words.

THE HILLIES

John Updike

The town of Tarbox was founded, in 1634, on the way north from Plymouth, by men fearful of attack. They built their fortified meetinghouse on a rocky outcropping commanding a defensive view of the river valley, where a flotilla of canoes might materialize and where commerce and industry, when they peaceably came, settled of their own gravity. Just as the functions of the meetinghouse slowly split between a town hall and a Congregational church, the town itself evolved two centers: the hilltop green and the downtown. On the green stands the present church, the sixth successive religious edifice on this site, a marvel (or outrage, depending upon your architectural politics) of poured concrete, encircled by venerable clapboarded homes that include the tiny old tilting post office (built 1741, decommissioned 1839) and its companion the onetime town jail, recently transformed into a kinetic-art gallery by a young couple from Colorado. Downtown, a block or more of false fronts and show windows straggles toward the factory—once productive of textiles, now of plastic "recreational products" such as inflatable rafts and seamless footballs. The street holds two hardware stores, three banks, a Woolworth's with a new façade of corrugated Fiberglas, the granite post office (built 1933) with its Japanese cherry trees outside and its Pilgrim murals inside, the new two-story Town Hall of pre-rusted steel and thick brown glass, and a host of retail enterprises self-proclaimed by signs ranging in style from the heartily garish to the timidly tasteful, from 3-D neo-Superman to mimicry of the pallid script incised on Colonial tombstones. This downtown is no uglier than most, and its denizens can alleviate their prospect by lifting their eyes to the hill, where the church's parabolic peak gleams through the feathery foliage of the surviving elms. Between the green and the downtown lies an awkward steep area that has never been, until recently, settled at all. Solid ledge, this slope repelled buildings in the early days and by default became a half-hearted park, a waste tract diagonally skewered by several small streets, dotted with various memorial attempts—obelisks and urns—that have fallen short of impressiveness, and feebly utilized by a set of benches where, until recently, no one ever sat. For lately these leaden, eerily veined rocks and triangular patches of parched grass *have* been settled, by flocks of young people; they sit and lie here overlooking downtown Tarbox as if the spectacle is as fascinating as Dante's rose. Dawn finds them already in position, and midnight merely intensifies the murmur of their conversation, marred by screams and smashed bottles. The town, with the wit anonymously secreted within the most pedestrian of populations, has christened them "the hillies."

They are less exotic than hippies. Many are the offspring of prominent citizens; the son of the bank president is one, and the daughter of the meatmarket man is another. But even children one recognizes from the sidewalk days when they peddled lemonade or pedalled a tricycle stare now from the rocks with the hostile strangeness of marauders. Their solidarity appears absolute. Their faces, whose pallor is accented by smears of dirt, repel scrutiny; returning their collective stare is as difficult as gazing into a furnace or the face of a grieving widow. In honesty, some of these effects—of intense embarrassment, of menace—may be "read into" the faces of the hillies; apart from lifting their voices in vague mockery, they make no threatening moves. They claim they want only to be left alone.

When did they arrive? Their advent merges with the occasional vagrant sleeping on a bench, and with the children who used to play here while their mothers shopped. At first, they seemed to be sunning; the town is famous for its beach, and acquiring a tan falls within our code of coherent behavior. Then, as the hillies were seen to be sitting up and clothed in floppy costumes that covered all but their hands and faces, it was supposed that their congregation was sexual in motive; the rocks were a pickup point for the lovers' lanes among the ponds and pines and quarries on the dark edges of town. True, the toughs of neighboring villages swarmed in, racing their Hondas and Mustangs in a preening, suggestive fashion. But our flaxen beauties, if they succumbed, always returned to dream on the hill; and then it seemed that the real reason was drugs. Certainly their torpitude transcends normal physiology. And certainly the afternoon air is sweet with pot, and pushers of harder stuff come down from Boston at appointed times. None of our suppositions has proved entirely false, even the first, for on bright days some of the young men do shuck their shirts and lie spread-eagled under the sun, on the brown grass by the Civil War obelisk. Yet the sun burns best at the beach, and sex and dope can be enjoyed elsewhere, even—so anxious are we parents to please—in the hillies' own homes.

With the swift pragmatism that is triumphantly American, the town now tolerates drugs in its midst. Once a scandalous rumor on the rim of possibility, drugs moved inward, became a scandal that must be faced, and now loom as a commonplace reality. The local hospital proficiently treats fifteen-year-old girls deranged by barbiturates, and our family doctors matter-of-factly counsel their adolescent patients against the dangers, such as infectious hepatitis, of dirty needles. That surprising phrase woven into our flag, "the pursuit of happiness," waves above the shaggy, dazed heads on the hill; a local parson has suggested that the community sponsor a "turn-on" center for rainy days and cold weather. Yet the hillies respond with silence. They pointedly decline to sit on the green that holds the church, though they have been offered sanctuary from police harassment there. The town discovers itself scorned by a mystery beyond drugs, by an implacable "no" spoken between its two traditional centers. And the numbers grow; as many as seventy were counted the other evening.

We have spies. The clergy mingle and bring back reports of intelligent, uplifting conversations; the only rudeness they encounter is the angry shouting ("Animals!" "Enlist!") from the passing carfuls of middle-aged bourgeoisie. The guidance director at the high school, wearing a three days' beard and blotched bluejeans, passes out questionnaires. Two daring young housewives have spent an entire night on the hill, with a tape recorder concealed in a picnic hamper. The police, those bone-chilled sentries on the boundaries of chaos, have developed their expertise by the intimate light of warfare. They sweep the rocks clean every second hour all night, which discourages cooking fires, and have instituted, via a few quisling hillies, a form of self-policing. Containment, briefly, is their present policy. The selectmen cling to the concept of the green as "common land," intended for public pasturage. By this interpretation, the hillies graze, rather than trespass. Nothing is simple. Apparently there are strata and class animosities within the hillies—the "grassies," for example, who smoke marijuana in the middle area of the slope, detest the "beeries," who inhabit the high rocks, where they smash their no-return bottles, fistfight, and bring the wrath of the town down upon them all. The grassies also dislike the "pillies," who loll beneath them, near the curb, and who take harder drugs, and who deal with the sinister salesmen from Boston. It is these pillies, stretched bemused between the Spanish-American War memorial urns, who could tell us, if we wished to know, how the trashy façades of Poirier's Liquor Mart and Leonard's Pharmaceutical Store appear when deep-dyed by LSD and ballooned by the Eternal. In a sense, they see an America whose glory is hidden from the rest of us. The guidance director's questionnaires reveal some surprising statistics. Twelve per cent of the hillies favor the Vietnam war. Thirty-four per cent have not enjoyed sexual intercourse. Sixty-one per cent own their own automobiles. Eighty-six per cent hope to attend some sort of graduate school.

Each week, the Tarbox *Star* prints more of the vivacious correspondence occasioned by the hillies. One taxpayer writes to say that God has forsaken the country, that these young people are fungi on a fallen tree. Another, a veteran of the Second World War, replies that on the contrary they are harbingers of hope, super-Americans dedicated to saving a

mad world from self-destruction; if he didn't have a family to support
he would go and join them. A housewife writes to complain of loud
obscenities that wing outward from the hill. Another housewife promptly
rebuts all such "credit-card hypocrites, installment-plan lechers, and
Pharisees in plastic curlers." A hillie writes to assert that he was driven
from his own home by "the stench of ego" and "heartbreaking lascivi-
ousness." The father of a hillie, in phrases broken and twisted by the
force of his passion, describes circumstantially his child's upbringing in an
atmosphere of love and plenty and in conclusion hopes that other parents will benefit from the hard lesson of his present disgrace—a punishment he "nightly embraces with grateful prayer." Various old men write
in to reminisce about their youths. Some remember hard work, bitter
winters, and penny-pinching; others depict a lyrically empty land where a
boy's natural prankishness and tendency to idle had room to "run their
course." One "old-timer" states that "there is nothing new under the
sun"; another sharply retorts that *everything* is new under the sun, that
these youngsters are "subconsciously seeking accommodation" with
unprecedented overpopulation and "hypertechnology." The Colorado
couple write from their gallery to agree, and to suggest that salvation lies
in Hindu reposefulness, "free-form creativity," and wheat germ. A downtown businessman observes that the hillies have become something of a
tourist attraction and should not be disbanded "without careful preliminary study." A minister cautions readers to "let him who is without sin
cast the first stone." The editor editorializes to the effect that "our" generation has made a "mess" of the world and that the hillies are register-
ing a "legitimate protest"; a letter signed by sixteen hillies responds that
they protest nothing, they just want to sit and "dig." "Life as it is," the
letter (a document mimeographed and distributed by the local chapter of
PAX) concludes, "truly grooves."

The printed correspondence reflects only a fraction of the opinions expressed orally. The local sociologist has told a luncheon meeting of the
Rotary Club that the hillies are seeking "to reemploy human-ness as a
non-relative category." The local Negro, a crack golfer and horseman
whose seat on his chestnut mare is the pride of the local hunt club, cryp-
tically told the Kiwanis that "when you create a slave population, you
must expect a slave mentality." The local Jesuit informed an evening
meeting of the Lions that drugs are "the logical end product of the per-
nicious Protestant heresy of the 'inner light.'" The waitresses at the local
restaurant tell customers that the sight of the hillies through the plate-
glass windows gives them "the creeps." "Why don't they go to *work*?"
they ask; their own legs are blue-veined from the strain of work, of waiting and hustling. The local Indian, who might be thought sympathetic,
since some of the hillies affect Pocahontas bands and bead necklaces, is

savage on the subject: "Clean the garbage out," he tells the seedy crowd that hangs around the liquor mart. "Push 'em back where they came from." But this ancient formula, so often invoked in our history, no longer applies. They came from our own homes. And in honesty do we want them back? How much a rural myth is parental love? The Prodigal Son no doubt became a useful overseer; they needed his hands. We need our self-respect. That is what is eroding on the hill—the foundations of our lives, the identities our industry and acquisitiveness have heaped up beneath the flag's blessing. The local derelict is the only adult who wanders among them without self-consciousness and without fear.

For fear is the mood. People are bringing the shutters down from their attics and putting them back on their windows. Fences are appearing where children used to stray freely from back yard to back yard, through loose hedges of forsythia and box. Locksmiths are working overtime. Once we parked our cars with the keys dangling from the dashboard, and a dog could sleep undisturbed in the middle of the street. No more. Fear reigns, and impatience. The downtown seems to be tightening like a fist, a glistening clot of apoplectic signs and sunstruck, stalled automobiles. And the hillies are slowly withdrawing upward, and clustering around the beeries, and accepting them as leaders. They are getting ready for our attack.

RED-DIRT MARIJUANA

Terry Southern

The white boy came into the open-end, dirt-floor shed where the Negro was sitting on the ground against the wall reading a *Western Story* magazine.

In one hand the boy was carrying a pillowcase that was bunched out at the bottom, about a third filled with something, and when the Negro looked up it appeared from his smile that he knew well enough what it was.

"What you doin', Hal', bringin' in the *crop*?"

The white boy's name was Harold; the Negro pronounced it *Hal'*.

The boy walked on over to one side of the shed where the kindling was stacked and pulled down an old sheet of newspaper which he shook out to full size and spread in front of the Negro. He dumped the gray-grass contents of the pillowcase onto the paper and then straightened up to stand with his hands on his hips, frowning down at it. He was twelve years old.

The Negro was looking at it, too; but he was laughing. He was about thirty-five, and he laughed sometimes in a soft, almost soundless way, shaking his head as though this surely were the final irony, while his face, against very white teeth, gleamed with the darks of richest pipebriar. His name was C.K.

"*Sho'* is a lotta gage," he said.

He reached out a hand and rolled a dry pinch of it between his thumb and forefinger.

"You reckon it's dried out enough?" the boy asked, nasal, sounding almost querulous, as he squatted down opposite. "Shoot, I don't wannta leave it out there no more—not hangin' on that dang sycamore any-way—it's beginnin' to *look* too funny." He glanced out the end of the shed toward the big white farmhouse that was about thirty yards away. "Heck, Dad's been shootin' dove down in there all week—I was down there this mornin' and that damned old dog of Les Newgate's was run-nin' around with a piece of it in his *mouth!* I had to git it away from 'im 'fore they seen it."

The Negro took another pinch of it and briskly crushed it between his flat palms, then held them up, cupped, smelling it.

"They wouldn't of knowed what it was noway," he said.

"You crazy?" said Harold, frowning. "You think my Dad don't know *Mex'can loco-weed* when he sees it?"

"Don't look much *like* no loco-weed now though, do it?" said the Negro flatly, raising expressionless eyes to the boy.

"*He's* seen it dried out, too, I bet," said the boy, loyally, but looking away.

"*Sho'* he is," said C.K., weary and acid. "Sho', I bet he done *blow* a lot of it too, ain't he? Sho', you daddy pro'bly one of the biggest ole hop-heads in Texas—why I bet he *smoke* it an' *eat* it an' jest anyway he can git it into his ole haid! Hee-hee!" He laughed at the mischievous image. "Ain't *that* right, Hal'?"

"You *crazy?*" demanded Harold, frowning terribly; he took the Negro's wrist. "Lemme smell it," he said.

He drew back after a second.

"I can't smell nothin' but your dang sweat," he said.

"'Course not," said C.K., frowning in his turn, and brushing his hands, "you got to git it jest when the *flower* break—that's the *boo*-kay of the plant, you see; that's what we call that."

"Do it again," said Harold.

"I ain't goin' *do* it again," said C.K., peevish, closing his eyes for a moment, ". . . it's jest a waste on you—I do it again, you jest say you smell my *sweat*. You ain't got the nose for it noway—you got to know you business 'fore you start foolin' round with *this* plant."

"I can do it, C.K.," said the boy earnestly, ". . . *come* on, dang it!"

The Negro sighed, elaborately, and selected another small bud from the pile.

"Awright now when I rub it in my *hand*," he said sternly, "you let out you breath—then I *cup* my hand, you put your nose in an' smell strong . . . you got to suck in *strong* thru you nose!"

They did this.

"You smell it?" asked C.K.

"Yeah, sort of," said Harold, leaning back again.

"That's the *boo*-kay of the plant—they ain't no smell like it."

"It smells like tea," said the boy.

"Well, now that's why they calls it that, you see—but it smell like somethin' *else* too."

"What?"

"Like mighty fine gage, that's what."

"Well, whatta you keep on callin' it *that* for?" asked the boy crossly, ". . . that ain't what that Mex'can called it neither—he called it '*pot*.' "

"That ole *Mex*," said C.K., brushing his hands and laughing, "he sho' were funny, weren't he? . . . thought he could pick *cotton* . . . told *me* he use to *pick-a-bale-a-day!* I had to laugh when he say that . . . oh, sho', you didn't talk to that Mex'can like I did—he call it *lotta* things. He call it '*baby*,' too! Hee-hee. Yeah, he say: 'Man, don't forget the *baby* now!'

He mean bring a few *sticks* of it out to the field, you *see*, that's what he mean by that. He call it '*charge*,' too. Sho'. Them's *slang* names. Them names git started people don't want the *police* nobody like that to know they business, you see. Sho', they make up them names, go on an' talk about they business nobody know what they *sayin'*, you see what I mean."

He stretched his legs out comfortably and crossed his hands over the magazine that was still in his lap.

"Yes indeed," he said after a minute, staring at the pile on the newspaper, and shaking his head, "I tell you right now, boy—that sho' is a lotta gage."

About two weeks earlier, on a day when C.K. wasn't helping Harold's father, they had gone fishing together, Harold and C.K., and on the way back to the house that afternoon, Harold had stopped and stood looking into an adjacent field, a section of barren pasture land where the cows almost never went, but where there was a cow at that moment, alone, lying on its stomach, with its head stretched out on the ground in front of it.

"What's wrong with that dang *cow*?" he demanded, not so much of C.K., as of himself, or perhaps of God—though in a sense C.K. was responsible for the stock, it being his job at least to take them out to pasture and back each day.

"Do look like she takin' it *easy*, don't it?" said C.K., and they went through the fence and started toward her. "*Look* like ole Maybelle," he said, squinting his eyes at the distance.

"I ain't never seen a cow act like *that* before," said Harold crossly, ". . . layin' there with her head on the ground like a damned old hound-dog."

The cow didn't move when they reached it, just stared up at them; she was chewing her cud, in a rhythmic and contented manner.

"*Look* at that dang cow," Harold muttered, ever impatient with enigma, ". . . it is old Maybelle, ain't it?" He felt of her nose and then began kicking her gently on the flank. "Git up, dang it."

"Sho' that's ole Maybelle," said C.K., patting her neck, "what's the matter with you, Maybelle?"

Then C.K. found it, a bush of it, about twenty feet away, growing in the midst of a patch of dwarf-cactus, and he was bent over it, examining it with great care.

"This here is a *full-growed* plant," he said, touching it in several places, gently bending it back, almost caressingly. Finally he stood up again, hands on his hips, looking back at the prostrate cow.

"Must be mighty fine gage," he said.

"Well, I ain't never seen loco-weed make a cow act like *that*," said Harold, as if that were the important aspect of the whole incident, and he began absently kicking at the plant.

"That ain't no ordinary loco-weed," said C.K., ". . . that there is *red-dirt marihuana*, that's what *that* is."

Harold spat, frowning.

"Shoot," he said then, "I reckon we oughtta pull it up and burn it."

"I reckon we oughtta," said C.K.

They pulled it up.

"Don't gen'lly take to *red-dirt*," C.K. remarked, casually, brushing his hands, ". . . they say if it *do*, then it's might fine indeed—they reckon it's got to be *strong* to do it, you see."

"Must be pretty dang *strong* awright," Harold dryly agreed, looking back at the disabled cow, "you think we oughtta git Doc Parks?"

They walked over to the cow.

"Shoot," said C.K., "they ain't nothin' wrong with *this* cow."

The cow had raised her head, and her eyes followed them when they were near. They stared down at her for a minute or two, and she looked at them, interestedly, still chewing.

"Ole Maybelle havin' a *fine* time," said C.K., leaning over to stroke her muzzle. "Hee-hee. She *high*, that's what she is!" He straightened up again. "I tell you right now, boy," he said to Harold, "you lookin' at a *ver'* contented cow there!"

"You reckon it'll ruin her milk?"

"Shoot, that make her milk all the more *rich!* Yeah, she goin' give some Grade-A milk indeed after *that* kinda relaxation. Ain't that right, Maybelle?"

They started back to the fence, Harold dragging the bush along and swinging it back and forth.

"Look at the ole *root* on that plant," said C.K., laughing, ". . . big ole juicy root—sho' would make a fine soup bone I bet!"

He had twisted off a branch of the plant and plucked a little bunch of leaves from it which he was chewing now, like mint.

"What's it taste like?" asked Harold.

C.K. plucked another small bunch and proffered it to the boy.

"Here you is, my man," he said.

"Naw, it jest makes me sick," said Harold, thrusting his free hand in his pocket and making a face; so, after a minute, C.K. put that piece in his mouth too.

"We could dry it out and smoke it," said Harold.

C.K. laughed a short derisive snort.

"Yes, I reckon we could."

"Let's dry it out and sell it," said the boy.

C.K. looked at him, plaintive exasperation dark in his face.

"Now Hal' don't go talkin' without you knows what you talkin' *about*."

"We could sell it to them Mex'can sharecroppers over at Farney," said Harold.

"Hal', what is you *talkin'* about—them people ain't got no money."

They went through the fence again, silent for a while.

"Well, don't you wantta dry it out?" Harold asked, bewildered, boy of twelve, aching for action and projects—*any* project that would bring them together.

C.K. shook his head.

"Boy, you don't catch me givin' no advice on that kinda business— you daddy run me right off this place somethin' like that ever happen."

Harold was breaking it up.

"We'd have to put it some place where the dang stock wouldn't git at it," he said.

So they spread the pieces of it up in the outside branches of a great sycamore, where the Texas sun would blaze against them, and then they started back on up to the house.

"Listen, Hal'," said C.K. about halfway on. "I tell you right now you don't wanta say nothin' '*bout* this to nobody up at the house."

"You crazy?" said the boy, "you don't reckon I *would* do you?"

They walked on.

"What'll we do with it when it's dried out, C.K.?"

C.K. shrugged, kicked at a rock.

"Shoot, we find *some* use for it I reckon," he said, with a little laugh.

"You think it's dried *out* enough?" Harold was asking, as they sat with the pile of it between them, he crumbling some of it now in his fingers, scowling at it.

C.K. took out his sack of *Bull Durham*.

"Well, I tell you what we goin' have to do," he said with genial authority, ". . . we goin' have to *test* it."

He slipped two cigarette papers from the attached packet, one of which he licked and placed alongside the other, slightly overlapping it.

"I use *two* of these papers," he explained, concentrating on the work, "that give us a nice *slow*-burnin' stick, you see."

He selected a small segment from the pile and crumpled it, letting it sift down from his fingers into the cupped cigarette paper; and then he carefully rolled it, licking his pink-white tongue slowly over the whole length of it after it was done. "I do that," he said, "that seal it in good, you see." And he held it up then for them both to see; it was much thinner than an ordinary cigarette, and still glittering with the wet of his mouth.

"That cost you a half-a-*dollah* in *Dallas*," he said.

"Shoot," said the boy, uncertain.

"Sho' would," said C.K., ". . . oh you git you three for a dollah, you *know* the man—'course that's mighty good gage I'm talkin' 'bout you pay half-a-dollah . . . that's you *quality* gage. I don't know how good quality this here is yet, you see."

He lit it.

"Sho' *smell* good though, don't it?"

Harold watched him narrowly as he wafted the smoking stick back and forth beneath his nose.

"*Taste* mighty good too! Shoot, I jest bet this is *ver'* good quality gage. You wanta taste of it?" He held it out.

"Naw, I don't want none of it right now," said Harold. He got up and walked over to the kindling stack, and drew out from a stash there a package of Camels; he lit one, returned the pack to its place, and came back to sit opposite C.K. again.

"*Yeah*," said C.K. softly, gazing at the thin cigarette in his hand, "I feel this gage awready . . . this is *fine.*"

"What does it feel like?" asked Harold.

C.K. had inhaled again, very deeply, and was holding his breath, severely, chest expanded like a person who is learning to float, his dark brow slightly knit in the awareness of actually *working* at it physically.

"It feel *fine*," he said at last, smiling.

"How come it jest made me *sick*?" asked the boy.

"Why *I* tole you, Hal'," said C.K. impatiently, " 'cause you tried to fight *against* it, that's why . . . you tried to *fight* that gage, so it jest make you *sick!* Sho', that was *good* gage that ole Mex had."

"Shoot, all I felt besides gittin' sick at my stomach was jest right *dizzy.*"

C.K. had taken another deep drag and was still holding it, so that now when he spoke, casually but without exhaling, it was from the top of his throat, and his voice sounded odd and strained:

"Well, that's 'cause you *mind* is young an' un*formed* . . . that gage jest come into you mind an' *cloud* it over!"

"My *mind*?" said Harold.

"Sho', you *brain*!" said C.K. in a whispery rush of voice as he let out the smoke. "*You* brain is young an' un*formed*, you see . . . that smoke come in, it got no where to go, it jest *cloud* you young brain over!"

Harold flicked his cigarette a couple of times.

"It's as good as any dang nigger-brain I guess," he said after a minute.

"Now boy, don't *mess* with me," said C.K., frowning, ". . . you ast me somethin' an' I tellin' you! *You* brain is young an' un*formed* . . . it's all *smooth*, you brain, smooth as that piece of shoe-leather. That smoke jest come in an' cloud it over!" He took another drag. "Now you take a full-*growed* brain," he said in his breath-holding voice. "It *ain't* smooth —it's got all *ridges* in it, all over, go this way an' that. Shoot, a man know what he doin' he have that smoke runnin' *up* one ridge an' *down* the other! He *con*trol his high, you see what I mean, he don't fight against it. . . ." His voice died away in the effort of holding breath and speaking at the same time—and, after exhaling again, he finished off the cigarette in several quick little drags, then broke open the butt with lazy care and emptied the few remaining bits from it back onto the pile. "*Yeah* . . ." he said, almost inaudibly, an absent smile on his lips.

Harold sat or half reclined, though somewhat stiffly, supporting himself with one arm, just staring at C.K. for a moment before he shifted about a little, flicking his cigarette. "Shoot," he said, "I jest wish you'd tell me what it *feels* like, that's all."

C.K., though he was sitting cross-legged now with his back fairly straight against the side of the shed, gave the appearance of substance wholly without bone, like a softly filled sack that has slowly, imperceptibly sprawled and found its final perfect contour, while his head lay back against the shed, watching the boy out of half-closed eyes. He laughed.

"Boy, I done *tole* you," he said quietly, "it *feel* good."

"Well, that ain't nothin', dang it," said Harold, almost angrily, "*I aw-ready* feel good!"

"Uh-huh," said C.K. with dreamy finality.

"Well, I *do*, god-dang it," said Harold, glaring at him hatefully.

"That's right," said C.K., nodding, closing his eyes, and they were both silent for a few minutes, until C.K. looked at the boy again and spoke, as though there had been no pause at all: "But you don't feel as good now as you do at *Christmas*time though do you? Like when right after you daddy give you that new *Winchester*? An' then you don't feel as *bad* as that time he was whippin' you for shootin' that doe with it neither do you? Yeah. Well now that's how much difference they *is*, you see, between that cigarette you got in you hand an' the one I jest put out! Now that's what I tellin' *you.*"

"*Shoot*," said Harold, flicking his half-smoked Camel and then mashing it out on the ground, "you're crazy."

C.K. laughed. "Sho' I is," he said.

They fell silent again, C.K. appearing almost asleep, humming to himself, and Harold sitting opposite, frowning down to where his own finger traced lines without pattern in the dirt floor of the shed.

"Where we gonna keep this stuff at, C.K.?" he demanded finally, his words harsh and reasonable, "we can't jest leave it sittin' out like this."

C.K. seemed not to have heard, or perhaps simply to consider it without opening his eyes; then he did open them, and when he leaned forward and spoke, it was with a fresh and remarkable cheerfulness and clarity:

"Well, now the first thing we got to do is to *clean* this gage. We got to git them *seeds* outta there an' all them little sticks. But the *ver'* first thing we do . . ." and he reached into the pile, "is to take some of this here *flower*, these here *ver'* small leaves, an' put them off to the side. That way you got you *two* kinds of gage, you see—you got you a *light* gage an' a *heavy* gage."

C.K. started breaking off the stems and taking them out, Harold joining in after a while; and then they began crushing the dry leaves with their hands.

"How we ever gonna git all them dang seeds outta there?" asked Harold.

"Now I show you a *trick* about that," said C.K., smiling and leisurely getting to his feet. "Where's that pilly-cover at?"

He spread the pillowcase flat on the ground and, lifting the newspaper, dumped the crushed leaves on top of it. Then he folded the cloth over them and kneaded the bundle with his fingers, pulverizing it. After a minute of this, he opened it up again, flat, so that the pile was sitting on the pillowcase now as it had been on the newspaper.

"You hold on hard to that end," he told Harold, and he took the other himself and slowly raised it, tilting it, and agitating it. The round seeds started rolling out of the pile, down the taut cloth and onto the ground. C.K. put a corner of the pillowcase between his teeth and held the other corner out with one hand; then, with his other hand, he tapped gently on the bottom of the pile, and the seeds poured out by the hundreds, without disturbing the rest.

"Where'd you learn all that at, C.K.?" asked Harold.

"Shoot, you got to know you business you workin' with *this* plant," said C.K., ". . . waste our time pickin' out them ole seeds." He stood for a moment looking around the shed. "Now we got to have us somethin' to *keep* this gage in—we got to have us a *box*, somethin' like that, you see."

"Why can't we jest keep it in that?" asked Harold, referring to the pillowcase.

C.K. frowned. "Naw we can't *keep* it in that," he said, ". . . keep it in that like ole sacka turnip . . . we got to git us somethin'—a nice little *box*, somethin' like that, you see. How 'bout one of you empty shell boxes? You got any?"

"They ain't big enough," said Harold.

C.K. resumed his place, sitting and slowly leaning back against the wall, looking at the pile again.

"They sho' ain't, is they," he said, happy with that fact.

"We could use two or three of 'em," Harold said.

"Wait a minute now," said C.K., "we talkin' here, we done forgit about this *heavy* gage." He layed his hand on the smaller pile, as though to reassure it. "One of them shell boxes do fine for that—an' I *tell* you what we need for this *light* gage now I think of it . . . is one of you momma's quart *fruit* jars!"

"Shoot, I can't fool around with them dang jars, C.K.," said the boy.

C.K. made a little grimace of impatience.

"*You* momma ain't begrudge you one of them fruit jars, Hal'—she *ast* you 'bout it, you jest say it got *broke!* You say you done *use* that jar put you fishin' minners in it! *Hee-hee* . . . she won't even *wanta* see that jar no more, you tell her *that*."

"I ain't gonna fool around with them jars, C.K."

C.K. sighed and started rolling another cigarette.

"I jest goin' twist up a few of these sticks now," he explained, "an' put them off to the side."

"When're you gonna smoke some of the other?" asked Harold.

"What, that *heavy* gage?" said C.K., raising his eyebrows in surprise at the suggestion. "Shoot, *that* ain't no workin'-hour gage there, that's you *Sunday* gage . . . oh you mix a little bit of that *into* you light gage now and then you *feel like* it—but you got to be sure ain't nobody goin' to mess with you 'fore you turn *that* gage full on. 'Cause you jest wanta lay back then an' take it *easy*." He nodded to himself in agreement with this, his eyes intently watching his fingers work the paper. "You see . . . you don't *swing* with you heavy gage, you jest *goof* . . . that's what you call that. Now you light gage, you *swing* with you light gage . . . you *control* that gage, you see. Say a man have to go out an' *work*, why he able to enjoy that work! Like now you seen me turn on some of this light gage, didn't you? Well, I may have to go out with you *daddy* a little later an' lay on that fence wire, or work with my post-hole digger. Why I able to *swing* with my post-hole digger with my light gage on. Sho', that's you *sociable* gage, you light gage is—this here other, well, that's what you call you *thinkin'* gage. . . . Hee-hee! Shoot, I wouldn't even wanta *see* no post-hole digger I turn *that* gage full on!"

He rolled the cigarette up, slowly, licking it with great care.

"Yeah," he said half aloud, ". . . ole fruit jar be *fine* for this light gage." He chuckled. "That way we jest look right in there, know how much we got on hand at all time."

"We got *enough* I reckon," said Harold, a little sullenly it seemed.

"Sho' is," said C.K., "mor'n the law allows at that."

"Is it against the law then sure enough, C.K.?" asked Harold in eager interest, ". . . like that Mex'can kept sayin' it was?"

C.K. gave a soft laugh.

"I jest reckon it *is*," he said, ". . . it's against all kinda law—what we got here is. Sho', they's one law say you can't have *none* of it, they put you in the jailhouse you do . . . then they's another law say they catch you with more than *this* much . . ." he reached down and picked up a handful to show, "well, then you in *real* trouble! Sho', you got more than *that* why they say: 'Now that man got more of that gage than he *need* for his personal use, he must be *sellin'* it!' Then they say you a *pusher*. That's what they call that, an' boy I mean they put you way back in the jailhouse then!" He gave Harold a severe look. "I don't wanta tell you you business, nothin' like that, Hal', but if I was you I wouldn't let on 'bout this to nobody—not to you frien' Big Law'ence or *any* of them people."

"Heck, don't you think I know better than to do that?"

"You ain't scared though, is you Hal'?"

Harold spat.

"Shoot," he said, looking away, as though in exasperation and disgust that the thought could have occurred to anyone.

C.K. resumed his work, rolling the cigarettes, and Harold watched him for a few minutes and then stood up, very straight.

"I reckon I could git a fruit jar outta the cellar," he said, "if she ain't awready brought 'em up for her cannin'."

"That sho' would be fine, Hal'," said C.K., without raising his head, licking the length of another thin stick of it.

When Harold came back with the fruit jar and the empty shell box, they transferred the two piles into those things.

"How come it's against the law if it's so all-fired good?" asked Harold.

"Well, now I use to study 'bout that myself," said C.K., tightening the lid of the fruit jar and giving it a pat. He laughed. "It ain't because it make young boys like you sick, I tell you *that* much!"

"Well, what the heck is it then?"

C.K. put the fruit jar beside the shell box, placing it neatly, carefully centering the two just in front of him, and seeming to consider the question while he was doing it.

"I *tell* you what it is," he said then, "it's 'cause a man *see* too much when he git high, that's what. He sees right *through* ever'thing . . . you understan' what I say?"

"What the heck are you talkin' about, C.K.?"

"Well, maybe you too young to know what I talkin' 'bout—but I tell you they's a lotta trickin' an' lyin' go on in the world . . . they's a lotta ole *bull-crap* go on in the world . . . well, a man git high, he see right through all them tricks an' lies, an' all that ole bull-crap. He *see* right through there into the *truth* of it!"

"Truth of *what?*"

"*Ever'*thing."

"Dang you sure talk crazy, C.K."

"Sho', they got to have it against the law. Shoot, ever'body git high, wouldn't be nobody git up an' feed the chickens! Hee-hee . . . ever'body jest *lay in bed*! Jest lay in bed till they *ready* to git up! Sho', you take a man high on good gage, he got no use for they ole bull-crap, 'cause he done *see* right through there. Shoot, he lookin' right down into his ver' *soul!*"

"I ain't never heard nobody talk so dang crazy, C.K."

"Well, you young, boy—you goin' hear plenty crazy talk 'fore you is a growed man."

"Shoot."

"Now we got to think of us a good place to *put* this gage," he said, "a *secret* place. Where you think, Hal'?"

"How 'bout that old smokehouse out back—ain't nobody goes in there."

"Shoot that's a *good* place for it, Hal'—you sure they ain't goin' tear it down no time soon?"

"Heck no, what would they tear it down for?"

C.K. laughed.

"Yeah, that's right," he said, "well, we take it out there after it gits dark."

They fell silent, sitting there together in the early afternoon. Through the open end of the shed the bright light had inched across the dirt floor till now they were both sitting half in the full sunlight.

"I jest wish I knowed or not you daddy goin' to work on that south-quarter *fence* today," said C.K. after a bit.

"Aw him and Les Newgate went to *Dalton*," said Harold, ". . . heck, I bet they ain't back 'fore dark. You wanta go fishin'?"

"Shoot, that sound like a *good* idee," said C.K.

"I seen that dang drumhead jumpin' on the west side of the pond again this mornin'," said Harold, ". . . shoot, I bet he weighs seven or eight pounds."

"I think we do awright today," C.K. agreed, glancing out at the blue sky and sniffing a little, ". . . shoot, we try some calf liver over at the second log—that's jest where that ole drumhead is 'bout now."

"I reckon we oughtta git started," said Harold, "I guess we can jest leave that dang stuff here till dark . . . we can stick it back behind that firewood."

"Sho'," said C.K., "we stick it back in there for the time bein'—I think I jest twist up one or two more 'fore we set out though . . . put a taste of this heavy in 'em." He laughed as he unscrewed the lid of the fruit jar. "Shoot, this sho' be fine for fishin'," he said, ". . . ain't nothin' like good gage give a man the strength of patience—you want me to twist up a couple for you, Hal'?"

Harold spat.

"Aw I guess so," he said, ". . . you let *me* lick 'em though, dang it, C.K."

HECTOR RODRIGUEZ

Jeremy Larner

I started taking narcotics in the Bronx, when I was eleven. I was curious, but I wasn't using them that much—I was just taking marijuana once in a while and snorting; I wasn't shooting it up, I was just skinning it then. Skinning is just where you hit anywhere in your body and shoot the dope in. That's with heroin. And snorting is where you snort it up your nose, just like if you're sniffing something. And burning marijuana, that's just like smoking a cigarette, the only thing you inhale it, you don't let it out, you just try to hold it in.

I was using it up there, and then when I moved down here, I was still using it, you know, but I didn't have no habit or nothing. Like when I started going to school, I would go to school high, and I learned how to read a little high. You know, like I wanted to learn something, the things I need in life, but the teachers wouldn't teach me. They used to ignore me, and pay attention to the other kids. Then when I didn't want to learn, they used to come and try to teach me how to learn. Like I couldn't see that; it used to burn me up. I used to go to school high and start nodding all over the classroom, get drowsy, and that's when I started staying out of school; I didn't go to school no more than three or four months in a year.

That's when I started mainlining, when I got to be fifteen; I started mainlining like a dog. Then when I was sixteen, about three or four months ago, I told my mother I was on narcotics. She started crying, but I told her don't cry, if I was another kid I would probably keep it to myself and die by myself. All I want you to do is give me your signature. That way I can go away to Riverside and help myself. The day that I was going away my mother came and gave me some money, my sister gave me some money, and my mother said, I can't see you go, and I said, well go home, 'cause I can't see myself go, 'cause I love you and I know I done one of the most stupidest mistakes in my life. My mother left crying and that hurt me, you know, but I had to take it like a man, because I knew that I stepped into something that was bigger than myself.

Then when I went to Riverside, it wasn't that bad kicking, because they give you medication to calm down your sickness, and that way you can kick in peace. I was wrapped up in a blanket for five days with cold sweats, and when they came to bring my food I couldn't eat. Then after five days I started out with soup and milk, and I couldn't hold that in my system. After that when I started eating, I started going down to my social worker, having my team meetings.

I was on Team Two. Mr. W. was my social worker, Mr. Z. was my psychiatrist; then I had Mr. P. my psychologist, and I had a few other people there that I forgot their names. I used to go down and tell them my troubles and when they asked me how come I started using narcotics, I told them I was curious, because that was the truth; it wasn't because I had a problem or nothing, I was just curious, I played it stupid. I used to see my friends using it, I used to see them having fun, and I wanted to know what it was. When I got my hands on it I started to like it, so then it was too late to back out of it. So then I turned myself over to Riverside. They understood it, and at first they wanted to keep me six months, but I told them I wanted to come out, I wanted to start straight, see if I could get me a job, you know, to help out my parents. With a job I could occupy my time, kill time, stay away from everything. So they let me out, and every Thursday at six o'clock I got to check into the after-care clinic. I'm on three years' probation, and if I get caught with narcotics, I get taken in again, and this time they hit me with six months. And if I keep getting in trouble, they give me a year or send me upstate.

Marijuana smells like tea and olive seasoning mixed up together. Once you got it in you it makes you feel drowsy and it makes you forget about things you don't even want to know about. Or it just brings you out so you can have a gay time. If you want to jump around, you jump around; if you want to sit down and just be in a world of your own, you just sit down and look for your own kicks on it. Like if you see somebody and they come talk to you and something strikes you funny, you just crack up laughing. And you sit down, talk to a girl or boy, you know, like you got some company. You just stay sitting down in a corner and nobody can bother you, no trouble, no nothing. Since marijuana isn't habit-forming you can take it any time you feel like it. If you're in a good mood, you want to get gay, you haven't got nothing to do, you just go and buy yourself a couple of sticks, if you know anybody that sells it. You need to know the right person, 'cause you can go ask a cop for all I know, you need to know the right connection. If you get it, you just take it and there you are, in your own world.

I used to get it uptown, anywhere in Prospect Avenue, right in the streets. Like if you see a junkie and you know him, you just ask him where can I cop some pot? If he knows he'll take you, he'll cop for you. I paid 75 cents a stick, or a dollar for a bomb. A bomb is about as big as a Pall Mall and as fat as a Pall Mall. Like a regular cigarette. The other one is skinnier. I used to smoke it anywhere, like I coulda smoked it in a hallway, smoke it in my house, and if I wanted to just start walking down the street smoking it without nobody seeing me. Just cuff it up in my hand without nobody seeing me and keep on smoking it, just like if I'm smoking a cigarette. Like I would light up a cigarette and light up a joint, start smoking the joint, and everytime I would see a cop or a person coming up I would hide it in my hand or in my pocket and just take out the cigarette, keep on walking. That way nobody would suspect.

I was eleven when I started with marijuana and heroin, too. I stole the heroin off of some guys. I seen them put it up on a roof. I didn't like them because they push me around too much. And I said I don't know what it is, but the only way I can get even with them is by taking it. And I got two of my friends, you know, they were brothers; one of them was twelve and the other was thirteen, like they would shoot up and all. So I took it; since I had seen them doing it, I knew what it was already, more or less. I went and took it and then I knew what it felt like and I liked it. Then from there on I kept on using it.

When you snort heroin, you know, it got a bad bitter taste, like a taste that would turn your stomach inside out. It got some way-out taste. I couldn't snort because I couldn't take that taste; so I started shooting up. Shooting up you don't get the taste; all you get is a fast rush and a boss feeling, you know, like then you got a higher kick than marijuana. You feel drowsy, sit in a corner nodding, nobody to bother you, you're in your own world, in other words. You ain't got no problems whatsoever, you think freely, you don't think about things you were thinking about before shooting up, like you're in your own world, nobody to bother you or nothing.

The first time I skinned, like I wouldn't hit the vein, just pick up the spike and shove it in. Skin-popping, it takes quite a while before you feel it—take a couple of minutes, but it still do the same effect. Skin-popping you don't get no tracks or nothing. Now mainlining you get tracks, and you're hitting directly in the vein. You get a faster habit and while you're mainlining you can feel the stuff faster. Tracks are marks, black marks, like a long black streak coming down your arm directly over your vein; that comes from hitting in the same place so much. Now when you skin-pop you hit all over your body; you can't keep up with tracks. You lose them; they just keep falling off.

I was fifteen when I started mainlining. I got a set of works: a spike, a whisky bottle cap with a bobby pin around it to make like a handle, an eyedropper, and a baby's pacifier. Now when you cook the stuff you just put it inside the bottle cap, draw it up with the eyedropper, tie the dropper to the spike and just shoot it in your veins. You need water to cook it up—a lot of guys carry a little bottle. You have a special spot to shoot up, that's where you have your water stashed. You measure out the heroin into the water, light a match, and cook it up in the cooker just like when you're heating up a bowl of soup or something. They got a piece of cotton inside the cooker to help them draw it all up. They put the spike on the dropper, strap their arm up and wait till the veins come up and then just hit directly. You put the spike in slow, and the only way you know you got a hit is by watching the blood come up; then you just take off the strap and squeeze it in. Then you feel that rush all over your body and you got your high.

Once you squeeze it in, the drug circulates with your blood, it will come around your system, and all of a sudden your eyes will feel like they gonna close up on you. You feel drowsy, your mouth will dry up on you, your spit will turn into cotton balls, right?; then you just start nodding all over the place, take out the works, clean 'em and hide 'em. Then you got that boss feeling, man, like you're your own boss, there ain't nobody can tell you what to do in this world.

If you're weak-minded, if you get a habit, your body will like cramp up on you, your skin'll start shrinking up, you'll start getting sick and need a fix, you'll start sweating at the same time you'll feel cold, you'll be wrapped up in blankets. You'd do anything just to get a fix. For me to get my habit without mainlining it took me six months. I just kept on using it, and I kept on getting the money, right?, so I didn't have to worry about me getting sick. When I started to get sick and I needed the money for a fix, I would go tell my Mom, look I have to buy my girl a present, this and that, and my Mom would fall for it. She would give me the money, I would run down for a shot, take off, and my body would feel relieved, feel at ease. You know, I don't cramp up, then I feel boss. Then when I had money I got my works, and anybody want to use them have to give me a taste of their junk, and somehow I kept up with my habit. Till I finally realized that I didn't want to use it no more, I wanted to straighten up, I wanted to go to work, help out my parents.

I have my own works, right? Now you're using junk yet you ain't got your own works. Well, you will come to use mine, 'cause you can't snort and you need a shoot-up. Now I'll tell you you have to give me a fix before using my works. You ain't got no choice, you have to give me a fix or go on without one. I had a bathroom in Henry Street and then I had a roof in Henry Street. Inside the bathroom they got that box upstairs, the clean water, fresh water comes down to wash out the bowl; well we just take a canful and bring it down. I had a special rule, you know: nobody could come up and get me till after nine o'clock in the morning, 'cause I was out all night. I had two sets of works—the one at home and the one I lend out to the people. Now sometimes I tell them, look, I've already shot up, I don't want to shoot up, just put a little bit inside of this bag—and I'll go shoot that home. Then we would shoot up in that bathroom or up on the roof. After that I would stash the works downstairs where nobody could see me, go home and during the night when I'm sick I have my own works home. I would lock myself in the bathroom where nobody see me and shoot up there, all by myself.

That bowl, you know, in the bathroom—I used to move it, and we had like a loose brick where I stash them; and the minute I move it back in place it look like it was built there and nobody could move it. Now before I hide them I tell my fellas, okay now go downstairs, and I start walking upstairs. They would think that I'm hiding upstairs and I would just watch them leave, and then I would just run down and hide them, go upstairs and come down through the next building. That way they wouldn't know where I had them.

The works that I had home, I used to clean up the spike and wrap it up in a piece of aluminum paper. Then I would wrap up the cooker in a piece of aluminum paper. The eye-dropper I would wrap in in a piece of bag paper, and put it all inside a box of Marlboro, you know, an empty pack of cigarettes, keep those home. Now the other works I used to wrap them up the same but wrap them up in a hanky and stash them. I kept this up till I was ready to go to Riverside, then I threw the works away, flushed them down the bowl piece by piece.

During a day I would take up two at a time; altogether it would come out to about sixteen fellas. Now you know if I was high, I wasn't gonna shoot up sixteen times, so I say okay, just start putting what you gonna give me inside this bag; then I just used to save it all up, and the next day I have my fix. I didn't have to worry about getting money or nothing.

The others couldn't get works. I had to steal my spike out of the hospital. Like when I went to the hospital for my penicillin shot when I had the Asiatic Flu, as the nurse walked out I seen where she threw the spike, inside a big jug full of alcohol. I just put my hand in and grabbed a whole bunch of spikes. I came out and I sold a whole lot of them to a whole lot of guys. And they lost them. But I still had two of them left, and I had my two sets of works, one home and one at the bathroom. And everybody after they lost theirs started coming to me. And I just kept collecting fixes.

I kept earning. I wouldn't sell nothing out. I figured if I sold something, I would spend the money, and later on like I be sick and nobody will come to give me a fix and I be stuck right there. So I used to keep taking in but I wouldn't give none out. A bag would be about a square inch—of that bag they would give me about a third. Now I would shoot up about four bags a day, right? The rest I would save and then I would have me about two more bags. I had it in my house stashed under the bureau. Or in the bathroom under the toilet bowl. I looked a long time before I found that place.

If one of them was nervous and he couldn't hit himself, if he would ask me I would hit him myself. I hit a lot of guys in my days. Now if a fella is capable to hit his own self, I would let him, I would let him judge his own self. Now I tell you I used to hit my own self. I wouldn't let no one hit me, I wouldn't take the chance. They might be nervous and run right through my vein, and who's gonna get messed up? Me.

In the morning, that's when everybody comes out sick, you know, to cop, and that's when I used to be ready with my works, just waiting for these people to come over my way. They used to come, boom! I would be collecting right there and then. They meet me in Henry Street. I wouldn't take nobody up to my house to shoot up, because I didn't want my parents to get a bad name. If I had a bad name why mess it up for my parents? I have to clear that up in my own ways. I would wait next to La Guardia Park, let 'em meet me there. When they come on I would say okay, go ahead, you know where to meet me. When they walk I would just run ahead, have the works and everything ready. I had a short-cut and I'd be there waiting for them.

About the junk itself, it is different depending on where and who you get it from. Now if one of these big operators, you know, the brain of the gang, if he would go and cop, and if he cops a piece that already been cut, he won't have to mess around with it unless he want to mess it up, you know, to make a little more out of it. Now if he go and cop a pure piece, that piece ought to be cut six and one, but he would come down and cut it two and one, make it nice and strong. Right there and then you got good junk, good heroin. Now if he were going to mess it up to get more junk than what he's supposed to get, he'll cut it up six and four, he'll loosen it up and make it weak, like guys won't cop off of him every day. By six and four I mean cutting it one spoon of pure heroin and six or four of sugar. They say it's supposed to be six and one, but if the dealer is wise, he wants everybody to keep coming to him, and he wants to give them a nice count so they can fall out, he will go and cut it two and one, or three and one, make it nice and strong.

Uptown they had this broad, you know, she was a woman already, she was married and she had three kids. She was a junkie and every time she would send somebody out to cop for her—'cause she wouldn't take the chance of going and buying for herself—they would beat her out of her money. And she started marking down the people who started doing that. And she lost her head. So she went and bag up a couple of bags full of rat poison, and when the guys came, you know, she told 'em, well I'm dealing now; and when they cop off her she say, well this guy didn't beat me or nothing, he didn't take my money, so she gave him a good bag. And she say, why this guy beat me, six times, so far he got 150 of my money. Boom! We'll give him a bag of rat poison and mess him up. Now if the guy taste it and know it's rat poison he can't do nothing about it, 'cause he beat her. If he shoots it up he's gonna die instantly.

I taste every bit of junk myself before I use it. I wouldn't take the chance—somebody could be sick, and they might want to get my money so they could get their real cure, and they might sell me a bag of Ajax or a bag of rat poison. And if I wouldn't taste it, if I would play stupid, I would just shoot it up, and like I would go out. Because rat poison cooks up. Now Ajax it cakes up on you, like it bubbles up, and I know if it's junk or not. I make a practice of tasting it, so I know what I'm getting and no one beats me for my money or tries to mess me up.

I had two overdoses in my life. One of them I had in Henry Street when I shot up, but it didn't hit me then, I didn't feel nothing till I walk downstairs. Boom! As soon as I hit the street I passed out. A guy took me up to his house, to his girl's house, and they woke me up. Then the second time I took too much, we were driving around inside a car and we were shooting up inside the car. I wind up in Jackson Park, unconscious, I done passed out, and the guys took me all the way back to Henry Street, took me up to a girl's house, gave me a salt shot, made me drink milk, forced milk down my system while I was out. Then they gave me some more salt shots and started slapping me out of it. Then when I opened one eye, they started walking me around. I was bleeding through my nose like a dog. After I woke up I thought I wasn't myself, because I was more than high. I still had that junk inside my system, and I was drowsy all over the street, I couldn't see where I was going.

It's very dangerous. If you go and shoot up someplace by yourself and you take an O.D. and you ain't got nobody to give you a salt shot, to help you out one-two-three, you'll die right there. You'll have white foam coming out of your mouth, you'll be bleeding. . . . This boy called Bobby, he died in a bathroom up here in Henry Street. He took an O.D. It was where Paul used to live. Paul came down and he was dead and Paul just stepped right over him. I know a lot of people died of overdoses.

I almost got yellow jaundice twice. I was here in Henry Street, and I was nodding. My friend came up and told me, hey, like your face is real yellow, man. Your whole body is yellow. Then when I went to the bathroom, my urinal came out like the color of tea. And the fellas told me, you know you could have yellow jaundice, and I told them no. And they looked at my eyes, made me stick out my tongue, and they said could you eat? And I told them no, and they said you got the reflex toward yellow jaundice, but we can't say for sure you got it. And like I didn't have it. I almost had it those two times, but I didn't get it. I didn't make it because I cut out in time.

I knew this Italian fellow who died of yellow jaundice in Bellevue. Like I knew George from Monroe Street. He had yellow jaundice, his eyes were all yellow; all you could see was a little black pit and the rest was all yellow. He went to the hospital and he came out all right, thank God. And a guy almost got his arm contaminated, they almost had to cut it off, because he blew air inside. He put air inside his veins and puffed them up. He was in the hospital for quite a while.

I've been walking around since I've been back, but I ain't seen none of the fellows who used to use my works. Except one, and he got popped the other day. He got picked up. I'm lucky I kicked.

PART 4

_____ Property Offenses

Property is important in our culture not only for its intrinsic value but also as a symbol of success and an expression of the owner's identity. As a result, many people think of violations against their property as violations against themselves, and so laws that protect property are enforced zealously and rigorously. The property offenses most frequently committed by juveniles are shoplifting, vandalism, motor-vehicle theft, burglary, and robbery—and these are committed most often by groups rather than individuals. Shoplifting (perhaps because merchandise is displayed in an invitingly accessible way) is one of the most common property offenses. Very often, groups or individuals develop specialties, such as stealing cars, clothing, or phonograph records. Occasionally, youngsters steal because they have no other way of fulfilling their basic needs. Sometimes, something is stolen simply for the profit it brings or as a means of showing to others one's courage and skill in performing a risky task. In the case of automobile thefts, a "joy ride" is usually sought, not the permanent possession of the vehicle. Often the skills developed in successful petty thefts by younger delinquents are used to perform more serious crimes when they are older. Although the motivations for property offenses are different, they all ultimately result in someone's property being partially or completely destroyed or taken without the owner's consent.

The stories in this section have been chosen because they explore in depth the more common property offenses and the motives of juveniles for committing them. It is an unusual day when one picks up a newspaper and does not read an account of at least one of these delinquent behaviors: shoplifting, a cash drawer pilfered, property vandalized, a car theft, a home burglarized, or someone robbed on the street.

During the last decade shoplifting has increased to epidemic proportions and has been written about often. Stories about shoplifting have changed considerably over the last half century. In those written during the 1930s, '40s, and '50s, most juvenile shoplifters were known by the store owners who apprehended them, and this acquaintanceship had a softening effect on the punishment, if punishment was imposed at all. Young shoplifters, after having been frightened with threats of legal action, usually were turned over to their parents, who promised to punish the offender and make proper financial recompense. Shoplifters were not viewed as skillful, premeditating criminals but as youngsters giving into a childish impulse and executing their theft so inexpertly as to be caught. The stories of the 1960s and '70s describe a different breed of shoplifter: affluent middle- and upper-class youngsters (possessing all the luxuries they could want) discover shoplifting as an exciting game, which supplies additional clothes, records, and other trinkets. Shop owners in current stories do not hesitate to call in the law to arrest the offenders, who are often brought to trial. What was considered at one time a petty offense is now not so cavalierly dismissed.

"The Parsley Garden" looks back to a more innocent time when childish impulses were the main cause for shoplifting. Surely the reader must feel a certain sympathy for young Al Condraj, from an impoverished neighborhood and "without a penny to spend," who is suddenly "possessed with longing" to have a hammer he sees in a store. After he has been apprehended for stealing it, the only defense he can give for his action is pathetic and guileless: " 'I didn't mean to steal it. I just need it and I haven't got any money.' " Not being a thief by nature, Al's humiliation is intense when he is identified as one— and his final revenge on the store owner is subtle beyond his years in the way it reestablishes his sense of self-esteem.

The youthful offender in "A Criminal's Christmas" is as ingenuous as Al Condraj and is motivated by basically the same impulse when he pilfers six dollars from the open cash drawer of his employer. The aftermath of his theft—an agonized conscience, remorse, and the return of most of the money—hardly reflects the feelings and actions of a hardened thief. Yet, shoplifting a hammer is one thing and stealing money from a cash drawer is another; the reader can well imagine the consequences the latter youthful offender might suffer if apprehended, and how devastating the effects would be on his life. "A Criminal's Christmas" is not simply about stealing but also very much those misdeeds most of us have committed in a weak moment that have gone undetected.

The delinquent behavior of females is much less frequent and direct than that of males. Stories of female delinquency are unusual and even more so when they focus on vandalism. In "The Boats," Joan's middle-class status at a summer resort, though not the social pinnacle of some of the residents who vacation there, is considerably better than the impoverished environments of "The Parsley Garden" and "A Criminal's Christmas." Joan's vandalism of the expensive pleasure boats of her neighbors is obviously motivated by something other than financial need. Her indirect revenge on those who have snubbed her and her need for attention in no way lessen the serious consequences of her actions, which have resulted in extensive property damage.

The impact of the automobile on American adolescent culture has been profound and has been much written about by fiction writers and behavioral scientists. The automobile is important to contemporary adolescents as a status symbol, a means of independent mobility, an extension of their personality, an enclosed space within which to be alone, and a private parlor in which to court. Because cars are easy to steal and the desire for them is so great, they are frequently stolen. In fact, car theft forms something of a separate category of criminality among the young; it cuts across all social strata, though lower-class juveniles steal cars more frequently than advantaged youngsters do.

Juveniles steal cars for a number of reasons. Some youngsters come from families too poor to own a car and steal cars in order to drive. Many adolescents are too young to drive legally, yet have a precocious desire to emulate the confidence and skill of older drivers; to do so, they occasionally "borrow" a car. Other adolescents, of all ages and socioeconomic groups, are fascinated by the thrill of a spine-tingling "joy ride" that sometimes results in an accident, sometimes in arrest, and sometimes in the car's being returned to the place where it was stolen.

Eddie's and Brian's experiences as car thieves in "The Criminal Type" is typical of many car-theft stories. The attraction of a new car with a carelessly unlocked door and key in the ignition are all that are needed to make possible their joy ride. And though they are only fourteen and too young to drive, they enjoy the adult pleasure of driving around in an expensive car. As in many similar stories, their easy success in stealing results in carelessness—a wallet, a coat with a name in it, and fingerprints are left behind in a car and traced to them. Eddie and Brian are apprehended and must face trial, but these prep school boys have professional adult acquaintances who act as character witnesses for them and so they are placed on probation. Boys from less privileged backgrounds often fare much worse and are sent perfunctorily to reform schools, even when they have stolen the same number of cars as their prep school counterparts and are equally repentent.

Stories about robbery divide roughly into two categories: those in which store owners are held up and those in which an individual is singled out and robbed, usually on the street. In the first category the robbers are invariably armed, knowing that store owners are likely to have a concealed weapon. Robbing an isolated individual on the street does not always require a weapon, as you will see in "Never Lose Your Cool." Large physical size or an overwhelming number of robbers often makes the use of weapons unnecessary. William, inexpertly brandishing his pocket knife, is overcome and robbed by an unarmed pair of juveniles, "craftsmen working at their craft, sharp, delicate, not one crude step, not one faulty movement." William is an easy mark for the stronger boys, who beat him and take what small change he has. The scared onlookers, seeing him robbed, fail to report the incident to the police; this is not the course of events when stores are robbed, for store owners, with a large financial investment at stake, call in the law immediately. In most stories, robbers display an unusual proficiency and arrogant confidence; William's prankish theft after he is robbed is in part a testimony to the aplomb of his robbers, which he unsuccessfully tries to imitate.

Stories about property offenses are fascinating in their detailed accounts of how they are committed; more important, they give penetrating insights into the personalities and motivations of youthful offenders. Most property offense stories take place in the city. Those few that occur in the country are usually concerned with minor acts of vandalism committed out of revenge for some injury.

THE PARSLEY GARDEN

William Saroyan

One day in August Al Condraj was wandering through Woolworth's without a penny to spend when he saw a small hammer that was not a toy but a real hammer and he was possessed with a longing to have it. He believed it was just what he needed by which to break the monotony and with which to make something. He had gathered some first-class nails from Foley's Packing House where the boxmakers worked and where they had carelessly dropped at least fifteen cents' worth. He had gladly gone to the trouble of gathering them together because it had seemed to him that a nail, as such, was not something to be wasted. He had the nails, perhaps a half pound of them, at least two hundred of them, in a paper bag in the apple box in which he kept his junk at home.

Now, with the ten-cent hammer he believed he could make something out of box wood and the nails, although he had no idea what. Some sort of a table perhaps, or a small bench.

At any rate he took the hammer and slipped it into the pocket of his overalls, but just as he did so a man took him firmly by the arm without a word and pushed him to the back of the store into a small office. Another man, an older one, was seated behind a desk in the office, working with papers. The younger man, the one who had captured him, was excited and his forehead was covered with sweat.

"Well," he said, "here's one more of them."

The man behind the desk got to his feet and looked Al Condraj up and down.

"What's *he* swiped?"

"A hammer." The young man looked at Al with hatred. "Hand it over," he said.

The boy brought the hammer out of his pocket and handed it to the young man, who said, "I ought to hit you over the head with it, that's what I ought to do."

He turned to the older man, the boss, the manager of the store, and he said, "What do you want me to do with him?"

"Leave him with me," the older man said.

The younger man stepped out of the office, and the older man sat down and went back to work. Al Condraj stood in the office fifteen minutes before the older man looked at him again.

"Well," he said.

Al didn't know what to say. The man wasn't looking at him, he was looking at the door.

Finally Al said, "I didn't mean to steal it. I just need it and I haven't got any money."

"Just because you haven't got any money doesn't mean you've got a right to steal things," the man said. "Now, does it?"

"No, sir."

"Well, what am I going to do with you? Turn you over to the police?"

Al didn't say anything, but he certainly didn't want to be turned over to the police. He hated the man, but at the same time he realized somebody else could be a lot tougher than he was being.

"If I let you go, will you promise never to steal from this store again?"

"Yes, sir."

"All right," the man said. "Go out this way and don't come back to this store until you've got some money to spend."

He opened a door to the hall that led to the alley, and Al Condraj hurried down the hall and out into the alley.

The first thing he did when he was free was laugh, but he knew he had been humiliated and he was deeply ashamed. It was not in his nature to take things that did not belong to him. He hated the young man who had caught him and he hated the manager of the store who had made him stand in silence in the office so long. He hadn't liked it at all when the young man had said he ought to hit him over the head with the hammer.

He should have had the courage to look him straight in the eye and say, "You and who else?"

Of course he *had* stolen the hammer and he had been caught, but it seemed to him he oughtn't to have been so humiliated.

After he had walked three blocks he decided he didn't want to go home just yet, so he turned around and started walking back to town. He almost believed he meant to go back and say something to the young man who had caught him. And then he wasn't sure he didn't mean to go back and steal the hammer again, and this time *not* get caught. As long as he had been made to feel like a thief anyway, the least he ought to get out of it was the hammer.

Outside the store he lost his nerve, though. He stood in the street, looking in, for at least ten minutes.

Then, crushed and confused and now bitterly ashamed of himself, first for having stolen something, then for having been caught, then for having been humiliated, then for not having guts enough to go back and do the job right, he began walking home again, his mind so troubled that he didn't greet his pal Pete Wawchek when they came face to face outside Graf's Hardware.

When he got home he was too ashamed to go inside and examine his junk, so he had a long drink of water from the faucet in the back yard. The faucet was used by his mother to water the stuff she planted every

year: okra, bell peppers, tomatoes, cucumbers, onions, garlic, mint, egg-
plants and parsley.

His mother called the whole business the parsley garden, and every
night in the summer she would bring chairs out of the house and put
them around the table she had had Ondro, the neighborhood handy-
man, make for her for fifteen cents, and she would sit at the table and
enjoy the cool of the garden and the smell of the things she had planted
and tended.

Sometimes she would even make a salad and moisten the flat old-
country bread and slice some white cheese, and she and he would have
supper in the parsley garden. After supper she would attach the water
hose to the faucet and water her plants and the place would be cooler
than ever and it would smell real good, real fresh and cool and green, all
the different growing things making a green-garden smell out of themselves and the air and the water.

After the long drink of water he sat down where the parsley itself was
growing and he pulled a handful of it out and slowly ate it. Then he went
inside and told his mother what had happened. He even told her what he
had *thought* of doing after he had been turned loose: to go back and
steal the hammer again.

"I don't want you to steal," his mother said in broken English. "Here is
ten cents. You go back to that man and you give him this money and
you bring it home, that hammer."

"No," Al Condraj said. "I won't take your money for something I
don't really need. I just thought I ought to have a hammer, so I could
make something if I felt like it. I've got a lot of nails and some box wood,
but I haven't got a hammer."

"Go buy it, that hammer," his mother said.

"No," Al said.

"All right," his mother said. "Shut up."

That's what she always said when she didn't know what else to say.

Al went out and sat on the steps. His humiliation was beginning to
really hurt now. He decided to wander off along the railroad tracks to
Foley's because he needed to think about it some more. At Foley's he
watched Johnny Gale nailing boxes for ten minutes, but Johnny was too
busy to notice him or talk to him, although one day at Sunday school,
two or three years ago, Johnny had greeted him and said, "How's the
boy?" Johnny worked with a boxmaker's hatchet and everybody in
Fresno said he was the fastest boxmaker in town. He was the closest
thing to a machine any packing house ever saw. Foley himself was proud
of Johnny Gale.

Al Condraj finally set out for home because he didn't want to get in the
way. He didn't want somebody working hard to notice that he was being

watched and maybe say to him, "Go on, beat it." He didn't want Johnny Gale to do something like that. He didn't want to invite another humiliation.

On the way home he looked for money but all he found was the usual pieces of broken glass and rusty nails, the things that were always cutting his bare feet every summer.

When he got home his mother had made a salad and set the table, so he sat down to eat, but when he put the food in his mouth he just didn't care for it. He got up and went into the three-room house and got his apple box out of the corner of his room and went through his junk. It was all there, the same as yesterday.

He wandered off back to town and stood in front of the closed store, hating the young man who had caught him, and then he went along to the Hippodrome and looked at the display photographs from the two movies that were being shown that day.

Then he went along to the public library to have a look at all the books again, but he didn't like any of them, so he wandered around town some more, and then around half-past eight he went home and went to bed.

His mother had already gone to bed because she had to be up at five to go to work at Inderrieden's, packing figs. Some days there would be work all day, some days there would be only half a day of it, but whatever his mother earned during the summer had to keep them the whole year.

He didn't sleep much that night because he couldn't get over what had happened, and he went over six or seven ways by which to adjust the matter. He went so far as to believe it would be necessary to kill the young man who had caught him. He also believed it would be necessary for him to steal systematically and successfully the rest of his life. It was a hot night and he couldn't sleep.

Finally, his mother got up and walked barefooted to the kitchen for a drink of water and on the way back she said to him softly, "Shut up."

When she got up at five in the morning he was out of the house, but that had happened many times before. He was a restless boy, and he kept moving all the time every summer. He was making mistakes and paying for them, and he had just tried stealing and had been caught at it and he was troubled. She fixed her breakfast, packed her lunch and hurried off to work, hoping it would be a full day.

It was a full day, and then there was overtime, and although she had no more lunch she decided to work on for the extra money, anyway. Almost all the other packers were staying on, too, and her neighbor across the alley, Leeza Ahboot, who worked beside her, said, "Let us work until the work stops, then we'll go home and fix a supper between us and eat it in your parsley garden where it's so cool. It's a hot day and there's no sense not making an extra fifty or sixty cents."

When the two women reached the garden it was almost nine o'clock, but still daylight, and she saw her son nailing pieces of box wood together, making something with a hammer. It looked like a bench. He had already watered the garden and tidied up the rest of the yard, and the place seemed very nice, and her son seemed very serious and busy. She and Leeza went straight to work for their supper, picking bell peppers and tomatoes and cucumbers and a great deal of parsley for the salad.

Then Leeza went to her house for some bread which she had baked the night before, and some white cheese, and in a few minutes they were having supper together and talking pleasantly about the successful day they had had. After supper, they made Turkish coffee over an open fire in the yard. They drank the coffee and smoked a cigarette apiece, and told one another stories about their experiences in the old country and here in Fresno, and then they looked into their cups at the grounds to see if any good fortune was indicated, and there was: health and work and supper out of doors in the summer and enough money for the rest of the year.

Al Condraj worked and overheard some of the things they said, and then Leeza went home to go to bed, and his mother said, "Where you get it, that hammer, Al?"

"I got it at the store."

"How you get it? You steal it?"

Al Condraj finished the bench and sat on it. "No," he said. "I didn't steal it."

"How you get it?"

"I worked at the store for it," Al said.

"The store where you steal it yesterday?"

"Yes."

"Who give you job?"

"The boss."

"What you do?"

"I carried different stuff to the different counters."

"Well, that's good," the woman said. "How long you work for that little hammer?"

"I worked all day," Al said. "Mr. Clemmer gave me the hammer after I'd worked one hour, but I went right on working. The fellow who caught me yesterday showed me what to do, and we worked together. We didn't talk, but at the end of the day he took me to Mr. Clemmer's office and he told Mr. Clemmer that I'd worked hard all day and ought to be paid at least a dollar."

"That's good," the woman said.

"So Mr. Clemmer put a silver dollar on his desk for me, and then the fellow who caught me yesterday told him the store needed a boy like me every day, for a dollar a day, and Mr. Clemmer said I could have the job."

"That's good," the woman said. "You can make it a little money for yourself."

"I left the dollar on Mr. Clemmer's desk," Al Condraj said, "and I told them both I didn't want the job."

"Why you say that?" the woman said. "Dollar a day for eleven-year-old boy good money. Why you not take job?"

"Because I hate the both of them," the boy said. "I would never work for people like that. I just looked at them and picked up my hammer and walked out. I came home and I made this bench."

"All right," his mother said. "Shut up."

His mother went inside and went to bed, but Al Condraj sat on the bench he had made and smelled the parsley garden and didn't feel humiliated any more.

But nothing could stop him from hating the two men, even though he knew they hadn't done anything they shouldn't have done.

A CRIMINAL'S CHRISTMAS:
THE CONFESSIONS OF A YOUTHFUL OFFENDER WHO, IN LATER LIFE, BECAME AN AUTHOR

Sherwood Anderson

Every man's hand against me. There I was in the darkness of the empty house. It was cold outside and snow was falling. I crept to a window and raising a curtain peered out. A man walked in the street. Now he had stopped at a corner and was looking about. He was looking toward the house I was in. I drew back into the darkness.

Two o'clock, four o'clock. The night before Christmas.

Yesterday I had walked freely in the streets. Then temptation came. I committed a crime. The man hunt was on.

Always men creeping in darkness in cities, in towns, in alley-ways in cities, on dark country roads.

Man wanted. The man hunt. Who was my friend? Whom could I trust? Where should I go?

It was my own fault. I had brought it on myself. We were hard up that year and I had got a job in Willmott's grocery and general store. I was twelve years old and was to have fifty cents a day.

During the afternoon of the day before Christmas there was a runaway on Main Street. Every one rushed out. I was tying a package and there—right at my hand—was an open cash drawer.

I did not think. I grabbed. There was so much silver. Would any one know? Afterward I found I had got six dollars, all in quarters, nickels and dimes. It made a handful. How heavy it felt. When I put it in my pocket what a noise it made.

No one knew. Yes, they did. Now wait. Don't be nervous.

You know what such a boy—twelve years of age—would tell himself. I wanted presents for the other kids of our family,—wanted something for mother. Mother had been ill. She was just able to sit up.

When I got out of the store that evening it was for a time all right. I spent a dollar seventy-five. Fifty cents of it was for mother—a lacy looking kind of thing to put around her neck. There were five other children. I spent a quarter on each.

Then I spent a quarter on myself. That left four dollars. I bought a kite. That was silly. You don't fly kites in the winter. When I got home and before I went into the house I hid it in a shed. There were some old boxes in a corner. I put it in behind the boxes.

It was grand going in with the presents in my arms. Toys, candy, the lace for mother.

Mother never said a word. She never asked me where I got the money to buy so many things.

I got away as soon as I could. There was a boy named Bob Mann giving a party. I went there.

I had come too early. I looked through a window and saw I had come long before the party was to start so I went for a walk.

It had begun to snow. I had told mother I might stay at Bob Mann's all night.

That was what raised the devil—just walking about. When I had grabbed the money out of the cash drawer, I did not think there was a soul in the store. There wasn't. But just as I was slipping it into my pocket a man came in.

The man was a stranger. What a noise the silver made. Even when I was walking in the street that night, thinking about the man, it made a noise. Every step I took it jingled in my pocket.

A fine thing to go to a party making a noise like that. Suppose they played some game. In lots of games you chase each other.

I was frightened now. I might have thrown the money away, buried it in the snow, but I thought . . .

I was full of remorse. If they did not find me out I could go back to the store next day and slip the four dollars back into the drawer.

"They won't send me to jail for two dollars," I thought, but there was that man.

I mean the one who came into the store just when I had got the money all safe and was putting it into my pocket.

He was such a strange acting man. He just came into the store and then went right out. I was confused of course. I must have acted rather strange. No doubt I looked scared.

He may have been just a man who had got into a wrong place. Perhaps he was a man looking for his wife.

When he had gone all the others came back. There had been a rush before the runaway happened and there was a rush again. No one paid any attention to me. I never even asked whose horse ran away.

The man might however have been a detective. That thought did not come until I went to Bob Mann's party and got there too early. It came when I was walking in the street waiting for the party to begin.

I never did go to the party. Like any other boy I had read a lot of dime novels. There was a boy in our town named Roxie Williams who had been in a reform school. What I did not know about crime and detectives he had told me.

I was walking in the street thinking of that man who came into the store just as I stole the money and then, when I began to think of detectives, I began to be afraid of every man I met.

In a snow like that, in a small town where there aren't many lights, you can't tell who any one is.

There was a man started to go into a house. He went right up to the front door and seemed about to knock and then he didn't. He stood by the front door a minute and then started away.

It was the Musgraves' house. I could see Lucy Musgrave inside through a window. She was putting coal in a stove. All the houses I saw that evening, while I was walking around, getting more and more afraid all the time, seemed the most cheerful and comfortable places.

There was Lucy Musgrave inside a house and that man outside by the front door, only a few feet away and she never knowing. It might have been the detective and he might have thought the Musgrave house was our house.

After that thought came I did not dare go home and did not know where I could go. Fortunately the man at the Musgraves' front door hadn't seen me. I had crouched behind a fence. When he went away along the street I started to run but had to stop.

The loose silver in my pocket made too much racket. I did not dare go and hide it anywhere because I thought, "If they find and arrest me and I have four dollars to give back maybe they'll let me go."

Then I thought of a house where a boy named Jim Moore lived. It was right near Buckeye Street—a good place. Mrs. Moore was a widow and only had Jim and one daughter and they had gone away for Christmas.

I made it there all right, creeping along the streets. I knew the Moores hid their key in a woodshed, under a brick near the door. I had seen Jim Moore get it dozens of times.

It was there all right and I got in. Such a night! I got some clothes out of a closet to put on and keep me warm. They belonged to Mrs. Moore and her grown up daughter. Afterward they found them all scattered around the house and it was a town wonder. I would get a coat and skirt and wrap them around me. Then I'd put them down somewhere and as I did not dare light a match would have to get some more. I took some spreads off beds.

It was all like being crazy or dead or something. Whenever any one went along the street outside I was so scared I trembled all over. Pretty soon I had got the notion the whole town was on the hunt.

Then I began thinking of mother. Perhaps by this time they had been to our house. I could not make up my mind what to do.

Sometimes I thought,—well, in stories I was always at that time reading—boys about my own age were always beginning life as bootblacks and rising to affluence and power. I thought I would slide out of town before daylight and get me a bootblack's outfit somehow. Then I'd be all right.

I remember that I thought I'd start my career at a place called Cairo, Illinois. Why Cairo I do not know.

I thought that all out, crouching by a window in the Moores' house that Christmas eve, and then, when no one came along the street for a half hour and I began to be brave again, I thought that if I had a pistol I would let myself out of the house and go boldly home. If, as I supposed, detectives were hid in front of the house, I'd shoot my way through.

I would get desperately wounded of course. I was pretty sure I would get a mortal wound but before I died I would stagger in at the door and fall at mother's feet.

There I would lie dying, covered with blood. I made up some dandy speeches. "I stole the money, mother, to bring a moment of happiness into your life. It was because it was Christmas eve." That was one of the speeches. When I thought of it—of my getting it off and then dying, I cried.

Well, I was cold and frightened enough to cry anyway.

What really happened was that I stayed in the Moores' house until daylight came. After midnight it got so quiet in the street outside that I risked a fire in the kitchen stove but I went to sleep for a moment in a chair beside the stove and falling forward made a terrible burned place on my forehead.

The mark of Cain. I am only telling this story to show that I know just how a criminal feels.

I got out of the Moore house at daylight and went home and got into our house without any one knowing. I had to crawl into bed with a brother but he was asleep. Next morning, in the excitement of getting all the presents they did not expect, no one asked me where I had been. When mother asked me where I had got the burn I said "at the party," and she put some soda on it and did not say anything more.

And on the day after Christmas I went back to the store and sure enough got the four dollars back into the drawer. Mr. Willmott gave me a dollar. He said I had hurried away so fast on Christmas eve that he hadn't got a chance to give me a present.

They did not need me any more after that week and I was all right and knew the man that came in such an odd way into the store wasn't a detective at all.

As for the kite, in the spring I traded it off. I got me a pup but the pup got distemper and died.

THE BOATS

Constance Crawford

Everyone had to come to Walt Pener's boathouse eventually since it was the only place on the lake which sold gasoline for the speedboats and repaired them when they leaked, sputtered, or would not go fast enough. The boathouse leaned back against the steep sandstone cliff, and docks were strung along the shore, flapping and creaking as the wind pushed the water under and between the metal barrels which floated them. The docks and the yard were usually in a state of workmanlike confusion, and on weekends the slips by the gasoline pumps were so crowded that there were always several people circling their boats slowly, offshore, waiting their turn. The men in loud shirts and boys with backs the color of their mahogany speedboats were always bustling in and out, discussing horsepower and varnishes and racing technique with the big husky Swedes Walt Pener hired as mechanics and dock boys. The few sailboat owners who came to have sails mended or rudders repaired were quiet and a little out of place.

Everybody seemed to know everybody else at the boathouse, and Joan Halderman liked to come here, especially lately, and watch, pretending that she, also, knew everybody and they knew her. Now she sat on a pile of boards, facing away from the blinding late-afternoon glare of the water. The sun was warm on her back, browning it still deeper, but the wind off the lake was rising, rustling the row of poplars, rushing in the pines on top of the cliff. Her shadow lay before her on the asphalt of the yard, and she watched the wind pick up long strands of her hair and wave them out from her head—like flames.

Wondering if her hair had grown to reach her waist yet, she bent her head back and her hair fell down, soft and thick and tickling. By twisting her arm behind her, Joan could feel that the longest hairs came all the way to her waist. But she jerked her head up quickly when she remembered that Ed might be watching and think she was foolish and a sissy. Ed was a friend of hers who worked with boats better than anyone, better, even, than Walt Pener himself. Ed had beautiful lumpy, strong arms and Joan wondered if he ever noticed how long and wavy her hair was and how well she could judge boats herself.

Then, with a shiver of anticipation, Joan saw that the thing she had been waiting for was going to begin, and she forgot about her hair. The gray work boat had reached the dock, towing a big speedboat that was listing badly. It belonged to Mr. DeYoung, Joan knew, who was a Yacht Club officer. This afternoon the boat had been found loose, banging against the rocks in a windy, deserted bay on the north shore. Now one man floated the boat onto the carriage, which was on a steep track leading down under the water. Ed started the mechanical winch, and the carriage was drawn up the track into the yard. The boat was glossy and dripping, and water spouted from the cracked bottom. Above the water line was a great splintered hole. Joan stood up to see better as Ed started to work, taking out the ruined plank. He was deft and strong.

"What happened this time, Ed?" she asked, and he glanced at her, squinting against the sun.

"You here again, kid? Look out now." He wrenched a piece of wood free and Joan could peer through the wound into the boat's very insides. "Found her banging on the rocks somewhere. Fifth time this *week* a boat's been turned loose. People better start buying locks. Yes, sir." His voice trailed off, and he was absorbed in his work.

"Yeah," said Joan, sitting down again. "They've all been nice boats, too, you notice?" She waited for an answer and then continued. "This has a hundred and seventy-five horse Fireball, doesn't it?"

"Yeah," he said. "Say, girls aren't supposed to know about engines." But he said it slowly, still working, as though he weren't even thinking about her.

"But *I* do," Joan said.

"H'm. How old are you?"

"Thirteen. Well, really nearly fourteen," she said, knowing he would believe her, for she looked much older than twelve and a half.

But he only said, "H'm."

Ed swooped the plane again and again along a plank, and the shavings curled up and dropped off as though his swinging movements had made them grow, by magic, out of the metal tool. His arms were strong and brown, with yellow hair on them. Joan imagined him wrapped in a red and gold cloth, stalking through a green jungle, cutting the creepers and twining things from his path with a long knife. "When I was little," she said, "about eight, my father and I sailed a boat around in the South Seas. That's where I learned it all. About boats." She was going to go on, but Ed straightened and looked up the road which led down from the top of the cliff.

A yellow Cadillac stopped in the yard, and a man in bright Hawaiian-print trunks and shirt got out and came over to Ed. The man took the cigar from between his teeth and puffed the air out of his red-veined cheeks with a hiss of exasperation as he saw the hole in the side of the boat. He grunted. "They'll jew me plenty again this time. Huh, Ed?"

"At least it didn't get to the motor, Mr. DeYoung," said Ed.

"Your boss'd say that's a damn shame." The man laughed, belching a cloud of smoke into the air. Joan sat on the pile of boards and listened only halfway to their voices. She studied Mr. DeYoung's feet in their leather sandals, and then his knobby, hairy knees. His shirt was open, hanging on each side of his round stomach. The smell of his cigar called up from somewhere, far back, the remembrance of her father, who had once scooped her up from the floor and set her on the table, which was wet from a glass someone had spilled. Everyone had laughed, and the smell of the cigars had hung all through the room. Joan hadn't thought of her father for a long time—maybe for the whole summer—and she wondered a little what he was doing, if perhaps he *could* be hunting big game or horse racing as she sometimes told the people who asked.

"Son of a bitch," muttered Mr. DeYoung, running his hand over the chrome strip on the hull. Joan began to listen, knowing he was thinking of the person who had turned his boat loose to drift. She watched with pleasure as he winced, noticing another deep scratch on the side. He groaned again. "The cops are going to get that guy, believe me."

"I guess people will have to begin buying locks," said Ed quietly, and Joan hid her smile behind her hand. She hoped Mr. DeYoung would scream and threaten the culprit with death, but he only muttered, "Son of a bitch," and "Who the devil . . . ?" a few times more, slapped Ed on the shoulder, and drove away. The tires of the Cadillac skidded on the gravel as he turned onto the main road at the top.

Joan watched Ed for a while longer. She hugged her knees and kept her feet up off the cold asphalt, listening to the roar of the wind. She dreamed of speed—flying, running, riding on a wild black horse, the biggest and wildest horse.

"Time to quit," said Ed, putting his tools in a box. "So long, kid."

The wind had begun to cut through the sun's warmth on Joan's back, and she was glad to get up. "So long, Ed." Though the boards were splintery, she skipped down the docks, because Ed was her friend and it had been an exciting afternoon. She decided to walk along the beach instead of taking the regular trail that ran through the pines and was smooth and civilized for the city people. The sand was cold, but, to show herself that she was tough, she ran where the water was ankle-deep. The golden spray shot up all around, and the drops, when they struck her, stung like hailstones. At the point, the wind always drove the foaming water onto the sand in miniature breakers which, if she watched long enough, would turn into real ones, salty and roaring. The rocks here, now turning bluer and colder as the sun sank, were jumbled down the beach and out into the water. Joan always thought it was as though a giant had sat once on top of the sandstone cliff and let gravel trickle idly through his fingers.

Since the sun was still up, Joan knew it must not even be six-thirty, and her mother and Steve would be having just their first highballs. It was too early to go home, for if she did, she would get there before dinner and they would think that she had nothing to keep her busy. In the next inlet, the public beach would be empty now. Joan decided to go around and sit on the diving board for a while and watch the seaweed which always twirled around the string of floats used to keep the dude swimmers in the shallow water.

Back in the bay, the water, sheltered by the point, became quiet suddenly, smeared with green reflections from the opposite shore. Joan lay on her stomach and dangled her arms over the sides of the diving board, feeling her hands grow heavy. She hung her head over the end, looking back at the beach, making herself believe that the sky and the sand had changed places and that the trees here were rooted by their slender tops. Then three boys came onto the sand, intruding into that strange world, destroying the illusion that it was the earth, and not she, that had turned upside down. Joan sat up quickly, and, hugging her knees, stared past the boys with cool, gray eyes to show her unconcern. They sounded like little children, giggling loudly. They, who could not possibly have understood, had interfered with her. The breeze lifted her hair softly, and she felt solitude around her like a cloak. But when the boys began skipping rocks over the water, she watched in spite of herself.

One of them they called Mort, and he had red hair which jerked in front of his eyes whenever he drew his long, freckled arm back to throw. Once the smallest boy took such a running windup that he splashed into the water, soaking his tennis shoes. They all laughed loudly, the other two patting the little one on his back. Joan no longer was protected by her isolation, but felt shut out of their gaiety. She let her legs down over the side of the diving board and swung them rapidly, gazing up at the pines bordering the beach, but the boys did not even glance at her. They had seen a frog squatting on a rock which jutted out of the water, some distance from shore. The frog stared arrogantly from bulging, half-closed eyes.

"O.K., ol' frog," the boys said, but even when the stones started splashing into the water around him, the frog sat motionless, disdainful. The boys became more earnest, gathering handfuls of rocks, taking careful aim, but always missing their target. They can't do it, Joan thought, they can't do it. She leaned back and contemplated the opposite shore. Out of the corners of her eyes she could see the boys were getting exasperated, and their throws became wilder and wilder. Two of them finally gave up, and only the red-haired boy kept on.

Joan got up slowly, dropped onto the sand, and chose her rock. A round one with enough roughness to give a good grip, she made sure. Scuffing her feet a little, she walked down the beach to get a better aim. She noticed with pride how quiet and steady her heart beat against her

ribs. She was the heroine who, with only a whip and a chair, approaches
the ferocious tiger. She took aim, and the boys turned to watch her. She
missed the frog, but her stone struck the bigger rock just at the water line
with a hard *splut* sound which Joan remembered clearly afterward. The
frog leapt upward with a little squawk, flopped into the water belly first,
and disappeared.

Placing her feet deliberately, looking straight ahead, Joan walked away
up the beach, as a heroine should, curbing her urge to run and laugh,
until she was on the trail, hidden in the pines. Then she ran as hard as
she could, and as gracefully, beautifully. Horrid, stupid boys. But she
hoped she would see them again and they would ask her who she was.
Her legs obeyed her especially well tonight, gathering up, loosening out,
taking the ground with great strides, great—powerful—strides. It was
what they said about race horses.

In front of the Yacht Club dock the trail tipped downhill and threaded
between the boulders. Joan disdained the people who took the easy
way, and she could run straight over the pile of rocks without slackening
speed. Little rock, big rock, one with moss, black one, cracked one, jump
across—the words always chanted themselves through her head, and tonight they had to go faster than ever to keep up with her feet. Her hair
flew and jerked and swished over her back. The rocks blurred by under
her and she landed lightly on the pine needles on the other side, breathing hard with excitement.

Here the houses began, and Joan could see their lights blinking on, up
the hill. The wild part of the trail was past, and so she walked slowly, as
quiet as an Indian, through the darkening columns of the tree trunks. She
was a scout, and if any of the white men, in their hillside forts, should
look out, searching, they would glimpse a shadow, only for an instant,
and would hear no sound.

Before climbing the hill to her own house, Joan stopped and looked
past the docks, out over the open water, where the bats were darting to
and fro in the half-light. She heard the rising rush of the wind far away in
the trees on the opposite shore, and even here, on the sheltered side, the
water was slapping against the creaking docks. She decided that later
tonight she would walk clear around to Forster's, where the hills were low
and the wind swept down across the bay.

Climbing the hill toward the houses, Joan realized how cold her feet
were and how hungry she had become, but she did not hurry. In this
neighborhood only the lake-front houses had great terraces and wide
windows, and the farther Joan got from these, the smaller the houses
were. Now there were dinner smells in the air, and people were sitting
inside, in the flat yellow electric light of their dining rooms. Mrs. Ketcham,
a blue bandanna around her head, greeted Joan from her kitchen win-

dow. Finally deciding to answer, Joan said, "Hello," and walked on. Jim Cannon, who had one of the fastest boats on the lake, was in his yard, hurriedly putting varnish on a water ski. He had never given Joan a ride in his boat, and she was glad he did not notice her now.

Then she saw the lights of her own house. She disliked their cabin, for that was what it was, a cabin, with blue trim and a steep little roof. There was only one real bedroom downstairs for her mother and Steve, and Joan had to use the slant-walled, half-finished room upstairs. Her windows were not wide casements opening out over the water but dormer windows looking at the steep side of the hill and at the main road just above, where, on week ends, the drunks squealed their tires going around the mountain curves.

When Joan opened the front door, her mother was stretched out on the bamboo chaise longue, and Joan could see that she was not in a good mood, even though the glass in her hand was nearly empty.

"*Well,* the wanderer returneth," her mother called to Steve, whom Joan could see through the open kitchen door. He was stirring something in a pan on the stove and had a dish towel tied around his waist. He turned and glanced at Joan. "Here, set the table, will you, Joan? This damn gravy won't thicken."

Joan was annoyed; she *had* come back too soon. As she got the spoons out of the drawer in the kitchen, she noticed that Steve's mustache looked ragged and his blond hair fell over his sweaty forehead. When Steve had first come to live with them, and they had moved to the mountains, Joan had thought he was very handsome, with his smooth blond hair, jutting eyebrows, and shoulders like the men in magazines. But lately, since he went around in his shirt sleeves most of the time, his shoulders were narrower than Joan had thought. "Don't forget the milk," he said.

"Do we *always* have to . . ."

"*You* should have milk—yes, always."

Joan opened the icebox door and slammed it back against the sink. Steve was always treating her like a child. Still, she got the milk bottle out and brought it to the table in the living room, where they ate. She and Steve did have lots of fun, sometimes. Joan stood by the table and looked at her mother. "Are you sick again?" Joan asked.

"Exhausted," said her mother. "So sweet old Steve is fixing dinner. Have you ever thought, Joan, where you and I would be without Steve?"

"Cut it out, Marcia," said Steve quietly, carrying dishes to the table.

Joan had noticed that ever since her mother had left the rest home last winter she was always tired, although she got more beautiful all the time. Joan wondered if she would ever be so beautiful that a man would work

for her the way Steve did for her mother. Even so, she didn't like having
Steve with a towel around his waist. "Why don't we get a maid?" Joan
asked, after a long silence. "The Bergen kids are always talking about
their maid."

Her mother smiled, showing her even, white teeth. "Why, what a little
snob you're getting to be!" Her smile faded. "Well, I'd like one, too, but
where would we put her? And Steve thinks we should conserve my
money." Steve turned and went into the kitchen. Joan's mother got up
and came to the table. She had on the dress that Joan liked the best of
all. It was bright blue and startling against her white skin and the dark,
perfect waves of her hair. Joan had hated her own long, light, tangled
hair until one day when Steve and her mother had been laughing and
having fun together, and in a loud, jolly voice Steve had called Joan "the
gray-eyed, golden-haired goddess, Athena." Joan wondered where he
had got the name Athena, but she liked it and thought of changing her
name when she grew up. Athena Halderman. Ever since then, studying
her face in the mirror, she had seen new things, and she knew that she
was beautiful, almost like her mother.

Steve brought in the dish of stew and they sat down. Joan poured
herself a glass of milk, hoping Steve would notice how she scowled.
When her mother started to eat, Joan noticed a bandage around the tip
of her index finger. It looked strange beside the other long, scarlet fingernails.

"Another one broke?" said Joan regretfully.

"Don't remind me," said her mother, putting her hand out of sight.
"I'm so mad I could scream. I did it on the damn garbage can." Joan
knew her mother had been letting her fingernails grow ever since she had
been sick. They made her long, blue-veined hands ever more graceful,
and sometimes when she let her hands droop over the arms of her chair,
Joan thought the nails looked like the polished claws of a tiger or a lion.
Joan wanted to tell her mother how sorry she was about the broken one,
but they were talking of something else and she knew they would not
listen to her.

Joan played with her food, eating only when she thought Steve would
not see. Wishing they would pay attention to her, she puckered her
forehead, trying to draw her eyebrows up in the middle as her mother
did when she was disturbed. Sometimes Joan even put on special clothes
or combed her hair differently to make them notice, but Steve had never
called her gray-eyed Athena again.

Then Joan remembered how the frog had jumped off the rock this
afternoon, frightened by her miraculous throw. Those stupid boys must
have stared and gaped and wondered who she was as she walked coolly
away, not giving them even so much as a glance. She wondered if Steve

and her mother would realize how magnificent it had been if she told them about it. But they were talking about people Joan had never heard of, and Steve only looked at her once and said, "Joan, stop fooling around and eat."

All right, she would eat and they could go to hell. She would keep all her secrets—and she had plenty. Joan began stuffing the food into her mouth, gulping and chewing as noisily as she could. A piece of cold carrot fell off her spoon and slid down her bare leg. She would not even tell them the biggest, best secret of all. Just thinking about it made her heart beat faster with excitement. She knew other ways than talking to make people notice her, she thought.

Suddenly, in the middle of their incomprehensible talk, Joan's mother turned to her and said, "Maybe *Joan* said something. Has anyone been asking you about your father?"

"No," Joan said, "but those Bergen kids kept talking about how *their* father did this and *their* father did that. So I just told 'em something about *my* father, for a change." Joan remembered with pleasure that they had believed it all, even the part about Alaska. "Where is he anyway?" she asked, half afraid of a disappointing answer.

But her mother only said, "So that's it. I suppose Mrs. Bergen heard this conversation, too?"

Joan watched her mother's eyes, so dark that behind the reflections of light in them you could not even guess how deep they went. She enjoyed having her mother look at her so closely. "I don't know what I said," Joan answered, slowly, to keep her mother's eyes on her.

Her mother gave a breathy, mirthless little laugh. "And I suppose you forgot that my name is Mrs. Walch now, and not Mrs. Halderman."

"I don't know," said Joan again, suddenly not caring.

Her mother stood up, her mouth set in a smile, but Joan saw that where the dimples usually came, there were only dark lines instead. "Well, it makes no difference," her mother said. "I was a fool to think Lake Benton would be any different from any other place. They're *all* full of catty women."

I don't see why getting into their stupid Yacht Club is anything to be desired," said Steve. "You wouldn't *like* them, even if they did ask you to play bridge. Now let's go somewhere and forget about it."

"All right," she said lightly. "Where shall it be? To the club for drinks and dancing? To the lovely house of some of our many friends for sparkling conversation? To a lively party, overlooking the lake?"

Steve stood up and smiled at her—a little sadly, Joan saw with bewilderment. "Why not the theater," he said, "joining the gay, after-dinner crowds?"

"Perfect!" said Joan's mother. "There's a new thing with John Wayne and Maureen O'Hara, isn't there? The critics *raved* about it." They both laughed together, quietly, leaning against the table.

Joan could not understand; they had a secret and she was left out. Then she remembered the secret *she* had from them, from everybody, and she began to laugh, too. It was hard at first but then came easier until the tears filled her eyes. But somehow, nothing was funny.

Then Joan's mother went into the bedroom to get her coat, and the laughter subsided. Joan was still vaguely troubled. "Want to come to the movie, Joan?" asked Steve. "You've been getting to bed early lately."

"No, I think I'll stay home," said Joan. "I have some things I want to do."

"O.K.," he said. "So long." And they went out.

Joan waited until she heard the car start outside and then ran up the stairs, two at a time, to her bedroom. She did not switch on the light but got the package of matches which she kept hidden under her mattress. She lit the candle which she had stood in a saucer on the old chiffonier. Joan loved the way the glow filled the long mirror, as though from under water. She took off her faded bathing suit, got the green one from the bottom drawer, and put it on. It hugged her tightly, and in the candle light it had a soft, half-sheen. She liked to run in this bathing suit; it seemed to stretch and relax with her, helping her. She shook her hair down, admiring it. Moving close to the mirror, she smoothed her eyebrows and looked for a long time into the gray eyes in the reflection. The candle was a tiny flame in each one. Finally she blew out the candle and went to the window. She knew the branches of the pine tree outside by heart, and could let herself down to the ground even on moonless, cloudy nights. She never went down the stairs, even when Steve and her mother were gone.

The air was cold now, and Joan shivered standing by the corner of the house, trying to decide where to go. Somehow, this time, it was different. The excitement of the afternoon had left her. The wind had risen, as she had thought it would, but it only made her colder; the moon was thin, already close to the jagged treetops on Wheeler Ridge. Then Joan remembered her resolve to go clear to Forster's on the big bay, and she started down the hill, trotting to keep warm. She tried leaping the ferns, and she noticed that her feet were now so tough that the pine needles only felt slippery and never pricked her as they used to. By the time she was on the trail by the shore, she felt much better, and began watching, as usual, for strange animal eyes and lurking danger. Thinking how surprised her mother and Steve would be if they knew, she almost laughed aloud, but then remembered how important it was for her to keep perfectly silent. The familiar excitement returned, tightening her muscles and making her ready, she felt, to perform miraculous feats of agility and daring if necessary.

But it was farther to the bay than she had thought. The woods became thicker, and the lights of the houses retreated far back in the trees. At one place, the trail crossed a wide stretch of sand where a stream, now dry, ran down from the hills in the spring, when the snow melted. The sand glimmered faintly around her. The wind carried the smell of the marshy plants which grew in the mud where the lake had receded through the rainless summer. Joan shivered; when she was nearly across the sand and into the trees again, a loud grating, rasping cry boomed from the shore where the row of docks floated on the black water. Joan gasped and stood rigid; the sound came again, like a groaning voice. And suddenly, from the trees, great, dark creatures rose into the sky with a rush of air all around, covering the sliver of moon. Joan cried out and ran, hardly realizing she had done so until she found herself standing among the tree trunks, her own scream echoing in her ears. Her heart filled her temples with pulse beats.

The lights of the Bergens' house showed a little distance up the hill, yellow and warm. While Joan looked at them, the sound came again. Then she knew it was only a fat bullfrog sitting somewhere in his cold, muddy world under the docks. And she must have frightened the cranes which always sat in the tops of the pine trees, like marble statues, until suddenly they would leap into the air with a rush of wings. Joan felt ridiculous standing, cold, in the middle of the trail, her knees shaking. Scared by a frog and some dumb cranes, like a city sissy, she thought with disgust. But she looked at the squares of yellow light from the Bergens' house, and longed to be inside with them. She knew that Mrs. Bergen sometimes read to the two girls and that they always had something good to eat in their hands when they came out to play. They were her friends. Joan started up the little path leading to the house.

But the Bergen girls had straight brown hair and tender feet. They bragged about their boat and the Yacht Club and their father. Joan remembered how they smirked at her sometimes, hating her. Often when she came to play, they wouldn't let her in the house and giggled at her from their bedroom window upstairs. Joan remembered, too, that, in some way, Mrs. Bergen had hurt her mother. Somehow she, like Joan, had been left out.

Joan smiled to herself in the dark, thinking how much the Bergens missed, even though they did have a fast boat. They never had adventures; they just sat and giggled. Those girls never knew how dark and thrilling it was at night, because they went inside and turned on all the lights. Joan forgot about going to Forster's, and she went back down the path quietly.

On the main trail, Joan stopped and listened, looking about her; there was nothing, no sound but the wind. She ran through the ferns down to the shore, out onto the Bergens' dock. It was littered with pieces of rope, a canoe paddle, a fishing pole, and several canvas chairs, one lying on its side. The Bergen girls never put away their things. Joan stood by the slip where the speedboat was tied—loosely tied, Joan saw, so that it banged against the dock when a gust of wind caught it. The canvas cover was thrown over the top of the boat and not fastened. She smoothed the cover and tied it down carefully, as if everything had belonged to her. Excitement flooded through her, more intensely than at any of the other times.

Joan unlooped the stern lines and then had to work over the knotted rope at the prow before it would loosen. Gripping the sides of the boat and bracing her feet against the cleats on the dock, Joan pushed with her full weight. The heavy boat started to slide out into the open water. When it was just free of the dock, she gave one last shove and the dark shape drifted out quietly, away from her. The momentum of her push spent itself, and the boat hung in a glassy strip of water for a moment, before the wind caught it. Then the stern swung crosswise to the wind, and the waves pushed against the mahogany sides. Joan watched until the boat disappeared in the darkness. Even though she held her hands over her mouth, she let out a high, thin little cry of exaltation.

THE CRIMINAL TYPE

Peter Brennan

I'll make this as short as I can, just enough so you can see for yourself what happened. The morning of the trial I walked across the wet blacktop court toward the old brick chemistry building and opened the door to the auditorium. It was warm and noisy inside and the whole hall was full of laughing and clapping. The play had already started. Every year on the last day before Christmas vacation the school put on a big play. I stood by one of the long radiators in the back and watched. It wasn't very funny, but everybody was laughing a lot. I guess I wasn't in the right mood really.

I was supposed to have given a speech, but it was canceled because I had to go to Juvenile Court that morning. The headmaster was just as happy. I don't think he would have been too pleased to see me up there on the stage when everybody in the whole school knew I'd been arrested for stealing cars. I was going to talk about the shepherds and how, when the angels came and started singing, they got so scared and wanted to beat it. What always interests me most is to think about what happened later, when they were old. I wonder if they forgot the whole thing and went back to being shepherds. It's kind of difficult to see how they could. Anyhow, it would have been a good speech because I'd worked on it for almost two weeks.

Mr. Burke saw me standing there and came back to talk to me.

"Are you going now?" he said.

"Yes, I better. My parents are up at the Juvenile Home now and I don't want to keep them waiting."

"How do they feel this morning? Have they calmed down at all?" I had told Mr. Burke how they had been yelling like crazy all week.

"I don't know, they didn't say much. I guess they're kind of scared."

"Can you blame them?"

"No, not really. I don't feel so good myself."

"Neither would I if I had to stand trial this morning."

There was another burst of laughing and shouting. I could see some of the guys in my class who were sitting near the back laughing like mad. In school, people will laugh at anything.

"Let's step outside so we can hear ourselves," Mr. Burke said. He opened the big auditorium door and we went out. It was really cold.

"Would you like a cigarette?"

"Thanks." It wasn't every day a teacher offered you a smoke. But then

170

Mr. Burke didn't seem like a regular teacher. He was only about twenty-five and was still studying to be a priest. That's why we called him "Mister" even though he wore a habit and looked just like a priest.

"Will you be able to come?"

"That depends," he said, checking his watch. "The play was late starting. It may take another hour. And then, of course, there's the headmaster's Christmas address, which should make it two hours. I may be late, but I'll be there as soon as I can."

He was going to be a character witness for me at the trial. Eddie Flynn and I both had to bring a couple of people to swear that we were really good, honest guys. I couldn't see much sense in it. If they were going to send you up, they'd do it no matter what the witnesses said.

"I spoke to the headmaster yesterday," he said. "He's agreed to let you back into school as long as there's nothing in the papers. You can return after Christmas vacation as though nothing had happened."

"If I'm not in jail."

"Don't worry, I'm sure everything will turn out all right."

"Yeah, I hope so."

"Please, Brian, for once remember to say 'Yes,' not 'Yeah.' "

"Okay." I wiped some loose hair out of my ear. I'd just gotten a haircut.

"And remember to use 'Sir' when you're speaking to the judge."

"Okay."

I could see he wanted to say something to kind of cheer me up.

"I asked the whole class to say a prayer for you this morning."

"Thanks," I said. The priests were always praying for you or asking somebody else to. It's funny really. They prayed for the basketball team and the baseball team and even the debating team. Whenever we had a test the teacher always sat up at his desk mumbling over a rosary. I think what they were really praying for was that when we cheated we'd be sneaky enough not to get caught. Teachers always hated to have to catch you.

"Well, you better get going," he said. "Besides, I'm beginning to freeze out here. I'll be up as soon as I'm free."

We shook hands and he turned to go back in.

"And you better put that out before someone sees you." He pointed to my cigarette.

You weren't supposed to smoke anywhere on the school grounds. But everybody did, especially down in the lavatory and behind the lockers in the locker room. I stepped on the cigarette and ran around the old brick building, back across the yard, and out the gate that said Slokum Prep on it.

It was only about two blocks from the school that Eddie and I stole the
first car. It was a Friday afternoon, and we were cutting through an alley
on our way to York's diner. Eddie spotted a pack of cigarettes sitting on
the dashboard of a parked car. It was one of those new models, so you
could see them a mile away.

"Hey, you want a couple smokes?"

"It's probably locked," I said.

"Let's see." He tried the door and it opened. There was no one coming, so he grabbed the smokes and we ran up the alley. When we were
out of breath we stopped.

"Let's have one." He took them out of his pocket and we lit up.

"You know," he said, "the keys were in that car."

"That means the owner'll be back in a minute. Let's keep moving."

"No, wait a minute. I'll bet that car's been there all day. Plenty of
people park in this alley."

We walked back to the car carefully, looking behind us all the time.

"Hold my books a second," Eddie said. He climbed in and fiddled
with the key. The car started up with a noise loud enough to be heard for
blocks.

"Come on. Hurry up. Get in."

I hopped in, still holding two sets of books. He pushed the gas pedal
and the car jumped away from the side of the building and headed down
the alley.

"Jesus Christ! Here we go!"

"Take a look out the back window and see if anybody's following us."

I looked and the alley was empty.

"What are we going to do now?" I asked.

"Go for a ride."

If there was one thing Eddie could do, it was drive. He wasn't so sharp
in school, but he knew all about cars. I don't know how he learned
because we were both fourteen and too young to get a driver's license.
The only trouble was that he was too short. He had to stop and pull up
the seat and that wasn't enough so he wadded up his coat and sat on it.

"Did you ever do this before?"

"Sure, a couple times." The way he said it I didn't know whether to
believe him or not.

"Anything happen?"

"What do you mean?"

"Did you get caught or anything?"

"Naw. It's perfectly safe, just so long as you know what you're doing
and you're careful about it."

"What do you do with it when you're finished?"

"Don't worry," he said, "we'll just leave it somewhere."

I'll have to admit it was fun having your own car—that is, after I stopped being so nervous. We turned the radio up real loud and smoked all the guy's cigarettes and honked at every chick we saw. Just to be safe, we left the city and drove up the big highway that runs along the mountain. From there you can see all of Slokum below you, and it looks a lot better from above. After a couple hours we came back and left the car down by a culm pile and went home for supper.

The next night I was sitting in the movies with a couple guys from school, and Eddie came in. He said he found another car; the other guys didn't want to go, so we went for a ride by ourselves. It was a lot better at night. There're more girls walking around. We didn't pick any of them up, but we spent a few hours trying and it was fun anyhow.

After that we took a car every weekend. We didn't take any old ones either, only ones that were pretty new. They weren't hard to find because we knew a couple of parking lots where they left the keys in the cars. Sometimes we found one on the street that didn't need a key to start it, like a Chevy.

Once, when it was snowing, Eddie skidded and hit a parked car. We figured we were through for sure. But it was some guy with his girl, and before he could get untangled and get his car started, we had disappeared. Aside from a few things like that, it was like owning your own car. You could go anywhere you pleased, drive as fast as you liked, and leave the thing anywhere. There was never a parking problem, you just got out and left it.

The last one we took was from a used-car lot. It was late so the place was closed up and dark. We were walking up the street when we saw this big, white Buick convertible sitting there.

"Let's just give it a check," Eddie said.

I stood on the sidewalk and watched while he went to see if perhaps the keys were in it. Of course they weren't.

He came back.

"Have you got a nickel?"

"How about a dime?"

"Nope, it won't fit."

"Here we are." I gave him the nickel and he ran back to the car. I could see him bent down under the steering wheel. Suddenly the thing started and came roaring out of the lot. I jumped in while it was still moving.

"How did you get her started?"

"It wasn't easy. They got this damn dashboard that curls around at the bottom. But I got the nickel in between the two terminals and bingo! she starts."

"Yeah?"

"But you should have seen the shock I got."

When we got far enough away we put the top down, even though it was December. But it got too cold, so we put it up again.

"Let's pick up some girls," I suggested, like I did every time.

"Okay, let's give it a try."

We drove to a high school outside of Slokum that was having a dance. The guy at the door wasn't going to let us in because we didn't go to school there, but finally he gave in. It was a pretty lousy dance. After about an hour we picked up these two girls who wanted to go for a ride. They didn't believe that it was really our car, but they came anyhow. They were both pretty ugly; I think they were sisters or something. The one I had was fat. Her face was fat and she had a roll of flab around her stomach like an inner tube. She must've weighed about a hundred pounds more than me, but she was all right in the back seat. She didn't mind at all when I slipped my hand in around her inner tube.

Eddie was mad because he had to drive. He was going back through town, headed for the park, when we heard sirens behind us. At first I thought it was probably an ambulance, but it kept coming down on us.

"Let's get out of here," I shouted to Eddie.

"What's the matter?" the fat girl kept saying. "You see, I knew it wasn't your car. It's stolen, isn't it? I knew it."

Eddie started going faster, and the girls got scared and began to scream. So, when we turned a corner, we got rid of them and kept going. The way Eddie drove I figured we were both going to get killed. He went right through stop signs and red lights and the sirens kept coming. We nearly killed about a dozen people who were trying to cross the street. Eddie drove down a long, bright street, and when we were far enough ahead, he pulled in behind a factory. There was a big vacant lot in back. We jumped out, and the car kept going and came to a stop in a little ditch. The lot was empty except for a big truck parked right in the middle.

"Follow me," Eddie said, grabbing me by the sleeve.

We crawled under the truck. A second later the cop car pulled in with its siren screaming. The cops got out and looked in the empty car. Then they came toward the truck. I could hear their feet on the gravel. My heart was thumping so loud I thought they'd hear me.

"We know you're in there. Come out."

I figured they had us now. I put my head between my knees so they couldn't hear my breathing. I was so scared I couldn't think of anything besides the sounds my body was making. They walked all around the truck and lifted the canvas flap in the back. They flashed their flashlights in and then walked around the truck again and looked in the cab. When I raised my head I could see the cop's black boot about three feet away from my head. But he didn't bother to bend over and look underneath.

"The bastards must've gone over that fence."

"We'll get them anyhow," the other cop said.

They went back to their car and talked on the phone for a while and then drove away. The headlights of their car flashed under the truck but they didn't see us.

We waited for a few minutes and crawled out. My mouth was all pasty and I couldn't swallow so well. I thought maybe I'd caught something from that girl. I've heard of other people getting things just from kissing. We ran along the side of the factory and down a street toward the river. We must've run about ten miles without saying a word and without stopping once.

That was on a Friday night. Sunday afternoon a detective came to the house. I was upstairs in my room and I could hear him talking to my father.

"Brian, come down here," my father called.

I came downstairs as though nothing was wrong.

"Brian, the officer has some disturbing news."

"Oh yeah," I said, "how's that?"

"I just came from your pal Eddie Flynn's house." The detective was a tall guy and spoke very solemnly.

"Why, did Eddie get hurt?"

"He's been arrested."

"Really? What for?"

"I'm afraid he was involved in a car theft last Friday night."

"I don't believe it," I said. "Not Eddie Flynn."

"His coat was found in the car, with his wallet and identification in it."

I had to sit down in a big chair. How could he be so stupid to leave his coat in the car? He must've taken it off when we picked up the girls and then forgotten about it.

"He's already admitted stealing the car. He claims that you were with him. You'll have to come along now to Juvenile Home for questioning."

"Just a minute," my father said. "The boy hasn't confessed to anything."

"I'm sorry, sir, but the boy is under arrest."

"Brian, tell me the truth," my father said. "Were you involved in this?"

That was a bad question. What could I say?

"I don't know anything about it. I was at a dance Friday night."

"With whom?"

That was another difficult one.

"I went alone."

"If that's the truth, we can check it out," the detective said. "But you'll have to come with me now."

My father tried to argue, but the detective was insistent, so I got my coat and went with him. As we were leaving he grabbed me by the arm, right in my own living room, like I was a real criminal.

We didn't say a word all the way. He took my arm again when we got to the Juvenile Home. It was an old private house that they'd converted into a prison. I had to take off my shoes and belt and watch, and empty out my pockets. I had about a buck in change and they took that too.

Then this old guy with a limp and a flat, pink scar on his cheek led me through a bunch of doors and into the prison section.

"You'll like it here," he said. "We've got clean rooms, good food, and plenty of toilet facilities. It's a very clean place. Just like home, the boys always say."

"I'm only staying long enough to be questioned," I said.

He put me in a cell and locked the door. I heard it click, and then he walked away. I had never been locked in a room before. It was awfully small, only about five feet long. The walls were covered with green tile, like a bathroom. The only things it had in it were a cot and a toilet. But the toilet didn't have any seat and you could only flush it by pushing a little chrome button in the wall. There was a window all screened over, and the door had a narrow slot in it, hardly big enough to get your hand through.

"Hey, Brian, is that you?"

"Who is it?"

"Me. Eddie."

"Where are you?"

"Next door. Put your face against the hole in the door and we can talk."

I pushed my face up against the slot. I couldn't see anywhere but straight ahead.

"When did they get you?" Eddie said.

"Just now. They came to my house."

"They got me this morning, on my way home from church. Hey, you're not pissed-off are you?"

"I don't know," I said. I really hadn't thought about it yet. "Why'd you tell them?"

"I couldn't help it. They had my coat and everything."

"Why didn't you say you did it alone?"

"Listen, I tried to, but they saw two of us. They were going to beat my head in unless I told them. It wasn't my fault. They had me dead to rights."

"I guess they did."

I didn't feel like talking anymore, so I went back and sat on the cot.

After several hours of getting up and going to the door and flushing the toilet and sitting down again, I heard the clump-tap, clump-tap of the old guy coming down the hall. He unlocked my door.

"Time for dinner," he said, like he was a butler.

He unlocked Eddie and a few other guys, and we all walked down to the end of the hall and into a room that was bare except for a wooden table and a few chairs. We sat down and an old woman in a white uniform brought in the food. It was pretty terrible stuff, some kind of tough meat that was cooked too much and a pot of boiled potatoes. I didn't feel much like eating anyway.

The old man kept limping around the table saying, "Isn't it delicious? Some of the boys think the food is so good they come back year after year. Yes sir, a prince could dine here and feel at home."

Eddie must've been hungry because he was eating. Across the table was a skinny guy with long black hair who looked kind of undernourished. The guy next to him had a round face and red hair.

"What are you in for?" Eddie asked the skinny guy.

"Setting a fire," he said without interrupting his eating.

"To what?"

"A building."

"He burned down his house with the whole family in it," the round-faced guy said.

"Shut up!" yelled the skinny guy. He looked pretty mad.

After that, nobody said anything else.

When dinner was over they gave us each one cigarette and then put us back in our cells. It got dark outside, and the old man came around and told us all to get into bed. I couldn't sleep much and kept waking up, and then I'd remember where I was and get scared and stay awake for a while.

In the morning, after we'd all been taken down to the lavatory to wash, they sent for Eddie, and when he got back, they sent for me. I was taken into an office on the first floor. There was a woman at the desk about the same age as my mother, or maybe a little older. I figured she'd be easy on me. But she wasn't; she was a regular cop. She said Eddie had confessed to the whole thing, all seven cars, and she kept reading from a paper he'd signed. It had the dates they were taken and a description of each car and everything. I tried to deny the whole thing, but she didn't even give me a chance.

"If you refuse to cooperate," she said, "the judge will have no choice but to send you to reform school. I don't imagine you would like that."

I didn't say anything.

"Well, do you want to go to reform school?"

"No."

"All right, let's get down to business. How many of these thefts were you a party to?"

I broke down and told her everything. I even started crying and asked her not to tell my parents. She promised she wouldn't. Then she typed out a paper and made me sign it. It was one thing to tell her about it and another thing to see it typed out. On paper it sounded a lot worse. But I signed it.

She phoned my father to come down and get me. As soon as he came, she showed him the paper and told him everything I'd said. She even told him about me asking not to let my parents know, which really got me mad.

They let me out in the custody of my parents until the trial. So I went back to school for a few days. Everybody there knew about it. That's because Eddie kept telling the whole story, only he told it differently than I'm telling it right now. He made it sound as though we were a pair of real professional gangsters who'd been doing this sort of thing for years. During lunch period he'd sit around and talk about all the girls we picked up with the cars. Actually, we only got those two sisters, but he didn't say that. He'd say how we fooled the cops, and how, when they finally succeeded in catching us, we wouldn't say a word; they had to beat us up to make us talk. Even then we only told them part, there were a lot more cars they didn't know about. It sounded pretty funny the way he told it, because Eddie knows how to tell a good story.

Everybody started asking me a lot of questions. Guys I didn't even know before came up to me and wanted to know all about it. You know how it is, so little ever happens around Slokum Prep that when they hear about something, they want all the details. It seemed as though everybody was getting a lot of fun out of it. Even Eddie. It was like when somebody comes to school with a hole in his pants. Everybody laughs except the guy with the hole and he gets kind of mad to see everybody enjoying it so much.

Naturally my teachers found out about it. They always do. You can tell by the way they look at you. It's one of those long, distrustful looks, the kind you get when the teacher thinks you're cheating in a test.

That's when I first got friendly with Mr. Burke. He kept me after class and asked me to tell him what had happened. I did, but I left out the part about the fat girl. He didn't even ask me why I did it, which was all my parents could say for about three days. "Why did you do such a stupid thing? Do you want to be a criminal? Are you crazy? Why?" But Mr. Burke was different. Before I even asked, he volunteered to be a character witness. He also said he'd speak to the headmaster, to keep me from getting thrown out of school.

It was a good thing he did, because the next day we got called in. Eddie and I just stood there in his office twitching and coughing while the headmaster told us what a serious sin stealing cars was and how we better go to confession as soon as we could. He said that even if we did get off, we'd be punished by God and probably by everybody else too.

I thought a lot about running away then. But Eddie said that since it was our first offense we would get off easy, and if we ran away and got caught, then we'd be sent up for sure. Anyway, I couldn't have gone any place if I'd wanted to. I only had about twenty-five dollars, and that was in a bank account. So, I just waited around until Friday, the day of the trial.

When I got to the Juvenile Home my parents were sitting in the waiting room on one of those long benches. I could see they were pretty uncomfortable. My mother tried to smile as I came in, but my father didn't say anything. I sat by them and didn't say anything either.

After a while Eddie came in with his parents. He was all dressed up in a new suit.

Then some men started coming in one at a time, all well dressed and looking like lawyers. They were friends of my father who were going to serve as character witnesses for me, but I didn't know any of them. My father introduced me to them and we shook hands. When my father thanked them for coming, they all said something like: "No, please don't mention it. You know I'm always glad to help." Everytime they talked they would smile very sympathetically and then look serious and really worried. I kept hoping Mr. Burke would show up.

We waited about half an hour. Finally a very fat bald guy with a ring of dark hair around his head like a monk came out and asked us all to go into the courtroom. It wasn't a regular courtroom, just a big room with a desk and two American flags.

The judge was sitting at the desk. He didn't look like what I'd expected. He was a thin little man of about sixty and he wore those glasses with the wire rims. He looked like the type that didn't drink or smoke all his life, because he didn't smile once the whole time. There was a big pitcher of water on the desk and he kept pouring himself a glassful.

Eddie and I stood in front of the desk, two feet away from him, and our parents and all the witnesses stood behind us.

The fat guy came in and read a big official proclamation about how in the case of the state against Edward Flynn and Brian Doherty we had pleaded guilty and submitted signed confessions to the court and everything. It sounded like we were real criminals, like we'd murdered somebody. That's what I couldn't understand; I mean we weren't really criminals, but everybody acted like we were. Taking a few cars wasn't that bad. It happened all the time. Everybody got them back, and we didn't damage them or smash them up. I wouldn't be that mad if somebody took my car.

The judge started asking us a lot of questions, about what our fathers did for a living and where we went to school and everything. I don't know why he was asking all that stuff, he already knew it. It was all typed out on a sheet of paper on his desk.

"Now boys," he said, taking off his glasses, "I want you to consider the seriousness of your crime, a crime for which an older man would be sentenced to four or five years in the state penitentiary. Do you realize what you have done?"

He sounded just like the headmaster. Eddie and I kind of looked at each other, wondering if he wanted an answer.

"You are guilty of grand larceny. Do you know the punishment for that crime?"

This time Eddie and I nodded our heads yes.

"Under the law it is my responsibility to protect the citizens of this community by removing you from society."

I figured for sure he was going to send us up. Then I started thinking about spending four or five years in reform school. I'd be in a cell all the time and I'd have to talk to everybody through a little hole and there'd be lots of guys around like the guy who burned down his house. After a while I'd probably go crazy and hang myself with my belt—if they hadn't already taken that away from me.

"Perhaps this sounds harsh, but what guarantee do I have that you won't steal another car? And the next time you may cause an accident and kill an innocent person."

"I wouldn't take another car," Eddie said.

"Can you give me any assurance of that?"

"I promise," he said. "Honest I won't, sir."

"Well, considering your family backgrounds, I'll give you a choice. If you think you are capable of reforming yourselves, then I'll suspend your sentence. You must promise this court that you will stay out of trouble and become decent, obedient members of this community. Otherwise, I will be forced to commit you to a reformatory."

All of a sudden I began to get real angry. I don't know why, but I did. He wasn't saying we even deserved to be let off; he was saying we were really criminals and ought to be put away, but he'd be a nice guy and let us go if we pestered him a bit and promised not to be criminals anymore.

"Can you promise that?"

"Yes, yes sir, I promise," Eddie said.

"And you?"

I felt like saying no, you can't pull this stuff on me, I see what you're doing. If you really think we're so guilty, then send me up, lock me in, hang me, but don't give me any of this good-guy stuff. I think I really wanted to go to reform school. Then they could punish me for being guilty, and I'd be sure of it.

"Well?"

"I don't know," I said.

"What?"

"I don't know if I can be any different."

There was a shuffle behind me; I guess it was my parents.

"In other words you intend to steal more cars?"

"No sir," I said.

"Can you promise this court that you will not?"

"Yes."

"Then what's the problem?"

"I'm not sure, sir."

He looked at me for a moment. You could see he was impatient to get it over.

"You will be given a chance to prove yourselves. This court places you on probation until such a time as you have demonstrated that you can conduct yourselves as responsible young men."

Then he said something about the seventh commandment and let us go. When we turned to leave, Eddie said thank you. I couldn't figure out why anybody should really want to thank him.

Walking out of the courtroom, I felt my shirt and it was all wet from sweating, even the inside of my jacket was wet. My parents went around shaking hands with all the witnesses who'd never even been called on to testify, and when we left, they were standing around in thankful little circles smoking.

All that happened a couple months ago and it's nearly spring now. Every Friday I go to the headmaster's office to get my school attendance cards signed and I hand them in at the Juvenile Home on Saturday morning. The woman down there says they'll probably let me off in six months. Even if they do, it won't change anything. Because once everybody thinks you're a criminal, there's no escaping it. The only thing you can do is tell them that being a criminal is not as easy as it looks. You've got to go through a lot before they decide to make you one, and even then it's a lot of work just to keep telling everybody what really happened.

NEVER LOSE YOUR COOL

Paul Friedman

I

He turned an unfamiliar corner and heard footsteps quickly coming up
on him. He started to run. He ran, people saw him run, they saw the two
boys chasing him. The people did not try to stop the chase. William saw
a vacant lot and started to cut through it, fell, was overtaken. When he
got up they were standing right in front of him, two long haired, long
sideburned boys, about his age, in their middle teens.

Although the two boys had been running hard, when they spoke it was
as if they had not exerted themselves in the chase; they were not out of
breath, they were not panting.

"Okay man, all I want is your wallet, hand it across."

"I don't have any bread."

"That ain't what I asked Jack. I just want to see your wallet."

"I don't have one."

"Sure Ace, but I'm going to take a look."

"Look man, why don't you just cool it and do like he says? There
won't be trouble that way."

"That's right Ace, what do you want trouble for? You're just asking for
trouble. What are you going to do with trouble when you get it?"

"Yeah, we want the wallet," explained the boy. "We don't want trouble. How come you want trouble?"

"Man, I can't understand these cats that go around looking for trouble."

"Well, I guess some cats just got eyes for trouble. I can't understand it
either."

They talked slowly, clearly, so deliberately. As they took a step toward
him he took two steps back. They came in slowly, seemingly carelessly
yet actually carefully. They were positioning for the attack: craftsmen
working at their craft, sharp, delicate, not one crude step, not one faulty
movement. William kept backing up. He was about five feet from the
wall when he pulled out his knife.

William did not carry the knife for protection and he didn't carry it for
fun, although he used it for both; he carried it because he liked to put his
hand inside his pocket and feel it.

The two boys stopped. They didn't turn and run when they saw the
knife. William was frightened. They did not look at him any more. They
ignored him almost completely. They paid no attention to the people on

the street who could see everything. They spread out a little and while talking between themselves they forced him to back up, even more, even with his knife, even though they acted as if he were not there; back up, back up, more, ever so slowly.

"What do you think of a cat that pulls a blade?"

"I think he might be forcing someone to get cut."

"Yeah, that's what I think. Do you want to get cut?"

"Well, to tell you the truth, no, I don't think that I want to get cut."

"Man, I *know* I don't want to get cut."

"Yeah, that's right, I definitely don't want to get cut."

"Don't look like we'll get cut on then, does it?"

"No. I'll tell you something man, now that I've thought about it I'm damn glad that I'm not going to get cut because that can really be nasty, you know what I mean?"

"Man, I've seen some cats that look so ugly they hurt my eyes." He waited a moment then continued. "Do you know why?"

"Because they got cut on?"

"Right where people could see the scars."

"That's awful. But if there's a blade and if I'm not going to get cut, and you say you're not going to get cut, and it looks like someone might get cut, who do you figure is going to get cut on?"

"Well, it might be that cat that started all the action with the blade in the first place."

"That's just what I was thinking."

Slow, soft talk, purring, almost velvet talk, almost comical talk but talk that is electric and serious and adult. Walking in on William, spreading out on him, closing in a little, shuffling, positioning, forcing William back, all the way back now, still ignoring him.

"If the man had any smart he'd just drop the blade. He'd drop the blade and give us his bread."

"But if the man had any smart he never would have shown the blade, ain't that so?"

"Yeah, that's right."

"I guess the cat just don't have any smart."

Then one of the boys, with his head slightly down, lifted his eyes and looked at William. Directly. William could no longer move.

"C'mon my man, you made a couple of mistakes so far, you going to make another one now? Now what are you going to do?"

William could not keep his knees still; his nose started to run, his eyes were watering, and his cheek twitched. He wanted to urinate; a few drops escaped and slid down his leg.

"Look man, you're holding a blade, you don't want to do anything with it, why don't you just drop it?"

"Yeah, no one's going to help you. I'm not, he's not. You're going to have to help yourself because you're the only one on your side. Now, what are you going to do?"

William dropped his knife. As he did this the boy slapped him in the face, gently, playfully, like he'd pat a puppy. William felt a knee blast his stomach, then a thunderous blow on the back of his neck. He sagged down; not passed out. Not quite.

They kicked William. They took William's knife. They took the few pennies he had and then they sauntered off. He watched them walk away, unconcernedly; they walked with a certain air, an air that included pistol pockets and saddle stitching; he watched the people walking by on the street, the people who had witnessed this episode and who had walked right on by, the people who had averted their eyes after realizing what it was that they were seeing, the people who had been afraid to try and stop it, afraid to even call the police.

The two boys who had beaten him up were well trained, intuitively William grasped this, the people walking by were well trained, housebroken, William saw and accepted this. He was now determined that one day he too would be well trained, proficient, so proficient that he would have the power to turn strangers into sniveling and blind housebroken puppies.

William felt a profound admiration for those two boys. He desired their power.

The disdain they showed for everyone and everything; the sneer attitude they carried like a sign on their bodies and faces; the attitude that said we can do what we want and when we want and how we want and if you don't think so why don't you step up here and try to stop us; they didn't respect anything, they didn't sweat anyone.

The way they walked; a slight bounce to every step, a litheness, a gliding more than walking. Not one clumsy movement. Surety. . . . Cool.

II

William felt like punching someone, anyone. Blast, hard, in the mouth. There would be blood and spitting teeth; his hand would be cut and it would be painful. He wanted to feel a part of him hurt. William wanted to strike out. He felt the knot grow in his stomach.

He walked down the block to his car. Some of the people he passed were aware of him. William was starting to make it. He hadn't been tested yet; before the test comes you have to be worthy of a test. He had been proving that he was.

William got into his car. Not a hotrod with a packed hood and dual exhausts and an aerial that extended three feet over the roof of the car.

Not a new black Fleetwood either. He was just starting to move up, he was ready to prove it.

Eighteen years old. William felt old, mature. Out of school for a year and a half, had a few hustles going, making good money, had a hard reputation, was respected. He learned his lessons well in high school and he had learned all that high school had to teach him by the time he was thrown out.

He parked the car in front of the school and smoked a cigarette. His hand did not shake as he smoked but he inhaled jerkily. He finished, locked the car door, and walked toward the gymnasium.

William was wearing a light blue topcoat with wide lapels. A belt was loosely strung around the outside of his coat and he had a thick loose knot tied in front of him. His pants were black, slightly pegged and sharply creased; his shoes had pointed toes and were gleaming black, polished to perfection. His hair was long and slicked back. William knew that he looked cool.

There was a basketball game scheduled today and William knew the gymnasium would be packed. William had seen many things happen at high school athletic events; he had participated in many of the happenings. He still retained a vivid picture of the football game he'd attended two years ago: the opposing school's side of the grandstand started to move, en masse, and like a wave they flowed from their side of the stands, through the end zone section, and toward his school's side of the stands. They met. Razor blades were shot from rubber bands. Brass knuckles appeared from back pockets. Lengths of lead pipe wrapped in tape connected with human shapes and caused dull thuds. The dull cracks of blackjacks. The screams of captured girls who were being toyed with under the grandstand. The game was forgotten, hysteria grabbed the crowd, the students surged forward, seeking the safety of the playing field. (This was a student body that was used to fights and flare-ups at athletic events, that expected and, by and large, looked forward to them, but the viciousness and savagery that were evident at that game were too much for most of them. They did not want to be involved, at all, this time.)

The feeling that William had (being a part of the small force that did not desert the stands) was a feeling that he could not forget. Standing there defiantly, not running, not moving, waiting, bouncing up and down confidently, trying to spot an enemy trooper within range, sensing that hundreds of people were watching him, or rather, watching all of the men who stayed in the stands, this was something he would never forget. This is what he thought about at night, in bed, alone, unable to sleep, when he wanted to think about the nicest thing that had ever happened to him.

On other occasions William had succeeded in partially recapturing that feeling, but never completely; either the audience was too small or the feat was not significant enough. He often imagined what it would be like if, instead of waiting for the enemy to advance, he were the aggressor, and if, instead of being a cog in the advancing machine, he were the whole machine. William spent many hours speculating on this unknown sensation, its rewards, the hazards presented by the difficulty of the task; he wondered, and he told himself that one day he would find out.

William was waiting, and after the wait was over, and after the feat was performed, he was going to tell the whole damn world, "Listen, I'm me and I'm the swinging cat. I'm cool, watch if you don't believe me, or ask someone who's seen me, he'll tell you, you'll find out. I'm cool, so my way is the cool way, don't try and mess up because remember what happened to the last cat who tried. I'm not a punk. I worked hard to get where I am and now I am here baby so dig, I do what I want, you do what I want. What I say, me. I'm cool, remember that. Watch."

As he was on his way into the gymnasium he noticed a group of students standing in the hallway outside the gym entrance. He lit a cigarette, stopped to smoke it. The students saw him, and watched him, and their conversation slowly evaporated. The air thickened with the smoke from William's cigarette. William inhaled. One hand went into a big patch pocket on his topcoat. The other hung almost limply at his side. The cigarette hung between his lips. The smoke from the cigarette made his eyes squint. He snapped his thumb and middle finger together, rhythmically, as if keeping time to a rock tune. He nodded his head in time to the beat of his thumb and middle finger. He moved his left knee back and forth. The movement of his head, of his knee, of his whole body, was almost but not quite, imperceptible. He looked sensual, lazy, ready to uncoil, cool.

William walked through the crowd of students and opened the door to the gym. A boy sitting behind a desk at the entrance was collecting admissions.

"Half a rock pal."

William laughed; a low, calculated, and controlled laugh.

"Sure." He made no move to pay. He stood right where he was, not looking at the boy, but letting his eyes rove through the crowd that was already seated.

The game was just starting. Not many people had their eyes on the entrance, most of them were watching the jump at mid-court, but those few who did happen to see William saw not only an ex-student but also a person who had not come to watch a basketball game. They sensed this and they prodded the person sitting next to them. Slowly the crowd's attention was transferred from the court to the entrance.

William was well known. To these high school people he stood for fear on one hand and freedom on the other. Freedom through defiance. The stands were full of people who nurtured the same dream he nurtured, but he was more advanced than they were. William felt the eyes on him.

"C'mon, it's a half a dollar."

William turned to face the boy. William's head bobbed slightly now. He opened his mouth wide, raised his eyebrows, sneered, and shook his head.

The boy did not know what to do. He wished that one of the teachers would come over. He was sure that the teachers knew what was going on. He also knew that teachers never tried to break up fights in the locker room. The teachers had been teaching in this high school long enough to know when it is wisest to stay away, when it is time to keep the eyes straight ahead and unseeing. The teachers were hoping that William would just go and sit down. They didn't want his fifty cents. It wasn't worth it.

William was savoring every moment of the boy's indecision. He wanted the boy to ask him for the money, again. He wanted to hear that quivering voice, again. He felt powerful, knowing that the boy's voice did not ordinarily quiver. William knew that by now more people were watching him than were watching the game. He sensed the admiration, the adulation, the intense jealousy, the hatred. He gloried in it all. The boy's lips started to move. William wanted to expand his chest. He wanted to make his biceps bulge. Suddenly, tiring of the warm-up game, he walked away; a time-out had been called on the floor.

William walked out there. The cheerleaders who had run onto the court quickly headed back to the sideline. He headed for the referee. Tense inside, but loose and agile on the outside. He wished that he had a piece of gum to chew on. He felt that his walk was right. From the quiet of the crowd he knew that it was. The referee, out of a corner of his eye, could see William coming at him. He did not turn around to face William, to meet him head on, to look him in the eye, to try and stare him down, to intimidate him with age and righteousness. He did not want to. William reached him, tapped him on the shoulder, gently, two times. Very, very . . . lightly . . . politely. The referee stiffly turned. He seemed startled that it was William and not a fellow in a basketball uniform. The referee had known that William was going to force him to turn around; he had tried to hope that it was a player who was touching him.

No one moved. Anywhere. There were at least two hundred high school pupils. They sat, transfixed. Dreaming. Envious. The few instructors who were there sat shamed and afraid. William had everything in the palm of his hand. He knew it.

William pointed, almost daintily, at the whistle that hung around the referee's neck. He moved his finger back and forth, in pantomime, telling the referee and the crowd and the whole goddam world that he, William Baronofsky, wanted that silly goddam whistle that hung around that frightened goddam referee's neck. And everyone knew he wanted it. And everyone knew that he wanted it for nothing; and everyone knew that if he got it he could have everything.

William realized that if he made a mistake now he would have less than nothing. The referee did not know what to do. William waited, bouncing on the balls of his feet. Laughing inside a little, happy that the timekeeper would be messed up, happy that the ballplayers were not on the court even though the time-out was over. William wondered if this extra time-out could be considered an official's time-out. William laughed a little more. He felt giddy. William still bounced on the balls of his feet. Patient so far, making everything simple. Not a complicated plan; not a complicated objective; everything was simple. The referee looked toward the benches where the coaches sat. They looked the other way. The referee waited. William bounced and waited. The crowd sat, frozen. William deliberated. Should he try and yank the whistle off the referee's neck? If the string did not break and the whistle did not come off with the first yank the picture would not appear smooth and unmarred. That flaw could change everything. It could break the spell. He decided. His hand flashed to the whistle and pulled it and the string up over the referee's head. The whistle was off and in his hand. Free. Nothing had been touched; nothing was ruptured.

The referee stood, paralyzed. The crowd gasped silently, in awe. The crowd did not utter a sound but the pride, and also the revulsion, they felt could be heard quite clearly. That instant they all wanted to be William, regardless of how they had felt fifteen minutes before they walked into the gymnasium, regardless of the way they felt toward adults, regardless of the way they felt toward their parents and going to church on Sunday and helping old ladies with packages; any one of them would have traded places with William right then, gladly. They all ached to be William.

William tossed the whistle up and down a few times. He tossed it neatly and caught it neatly. Nothing sloppy, nothing that was not clear, hard, cold. He balanced the whistle in the palm of his hand. He looked at it. And smiled. He looked at one of the baskets at the end of the court. He looked at the whistle again. Long, hard. He smiled again. William started to walk, slowly, lightly toward the basket, with his head still down, looking at the whistle, still balanced in the palm of his hand. When he was two feet from the basket he stopped. He threw the whistle, carefully, through the hoop. He caught it, glad that it had not touched the netting. After he caught it he looked at it again. Again he smiled; with his head down he almost started to laugh. He threw the whistle straight up and down a few times. He stopped doing this and thought about throwing it through the hoop again. He decided not to; it might touch the net and somehow spoil the picture. The picture he had created. He wondered what he should do now. The crowd was straining toward him, going with him, wanting him. Being him.

Turning, without thinking, without realizing what he was doing, he hurled the whistle against the wall. There had been no warning. The crowd screamed. Loud. Everyone was caught off guard, unprepared. William included. The hypnotic spell had been pierced but not completely broken. The whistle had sliced the air like a saber. The sound the whistle made when it hit the wall was like the sound of a man dying, not afraid of death, but unable to keep from crying out.

William had not planned on any movement as violent as the one that had just taken place. It just happened. He heard the noise and he felt his cool leaving him. He started to feel lonely and afraid. Tired and empty. He felt untidy, almost undressed. Undressed and dirty. He almost panicked and ran. He wanted to let himself panic. He wanted to run, away. He bit his tongue to keep control. He realized the faster he ran now, the longer and farther he would have to crawl later. He forced his body to move. Slowly, disconnectedly, heavily. William plodded. He was stiff instead of loose. He made an effort to walk self-assuredly. He looked up at the crowd. He was surprised to see that they were still sitting still, staring at him, watching him with care, taking in every detail. He tried to regain his loose and agile walk. His body reacted jerkily, no longer a well-oiled machine; but it did do what he wanted it to do, more or less. He was surprised.

William could not unlock his car door. He could not get the key into the lock. He had captivated and then fooled those people, but he knew that he had lost. He realized he had failed. He did not know why. He didn't know if it was a lack of training or a lack of ability or perhaps even a lack of desire. He did not know. He realized he had almost won.

He wondered why he missed.

PART 5 _____

Personal Offenses

Offenses against persons make provocative newspaper headlines and often exciting novels and short stories. Over the past twenty years there has been an increase in violent crimes against persons by juveniles. The notoriety of these offenses, however, is out of proportion to their actual number. Aggravated assault, homicide, rape, and armed robbery, taken together, account for about 15 percent of the serious crimes committed in the United States each year. It should also be kept in mind that crimes of this nature are more likely to be committed in crowded cities than in rural areas and that some ethnic groups have a higher incidence of violent crimes than do others. Most people fail to realize that more assaults against persons take place in homes or local meeting places (e.g., the corner bar) among people who know or are related to each other than take place among strangers. The reasons most often cited for personal offenses are emotions erupting out of control; unintended violence occurring while committing a crime; drunkenness; the effects of drugs; and conflicts between individuals or groups that lead to premeditated violence, as on those occasions when two individuals fight for the leadership position of a gang or two gangs fight to decide territorial rights.

Much violent behavior results from social disorganization and lack of social control. In many slums the institutional forms that regulate the behavior of family, neighborhood, and culture are fragmented—in extreme cases they do not exist at all. Youngsters cast adrift and thrown on their own resources become impulsive, unruly, and have few internal or external controls to govern their behavior. When these adolescents seek goals their social position will not allow them to achieve, they often learn to manipulate violence to acquire what they want illegally.

The violence of juveniles toward others is diverse in its range and degree of expression. The stories of this section consider an attempted murder, manslaughter, a multiple-murder spree, assault and battery, and homicide as part of an initiation rite. They explore in depth the complex interrelationships of circumstances and motives that give rise to the offenses.

In "The White Circle," it would seem on first inspection that the most unlikely thing a twelve-year-old would say is, "I was lying there with a towering, homicidal detestation, planning to kill Anvil—and the thought of it had a sweetness like summer fruit." The violence of youngsters should not be surprising to adults when they consider that those in their early teens are still learning to modify and direct their behavior according to acceptable cultural norms. Stories about young murderers, particularly those between the ages of eleven and fifteen, are remarkable in delineating how suddenly their emotions can be triggered to commit an act as extreme as murder. In most cases a physical assault, the theft of some prized possession, or the destruction of the youngster's pride and self-esteem are the incidents that cause a murderous retaliation, which, luckily, is usually unsuccessful. Young Tucker in "The White Circle" is a sensitive rural boy and the last person one would suspect of attempting to murder his disliked acquaintance. His failure to accomplish the task brings about the beginnings of regret and compassion in his actions. In some stories, the homicides of younger children (usually below the age of thirteen) are rationalized by adults as unavoidable, tragic accidents.

Bruno "Lefty" Bicek is not so lucky in "A Bottle of Milk for Mother." As often happens when older adolescents carry weapons, the unexpected events of a robbery cause Lefty to use his gun, and, though he does not intend to, he kills a man. Lefty's narration of the chain of events leading to his arrest shows how an unfortunate moment can lead to a charge of manslaughter or possibly first-degree murder. However, one must wonder, in listening to Lefty's account, what really happened, knowing that he has lied about his friend Benkowski's involvement in the wino's death and suspecting other lies have been told as well. And, as the story unfolds by means of the cat-and-mouse dialogue between Lefty and his police interrogators, one might ask who the victim in the story really is. Is it the man Lefty has shot? Or is it Lefty himself who is victimized by his environment?

Nothing seems to capture the attention of the public better than a murder spree, and few short stories record this type of crime as well as "Boys at a Picnic." The particulars are familiar: the stolen car, the brutal murders for what turns out to be pocket change. If a sequel to the story were written, it would undoubtedly include the sensational manhunt, the capture, the public outrage, and, of course, the question, What caused those kids to do something so insane? The question is important in probing the actions of Rafe, Kennie, and Dan, who murder two people for less than two and a half dollars. Unlike "A Bottle of Milk for Mother," which considers the aftermath of Lefty's crime, "Boys at a Picnic" concentrates on the crime itself—and prophesies in Rafe's words what will happen to them: " 'I'm goin' to die! I'm goin' to die!' " But before the spree ends, how many others will be victimized?

The high emotional pitch found in stories about fistfights and gang "rumbles" is explored in "The Last of the Spanish Blood" in which one group of boys assaults another group held defenseless at gunpoint. As in fistfights and rumbles, the anticipatory fear before the action begins gives way to a wild exhilaration during the conflict; and when the battle is over and the combatants have time to reflect on what they have done, a feeling of remorse and shame sets in—even for the winners. As the narrator of the story confides to Harry, " 'We all went kind of crazy. I didn't know I could do like that. I didn't know I could enjoy it.' " The large number of stories that detail the cruelty of children disproves the oft-held misconception that children are by nature innocent. When children discover the meaning of cruelty from personal experience, they are usually puzzled by the enjoyment they get from it.

The entrance requirements for gang membership vary, and in "A Point of Honor" Julio is required to kill a man who has insulted the gang and to bring back his victim's ears as proof of the murder. Even though Julio is a devout churchgoer and plans someday to become a druggist, his intense desire to join The Aces and the peer pressure of the gang are enough for him to agree to commit a murder. Although he is scared, he is driven to fulfill his assignment because of "what would be said, of all the eyes turned on him like ominous spotlights. The laughter he heard was what he hated most."

Offenses against persons seem for the most part to be caused by factors beyond the control of those who commit them; overpowering emotions, irresistible impulses, peer pressure, the consequences of a hostile environment, and the effects of alcohol and drug abuse. Rarely are these offenses carefully plotted out beforehand and rationally executed. No matter what the cause, the resulting bodily injury or death of the victim has far-reaching effects on both perpetrator and victim. In stories of personal offenses written before the 1950s the emphasis is on describing the offense in detail, especially as it

affects its victims; since that time, authors have been more concerned with the psychological effect of the offense on the juvenile
who commits it. Only in a few stories are the perpetrators without
serious remorse or an important insight into their motives, though
often these come too late to save them from prosecution.

THE WHITE CIRCLE

John Bell Clayton

As soon as I saw Anvil, squatting up in the tree like some hateful creature that belonged in trees I knew I had to take a beating and I knew the kind of beating it would be. But still I had to let it be that way because this went beyond any matter of courage or shame.

The tree was *mine*. I want no doubt about that. It was a seedling that grew out of the slaty bank beside the dry creek-mark across the road from the house, and the thirteen small apples it had borne that year were the thirteen most beautiful things on this beautiful earth.

The day I was twelve Father took me up to the barn to look at the colts—Saturn, Jupiter, Devil, and Moonkissed, the white-face. Father took a cigar out of his vest pocket and put one foot on the bottom plank of the fence and leaned both elbows on the top of the fence and his face looked quiet and pleased and proud and I liked the way he looked because it was as if he had a little joke or surprise that would turn out nice for me.

"Tucker," Father said presently, "I am not unaware of the momentousness of this day. Now there are four of the finest colts in Augusta County; if there are four any finer anywhere in Virginia I don't know where you'd find them unless Arthur Hancock over in Albemarle would have them." Father took one elbow off the fence and looked at me. "Now do you suppose," he asked, in that fine, free, good humor, "that if I were to offer you a little token to commemorate this occasion you could make a choice?"

"Yes sir," I said.

"Which one?" Father asked. "Devil? He's wild."

"No sir," I said. "I would like to have the apple tree below the gate."

Father looked at me for at least a minute. You would have to understand his pride in his colts to understand the way he looked. But at twelve how could I express how *I* felt? My setting such store in having the tree as my own had something to do with the coloring of the apples as they hung among the green leaves, it had something also to do with their ripening, not in autumn when the world was full of apples, but in midsummer when you *wanted* them; but it had more to do with a way of life that had come down through the generations. I would have given one of the apples to Janie. I would have made of it a ceremony. While I would not have said the words, because at twelve you have no such words, I would have handed over the apple with something like this in mind: "Janie, I want to give you this apple. It came from my tree. The tree

195

stands on my father's land. Before my father had the land it belonged to his father, and before that it belonged to my great-grandfather. It's the English family land. It's almost sacred. My possession of this tree forges of me a link in this owning ancestry that must go back clear beyond Moses and all the old Bible folks.''

Father looked at me for that slow, peculiar minute in our lives. "All right, sir," he said. "The tree is yours in fee simple to bargain, sell, and convey or to keep and nurture and eventually hand down to your heirs or assigns forever unto eternity. You have a touch of poetry in your soul and that fierce, proud love of the land in your heart; when you grow up I hope you don't drink too much.''

I didn't know what he meant by that but the tree was mine and now there perched Anvil, callously munching one of my thirteen apples and stowing the rest inside his ragged shirt until it bulged out in ugly lumps. I knew the apples pressed cold against his hateful belly and to me the coldness was a sickening evil.

I picked a rock up out of the dust of the road and tore across the creek bed and said, "All right, Anvil—climb down!"

Anvil's milky eyes batted at me under the strangely fair eyebrows. There was not much expression on his face. "Yaannh!" he said. "You stuck-up little priss, you hit me with that rock. You just do!"

"Anvil," I said again, "climb down. They're my apples."

Anvil quit munching for a minute and grinned at me. "You want an apple? I'll give you one. Yaannh!" He suddenly cocked back his right arm and cracked me on the temple with the half-eaten apple.

I let go with the rock and it hit a limb with a dull chub sound and Anvil said, "You're fixin' to git it—you're real-ly fixin' to git it."

"I'll shake you down," I said. "I'll shake you clear down."

"Clear down?" Anvil chortled. "Where do you think I'm at? Up on top of Walker Mountain? It wouldn't hurt none if I was to fall out of this runty bush on my head."

I grabbed one of his bare feet and pulled backwards, and down Anvil came amidst a flutter of broken twigs and leaves. We both hit the ground. I hopped up and Anvil arose with a faintly vexed expression.

He hooked a leg in back of my knees and shoved a paw against my chin. I went down in the slate. He got down and pinioned my arms with his knees. I tried to kick him in the back of the head but could only flail my feet helplessly in the air.

"You might as well quit kickin'," he said.

He took one of my apples from his shirt and began eating it, almost absent-mindedly.

"You dirty filthy stinkin' sow," I said.

He snorted. "I couldn't be a sow, but you take that back."

"I wish you were fryin' in the middle of hell right this minute."

"Take back the stinkin' part," Anvil said thoughtfully. "I don't stink."

He pressed his knees down harder, pinching and squeezing the flesh of my arms.

I sobbed, "I take back the stinkin' part."

"That's better," Anvil said.

He ran a finger back into his jaw to dislodge a fragment of apple from his teeth. For a moment he examined the fragment and then wiped it on my cheek.

"I'm goin' to tell Father," I said desperately.

" 'Father,' " Anvil said with falsetto mimicry. " 'Father.' Say 'Old Man.' You think your old man is some stuff on a stick, don't you? You think he don't walk on the ground, don't you? You think you and your whole stuck-up family don't walk on the ground. Say 'Old Man.' "

"Go to hell!"

"Shut up your blubberin'. Say 'Old Man.' "

"Old Man. I wish you were dead."

"Yaannh!" Anvil said. "Stop blubberin'. Now call me 'Uncle Anvil.' Say 'Uncle Sweetie Peetie Tweetie Beg-Your-Pardon Uncle Anvil.' Say it!"

"Uncle Sweetie . . . Uncle Peetie, Tweetie Son-of-a-Bitch Anvil."

He caught my hair in his hands and wallowed my head against the ground until I said every bitter word of it. Three times.

Anvil tossed away a spent, maltreated core that had been my apple. He gave my head one final thump upon the ground and said "Yaannh!" again in a satisfied way.

He released me and got up. I lay there with my face muscles twitching in outrage.

Anvil looked down at me. "Stop blubberin'," he commanded.

"I'm not cryin'," I said.

I was lying there with a towering, homicidal detestation, planning to kill Anvil—and the thought of it had a sweetness like summer fruit.

There were times when I had no desire to kill Anvil. I remember the day his father showed up at the school. He was a dirty, half crazy, itinerant knickknack peddler. He had a club and he told the principal he was going to beat the meanness out of Anvil or beat him to death. Anvil scudded under a desk and lay there trembling and whimpering until the principal finally drove the ragged old man away. I had no hatred for Anvil then.

But another day, just for the sheer filthy meanness of it, he crawled through a classroom window after school hours and befouled the floor.

And the number of times he pushed over smaller boys, just to see them hit the packed hard earth of the school yard and to watch the fright on their faces as they ran away, was more than I could count.

And still another day he walked up to me as I leaned against the warmth of the school-hack shed in the sunlight, feeling the nice warmth of the weatherbeaten boards.

"They hate me," he said dismally. "They hate me because my old man's crazy."

As I looked at Anvil I felt that in the background I was seeing that demented, bitter father trudging his lonely, vicious way through the world.

"They don't hate you," I lied. "Anyway I don't hate you." That was true. At that moment I didn't hate him. "How about comin' home and stayin' all night with me?"

So after school Anvil went along with me—and threw rocks at me all the way home.

Now I had for him no soft feeling of any kind. I passionately hated him as he stood there before me commanding me to stop blubbering.

"Shut up now," Anvil said. "I never hurt you. Stop blubberin'."

"I'm not cryin'," I said again.

"You're still mad though." He looked at me appraisingly.

"No, I'm not," I lied. "I'm not even mad. I was a little bit mad, but not now."

"Well, whattaya look so funny for?"

"I don't know. Let's go up to the barn and play."

"Play whut?" Anvil looked at me truculently. He didn't know whether to be suspicious or flattered. "I'm gettin' too big to play. To play much, anyway," he added undecidedly. "I might play a little bit if it ain't some sissy game."

"We'll play anything," I said eagerly.

"All right," he said. "Race you to the barn. You start."

I started running toward the wire fence and at the third step he stuck his feet between my legs and I fell forward on my face.

"Yaannh!" he croaked. "That'll learn you."

"Learn me what?" I asked as I got up. "Learn me what?" It seemed important to know. Maybe it would make some difference in what I planned to do. It seemed very important to know what it was that Anvil wanted to, and never could, teach me and the world.

"It'll just learn you," he said doggedly. "Go ahead, I won't trip you any more."

So we climbed the wire fence and raced across the burned field the hogs ranged in.

We squeezed through the heavy sliding doors onto the barn floor, and the first thing that caught Anvil's eye was the irregular circle that father had painted there. He wanted to know what it was and I said "nothing" because I wasn't yet quite ready, and Anvil forgot about it for the moment and wanted to play jumping from the barn floor out to the top of the fresh rick of golden straw.

I said, "No. Who wants to do that, anyway?"

"I do," said Anvil. "Jump, you puke. Go ahead and jump!"

I didn't want to jump. The barn had been built on a hill. In front the ground came up level with the barn floor, but in back the floor was even with the top of the straw rick, with four wide, terrible yawning feet between.

I said, "Nawh, there's nothin' to jumpin'."

"Oh, there ain't, hanh!" said Anvil. "Well, try it—"

He gave me a shove and I went out into terrifying space. He leaped after and upon me and hit the pillowy side of the straw rick and tumbled to the ground in a smothering slide.

"That's no fun," I said, getting up and brushing the chaff from my face and hair.

Anvil himself had lost interest in it by now and was idly munching another of my apples.

"I know somethin'," I said. "I know a good game. Come on, I'll show you."

Anvil stung me on the leg with the apple as I raced through the door of the cutting room. When we reached the barn floor his eyes again fell on the peculiar white circle. "That's to play prisoner's base with," I said. "That's the base."

"That's a funny-lookin' base," he said suspiciously. "I never saw any base that looked like that."

I could feel my muscles tensing, but I wasn't particularly excited. I didn't trust myself to look up toward the roof where the big mechanical hayfork hung suspended from the long metal track that ran back over the steaming mows of alfalfa and red clover. The fork had vicious sharp prongs that had never descended to the floor except on one occasion Anvil knew nothing about.

I think Father had been drinking the day he bought the hayfork in Colonial Springs. It was an unwieldy, involved contraption of ropes, triggers, and pulleys which took four men to operate. A man came out to install the fork and for several days he climbed up and down ladders, bolting the track in place and arranging the various gadgets. Finally, when he said it was ready, Father had a load of hay pulled into the barn and called the men in from the fields to watch and assist in the demonstration.

I don't remember the details. I just remember that something went

very badly wrong. The fork suddenly plunged down with a peculiar ripping noise and embedded itself in the back of one of the work horses.
Father said very little. He simply painted the big white circle on the barn
floor, had the fork hauled back up to the top, and fastened the trigger
around the rung of a stationary ladder eight feet off the floor, where no
one could inadvertently pull it.

Then he said quietly, "I don't ever want anyone to touch this trip rope
or to have occasion to step inside this circle."

So that was why I didn't now look up toward the fork.

"I don't want to play no sissy prisoner's base," Anvil said. "Let's find a
nest of young pigeons."

"All right," I lied. "I know where there's a nest. But one game of
prisoner's base first."

"You don't know where there's any pigeon nest," Anvil said. "You
wouldn't have the nerve to throw them up against the barn if you did."

"Yes, I would too," I protested. "Now let's play one game of prisoner's base. Get in the circle and shut your eyes and start countin'."

"Oh, all right," Anvil agreed wearily. "Let's get it over with and find
the pigeons. Ten, ten, double ten, forty-five—"

"Right in the middle of the circle," I told him. "And count slow.
How'm I goin' to hide if you count that way?"

Anvil now counted more slowly. "Five, ten, fifteen—"

I gave Anvil one last vindictive look and sprang up the stationary
ladder and swung out on the trip rope of the unpredictable hayfork with
all my puny might.

The fork's whizzing descent was accompanied by that peculiar ripping
noise. Anvil must have jumped instinctively. The fork missed him by several feet.

For a moment Anvil stood absolutely still. He turned around and saw
the fork, still shimmering from its impact with the floor. His face became
exactly the pale green of the carbide we burned in our acetylene lighting
plant at the house. Then he looked at me, at the expression on my face,
and his Adam's apple bobbed queerly up and down, and a little stream
of water trickled down his right trouser leg and over his bare foot.

"You tried to kill me," he said thickly.

He did not come toward me. Instead, he sat down. He shook his head
sickly. After a few sullen, bewildered moments he reached into his shirt
and began hauling out my apples one by one.

"You can have your stinkin' old apples," he said. "You'd do that for a
few dried-up little apples. Your old man owns everything in sight. I ain't
got nothin'. Go ahead and keep your stinkin' old apples."

He got to his feet and slowly walked out of the door.

Since swinging off the trip rope I had neither moved nor spoken. For a moment more I stood motionless and voiceless and then I ran over and grabbed up the nine apples that were left and called, "Anvil! Anvil!" He continued across the field without even pausing.

I yelled, "Anvil! Wait, I'll give them to you."

Anvil climbed the fence without looking back and set off down the road toward the store. Every few steps he kicked his wet trouser leg.

Three sparrows flew out of the door in a dusty, chattering spiral. Then there was only the image of the hayfork shimmering and terrible in the great and growing and accusing silence and emptiness of the barn.

A BOTTLE OF MILK FOR MOTHER

Nelson Algren

I feel I am of them—
I belong to those convicts and prostitutes myself,
And henceforth I will not deny them—
For how can I deny myself?

Whitman

Two months after the Polish Warriors S.A.C. had had their heads shaved, Bruno Lefty Bicek got into his final difficulty with the Racine Street police. The arresting officers and a reporter from the *Dziennik Chicagoski* were grouped about the captain's desk when the boy was urged forward into the room by Sergeant Adamovitch, with two fingers wrapped about the boy's broad belt: a full-bodied boy wearing a worn and sleeveless blue work shirt grown too tight across the shoulders; and the shoulders themselves with a loose swing to them. His skull and face were shining from a recent scrubbing, so that the little bridgeless nose glistened between the protective points of the cheekbones. Behind the desk sat Kozak, eleven years on the force and brother to an alderman. The reporter stuck a cigarette behind one ear like a pencil.

"We spotted him followin' the drunk down Chicago—" Sergeant Comiskey began.

Captain Kozak interrupted. "Let the jackroller tell us how he done it hisself."

"I ain't no jackroller."

"What you doin' here, then?"

Bicek folded his naked arms.

"Answer me. If you ain't here for jackrollin' it must be for strong-arm robb'ry—'r you one of them Chicago Av'noo moll-buzzers?"

"I ain't that neither."

"C'mon, c'mon, I seen you in here before—what were you up to, followin' that poor old man?"

"I ain't been in here before."

Neither Sergeant Milano, Comiskey, nor old Adamovitch moved an inch; yet the boy felt the semicircle about him drawing closer. Out of the corner of his eye he watched the reporter undoing the top button of his mangy raccoon coat, as though the barren little query room were already growing too warm for him.

"What were you doin' on Chicago Av'noo in the first place when you live up around Division? Ain't your own ward big enough you have to come down here to get in trouble? What do you *think* you're here for?"

"Well, I was just walkin' down Chicago like I said, to get a bottle of milk for Mother, when the officers jumped me. I didn't even see 'em drive up, they wouldn't let me say a word, I got no idea what I'm here for. I was just doin' a errand for Mother 'n—"

"All right, son, you want us to book you as a pickup 'n hold you overnight, is that it?"

"Yes sir."

"What about this, then?"

Kozak flipped a spring-blade knife with a five-inch blade onto the police blotter; the boy resisted an impulse to lean forward and take it. His own double-edged double-jointed spring-blade cuts-all genuine Filipino twisty-handled all-American gut-ripper.

"Is it yours or ain't it?"

"Never seen it before, Captain."

Kozak pulled a billy out of his belt, spread the blade across the bend of the blotter before him, and with one blow clubbed the blade off two inches from the handle. The boy winced as though he himself had received the blow. Kozak threw the broken blade into a basket and the knife into a drawer.

"Know why I did that, son?"

"Yes sir."

"Tell me."

" 'Cause it's three inches to the heart."

"No. 'Cause it's against the law to carry more than three inches of knife. C'mon, Lefty, tell us about it. 'N it better be good."

The boy began slowly, secretly gratified that Kozak appeared to know he was the Warriors' first-string left-hander: maybe he'd been out at that game against the Knothole Wonders the Sunday he'd finished his own game and then had relieved Dropkick Kodadek in the sixth in the second. Why hadn't anyone called him "Iron-Man Bicek" or "Fireball Bruno" for that one?

"Everythin' you say can be used against you," Kozak warned him earnestly. "Don't talk unless you want to." His lips formed each syllable precisely.

Then he added absently, as though talking to someone unseen. "We'll just hold you on an open charge till you do."

And his lips hadn't moved at all.

The boy licked his own lips, feeling a dryness coming into his throat and a tightening in his stomach. "We seen this boobatch with his collar turned inside out cash'n his check by Konstanty Stachula's Tonsorial Palace of Art on Division. So I followed him a way, that was all. Just break'n the old monotony was all. Just a notion, you might say, that come over me. I'm just a neighborhood kid, Captain."

He stopped as though he had finished the story. Kozak glanced over the boy's shoulder at the arresting officers and Lefty began again hurriedly.

"Ever' once in a while he'd pull a little single-shot of scotch out of his pocket, stop a second t' toss it down, 'n toss the bottle at the car tracks. I picked up a bottle that didn't bust but there wasn't a spider left in 'er, the boobatch'd drunk her dry. 'N do you know, he had his pockets *full* of them little bottles? 'Stead of buyin' hisself a fifth in the first place. Can't understand a man who'll buy liquor that way. Right before the corner of Walton 'n Noble he popped into a hallway. That was Chiney-Eye-the-Princinct-Captain's hallway, so I popped right in after him. Me'n Chiney-Eye 'r just like that." The boy crossed two fingers of his left hand and asked innocently, "Has the alderman been in to straighten this out, Captain?"

"What time was all this, Lefty?"

"Well, some of the street lamps was lit awready 'n I didn't see nobody either way down Noble. It'd just started spitt'n a little snow 'n I couldn't see clear down Walton account of Wojciechowski's Tavern bein' in the way. He was a old guy, a dino you. He couldn't speak a word of English. But he started in cryin' about how every time he gets a little drunk the same old thing happens to him 'n he's gettin' fed up, he lost his last three checks in the very same hallway 'n it's gettin' so his family don't believe him no more . . ."

Lefty paused, realizing that his tongue was going faster than his brain. He unfolded his arms and shoved them down his pants pockets; the pants were turned up at the cuffs and the cuffs were frayed. He drew a colorless cap off his hip pocket and stood clutching it in his left hand.

"I didn't take him them other times, Captain," he anticipated Kozak.

"Who did?"

Silence.

"What's Benkowski doin' for a living these days, Lefty?"

"Just nutsin' around."

"What's Nowogrodski up to?"

"Goes wolfin' on roller skates by Riverview. The rink's open all year round."

"Does he have much luck?"

"Never turns up a hair. They go by too fast."

"What's that evil-eye up to?"

Silence.

"You know who I mean. Idzikowski."

"The Finger?"

"You know who I mean. Don't stall."

"He's hexin' fights, I heard."

"Seen Kodadek lately?"

"I guess. A week 'r two 'r a month ago."

"What was *he* up to?"

"Sir?"

"What was Kodadek doin' the last time you seen him?"

"You mean Dropkick? He was nutsin' around."

"Does he nuts around drunks in hallways?"

Somewhere in the room a small clock or wrist watch began ticking distinctly.

"Nutsin' around ain't jackrollin'."

"You mean Dropkick ain't a jackroller but you are."

The boy's blond lashes shuttered his eyes.

"All right, get ahead with your lyin' a little faster."

Kozak's head came down almost neckless onto his shoulders, and his face was molded like a flatiron, the temples narrow and the jaws round-ed. Between the jaws and the open collar, against the graying hair of the chest, hung a tiny crucifix, slender and golden, a shade lighter than his tunic's golden buttons.

"I told him I wasn't gonna take his check, I just needed a little change, I'd pay it back someday. But maybe he didn't understand. He kept hol-lerin' how he lost his last check, please to let him keep this one. 'Why you drink'n it all up, then,' I put it to him, 'if you're that anxious to hold onto it?' He gimme a foxy grin then 'n pulls out four of them little bottles from four different pockets, 'n each one was a different kind of liquor. I could have one, he tells me in Polish, which do I want, 'n I slapped all four out of his hands. All four. I don't like to see no full-grown man drinkin' that way. A Polak hillbilly he was, 'n certain'y no citizen."

" 'Now let me have that change,' I asked him, 'n that wasn't so much t' ask. I don't go around just lookin' fer trouble, Captain. 'N my feet was slop-full of water 'n snow. I'm just a neighborhood fella. But he acted like I was gonna kill him 'r somethin'. I got one hand over his mouth 'n a half nelson behind him 'n talked polite-like in Polish in his ear, 'n he begun sweatin' 'n tryin' t' wrench away on me. 'Take it easy,' I asked him. 'Be reas'nable, we're both in this up to our necks now.' 'N he wasn't drunk no more then, 'n he was plenty t' hold onto. You wouldn't think a old boobatch like that'd have so much stren'th left in him, boozin' down Division night after night, year after year, like he didn't have no home to go to. He pulled my hand off his mouth 'n started hollerin', *'Mlody bandyta! Mlody bandyta!'* 'n I could feel him slippin'. He was just too strong fer a kid like me to hold—"

"Because you were reach'n for his wallet with the other hand?"

"Oh no. The reason I couldn't hold him was my right hand had the nelson 'n I'm not so strong there like in my left 'n even my left ain't what it was before I thrun it out pitchin' that double-header."

"So you kept the rod in your left hand?"

The boy hesitated. Then: "Yes sir." And felt a single drop of sweat slide down his side from under his armpit. Stop and slide again down to the belt.

"What did you get off him?"

"I tell you, I had my hands too full to get *anythin'*—that's just what I been tryin' to tell you. I didn't get so much as one of them little single-shots for all my trouble."

"How many slugs did you fire?"

"Just one, Captain. That was all there was in 'er. I didn't really fire, though. Just at his feet. T' scare him so's he wouldn't jump me. I fired in self-defense. I just wanted to get out of there." He glanced helplessly around at Comiskey and Adamovitch. "You do crazy things sometimes, fellas—well, that's all I was doin'."

The boy caught his tongue and stood mute. In the silence of the query room there was only the scraping of the reporter's pencil and the unseen wrist watch. "I'll ask Chiney-Eye if it's legal, a reporter takin' down a confession, that's my out," the boy thought desperately, and added aloud, before he could stop himself: " 'N beside I had to show him—"

"Show him what, son?"

Silence.

"Show him what, Left-hander?"

"That I wasn't just another greenhorn sprout like he thought."

"Did he say you were just a sprout?"

"No. But I c'd tell. Lots of people think I'm just a green kid. I show 'em. I guess I showed 'em now all right." He felt he should be apologizing for something and couldn't tell whether it was for strong-arming a man or for failing to strong-arm him.

"I'm just a neighborhood kid. I belonged to the Keep-Our-City-Clean Club at St. John Cant'us. I told him polite-like, like a Polish-American citizen, this was Chiney-Eye-a-Friend-of-Mine's hallway. 'No more after this one,' I told him. 'This is your last time gettin' rolled, old man. After this I'm pertectin' you, I'm seein' to it nobody touches you—but the people who live here don't like this sort of thing goin' on any more'n you 'r I do. There's gotta be a stop to it, old man—'n we all gotta live, don't we?' That's what I told him in Polish."

Kozak exchanged glances with the prim-faced reporter from the *Chicagoski*, who began cleaning his black tortoise-shell spectacles hurriedly yet delicately, with the fringed tip of his cravat. They depended from a black ribbon; he snapped them back onto his beak.

"You shot him in the groin, Lefty. He's dead."

The reporter leaned slightly forward, but perceived no special reaction and so relaxed. A pretty comfy old chair for a dirty old police station, he thought lifelessly. Kozak shaded his eyes with his gloved hand and looked down at his charge sheet. The night lamp on the desk was still lit, as though he had been working all night; as the morning grew lighter behind him lines came out below his eyes, black as though packed with soot, and a curious droop came to the St. Bernard mouth.

"You shot him through the groin—zip." Kozak's voice came, flat and unemphatic, reading from the charge sheet as though without understanding. "Five children. Stella, Mary, Grosha, Wanda, Vincent. Thirteen, ten, six, six, and one two months. Mother invalided since last birth, name of Rose. WPA fifty-five dollars. You told the truth about *that*, at least."

Lefty's voice came in a shout: "You know *what*? That bullet must of bounced, that's what!"

"Who was along?"

"I was singlin'. Lone-wolf stuff." His voice possessed the first faint touch of fear.

"You said, 'We seen the man.' Was he a big man? How big a man was he?"

"I'd judge two hunerd twenty pounds," Comiskey offered, "at least. Fifty pounds heavier 'n this boy, just about. 'N half a head taller."

"Who's 'we,' Left-hander?"

"Captain, I said, 'We seen.' Lots of people, fellas, seen him is all I meant, cashin' his check by Stachula's when the place was crowded. Konstanty cashes checks if he knows you. Say, I even know the project that old man was on, far as that goes, because my old lady wanted we should give up the store so's I c'd get on it. But it was just me done it, Captain."

The raccoon coat readjusted his glasses. He would say something under a by-line like "This correspondent has never seen a colder gray than that in the eye of the wanton killer who arrogantly styles himself the *lone wolf of Potomac Street.*" He shifted uncomfortably, wanting to get farther from the wall radiator but disliking to rise and push the heavy chair.

"Where was that bald-headed pal of yours all this time?"

"Don't know the fella, Captain. Nobody got hair any more around the neighborhood, it seems. The whole damn Triangle went 'n got army haircuts by Stachula's."

"Just you 'n Benkowski, I mean. Don't be afraid, son—we're not tryin' to ring in anythin' you done afore this. Just this one you were out cowboyin' with Benkowski on; were you help'n him 'r was he help'n you? Did you 'r him have the rod?"

Lefty heard a Ford V-8 pull into the rear of the station, and a moment later the splash of the gas as the officers refueled. Behind him he could hear Milano's heavy breathing. He looked down at his shoes, carefully buttoned all the way up and tied with a double bowknot. He'd have to have new laces mighty soon or else start tying them with a single bow.

"That Benkowski's sort of a toothless monkey used to go on at the City Garden at around a hundred an' eighteen pounds, ain't he?"

"Don't know the fella well enough t' say."

"Just from seein' him fight once 'r twice is all. 'N he wore a mouth-piece, I couldn't tell about his teeth. Seems to me he came in about one thirty-three, if he's the same fella you're thinkin' of, Captain."

"I guess you fought at the City Garden once 'r twice yourself, ain't you?"

"Oh, once 'r twice."

"How'd you make out, Left'?"

"Won 'em both on K.O.s. Stopped both fights in the first. One was against that boogie from the Savoy. If he woulda got up I woulda killed him fer life. Fer Christ I would. I didn't know I could hit like I can."

"With Benkowski in your corner both times?"

"Oh no, sir."

"That's a bloodsuck'n lie. I seen him in your corner with my own eyes the time you won off Cooney from the C.Y.O. He's your manager, jackroller."

"I didn't say he wasn't."

"You said he wasn't secondin' you."

"He don't."

"Who does?"

"The Finger."

"You told me the Finger was your hex-man. Make up your mind."

"He does both, Captain. He handles the bucket 'n sponge 'n in be-tween he fingers the guy I'm fightin', 'n if it's close he fingers the ref 'n judges. Finger, he never losed a fight. He waited for the boogie outside the dressing room 'n pointed him clear to the ring. He win that one for me awright." The boy spun the frayed greenish cap in his hand in a concentric circle about his index finger, remembering a time when the cap was new and had earlaps. The bright checks were all faded now, to the color of worn pavement, and the earlaps were tatters.

"What possessed your mob to get their heads shaved, Lefty?"

"I strong-armed him myself, I'm rugged as a bull." The boy began to swell his chest imperceptibly; when his lungs were quite full he shut his eyes, like swimming under water at the Oak Street beach, and let his breath out slowly, ounce by ounce.

"I didn't ask you that. I asked you what happened to your hair."

Lefty's capricious mind returned abruptly to the word "possessed" that Kozak had employed. That had a randy ring, sort of: "What possessed you boys?"

"I forgot what you just asked me."

"I asked you why you didn't realize it'd be easier for us to catch up with your mob when all of you had your heads shaved."

"I guess we figured there'd be so many guys with heads shaved it'd be harder to catch a finger than if we all had hair. But that was some accident all the same. A fella was gonna lend Ma a barber chair 'n go fifty-fifty with her shavin' all the Polaks on P'tom'c Street right back of the store, for relief tickets. So she started on me, just to show the fellas, but the hair made her sicker 'n ever 'n back of the store's the only place she got to lie down 'n I hadda finish the job myself.

"The fellas begun giv'n me a Christ-awful razzin' then, ever' day. God oh God, wherever I went around the Triangle, all the neighborhood fellas 'n little niducks 'n old-time hoods by the Broken Knuckle, whenever they seen me they was pointin' 'n laughin' 'n sayin', 'Hi, Baldy Bicek!' So I went home 'n got the clippers 'n the first guy I seen was Bibleback Watrobinski, you wouldn't know him. I jumps him 'n pushes the clip right through the middle of his hair—he ain't had a haircut since the alderman got indicted you—'n then he took one look at what I done in the drugstore window 'n we both bust out laughin' 'n laughin', 'n fin'lly Bible says I better finish what I started. So he set down on the curb 'n I finished him. When I got all I could off that way I took him back to the store 'n heated water 'n shaved him close 'n Ma couldn't see the point at all.

"Me 'n Bible prowled around a couple days 'n here come Catfoot Nowogrodski from Fry Street you, out of Stachula's with a spanty-new sideburner haircut 'n a green tie. I grabbed his arms 'n let Bible run it through the middle just like I done him. Then it was Catfoot's turn, 'n we caught Chester Chekhovka fer *him*, 'n fer Chester we got Cowboy Okulanis from by the Nort'western Viaduct you, 'n fer him we got Mustang, 'n fer Mustang we got John from the Joint, 'n fer John we got Snake Baranowski, 'n we kep' right on goin' that way till we was doin' guys we never seen before even, Wallios 'n Greeks 'n a Flip from Clark Street he musta been, walkin' with a white girl we done it to. 'N fin'lly all the sprouts in the Triangle start comin' around with their heads shaved, they want to join up with the Baldheads A.C., they called it. They thought it was a club you.

"It got so a kid with his head shaved could beat up on a bigger kid because the big one'd be a-scared to fight back hard, he thought the Baldheads'd get him. So that's why we changed our name then, that's why we're not the Warriors any more, we're the Baldhead True American Social 'n Athletic Club.

"I played first for the Warriors when I wasn't on the mound," he added cautiously, " 'n I'm enterin' the Gold'n Gloves next year 'less I go to collitch instead. I went to St. John Cant'us all the way through. Eight' grade, that is. If I keep on gainin' weight I'll be a hunerd ninety-eight this time next year 'n be five-foot-ten—I'm a fair-size light-heavy right this minute. That's what in England they call a cruiser weight you."

He shuffled a step and made as though to unbutton his shirt to show his proportions. But Adamovitch put one hand on his shoulders and slapped the boy's hand down. He didn't like this kid. This was a low-class Polak. He himself was a high-class Polak because his name was Adamovitch and not Adamowski. This sort of kid kept spoiling things for the high-class Polaks by always showing off instead of just being good citizens like the Irish. That was why the Irish ran the City Hall and Police Department and the Board of Education and the Post Office while the Polaks stayed on relief and got drunk and never got anywhere and had everybody down on them. All they could do like the Irish, old Adamovitch reflected bitterly, was to fight under Irish names to get their ears knocked off at the City Garden.

"That's why I want to get out of this jam," this one was saying beside him. "So's it don't ruin my career in the rope' arena. I'm goin' straight. This has sure been one good lesson fer me. Now I'll go to a big-ten collitch 'n make good you."

Now, if the college-coat asked him, "What big-ten college?" he'd answer something screwy like "The Boozological Stoodent-Collitch." That ought to set Kozak back awhile, they might even send him to a bug doc. He'd have to be careful—not *too* screwy. Just screwy enough to get by without involving Benkowski.

He scuffed his shoes and there was no sound in the close little room save his uneasy scuffling; square-toed boy's shoes, laced with a button-hook. He wanted to look more closely at the reporter but every time he caught the glint of the fellow's glasses he felt awed and would have to drop his eyes; he'd never seen glasses on a string like that before and would have given a great deal to wear them a moment. He took to looking steadily out of the barred window behind Kozak's head, where the January sun was glowing sullenly, like a flame held steadily in a fog. Heard an empty truck clattering east on Chicago, sounding like either a '38 Chevvie or a '37 Ford dragging its safety chain against the car tracks; closed his eyes and imagined sparks flashing from the tracks as the iron struck, bounced, and struck again. The bullet had bounced too. Wow.

"What do you think we ought to do with a man like you, Bicek?"

The boy heard the change from the familiar "Lefty" to "Bicek" with a pang; and the dryness began in his throat again.

"One to fourteen is all I can catch fer manslaughter." He appraised Kozak as coolly as he could.

"You like farm work the next fourteen years? Is that okay with you?"

"I said that's all I could get, at the most. This is a first offense 'n self-defense too. I'll plead the unwritten law."

"Who give you *that* idea?"

"Thought of it myself. Just now. You ain't got a chance to send me over the road 'n you know it."

"We can send you to St. Charles, Bicek. 'N transfer you when you come of age. Unless we can make it first-degree murder."

The boy ignored the latter possibility.

"Why, a few years on a farm'd true me up fine. I planned t' cut out cigarettes 'n whisky anyhow before I turn pro—a farm'd be just the place to do that."

"By the time you're released you'll be thirty-two, Bicek—too late to turn pro then, ain't it?"

"I wouldn't wait that long. Hungry Piontek-from-by-the-Warehouse you, he lammed twice from that St. Charles farm. 'N Hungry don't have all his marbles even. He ain't even a citizen."

"Then let's talk about somethin' you couldn't lam out of so fast 'n easy. Like the chair. Did you know that Bogatski from Noble Street, Bicek? The boy that burned last summer, I mean."

A plain-clothes man stuck his head in the door and called confidently: "That's the man, Captain. That's the man."

Bicek forced himself to grin good-naturedly. He was getting pretty good, these last couple days, at grinning under pressure. When a fellow got sore he couldn't think straight, he reflected anxiously. And so he yawned in Kozak's face with deliberateness, stretching himself as effortlessly as a cat.

"Captain, I ain't been in serious trouble like this before . . ." he acknowledged, and paused dramatically. He'd let them have it straight from the shoulder now: "So I'm mighty glad to be so close to the alderman. Even if he is indicted."

There. Now they knew. He'd told them.

"You talkin' about my brother, Bicek?"

The boy nodded solemnly. Now they knew who they had hold of at last.

The reporter took the cigarette off his ear and hung it on his lower lip. And Adamovitch guffawed.

The boy jerked toward the officer: Adamovitch was laughing openly at him. Then they were all laughing openly at him. He heard their derision, and a red rain danced one moment before his eyes; when the red rain was past, Kozak was sitting back easily, regarding him with the expression of a man who had just been swung at and missed and plans to use the provocation without undue haste. The captain didn't look like the sort who'd swing back wildly or hurriedly. He didn't look like the sort who missed. His complacency for a moment was as unbearable to the boy as Adamovitch's guffaw had been. He heard his tongue going, trying to regain his lost composure by provoking them all.

"Hey, Stingywhiskers!" He turned on the reporter. "Get your Eversharp goin' there, write down I plugged the old rumpot, write down Bicek carries a rod night 'n day 'n don't care where he points it. You, I go around slappin' the crap out of whoever I feel like—"

But they all remained mild, calm, and unmoved: for a moment he feared Adamovitch was going to pat him on the head and say something fatherly in Polish.

"Take it easy, lad," Adamovitch suggested. "You're in the query room. We're here to help you, boy. We want to see you through this thing so's you can get back to pugging. You just ain't letting us help you, son."

Kozak blew his nose as though that were an achievement in itself, and spoke with the false friendliness of the insurance man urging a fleeced customer toward the door.

"Want to tell us where you got that rod now, Lefty?"

"I don't want to tell you anything." His mind was setting hard now, against them all. Against them all in here and all like them outside. And the harder it set, the more things seemed to be all right with Kozak: he dropped his eyes to his charge sheet now and everything was all right with everybody. The reporter shoved his notebook into his pocket and buttoned the top button of his coat as though the questioning were over.

It was all too easy. They weren't going to ask him anything more, and he stood wanting them to. He stood wishing them to threaten, to shake their heads ominously, wheedle and cajole and promise him mercy if he'd just talk about the rod.

"I ain't mad, Captain. I don't blame you men either. It's your job, it's your bread 'n butter to talk tough to us neighborhood fellas—ever'body got to have a racket, 'n yours is talkin' tough." He directed this last at the captain, for Comiskey and Milano had left quietly. But Kozak was studying the charge sheet as though Bruno Lefty Bicek were no longer in the room. Nor anywhere at all.

"I'm still here," the boy said wryly, his lip twisting into a dry and bitter grin.

Kozak looked up, his big, wind-beaten, impassive face looking suddenly to the boy like an autographed pitcher's mitt he had once owned. His glance went past the boy and no light of recognition came into his eyes. Lefty Bicek felt a panic rising in him: a desperate fear that they weren't going to press him about the rod, about the old man, about his feelings. "Don't look at me like I ain't nowheres," he asked. And his voice was struck flat by fear.

Something else! The time he and Dropkick had broken into a slot machine! The time he and Casey had played the attention racket and made four dollars! Something! Anything else!

The reporter lit his cigarette.

"Your case is well disposed of," Kozak said, and his eyes dropped to the charge sheet forever.

"I'm born in this country, I'm educated here—"

But no one was listening to Bruno Lefty Bicek any more.

He watched the reporter leaving with regret—at least the guy could have offered him a drag—and stood waiting for someone to tell him to go somewhere now, shifting uneasily from one foot to the other. Then he started slowly, backward, toward the door: he'd make Kozak tell Adamovitch to grab him. Halfway to the door he turned his back on Kozak.

There was no voice behind him. Was this what "well disposed of" meant? He turned the knob and stepped confidently into the corridor; at the end of the corridor he saw the door that opened into the courtroom, and his heart began shaking his whole body with the impulse to make a run for it. He glanced back and Adamovitch was five yards behind, coming up catfooted like only an old man who has been a citizen-dress man can come up catfooted, just far enough behind and just casual enough to make it appear unimportant whether the boy made a run for it or not.

The Lone Wolf of Potomac Street waited miserably, in the long unlovely corridor, for the sergeant to thrust two fingers through the back of his belt. Didn't they realize that he might have Dropkick and Catfoot and Benkowski with a sub-machine gun in a streamlined cream-colored roadster right down front, that he'd zigzag through the courtroom onto the courtoom fire escape and—swish—down off the courtroom roof three stories with the chopper still under his arm and through the car's roof and into the driver's seat? Like that George Raft did that time he was innocent at the Chopin, and cops like Adamovitch had better start ducking when Lefty Bicek began making a run for it. He felt the fingers thrust overfamiliarly between his shirt and his belt.

A cold draft came down the corridor when the door at the far end opened; with the opening of the door came the smell of disinfectant from the basement cells. Outside, far overhead, the bells of St. John Cantius were beginning. The boy felt the winding steel of the staircase to the basement beneath his feet and heard the whining screech of a Chicago Avenue streetcar as it paused on Ogden for the traffic lights and then screeched on again, as though a cat were caught beneath its back wheels. Would it be snowing out there still? he wondered, seeing the whitewashed basement walls.

"Feel all right, son?" Adamovitch asked in his most fatherly voice, closing the cell door while thinking to himself: "The kid don't *feel* guilty is the whole trouble. You got to make them *feel* guilty or they'll never go to church at all. A man who goes to church without feeling guilty for *something* is wasting his time, I say." Inside the cell he saw the boy pause and go down on his knees in the cell's gray light. The boy's head turned slowly toward him, a pious oval in the dimness. Old Adamovitch took off his hat.

"This place'll rot down 'n mold over before Lefty Bicek starts prayin', boobatch. Prays, squeals, 'r bawls. So run along 'n I'll see you in hell with yer back broke. I'm lookin' for my cap I dropped is all."

Adamovitch watched him crawling forward on all fours, groping for the pavement-colored cap; when he saw Bicek find it he put his own hat back on and left feeling vaguely dissatisfied.

He did not stay to see the boy, still on his knees, put his hands across his mouth and stare at the shadowed wall.

Shadows were there within shadows.

"I knew I'd never get to be twenty-one anyhow," Lefty told himself softly at last.

BOYS AT A PICNIC

Joyce Carol Oates

They had been passing farmland for days. Fields sprawled up nearly to the road, with burnt, shabby weeds shooting out of the ditches. While they had still had the beer they had drunk it fast enough, and Kennie, who was sitting by the window, would throw the bottles back behind the car, so they would smash against the pavement. The dazzling glass would wink at them as they sped on, and Rafe, who was driving, would squint up through his sunglasses at the rear-view mirror, watching the slivers of brown glass disappear into the heat waves. He sang: "It's a long way from Texas it's a long way from home. It's a long way from Texas—"

Lately it did not seem so long. It seemed, instead, that distance had really stopped, that they were getting nowhere. Even time made no sense: there was daytime, and nighttime, but none of the three boys believed they were getting through time either, that they were really getting anywhere. About them the desolate pasture land stretched for miles—a gigantic floor of land—massive, complacent, binding them to it. Rafe sang angrily, shouting out the window, "It's a long way from home!" Beside him Dan sat chewing gum and nodding in time with Rafe's singing, his mouth sometimes going slack, his lips protruding, in a way he had. He had got the pose from a movie, probably, but it was more than just a pose—he had shown them that. He had shown them back at the garage. He supposed Rafe and Kennie would not forget that for a while. And now he just sat nodding a little, as if to show Rafe he still thought him boss, he didn't mean to challenge Rafe about anything. Unlike Rafe and Kennie, he wore no sunglasses, and so he sat with his eyes half shut, sleepy and cold-looking, his eyes brown slits against the glare of the sun. Next to him Kennie sat with his soft, delicate look: his hair grew down onto his neck and forehead and put people who looked at him in mind of an animal of some sort—a raccoon, a squirrel.

"That was a garage for you!" Rafe said suddenly. They fell in with his remark. Kennie giggled and Dan answered at once, "Yeah! It sure was!" Their answers seemed in accord with Rafe, in rhythm with his words. One of them felt a space, a lack of something—a syllable, maybe, it was hard to define—and grunted another "Yeah!" They squirmed in the brilliant heat. They were driving right into the sun, it seemed, and the heat flowed down upon them like water, easing into them; and their shouting only made it worse. "As hot as hell!" Rafe said. Kennie said "Yeah!" at once and Dan nodded a little faster, letting his jaw and lips go slack, to show he was thinking.

They passed no one on the road. It was a black-top road that would
turn into a highway later on. Rafe had said so, from looking at the map,
though Kennie wasn't sure and Dan had gotten mixed up with a railroad
that cut through the same part of the map. "You ain't doubtin' me, are
you?" Rafe had said, twitching his nose so the sunglasses slid further up
them. He had stared at Kennie and Dan; they had looked at the map and
had not answered. After a minute he had released them; they could feel
him release them. "Goddam back-country hillbillies," he had said. They
had continued to look at the map, trying to make sense out of the lines
and numbers and dots and symbols until Rafe had snatched it away,
though it was Kennie's, and folded it up, impatiently, getting the folds
wrong so many times he ended up by crushing the map together and
tossing it into the back seat. "I don't need no goddam map," he had
said. "I can do this-here trip by instruments."

They had liked the expression, though they did not know what it
meant. Dan had looked as if he were weighing the expression carefully
and deciding he liked it; Kennie had just grinned right away. "Sure," he
had said. "You just go any way you like. Me an' Dan's with you."

But now Rafe himself felt a little doubtful. The black-top ought to have
turned into the highway before this, or led onto a highway. Instead it just
kept going. It kept going through fields and hills and woods, everything
dusty, glaring with sunlight and heat, and never seemed to end. The boys
got thirsty. They thought of the beer they had had, and how fast they
had drunk it down, and they got thirstier. But Rafe never let on how he
felt. "It ought to be up that ways, where that woods is," he said mysteriously. He felt the other two staring up ahead, at a pencil-line of forest
that was almost imperceptible because of the glare. "You just wait on it."
They waited, and got thirstier.

"If it'd been more than two bucks there!" Kennie burst out sullenly.
They thought about it; it was the first time they had thought about it.
Dan, who had gone into the garage while the attendant—an old man of
about fifty with greasy overalls and a blue cotton cap that said JASON
FEED CO. on it—gave them gas, would certainly never have thought of it
by himself. There might have been two dollars or two hundred; it never
occurred to him to wish for more. He had squeezed himself behind the
garage door, and when the attendant came back in he had jumped out at
him. He used his fishing knife with the taped handle. When he came out
with the two dollars from the old cash register he never thought that it
might have been more. He had shown it to them and Rafe had taken it,
but nobody really thought then that Dan ought to have come out with
more. . . . He began chewing rapidly, angrily, thinking how they had
looked at him, how they had gaped, when he had come out with the
money just as if nothing had happened! How they had had to scramble

right out of the car and run in the garage and take a look for themselves! He thought of that with pleasure; he had surprised them. But right now he felt his thirst mount up painfully, ravagingly, as if to make fun of him. He wondered if the gum made it worse, but he kept chewing. "A goddam two bucks," Kennie said, sensing Rafe's agreement. "A goddam two bucks."

"We'll be fixed up just fine," Rafe said. "You just wait." He sang again. He shouted out at the wind. "There's a big horse runnin' alongside us," he said suddenly. He shook the steering wheel as if he wanted to break it off in his excitement. "You see that horse there?"

They were in scrubland now. The fields weren't tended or used for cattle but lay wild and cold-looking even in the agonizing heat. All the weeds were brown and dusty. Dan and Kennie gaped around but saw no horse. "Lookit that horse! A bastardly nice horse!" Rafe cried. He blew the old horn on the car; it sounded hoarse and surprised. "A big white horse with a long tail an' sharp feet. Now it's jumpin' the ditch there," Rafe said, "now it's poundin' along the road! Lookit it go!"

To Dan's surprise, Kennie gave a whooping sound. "There it is! It's beatin' you, Rafe! It's poundin' ahead! Lookit it go—a white one, ain't it?"

"It's beatin' me," Rafe said. His voice was pleased and strained. Dan stared at him. "It's beatin' me, beatin' me—"

"It's goin' further ahead," Kennie said. He was leaning forward, pounding at the cracked windshield with his palms. "C'mon, Rafe! C'mon! Beat it! Beat it! My God, a white son of a bitch of a horse— C'mon, Rafe! C'mon!"

"It's goin' so fast, an' them long legs!" Rafe said. He sounded as if he was going to cry. "Them long white legs an' sharp hoofs! My God, my God—It's beatin' me all to hell!"

He fell silent. The wind rushed past the car and inside, hot and stinging with dust. When Kennie said, "I ain't never seen a horse so fast," it sounded queer. Rafe did not reply. Kennie squirmed a little and looked out his window. Dan chewed again, slower. His throat felt as though he had swallowed a handful of dust.

It must have been about five in the afternoon when the old car turned off the road. There was a picnic or something going on a short distance away, around a church; the church steeple tilted up out of a clump of oaks and looked tarnished in the sun. Rafe shut off the engine with a quick sure turn of his wrist. He took a big breath and sat back, his arms up on the steering wheel. The others sat still, looking down at the picnic. Cars were parked tilted along the road, in the dusty grass, and a few children ran across the road just as they watched. They sat for a while and waited. Then Rafe said, "Let's get movin'."

Their legs were stiff. In the grass beside the road they stood awkwardly, stretching, stopping their yawns suddenly and looking around; they
avoided one another's eyes at first. Rafe caught sight of his car, suddenly,
as if he had just remembered it, and kicked the front wheel. "I expect my
pa'd like to know where this-here junker is, wouldn't he! Wouldn't he,
the old bastard!" Dan and Kennie giggled. They could see Rafe's old
man standing in the doorway of the old barn and gaping in at the dirt
floor and the cobwebs hanging from the ceiling and the piles of junk and
straw and some shabby chickens picking around, and nothing else. They
could see his popeyes and opened mouth. "Old bastard! A surprise for
him! I ought of set fire to the barn, too, to wake him up!"

Their thirst didn't allow them time to regret not having set fire to the
barn, though Dan, way in the back of his brain, had been regretting it all
along. "You follow me, now," Rafe said. He walked on ahead. He was
the oldest of the three, just turned eighteen, and the tallest, and he talked
the best, and everybody knew he was the smartest. Dan, who was thickly
built, who put even himself in mind of a white-faced steer, thought that
he was stronger than Rafe, but he never did anything about it; and Kennie, who was only fifteen, simply followed Rafe all over, the way he'd
been doing for ten years. Rafe walked ahead, fast, as if he knew right
where he was going. His boots were cracked and colorless in spots, but
they still looked good: black boots with white and red designs, a drawing
of a horse's hoof that looked ready to kick out. Walking through the
dried grass, Rafe put a hand out against cars as he passed them, familiar-
ly, complacently. He wore tight faded jeans and a belt with tarnished
silver ornaments on it, a white T-shirt stained under the arms, and a
droopy straw hat. He walked right for the picnic grounds as if he knew
somebody was waiting for him.

They drifted through the picnic. It was a Sunday afternoon and country people milled around and around, and children ran in and out of
crowds screaming with delight. The boys watched an over-and-under
game for a while. A man squatted on top of a table and shook the over-
sized dice in a tin cup and spilled them out, grimacing, rocking on his
heels, shouting "Ovah!" or "Undah!" so fast he must have known what
was coming every time. Farmers crowded around the table, fidgeting with
nickels and dimes. The man turned his big sweating face to the boys and
said, "Hey, there! Fellas! C'mon in here! C'mon with ya! Make some
money an' buy your girl friends a present! C'mon—ain't they handsome,
now, three of them in a row, like twins!"

The boys turned away. Even Rafe felt nervous. Dan and Kennie hurried to catch up with him; they pushed people aside blindly. At the out-
skirts of the grounds, by a bingo table, they slowed down. They wiped
their faces elaborately; they looked around slowly and without concern,

not glancing at one another. Sitting at the bingo table, women in brightly colored dresses worried kernels of corn around on the dirty cardboard squares. A man shouted numbers over a loud-speaker in a proud, nervous voice. The boys watched for a while, pretending interest, as their hearts slowed. Against their faces the hot air eased slowly, teasingly, carrying with it odors of hot dogs and beer and chowder mixed together with the sweet whine of country music. The boys swallowed. Rafe pulled his dirty hat down a little on his forehead and twitched his sunglasses up higher. The odor of food and the twang of music seemed to come stronger. Finally Rafe moved. "There she is," he said.

Dan and Kennie stared blankly at the crowd. "That-there girl. There she is," Rafe said quietly. He left them and followed along behind a young girl in a yellow sun dress. Dan and Kennie drifted after him. Their eyes burned and they were swallowing all the time, try as they could to forget about it. Rafe and the girl turned toward the outside of the picnic grounds, and now the girl was walking slowly alongside the church. She walked funny: none of them could say why, but it looked as if she had something wrong with her. She carried a red toy cane in one hand and a billfold in the other; the billfold hung from her fingers by a key chain. Dan and Kennie saw Rafe catch up with her. They didn't know what to do so they came closer, swallowing, pretending they didn't know Rafe. To their surprise they heard Rafe say, with a big grin, his voice all friendly, "There's my buddies. We just come to this place an' seen the picnic. I always loved a picnic. It sure is a nice one, ain't it?"

The girl blinked at him and at the other two boys. She wore glasses but her eyes were fine and large, blue, like a doll's eyes. Her lips were reddened and damp. As soon as she said, "I ain't seen you before," they knew she was younger even than Kennie.

They all nodded and grinned at once. "Just come by!" Kennie said in a rush of breath.

"We was wonderin' if you could—could walk a ways with us," Rafe said, grinning, with his face set so that Dan and Kennie could almost see his brain working behind it, so fast it made them all dizzy. "We was— lookin' for work," he said. "Hayfields mostly. You know anybody needs help?"

The girl giggled. "There might be some. I don't know. I just live with my mother," she said. She and Rafe walked on ahead, ambling, the girl ducking her head from time to time and twisting the cane around in the air. Dan and Kennie could hear her giggle and hear Rafe's voice. They walked behind, swallowing, their eyes fixed rigidly on the girl's small shoulders beneath the yellow dress. At the front of the church Rafe and the girl stopped. Rafe had his hands on his hips and was squinting and twitching his nose faster and faster. Dan and Kennie came up behind them, scuffing their feet and looking around, up at the weather-worn old church. "This is a Baptist one, is it?" Rafe said importantly, looking at the sign that said BAPTIST CHURCH. "Is that what it is?" The girl ducked her head a little and said yes. "Why, my folks are Baptist," Rafe said, "an' me too— Why, they'd just love for me to have a look inside. Is there anybody in there? Would the minister mind if I was—if we was— Maybe we could just step inside an'—" Rafe kept on talking, following the girl to the church door. He opened it for her and let her go in first, a bright movement of color beneath his arm, then he followed, glancing over his shoulder at Dan and Kennie. He made a sudden, violent face, as if all his features had suddenly run together in the effort to tell them something.

Right inside the door, in a hot musty corner, they saw a big cardboard box with clothes in it, all in a heap. "What's that for?" Rafe asked. He watched the girl's face. Dan and Kennie watched too; they waited for her to answer in the hot, still, empty silence of the old church. Her face looked small and smooth as a doll's, with her painted lips and blue eyes and the soft fringe of brown bangs on her forehead. She had time to say no more than "Clothes for poor folks—" when Rafe grabbed her. He put his big hand over her mouth and dragged her away from the door, back into the church. Dan had his fishing knife out and tried to grab hold of the girl, but Rafe pushed him away and struggled manfully with her himself. Her arms thrashed about him, beating at his shoulders, his head; then they stopped. Rafe swung her around viciously and slammed her head against one of the pews and let her drop.

Out in the sunlight the music and the smell of food were stronger. The boys walked back to the picnic. Rafe had the billfold in his pocket; he could feel it there. He was shaking. His hands were shaking so that he had to stuff them in his pockets. Dan and Kennie were already at the beer tent. They ordered three glasses and stood leaning against the counter, and Rafe paid the perspiring woman by counting out nickels and pennies onto the splintery counter. He took the coins one by one out of the pink billfold with his thick fingers, moving his lips to count; everyone waited patiently, watching him. When the woman took the thirty cents and left, Rafe stood quite still, his fingers caught in the change purse of the billfold. He looked down into it. "There ain't but eight cents left," he said softly.

Kennie had been drinking so fast that he swallowed wrong, and sputtered and coughed. When he could breathe again it was in short agonizing gasps. Dan wiped his mouth professionally and looked serious. "Eight cents," he said. He drank more beer. His eyes wandered around behind Rafe, lured by the music.

Rafe gulped at his beer. He put the billfold into his hip pocket. He leaned against the counter. Something had happened there in the church that hadn't been right; it had scared him. He wanted to tell Dan and

Kennie about it. But when he started to do so, when his words were all ready to begin, he took another sip of beer instead. "There's some hot dogs over there," Kennie said indifferently. "Over that way. I can smell them from here."

No one spoke. They finished their beer, sighing with satisfaction. On their way back to the car Rafe bought a bag of popcorn. The sign said POPCORN $.10¢ & $.25¢, but Rafe got a bag for eight cents by pretending he had lost two cents at the last minute, fishing through his pockets and standing with his mouth open. The fat woman in the little white trailer let him have the bag anyway, and they ran with it back to Rafe's father's old car.

After dark Rafe let Dan drive; it was the first time anyone but Rafe had driven at night. Rafe lay down in the back seat and tried to sleep. He fell asleep, finally, and woke up some time later to the jiggling of the car and a smell of grease and dampness. He grabbed at the front seat and shouted, "Where the hell are we! What are you bastards—" Dan's head jerked up as if someone had yanked it with a string, and Kennie slammed up against the glove compartment, half turned to gape at Rafe. The car swerved. Rafe's heart was pounding furiously; he stared at the road, saw it was a highway; his mind calmed a little. "I had a bad dream," he said.

"Jesus; you like to kilt us all," Dan said. But he spoke mildly. He watched the road and felt with his tongue around his teeth, and back in his mouth for the little piece of gum; but it was gone. "You been sleepin' an hour," he said.

Rafe stared past them at the road. "I tole you it was to be a highway," he said with weak enthusiasm. "You never believed me."

"It changed a few miles back," Kennie said. He rubbed his head where it had hit the windshield, and smiled sleepily at Rafe. "Like you showed us. On the map."

Rafe could not get calm. He kept thinking of something—that girl in the church. Something had happened there; Dan and Kennie didn't know. Rafe watched the highway whirl by beneath them. He leaned against the seat, his arms outstretched, almost hugging it. "It's a long way from Texas, it's a long way from home," he sang. "It's a—" He stopped. He watched the highway and the red clay shoulders bordering it. Then he said, "There was somethin' about that girl." He cleared his throat. When neither of the boys answered he went on, "She was sick or some-thin'. I expect she had a sickness."

Kennie looked around. He was still rubbing his head. "A sickness?" he said. "You mean like measles? You think you got it?"

"It was somethin' else," Rafe said. "How she walked, too, she never grew right—"

"I seen that," Kennie said.

"She never grew right, an' wasn't strong, an'—an'—" Rafe gulped for breath. "An' she just died, her heart give out, right before I did anything! Before I— She just give out by herself!" He blinked at Kennie. "She give out an' died an' I never needed to hit her—it was done—it was all over, just like that!"

Kennie nodded and sat back. Dan said nothing and drove on steadily, professionally, as if he were alone in the car. Rafe hugged the seat for a while, staring out at the highway. The night wind was cool and rushed against his hair. "We'll be comin' to the city tomorrow," Kennie said. "Won't we? Ain't that right?"

"That's right," Rafe said. He sat back and leaned to the window on his right, put his arm out and dragged it in the wind, and his face out too, the way dogs hang theirs out, riding in a car. He started to see a picture of the city, but it faded away. Then he started to see the stallion galloping alongside the car, its hooves pounding in the dirt, but that gave way, too. He leaned his head further out the window, as if to get at those lost images. His breath was sucked away from him. He wagged his fist at the rushing countryside, the dark, anonymous hills, the wasteland, and cried in rage and wonder: "I'm goin' to die! I'm goin' to die!" He shouted at the jumbled, empty land, at the rushing shapes and forms, all shadows, black against the lighter sky, "I'm goin' to die too—" until the wind tore his words away.

THE LAST OF THE SPANISH BLOOD

George Garrett

That was the summer my cousin Harry came to live with us. We weren't going anywhere that summer because the war was on. Harry's father had to have a serious operation and go all the way to Baltimore to have it. He would be in the hospital a long time. Aunt Jean would have to go and take a room near the hospital to be with him.

So Harry came to stay with us.

Harry was just my age, but I didn't know him at all. They seldom came to any of the family gatherings. Except, of course, the funerals. Everybody, cousins and uncles and aunts and pets, people you never heard of, showed up for funerals. A good-size family funeral was pure delight for the children, I remember. We ran free underfoot. There would be too many grownups around, and they'd be too stiff and sad and soft-footed to bother about scolding children. The only thing you had to do was to behave in the church. The rest of the time, the days before and after, was all yours. And I vaguely remember Harry from those times, dark, about my size, shabby, because his branch of the family was poor, quick-tempered, apt to throw a tantrum, but shy, too, as a wild animal is shy. Not timid, that is. Just not tame. I had a strange idea about him even then, the kind of notion a child will pick up and hold like a coin in the palm and flip, heads or tails, just for the fun of it. As I say, Harry and I were about the same age and size, but he had dark hair and I was red-headed; and in temperament and interests we were from the beginning just the opposite. So I used to think (if you can call the flow, the torment and joy, the visionary dance of a child's mind *thinking*) that we were really the same person somehow and that when I looked at him I was really looking at myself, changed and different, strange and wonderful, the way your own face and body comes back to you as a stranger from one of the crazy mirrors in the Funhouse at the Fair.

It was just a child's notion, and by the summer that Harry came to be with us I wasn't a child any more and not a man either. If I remembered that idea at all it was something to laugh at. Still, like all the other cock-eyed, cross-eyed visions from the knee-high world of children, it had some truth in its distortion.

Not a child any more and not yet a man. In the fall I would be sent back, according to the family custom still followed by those who could afford it, to military school. In that curious cold greenhouse the flowering from boy to man was supposed to be accomplished. I wasn't happy about it. I had been there. Suffered and survived. Conformed and thus gained some freedom. At least that was one lesson from the world of men, though you either learned it by accident, tripped over the truth as you might bump into and fall over a piece of furniture in a dark, but known room, or you were hurt and broken. What happened was that you stifled your impulse to rebel and followed an urge to conform. Very slowly it dawned on you that you were now anonymous. Nobody knew who you really were. You were just another pale-faced, gray-uniformed body passing up and down the cold stone halls of the barracks named for an Episcopal bishop, standing in ranks, marching on the parade ground, or sitting in a classroom with your compass and sharp pencil trying to prove that Euclid was right. Meanwhile you, the real you, were far away and somewhere else. You pushed the flesh and bones that bore your name through a thousand motions and activities every day. In a while these became routine and habit, and you could prod yourself along, all the separate and integral parts, careless and thoughtless as a shepherd with a flock of calm sheep grazing. You were free as a bird or a beast. The rebels charged windmills, battered at closed doors and high walls with their bare heads and were always bloodied and always finally bowed. You never had to bow. Of course your body did obeisance to custom and ceremony. But while your flesh knelt before some honored institution your spirit was dancing jigs and hornpipes and thumbing its nose at everything under the sun.

There was another lesson to be learned, not yet but soon after, as inevitable and abstract as those theorems and corollaries of Euclid: that the other survivors were doing exactly the same thing. That would be a chilly realization when you knew that all the others, like yourself, were ghosts in the flesh, countries and counties and continents populated by gray ghosts while, invisible, the world of spirits was a tumultuous chaos. Then you'd have to learn to live with that too.

But none of these things was much on my mind when Harry came to stay with us. I just thought that it would be good to have him around and show him things. I envied and admired him by that time. He had grown tall and slender and handsome. Everyone said he looked Spanish (the last of the Spanish blood in the family) and all agreed he was the best looking one in the whole family. He had his own car he had put together out of old parts from a junk yard, and he drove it down. (I still had a bike.) He brought guns and all kinds of fishing tackle with him. Up in his part of the state there was still lots of wild, wide, open country, and he had spent most of his spare time in the woods. When he arrived I helped him unload the car and carry all the stuff in the house and up to his room on the second floor. My father greeted him on the front porch and saw the rifles and the shotgun, and he didn't say anything but welcome.

When we got everything up to his room, Harry piled it all in a corner and flopped down on the big double bed and smoked. (I wasn't allowed to smoke yet.)

"Daddy must like you a lot," I said.

"How come? Why do you say that?"

"He doesn't allow any guns in the house. But he didn't say a word when he saw yours."

Harry laughed. "He doesn't care. He just feels *superior* and doesn't care."

"Oh, I don't think that's it."

"Or," Harry went on, ignoring my ideas, "maybe he just feels sorry for me. That makes me sick. It's exactly the same thing as feeling superior."

"I just think he wants you to feel at home."

"Well, it's a damn good thing," Harry said. "If he said anything about my guns I would've turned right around and hopped in the car and left."

"Where would you go to?"

Everything I said seemed to tickle Harry. He laughed at that too.

"Somewhere. Oh, I'd go somewhere," he said. He bounced up and down on the bed and then turned over on his stomach. "You know? I think I'm going to like it here. This has got my room at home beat a mile."

We were off for a summer of it, it seemed. Harry had lots of tales and plots and plans and ideas. Harry was bored and restless, fidgety and as calm as a stone in the sun at the same time. Harry had caught tarpon all by himself off the east coast, and he had killed more than one buck in the woods. He was a strange and wonderful kind of blood kin to have. He could make you want to show him everything you cared about in the whole country, and as you were showing it to him you knew all the time he'd be scornful and either by laughter or silence make you ashamed of every bit of it and yourself. Beautiful things could turn shoddy and cheap from one of his skeptical glances. He could laugh about anything. He even got the giggles when we went to St. Luke's Cathedral for Holy Communion. He held it all back while we were still kneeling at the altar, but when we went out the side door to go back to our pew, he ducked in the dark little room where they keep the vestments for the acolytes and started to laugh.

"What's the matter?"

"I can't help it," he said. "I got to thinking that's probably the only way I'll get a drink the whole time I'm here."

"That's sacrilegious."

"So what?"

"Don't you care?"

"Listen," he said. "If God was to walk in this room right now, I'd thumb my nose at Him."

Harry was brave, there was no doubt about that. He would take any kind of a dare my friends and I could come up with. He dived off the top of a high light-pole at Rock Springs and he didn't break his neck. He drove his car wide open up and down the main drag through all the red lights and the cops couldn't catch him. (Not *then*, anyway. They knew whose car it was all right.) He did whatever he felt like whenever he felt like it.

He used to talk a lot about wanting to be in the Army. (The real Army. He scorned military school.)

"I'll be glad when I can get in," he said. "I know everything there is about guns and I can really shoot a rifle."

The proof of that was that whenever he felt cranky and like being alone, he'd go down to the lake at the end of the street and shoot at snapping turtles. When they poked their little black heads above the surface he'd fire one shot and hit one most every time.

I thought it was fun to have him around.

That same summer Joe Childs came back from reform school. He was a lot older than we were, but he had been in the same grade with me all through the public schools until I went away to military school and he got sent off to the reform school at Raiford for trying to set fire to somebody's house. He was one of the barefooted, shambling, overage, shaggy-haired, snaggle-toothed, dull-eyed cracker boys, who always came to school in overalls and never took a bath. They brought their lunch in paper bags and ate outside under the trees by themselves instead of in the lunchroom where everybody else ate. Cornbread usually. They bullied everybody else, carried knives, were cruel to Negroes, cripples, stray dogs, and old maids. They smoked in the latrines. When they got caught at it the Principal beat them on the bare skin with a piece of rubber hose. But they were famous for never hollering or breaking into tears.

"*Him*? I don't pay him no never mind. *My* old man draws blood when *he* swings a strap."

Joe Childs was big and ugly and slow-witted. He had a lazy yellow smile all the time, but he could be cruel. When we were still in grammar school and his age and size made a lot more difference, he used to make some of us bring him a meat sandwich every day. If we didn't he beat us up. I used to beg my mother and Edna, the cook, for a meat sandwich. If they wouldn't make one for me I'd either have to play hookey that day or take a beating. I'd go dragging to school with my heart in my throat like a wad of sour grease and my feet like two heavy lead weights. It was hard to go ahead and go when you knew you were bound to take a beating.

Finally, after a long time of it, I broke down and told them why I had to have a meat sandwich every day.

My mother was really angry and all for telling the Principal, but the funny thing was that my father didn't get mad at all.

"That poor boy hasn't got anybody looking after him," he said. "Tell Edna to fix a meat sandwich every morning."

I'll never know, I guess, whether that was the right thing or not, or whether that was just feeling superior and sorry at the same time the way Harry said. At the time, anyway, it was a great relief. My father carefully explained to me that Joe Childs' father was a veteran of the First World War. He had been gassed and he couldn't do much work any more. His wife had run away and disappeared when Joe was still a baby. He drank a lot.

When Joe Childs got back from reform school, or anyway the first we knew about it was the day when some of us were out at the Old Fairgrounds, playing ball. (Harry didn't come with us. He couldn't see any point in games.) Joe Childs came running up out of a pit they had dug there years before, before the Depression, to put in a big municipal swimming pool. All they did was dig a hole in the ground. There were two other guys running along with Joe Childs. There were five of us, and I was standing with my back to the bushes around the pit knocking flies out to the others. I heard somebody or something thrashing in the bushes behind me and I twisted around to see what it was. And there stood Joe Childs, smiling that lazy yellow smile, and there were the two others, strangers to the town, on either side of him.

"Chunk me the ball." That was the first thing he said.

I threw it to him and he bounced it in his palm a few times and then put it in his pocket.

"All right," he said. "I'll take the bat too."

I wasn't going to give him the bat even if it meant a fight. He was big, but we had them five to three, and the other guys had run in from field and gathered around me.

"Don't you hear me, boy?"

I put the bat in my hands like a club.

"You'll have to take it if you want it."

All three of them reached in their pockets at one time and came up with big, long-bladed jackknives. I had had knives pulled on me before, and I was scared as soon as the sunlight hit the open blades and glanced off them brightly. All of them grinned at our surprise.

"Go on and give him the bat."

I handed it to him and he pushed me down.

"We don't want no kids from town coming out here and playing ball," he said. "You come out here again and we'll cut you wide open. Get!"

We turned around and started to walk across the field to where our bikes were parked, downcast and mad.

"Run, God damn you! Run!"

And we ran all the way to our bikes, hopped on, and pedaled away for all we were worth until we were out of sight.

I told Harry all about it that evening.

"You just let them walk over you like that?"

"What else could we do?"

"I'll tell you what you can do," he said. "You get another bat and a ball from somewhere and go back out there tomorrow afternoon."

"We couldn't do that."

"Don't worry," Harry said, laughing. "I'll come along too. Let's see if they'll try and pull a knife on *me*."

The next afternoon we piled into Harry's car and drove out to the lonely Old Fairgrounds. We started to play ball in the same spot. We played a little while, so tense and waiting for what we knew was going to happen we could hardly catch or hit the ball. Pretty soon, sure enough, the three of them came running out of the pit, blundering through the bushes like runaway animals. This time they had their knives out already.

"I thought I done told you all," Joe Childs said. He was red in the face he was so mad.

Harry came walking straight toward the three of them.

"What's the matter with you, waterhead?"

That made Joe Childs even madder. He *did* have a big head. He started for Harry, but before he could even move a couple of steps Harry calmly reached in his pocket and took out a little pistol. I didn't even know he had it with him. No wonder he was so sure of himself! He didn't wait or just wave it around either. When he pulled it out he shot— WHAM! (Every one of us jumped.)—about an inch or so in front of Joe Childs' bare foot. The three of them stopped like somebody had jerked them backwards on a leash. Joe Childs turned as pale as the belly of a catfish. One of his buddies broke out in a sweat all over and the other one wet his pants.

"Throw down them knives."

They dropped them in the grass.

"Okay," Harry said. "Let's all go down in the pit."

We picked up the knives and followed behind him. He marched them down in the pit and made them line up in a row with their hands up in the air. Just like the movies. We saw that they had built themselves a lean-to shack down there, and there were cans and bottles all around. They must have been living there.

"You know what you are?" Harry said.

They didn't say anything. The one who had wet his pants shook his head, but none of them said a thing.

"You're trash, white trash," he said. "I'd just as soon shoot you as not. Understand that?"

They all nodded.

"Now," he said. "All together: *We're trash! We're trash! We're trash!*"

They stood in front of him with their hands in the air and shouted over and over again that they were trash until Harry got tired of laughing and listening to them. He grabbed hold of my arm and pushed me right in front of Joe Childs.

"All right," he said. "Hit him."

I had been raised never to hit anyone first and especially somebody who couldn't hit you back. I couldn't do it. But Harry kept yelling in my ear until I finally hit him in the face.

"*Hit* him! I didn't say *tap* him. Hit him!"

I hit him a little harder. Joe Childs shook his head and had to spit on the ground. Harry kept on nagging at me until I hit the other two. The last I really teed-off on and he sat down. One by one we had to hit them, and after the first go-around we began to get in the mood for it. We were possessed by it. Round and around we went, hitting them until their faces were all cut and bruised and bloody, and they were begging us to quit. When they wouldn't get up off the ground to be hit again we kicked them until they would. We hit them until our hands hurt. When their faces got too bad we hit them in the stomach and the ribs. They got sick all over the ground and cried like babies.

In the end, once we had really got going, Harry had a hard time stopping us. They just lay on the ground and moaned. The strange thing was that all of us, who hadn't even dreamed of doing anything like that before, felt wild and exhilarated and good about it.

Harry kicked the lean-to over and we jumped up and down on it and smashed it to pieces. Then we piled everything they had on top of it and stuffed magazines and paper in wads underneath.

"You," Harry said to Joe Childs, prodding him with the point of his shoe. "Get up."

He struggled to his feet and moaned. He staggered and looked like a bear or a dog trying to walk on its hind legs, and we laughed at him.

"You're the one that plays with fire, ain't you?"

He kept both hands over his face and mumbled something.

Harry gave him a pack of matches and told him to start a fire. He knelt with trembling fingers and touched a match to the wadded paper. It caught and the dry wood caught too, and then there was a good crackling fire. After everything was burning good he made them empty their pockets and throw everything on the fire. Then we took them out of the pit and made them run, across the fairgrounds and away from town. They were weak, running and falling down. We yelled and hooted after them, and Harry shot at them a couple of times, over their heads. They picked up a great burst of speed when he did that, and we got to laughing so hard we fell on the ground and rolled over and over.

Then we climbed in Harry's car and drove it as fast as it would go, wildly, out in the country and all over the county. We laughed and sang and joked. It was just like being drunk.

It was only late that night when I was alone in my room trying to get to sleep that I started to feel real bad about it. I got up and went down the hall to Harry's room and woke him up to talk about it. He sat right up when I touched him, switched on the bedside light and smoked and listened to me. He laughed at my doubts and shame.

"They asked for it, didn't they, pulling knives like that?"

"Sure," I said. "It isn't that simple, though. It isn't that I feel sorry for them or anything. They probably would do the same to us if they could. It's just I didn't know I had it in me to act like that. We all went kind of crazy. I didn't know I could do like that. I didn't know I could enjoy it."

The answer he gave me has stuck, because, in a curious way, in the next years the whole world seemed to be asking itself the same question and getting the same answer. And once tasted, that doubt and shame is with you, on your tongue always. Harry puffed on his cigarette and looked at me. For once he wasn't smiling.

"Now you know," he said.

That ought to be the end of it, but it isn't. I don't know how I would have ended up feeling about Harry and myself if he had stayed on for the rest of the summer. I never found out. A few days later he got a telegram that his father was in a bad way, and he had to go to Baltimore. My father bought him a ticket on the plane and he left. And I didn't see him again. His father lived on through the summer and didn't die until I was already back at military school and couldn't come back for the funeral. I wrote him that I was sorry to hear about that, but I didn't get any answer.

Of course I thought about him and that one terrible thing we had done a lot. Since he wasn't there any more except as I chose to remember him, I usually made him the villain of the story, the one who had put us up to it, rather than simply the one who had made me see the potential of evil and violence in myself. For which, I guess, I should have been grateful.

Then along towards Christmas, not too long before vacation, I got a letter from home which said that Harry had accidently killed himself on a hunting trip. That seemed strange because he knew so much about guns and how to take care of himself. And I knew that the truth must be that he had killed himself, though I couldn't have said why. Except that maybe he knew too much about himself and other people too early.

But the strangest thing of all was how I felt when I surmised this. At first I was just plain numb, the way you always are about confronting a brute and sudden fact. But then one night after taps and after the midnight bed check when the beam of a flashlight crisscrossed our tranquil faces, I sat up in the cold dark and cried silently. It was a great deep loss to me all of a sudden. As much as I hated the memory of what had happened in the summer and still burned with shame at the injustice of his scorn and laughter, I felt that something had been taken away, stolen from me, that in some wordless way he had cheated me. I wept like a woman deceived and forsaken by a lover.

Then I felt better and turned over and went to sleep.

A POINT OF HONOR

Charles Beaumont

Today Mrs. Martinez did not practice on the organ, so St. Christopher's was full of the quiet that made Julio feel stange and afraid. He hated this feeling, and, when he touched the sponge in the fountain of Holy Water—brittle and gray-caked, like an old woman's wrist—he thought of sitting alone in the big church and decided that tomorrow would be time enough to pray. Making the Sign of the Cross, he put a dime and two pennies into the poor box and went back down the stone stairs.

The rain was not much. It drifted in fine mist from the high iron-colored clouds, freckling the dry streets briefly, then disappearing.

Julio wished that it would rain or that it would not rain.

He hurried over to the young man who was still leaning against the fender of a car, still cleaning his fingernails with a pocket knife. The young man looked up, surprised.

"So let's go," Julio said, and they started to walk.

"That was a quickie," the young man said.

Julio didn't answer. He should have gone in and prayed and then he wouldn't be so scared now. He thought of the next few hours, of Paco and what would be said if it were known how scared he really was.

"I could say your mom got sick, or something. That's what Shark pulled and he got out of it, remember."

"So?"

"So nothing, for Chrissakes. You want me to mind my own business —all right."

Danny Arriaga was Julio's best friend. You can't hide things from your best friend. Besides, Danny was older, old enough to start a mustache, and he'd been around: he had even been in trouble with a woman once and there was a child, which had shocked Julio when he first heard about it, though later he was filled with great envy. Danny was smart and he wasn't soft. He'd take over, some day. So Julio would have to pretend.

"Look, I'm sorry—okay by you?"

"Jimdandy."

"I'm nervous is all. Can't a guy get nervous without he's chicken?"

They walked silently for a while. The heat of the sun and the half-rain had left the evening airless and sticky, and both boys were perspiring. They wore faded blue jeans which hung tight to their legs, and leather flying jackets with THE ACES crudely lettered in whitewash on the backs. Their hair was deep black, straight and profuse, climbing down their necks to a final point on each; their shoes were brightly shined, but their

T-shirts were grimy and speckled with holes. Julio had poked the holes in his shirt with his finger, one night.

They walked across the sidewalk to a lawn, down the lawn's decline to the artificial lake and along the lake's edge. There were no boats out yet.

"Danny," Julio said, "why you suppose Paco picked me?"

Danny Arriaga shrugged. "Your turn."

"Yeah, but what's it going to be?"

"For you one thing, for another guy something else. Who knows? It's all what Paco dreams up."

Julio stopped when he saw that they were approaching the boathouse. "I don't want to do it, I'm chicken—right?"

Danny shrugged again and took out a cigarette. "I told you what I would've told Paco, but you didn't want to. Now it's too late."

"Gimme a bomb," Julio said.

For the first time, suddenly, as he wondered what he had to do tonight, he remembered a crazy old man he had laughed at once in his father's pharmacy on San Julian Street and how hurt his father had been because the old man was a shellshock case from the First World War and couldn't help his infirmity. He felt like the old man now.

"Better not crap around like this," Danny said, "or Paco'll start wondering."

"Let him wonder! All right, all right."

They continued along the edge of the lake. It was almost dark now, and presently they came to the rear door of the park's boathouse. Danny looked at Julio once, stamped out his cigarette and rapped on the door.

"Check the playboys," somebody said, opening the door.

"Cram it," Danny said. "We got held up."

"That's a switch."

Julio began to feel sick in his stomach.

They were all there. And Julio knew why: to see if he would chicken out.

Lined up against the far wall, Gerry Sanchez, Jesús Rivera, Manuel Morales and his two little brothers who always tagged along wherever he went; seated in two of the battery boats, Hernando and Juan Verdugo and Albert Dominguin. All silent and in their leather-jacket-and-jeans uniforms. In the center of the big room was Paco.

Julio gestured a greeting with his hand, and immediately began to fear the eyes that were turned on him.

Paco Maria Christobal y Mendez was a powerfully muscled, dark and dark-haired youth of seventeen. He sat tipped back in a wicker chair, with his arms stretched behind his head, staring at Julio, squinting through the cigarette smoke.

"What, you stop in a museum on the way?" Paco said. Everybody laughed. Julio laughed.

"What are you talking? I ain't so late as all that."

"Forty-five minutes is too late." Paco reached to the table and moved a bottle forward.

"Speech me," Julio said. "Speech me."

"Hey, listen, you guys! Listen, Julio's cracking wise."

"Who's cracking wise? Look, so I'm here, so what should I do?"

Danny was looking at his shoes.

Paco rubbed his face. It glistened with hot sweat and was inflamed where the light beard had caused irritations. "Got a hot job for Julio tonight," he said. "Know what it is?"

"How should I know?" Julio tried hard to keep his voice steady.

"Great kidders, you English," Paco said. "Hey, you guys, he don't know." He looked over at Danny Arriaga. "You didn't tell him?"

"For Chrissakes," Danny said.

"All right, all right, so. You still want in The Aces?"

Julio nodded.

"By which means you got to do whatever I say you got to do, no matter what, right? Okay." Paco drank from the bottle and passed it to Manuel Morales, who drank and gave the bottle to the younger of his brothers, who only wet his lips and gave it back.

Julio knew he'd have to wait, because he remembered Albert's initiation, and how Paco had stalled and watched to see how scared he got. They'd sent Albert to swipe a car that was owned by the manager of Pacific Fruit who always left the key in. That wasn't so bad, even if Albert did wreck the car the same night, driving it back to the club. Swiping a car would be all right.

But from the way Danny looked, it wasn't going to be anything like that. Paco had it in for him ever since he found out about his going to church. Though there must be more to it, because Julio knew that Hernando and Juan went to church, too.

Something deep and strange, hard to figure.

But strong.

"Pretty soon it's time," Paco said, leaning back in the chair. The others were smiling.

The boats rocked uneasily in the small currents, a short drifting.

Julio thought about Paco, about how he'd come to The Aces. It was Danny who joined first, long before, even before Julio was wearing jeans. Paco was later, a new guy on the street. Mr. Mendez was dead, and his mother worked in the Chinese grocery on Aliso Street with the dead cats in the window. No organization to the club, then. Paco moved in and organized. He beat up Vincente Santa Cruz, who was the strongest guy in the Heights, and he introduced the guys to marijuana and showed them where to get it. He'd been booked three times at the jail and was seen with girls tagging after him, even though he wasn't good-looking, only strong and powerful. Danny admired Paco. Julio didn't, but he respected him.

"Charge up, kid." Paco opened a pill box which contained four crude cigarettes.

"Afterwards," Julio said.

"So okay. Afterwards." Paco grinned and winked at the others.

There was silence again: only the water sloshing against the boats and the painful creak of the wicker chair straining back and forth.

The room was very small. THE ACES was whitewashed on the walls, and initials were carved in various places. Except Julio's. His were not on any of the walls. That distinction would come only when he'd finished his job.

No one seemed prepared to break the quiet.

Julio thought, Danny knows. He knew all along, but he wouldn't tell me. Danny was a full-fledged member now. He'd had to break windows out of Major Jewelry and swipe enough watches for the gang. A tough assignment, because of the cops who prowled and wandered around all the time. It took nerve. Julio had broken into a store himself, though—a tire shop—and so he knew he could do it again, although he remembered how afraid he had been.

Why wouldn't they tell him, for Chrissakes? Why stall? If they'd only tell him now, he'd go right out, he was sure. But, any later . . .

"Scared?" Paco asked, lighting another cigarette and taking off his jacket.

"Listen close—you'll hear me shaking," Julio said.

Danny smiled.

Paco frowned and brought his chair forward with a loud noise.

"What are you so cocky—I'll give you in the mouth in a minute. I asked a question."

"No, I ain't scared."

"That's a crock of shit. Who you trying to kid, anyway? Me?"

Suddenly Julio hated this leering, posturing Paco as he had never hated a person before. He looked at his friend Danny, but Danny was looking elsewhere.

"Mackerel snapper, isn't it, Julio?" Paco scratched his leg loudly. "What did you, go to confession today or was the priest busy in the back room?" He smiled.

Julio clenched his fists. "Gimme to do, already," he said; and, all at once, he thought of his father, Papa Velasquez. Papa would be working late right now, in the pharmacy, mixing sodas and prescriptions. Business was very good, with the new housing project and all the new trade.

Julio was going to be a pharmacist—everybody knew that, though no one believed it. No one but Father Laurent: he talked to Julio many times, softly, understandingly. And there were many times when Julio wanted to tell the priest what he had done—about the motorcycle or the time he helped the guys push tea—but he could never seem to get the words out.

He waited, hands tight together, listening to the breathing, and thinking: I could go right to the drugstore now, if I wanted. It was only a mile away. . . .

He cleared his throat. Albert Dominguin was staring at him.

And now Danny Arriaga was getting sore, too: Julio could tell.

"You want to know, huh? Guys—think I should tell him?"

"Tell him already," Danny snapped, rising to his feet. He looked a lot bigger than Paco, suddenly. "Now."

"Who asked for your mouth?" Paco said, glaring. He looked quickly away. "All right, Julio. But first you got to see this."

Paco reached in his pocket and took out a large bone-handled knife. Julio didn't move.

"Ever use one, kid?"

"Yeah."

"Hey, no shit? What do you think, guys—Julio's an expert!" Paco pressed a button on the knife with this thumb. A long silver blade flashed out, glittering in the greenish light of the boathouse.

"So?"

"So you're going to use it tonight, Julio," Paco said, grinning broadly and rocking in the chair. The others crouched and held their cigarettes in their mouths.

Danny seemed about to speak up, but he held himself in check.

"On what?" Julio said.

"No, kid—not on *what*. On *who*." Paco flipped the knife toward Julio's foot, but it landed handle-down and slid to a corner. Julio picked it up, pressed the button, folded back the blade and put the knife in his pocket.

"All right, who. On who?"

He remembered what the Kats had done to the old woman over on Pregunta. For eighty-three cents.

"A dirty son of a bitch that's got it coming," Paco said. He waited. "Hey, kid, what's wrong? You look sick."

"What are you talking, for Chrissakes? What do you want I should do?"

"Carry out a very important mission for our group, that's what. You're a very important man, Julio Velasquez. Know that?"

Near Cuernavaca, by the caverns of Cacahuamilpa, Grandfather had seen a man lying still in the bushes. The man was dead. But not only that—he had been dead for a long time. Grandfather used to sit after the coffee and tell about it; and it was always terrifying because Grandfather had a quiet way of talking, without emphasis, without excitement.

—*"Quien fué el hombre, Papá?"*

—*"Quien? Un hombre muy importante en el pueblo!"*

Always; then the slow description, unrolling like one of Mama's string-balls. The man had been a rich one of the village, influential and well liked, owner of a beautiful hacienda, over two thousand acres of land. Then one night he didn't come back when he should have, and the next night it was the same, and the next night, and after the searches, he was forgotten. It was Grandfather who found him. But the flies and the vultures had found him first.

—*"Comó murió el hombre?"* He had been murdered. The knife was still between his ribs and the flesh had softened and decayed around the knife.

Death. . . .

Julio always thought of death as the rich man from Cuernavaca.

"What'd he do?" Julio asked. "This guy."

"He got to *do* something?" Paco said, laughing. Then: "Plenty. You know when we all went to the Orpheum the other night and you had to stay home on account of your old man or something?"

"Yeah. Sure."

"Okay. They got Billy Daniels and a picture that's supposed to be good, y'know? Okay, we start to pay when the chick at the window picks up the phone and says, 'Wait a minute.' Pretty soon the brass comes out and starts to look us over, real cool, see, like he had a bug up or something. I talk to him and it's all right—we go in. Five goddam dollars. So—the show stinks, the movie: it's cornball, and we go to get our loot back. Guy at the window now, no broad. He says 'Nooo.' I ask to see the manager, but he's gone. They won't give us back our loot. What do we do? What would *you* do, Julio?"

"Raise a stink."

"You bet your sweet ass. That's what we do, what happens? Big Jew punk comes barrelin' down the aisle, says he's the assistant manager. We got to blow, see. But no loot, no, man. Then he took Albert by the hair and kicked him. Right, Albert?"

Albert nodded.

"So naturally this isn't for The Aces. I didn't say nothing after that, except I let the schmuck know he'd get his, later on. So we just casually walked out. And here's the thing—" Paco's eyes narrowed dramatically. "That louse is still walking around, Julio, like he never done a thing to anybody, like he never insulted all of us. Know what he said? Know what he called us, Julio?"

"What'd he call you?"

"Pachooks. Wetbacks. Dirty Mex bastards. Crapped his mouth off like that in front of everybody in the show.

"So you want him cut up?"

Paco rocked and smiled. "No, not just cut up. I want that liddle-Yiddle dead, where he can't crap off any more. That's your assignment, Julio. Bring back his ears."

Julio glanced at Danny, who was not smiling. The others were very quiet. They all looked at him.

"When's he get off?" Julio asked, finally.

"Ten-thirty. He walks down Los Angeles Street, then he hits Third, down Third till he's around the junction. It's a break, Julio. We followed him for three nights, and there's never anybody around the junction. Get him when he's passing the boon docks over to Alameda. Nobody'll ever see you."

"How will I know him?"

"Fat slob. Big nose, big ears, curly brown hair. Carries something, maybe his lunch-pail—you might bring that back with you. Albert'll go along and point him out, in case he wants to try to give you trouble. He's big, but you can take him."

Julio felt the knife in his pocket. He nodded.

"All right, so this is it. You and Albert take off in half an hour, wait and hang around the loading docks, but make sure nobody sees you. Then check the time and grab a spot behind the track next to Merchant Truck—you know where it is. He'll pass there around eleven. All right?"

Julio reached for the pill box and controlled his fingers as they removed the last cigarette. Paco grinned.

"So in the meantime, let's have our meeting. Whoever got what, lay it out on the floor."

The boys began reaching into bags and parcels, and into their pockets, and taking out watches and rings and handfuls of money. These items they spread on the floor.

The rich man, Julio thought, lying still in the bushes, with his fat dead face, waiting for the flies, waiting, while a little Mexican boy with red wet hands runs away, fast, fast. . . .

The grating sound of heavy machinery being pushed across cement came muffled through the wooden doors of the freight dock. There were a few indistinct voices, and the distant hum of other machines that never stopped working.

The night was still airless. Julio and Albert Dominguin walked along the vacant land by the boxcar, clinging to the shadows and speaking little.

Finally Julio said, "This guy really do all that that Paco said?"

"He got smart," Albert said.

"Kick you?"

"You could call it that. Just as good."

"So what kind of a stink you guys raise to cause all that?"

"Nothing."

"Nothing my ass."

"Aah, you know Paco. He got p-o'ed at the picture and started to horse around. Dropped a beer bottle off of the balcony or something, I don't know."

"Then this guy booted you guys out?"

"Yeah."

"Did Paco give him a fight?"

"No," Albert said, thoughtfully. They climbed up the side of a car and jumped from the top to the ground. "He's too smart for that. They would of called the cops and all that kind of crap. This way's better."

"Yeah."

"Nervous?"

"Yeah, real nervous. I'm dying to death, I'm so frigging nervous. Listen—when I get through tonight, Paco and all the rest of you guys better lay off me."

"Don't worry."

"So what is it?"

"Twenty-of. This is the place—he went by right over there."

Julio wondered if Albert could hear his heart. And if Albert could read his thoughts. . . .

He felt the greasy knife handle slip in his hands, so he took it out and wiped it on his trousers and tested it. He pushed the point of the blade into the soft wood of a car, pretending it was the Jewish boy's neck.

He pulled the knife out and didn't do that any more.

They sat on the cindery ground beside a huge iron wheel.

"Really a rat, huh?" Julio said.

"The most," Albert said.

"How old?"

"Who knows—twenty-five, thirty. You can't tell with them."

"You don't suppose he—I mean this guy—you don't think he's got a family or anything like that, do you?"

"What the hell kind of a thing is that to say? Christ, no! Who'd marry a greaseball slob like that?'' Albert laughed softly, and took from his leather jacket pocket a red-handled knife that had to be operated manually. He opened it and began to clean his fingernails. Every two or three seconds he glanced up toward the dark unpaved street.

"So nobody's going to miss *him,* right?'' Julio said.

"No. We're going to all break down and cry. What's the matter, you chickening out? If you are, I ain't going to sit here on my can all—''

Julio clutched Albert's shirt-front and gathered it in his fist. "Shut up. You hear? Shut your goddam face about that stuff or I'll break it for you.''

"Shhh, quiet down . . . we'll talk later. Let go. If you want to screw everything, just keep shooting your mouth.''

Julio felt the perspiration course down his legs.

He tried to stop the shudder.

"Okay,'' he said.

On the tracks a mile distant a string of freight cars lumbered clumsily out of a siding, punching with heavy sounds at the night. There were tiny human noises, too, like small birds high out of sight. Otherwise, there was only his own breathing.

"I want to hear 'mackerel snapper' when this is over,'' Julio said.

"You ain't done nothing yet,'' Albert said, looking away quickly.

"Screw you,'' Julio said. But his voice started to crack so he forced a yawn and stretched out his legs. "So when the hell we going to get a goddam sickle?'' he said.

Albert didn't answer.

"Kind of a gang is this, anyway, we don't have any goddam sickles?''

"Five-of. He ought to be along pretty quick now.''

Julio grinned, closed his knife, reopened it with a swift soft click, closed it again. His hands were moist and the knife handle was coated with a grimy sweat which made it slippery. He wiped it carefully along the sides of his jeans.

"The Kats have got sickles. Five, for Chrissakes.''

"Kats, schmats,'' Albert said. "Knock it off, will you?''

"What's the matter, Albert? Don't tell me you're scared!''

Albert drew back his fist and hit Julio's shoulder, then quickly put a finger to his lips. *"Shhh!''*

They listened.

It was nothing.

"Hey, little boy, hey, *Al*bert, know what?'' Julio combed his hair. "Know what I know? Paco, he don't think I'll do it. He wants you and I to come back so he can give with the big-man routine. He don't think I'll do it.''

Albert looked interested.

"He's real sharp. Having a great big ball right now. Where's it going to put him when we get back with that Jewboy's ears?" Julio laughed.

In the stillness, footsteps rang sharply on the ground, but ponderously as gravel was crunched and stones were sent snapping.

The footsteps grew louder.

Albert listened, then he rose slowly and brushed the dirt from his jeans. He opened his knife, looked at Julio and Julio got up. They hunched close by the shadow of the boxcar.

The steps were irregular, and for a moment Julio thought it sounded like a woman. For another moment he heard Grandfather's words and saw the carrion in the bushes.

The images scattered and disappeared.

"Dumb jerk don't know what he's walking into, right?" Julio whispered. The words frightened him. Albert wasn't moving. "Wetbacks. Greasers. Mex—right? Okay. Okay, Albert? Okay." The blade sprang out of the handle.

"Shut up," Albert whispered. "There he is. See him?"

There were no streetlamps, so the figure was indistinct. In the darkness it could be determined that the figure was that of a man: heavy set, not old, walking slowly, almost as if he were afraid of something.

"That's him," Albert said, letting out a stream of breath.

Julio's throat was dry. It pained him when he tried to swallow. "Okay," he said.

Albert said, "Okay, look. Go up and pretend you want a handout, y'know? Make it good. Then let him have it, right away."

"I thought I saw something," Julio said.

"What's that supposed to mean?"

"I thought I saw something, I thought I saw something. You mind?"

"Where?"

"I couldn't make out."

"Who you bulling? You want to go back?"

"All right, so I was wrong."

The figure had passed the boxcar and disappeared into shadows, but the footsteps were still clear.

"You ready?" Albert said.

Julio paused, then he nodded.

"The hell," Albert said. "You're scared green. You'll probably louse it all up. Let's go back."

Julio thought of going back. Of what would be said, of all the eyes turned on him like ominous spotlights. The laughter he heard was what he hated most.

Albert looked anxious; the footsteps were dying away.

"Screw you," Julio said. "You coming with, or not?" He put the knife up his sleeve and held it there with his palm cupped underneath.

Albert rubbed his hands along his shirt. "All right, I'll follow you—about a minute. Sixty seconds."

Julio listened. Suddenly he didn't tremble any more, though his throat was still dry. There were no more pictures in his mind.

He waited, counting.

Then he smiled at Albert and started to walk.

It will take only a few minutes, he thought. No one will see. No one will give Julio Velasquez the old crap about chicken after this. No one . . .

Up ahead, he could see the man. No one else: just the man who was a louse and who didn't deserve to live.

And the long shadows.

He looked over his shoulder once, but the darkness seemed alive, so he jerked his head around and walked faster, with less care.

At last he caught up with the man.

"Hey, mister," Julio said.

PART 6 _____

Treatment of Offenders

Few subjects are as controversial as the rehabilitation of juvenile delinquents. How should they be treated? What rehabilitation facilities should be provided for them? What are the duties of juvenile courts, probation officers, schools, and parents in dealing with delinquents? How effective are current reform techniques?

There is no consensus concerning the rehabilitation of juvenile delinquents, though three attitudes have been popular for some time. One holds that delinquents are taken into custody not to be punished but to be reformed; when they are returned to society, they should be law-abiding citizens and able to function as such. Another attitude maintains that delinquents should be institutionalized for a while in order to break a series of delinquencies, to keep them from negatively influencing others (or being negatively influenced by them), and to allow them to grow; after their release, they should be disinclined to return to their former delinquent behavior. A third group argues cynically that correctional institutions are corrupt schools in which less hardened delinquents are tutored in various criminal philosophies and practices by their more experienced peers; once offenders leave reform school, as it is conceived in this attitude, they are likely to commit more serious offenses. In addition to these three attitudes, others believe that all but the incorrigible should be severely reprimanded—to impress on them the seriousness of their offenses—and then should be put on a closely supervised probation. The probation officer would act as a counselor whenever possible, and for more serious problems, the delinquent could establish a dialogue with a psychologist or psychiatrist. Sometimes the probation officer would act as a go-between for delinquents and their parents and teachers.

For the most part, stories about reform schools are critical of the methods by which youthful offenders are rehabilitated. "Young Convicts," besides providing a vivid description of a lower-class immigrant neighborhood in the late 1940s, is an indictment of the poverty that causes delinquency and the juvenile court system that must deal with ghetto delinquents. When Tony and his gang are arrested for burglary, they are perfunctorily brought before an overburdened judge who is forced to hurry through her cases, thinking all the while "the cases had to be disposed of. Tomorrow there would be the same number. The juvenile problem was insoluble. There was no settlement of it." She simply has no time to "probe into the causes of these delinquencies," and it is implied that even if she could conduct a probe, there would not be much she or any other judge could do to solve the socioeconomic conditions causing so many children to be brought to trial. Part of Tony's gang is sent to the juvenile detention home, others are put on probation, some are released in the custody of their parents, and a few are reprimanded. It seems unlikely that any of them have been significantly changed for the better by the actions of the court; the implication is that some members of Tony's gang will appear again before the court. This, like so many stories of the 1940s, offers a bleak view of the juvenile courts of the time.

"The Divided House" presents a more encouraging picture of reformatory life. The story is set in South Africa, and the juvenile reform system described allows responsibility, dignity, and supervised freedom to the young inmates. The concern of the adults who work with their charges is sincere, and most of the youngsters profit by the treatment they are given; of course, a few do not or simply cannot. The story of young Jacky is by turns encouraging and sad. His talk with the principal indicates the principal's keen understanding of Jacky's problems. Yet, even the principal's best efforts are unable to save Jacky, who is torn between his conscious desire to become a priest and his unconscious impulses to break the law—hence his "divided house." Disheartening as it may be, some delinquents—even under the best conditions—are unable to rehabilitate their lives.

The bizarre violence of the girls in "The Universal Fears" makes one wonder if they can be reformed under any circumstances. Surely, the students of St. Dunster's Training School for Girls must sense the apparent concern of their teacher for them, and surely his actions in no way call for their near-fatal attack on him. Very likely, though, he represents the world of adults that has been partly responsible for what they are: "homeless, bad-off, unloved, semi-literate"; their assault is more against the world that has formed them than the man who stands in front of the class. Given the harrowing circumstances of his first meeting with his class, it is remarkable that the teacher chooses to return to it. What degree of success does he really expect to have with his students?

If the effectiveness of a rehabilitation program is to be measured by the behavior of those who are released from it, then Junior's eighteen-month confinement in "Hero's Return" has changed his outlook on life for the better. Indeed, Junior has learned his lesson well enough so that he directs his younger brother away from the life of a drug pusher. The story is unusual; similar stories often depict delinquents going home to their neighborhood and quickly returning to their former delinquencies. The majority of young delinquents are simply overwhelmed by their environment; many feel that their reform-school experiences have made them too clever to be caught again by the law. Few protagonists have the advantage of Jody's brother, who acts as a strong substitute father and counteracts the unhealthy influence others have on Jody, particularly the influence of King, the much admired local hustler.

Despite the pessimistic tone of many stories about reforming delinquents, the stories in this section offer hope for juvenile reform programs, which in fact accomplish more than is often apparent and too often are faulted for failing to accomplish the impossible. In "Young Convicts" there is the "hope that a few boys would be rescued from crime, and a few girls from the life of a prostitute." Even though the efforts of the principal in "The Divided House" fail to reform Jacky, they are bound to work with many other boys. The teacher's willingness in "The Universal Fears" to return to the classroom is noteworthy and offers hope to his students, and to himself. In "Hero's Return" the indirect influences of Junior's rehabilitation are evident in the way he shapes the life of his younger brother. We are left at last with an essential question: If present methods of coping with juvenile delinquency are inadequate, what constructive alternatives are there?

YOUNG CONVICTS

James T. Farrell

They were the children of Slavic immigrants and lived in the manufacturing district around Thirty-fifth and Morgan. Their fathers worked in the factories located in the area. Their sisters, even before they started to bloom and lose their gawky pre-puberty figures, also joined the ranks of those who trooped to the factories at six and seven in the morning. At six, seven, eight o'clock, rain or shine, morning after morning, their fathers, mothers, older brothers, sisters, all became part of the long line plodding to work.

There were six kids in this gang. Tony, the eldest, was a boy of twelve, and Stanley, the youngest, was eight. They all liked candy. They liked to go to the movies, especially on Saturday afternoons, when the serial was shown. They liked serials and movies of that type best because there was danger and adventure, shooting, robbing, train wrecks, bandits, outlaws, Indians, Mexicans, battles. And they scarcely ever had money for candy or for movies.

But they liked candy and they liked movies. And they liked to do dangerous, brave things, to pull off stunts like those pulled off by the older fellows in the neighborhood. They wanted to fight and steal and then brag about it, just as they heard their older brothers bragging. They could be heroes just like the older boys. And when they could steal, they could have money for candy and the movies.

Home to each of the kids in the gang was much the same. A wooden shack, one or two stories high, with an outside privy that smelled you out every time you wanted to take a leak. Three, four, five rooms, generally dirty, full of rags, papers, the smell of kerosene lamps. Dark bedrooms, old beds, dirty sheets, two, three, four, and five sleeping together in the same bed, and on cold nights there was always a fight for the blankets. A mother and a father who were generally overtired from work, and from raising a family. And the mother and father didn't speak English. They were greenhorns. And once every week, two weeks, three weeks, the mother and father would get drunk. They would curse and fight, throwing things at one another, shouting, even brandishing knives and cutting one another up, until the police came with a paddy wagon. These kids' homes were alike.

They didn't like school very much. They didn't like their studies, and in the classroom they groaned, twisted, squirmed, itched, dreamed of high deeds like those of the movie heroes and villains in the Saturday-afternoon serials, like those of the older fellows, like those of Al Capone. In school, they waited for the end of class. They were afraid of their teachers, and they neither liked nor trusted them. The teachers, some of them young girls from good families who were waiting until they found a husband, did not like the bad boys much either. Sometimes, in the hallways, the kids would hear one teacher tell another that she wished she would be transferred to another school where there was a better class of pupils than these incorrigible Polacks and Bohemians.

Often, they didn't learn their lessons. They bummed from school regularly, and went scavenging through vacant lots and streets, keeping their eyes peeled for the overworked truant officers. Or they went to the railroad yards with sacks and wagons for coal that was needed at home. In fact, they learned to steal in the railroad yards. The parents would send them out at night to get coal, and they'd go down to the yards and get it, one kid getting up in a car and throwing chunks down to the others. From the railroad yards they went to the stockyards, going over the fences and leaving with anything removable that could perhaps be sold. They stole everything they could, and finally stealing got to be a nightly occupation.

They knew about hold-ups. They knew that some of the older guys in the district had pulled off hold-ups, and that made them heroes. So they determined that they too would be heroes and pull hold-ups. That would get money for candy and movies. And they would be living like the heroes they saw in the movies. One night, Tony, the gang leader, picked out the Nation Oil filling station on Thirty-fifth Street. They played across the street from the station for two nights. They goofed about, ran, played tag by a closed factory, getting a line on what time the station closed and what time the cop on the beat passed by after it had closed. When they were sure of their time and their layout, they went to work. Young Stanley tossed a house brick through a side window. Tony then stood on a box, put his hand through the broken glass, and unlatched the window. He went in, followed by the others. The money was in the safe, and that could not be touched. So they tore the telephone box from the wall and scooted with it. They broke it open in a vacant lot and divided the nickels that were in it. The loot was three dollars, and, although it was to be divided evenly, Stanley was cheated out of a quarter.

Successful in their raid on the filling station, they made other raids. They robbed every filling station in the district, always running off with the telephone box, and they enjoyed the fruits of their robbery in candy, cigarettes, and movies. Tony liked it. He bossed his gang with an iron hand. Night after night he drove them in raid after raid. If they complained, he kicked them in the pants and slapped their faces. If they talked back to him, he cracked them. He saw himself as a young Al Capone. He dreamed of shootings, gang fights, submachine guns, robberies, money, automobiles, everything the gangsters had in the movies, everything Al Capone had in real life. And he always planned out the raids, instructing each kid in what he should do, going to the place in advance to get the lay of the land. He always had money and gave some of it away to younger kids, to girls whom he would try to bribe in order to get them alone with him in basements. He hung around the corners and the poolrooms late at night, watching the older fellows. He imitated them in walking, talking, gestures, held his cigarettes as they did, borrowed all their remarks. He pushed and pressed his gang constantly, always discovering new places to rob. One night they robbed a chain restaurant. Stanley threw a brick through the back window, and they entered and ran off with the cash in the till. Two nights later, they returned to the Nation Oil Company's filling station and again ran off with the telephone box full of nickels. This time they noticed that the attendant had gone home, leaving his safe open. In it, they saw bills, many of them, dollars and dollars, more money than they had ever seen before. They were so surprised by the sight of the money, so afraid, that they did not take it, satisfying themselves with only the small change in the safe. And on the night after this robbery they returned to the chain restaurant. They were caught by a watchman and a city policeman.

They were brought before Judge Katherine Henderson in the Juvenile Court; she was a woman jurist who was known beyond the city for her good work. The court was crowded with its usual array of young culprits and harassed, shamed parents. The boys had to wait their turn, and they sat with other boys, cowed and meek, and with their shabbily dressed immigrant parents. Nearly all those waiting to be tried were the children of working people, most of them of immigrants. Some were released, some placed on probation, some sentenced to the Juvenile Detention Home. Judge Henderson spoke crisply, hastily, perfunctorily, often in a scolding tone. She hurried through case after case, disposed of it, making instant decisions, bawling out parents, often telling immigrant fathers and mothers that they were responsible for the delinquent conduct of their children.

Judge Henderson just didn't have the time. The cases had to be disposed of. Tomorrow there would be the same number. The juvenile problem was insoluble. There was no settlement of it. The same boys were warned, but they were brought back. Parents were warned, but they were helpless. There was nothing to do but rush through from case to case, let so many off, put so many on probation, send so many to the Detention Home. Day after day, this must go on. The law must be upheld. There was no time for her to delay, study, probe into the causes of these delinquencies. All she could do was reach out and try, and hope that a few boys would be rescued from crime, and a few girls from the life of a prostitute. That was what she did. Lectures, warnings, scoldings, questions, sentences. Next. Next. Next. All morning. Next. All afternoon. Next. Tomorrow. More. Next.

Tony and the gang were called up. The bailiff rounded them up and prodded them in the back, his language curt and sharp. He shoved them up to the bar of justice. Judge Henderson read the papers on the case, closed her lips as she read, nodded her gray head. She raised her brows. Her benign face showed worry. She seemed to be wondering and thinking. She looked down sharply at the six boys before her. Their heads dropped. They were afraid to look her in the eye, just as they feared looking teachers, or policemen, in the eye. Her gaze shifted. She stared at their parents, who stood silently behind the boys. She asked each of the boys what his name was. The first answered that he was Clement Comorosky. Where was his mother? He shook his head. Again she asked where his mother was. Again he shook his head. More stridently, she asked where his father and mother were. He said that both were working and could not come down. Stanley's mother then spoke in Polish. An interpreter was called, and she spoke to him. He told the judge that the woman had said that the father and mother of the Comorosky boy worked in a factory and were afraid to stay out because they were too poor, and needed the day's wages, and they were afraid that if they didn't report for work they might be laid off. Please, she would take their place.

"All right. Now, do you boys know what you did?" the judge asked.

None of them answered. They stood with averted eyes.

"Can any of you talk? Can you talk?" she asked, sweeping her eyes from one to another, fixing them on Clement, who was ten years old.

He nodded his head affirmatively.

"Do you know that it's a crime to break into other people's homes and stores and to take things that don't belong to you?"

"I'm sorry . . . ma'am," Clement said.

"How long have you been doing this?"

"Just this time," Clement said.

She looked through the papers before her and called out Stanley's name.

"You were here before, and I told you that I didn't want to see you brought back. And why don't you go to school?"

He looked at her with large-eyed awe.

"Are your parents here?"

A small Slavic woman said that she was his mother; her face was lined, and an old black shawl covered her head. The judge asked her if she ever tried to keep her boy in at night. She shook her head, and said that she tried, but that he went out anyway. The judge looked down at Stanley, glowering.

"And what did you do?"

"Me? I thrun the brick through de window."

Many who heard him smiled. The judge continued to question them in a brusque manner which inspired fear. Their answers came slowly. They were evasive. They did not understand all of her questions. She became more brusque. She seemed annoyed. She listened, with increasing irritation, while the watchman who caught the boys gave his testimony. Then the gas station attendant testified that twice the station had been broken into, and the telephone box had been ripped off the wall on each occasion. The restaurant manager gave testimony also.

"You boys have to learn that you can't go on breaking into places and stealing money. That is not right, and it is not permitted. Do you hear me?"

Six heads nodded.

"Well, why did you do it?"

Her additional questions brought out the fact that Tony was the leader and inspiration of the gang, that Stevie Lozminski was his lieutenant, and that the raids and burglaries had been committed under their direction. Both had been in the court before for truancy and burglary, and the truant officer testified that all her efforts to do anything that would keep them in the classroom, where they belonged, were fruitless. Their teachers and the principal of the school had turned in written reports describing them as incorrigible. The judge continued her brusque questioning, directing some of it at the parents, who stood in silent awe and fear. She lectured the parents about taking care of their offspring and insisted that the interpreter translate her remarks so that they would surely be understood. Tony, Stevie, and Clement were all sentenced to six months in the Juvenile Detention Home, and the others were put on probation. The mothers cried. They looked with bewildered grief at the judge, their pleading eyes almost like those of sick animals. The boys were pulled from their parents' arms and taken off. Two of the mothers cried.

The next case, that of a colored boy caught stealing, was called.

The mill of the court continued.

THE DIVIDED HOUSE

Alan Paton

Of all the boys at the reformatory, Jacky was one of the strangest. He had once been a Pondo of Pondoland, but the big city was now in his blood. He was a closed-up, reserved kind of boy, and had no close companions, but he enjoyed a kind of popularity none the less, for he played a magnificent game of football. We gave him his freedom because no one knew much about him, not even the Tailoring Instructor who had worked with him for months. Of every hundred boys we made free, three absconded at once, the first time they were allowed to roam about the farm on their own. But another three had a conscience, and absconded only on the second or fifth or seventh occasion. Jacky was one of these, and one Sunday afternoon he failed to report back at five o'clock.

Some days after, I was visiting some boys who had been temporarily transferred to the non-European Hospital, and whom should I see in one of the wards, with an African constable sitting guard over him, but Jacky. I told the constable he was one of my boys, and asked if I might speak to him.

"What are you doing here, Jacky?"

He looked at me shamefacedly.

"I was shot, father," he said.

"How did you get shot?"

"I was breaking into a house, father."

Of course Jacky lost his freedom when the magistrate returned him to the reformatory, and he went back to the main building. But he was such a good tailor that he was allowed to return to his old work. When he had been back for a short time, he asked to see me, and the Tailoring Instructor brought him in.

"Jacky has a story to tell the Principal," he said, and then he looked at me apologetically. "It's a strange story," he said.

"Well, Jacky?"

"When I was in hospital, father, a voice spoke to me."

"A voice? What voice?"

"God's voice, father."

"And what did He say?"

"He said, 'Jacky, you won't die, your work is not yet finished.' "

"And what did you say?"

"I said, 'Father, what is the work?' "

"Yes?"

"And He said, 'Jacky, I want you to be a priest.' "

I sat and considered it, and then I said to him, "That's a new kind of work for you."

If there was any irony, he took no notice.

"It's a new kind of work," he said.

"How far have you been in school, Jacky?"

"Standard four, father."

"A priest has to go further than that."

"I'm ready," he said.

"You're asking," I said, "to go to the school?"

"Yes, father."

"Then you can go to the school."

So Jacky was put in Standard Five in the school, and though not brilliant, he worked hard and well.

In a few days he was back with the Head Teacher.

"What is it, Jacky?"

"Father, I am asking to go back to the free hostels."

"Absconders don't go back to the free hostels," I said. "They go back to the main building."

"I know," he said, "but I can't pray and study in the main building. There's too much noise."

I knew that Jacky was spending much time in prayer and study, when he wasn't playing football.

"You can go back to the hostels," I said. "Are you in earnest, Jacky?"

"I'm in earnest, father. I am determined to be a priest."

So Jacky went back to the hostels. He was an exemplary character, quiet and obedient, and spent much time by himself, praying and reading. The most extraordinary outward change was in his bodily cleanliness; he looked wholesome, and his face was shining. He washed and ironed his clothes every few days, which was really against the rules. He made more progress in school than his intelligence promised, and asked if he could preach in the hostels, where he had a small band of disciples. There was nothing extreme about it, for he spoke quietly of his own conversion, and asked others to follow his example before it was too late; in the meantime he went on playing his magnificent football. So he continued for some months, and it appeared that some deep change had taken place in his life, and that he thought nothing of the long period of training that stretched out before him, so long as he could become a priest.

Therefore it was a disappointment when he failed one day to appear at the evening parade of all free boys. The Head Teacher brought him to me.

"Why were you not at parade, Jacky?"

"It was the voice," he said.

"What did it tell you, Jacky?"

"It told me to go and pray, father."

"Where?"

"Down at the trees by the stables."

"A priest must obey the laws," I said.

"I know, father."

"Therefore," I said, "if this voice tells you again to go and pray, you will go at once and ask your teacher's permission."

"I promise it, father."

So Jacky continued again for some months, washing and ironing his clothes, working hard at school, playing hard at football, and preaching once a week at the hostels. Then he failed again to appear at the parade. The Head Teacher sent at once to the trees by the stables, but no Jacky was there.

"Have you thought, sir," asked the Head Teacher diffidently, "that he might be smoking *dagga*?"

Now although the smoking of *dagga* is common in our cities, and although it is one of the great reformatory enemies, I was shaken, and said, "What makes you think that?"

"Sometimes his manner is strange," he said.

And that of course is the great sign, after the smell of the weed itself; for the humble come out with sudden insolence, and the obedient with sudden disobedience, the open-hearted become secretive, the gay sullen.

The next morning he brought Jacky to me.

"Well, Jacky?"

"Father?"

"Where were you yesterday?"

"In the trees by the stables, father."

"Praying?"

"Yes, father."

I looked him in the eyes for some time, but he could not endure it.

"Jacky."

"Yes, father."

"We searched in the trees by the stables."

He did not maintain that we had searched inefficiently, nor did he pretend that he was in some other trees. He watched me anxiously, almost humbly.

"Would you lie to me?" I asked.

And he said in a subdued voice, "No, father."

"Have you been smoking *dagga*?"

He winced. The question was a hard blow to him. He would not look at me, but kept his eyes on the ground.

"Answer me, Jacky."

"I smoked it," he said.

I was silent a long time, so that he might feel that his admission had shocked me.

"You want to be a priest?"

"Yes, father."

"You want to be a priest," I said, "and you want to smoke *dagga* also."

My voice rose, and he turned his face away from me.

"But it cannot be done," I said.

He looked at me with anguish.

"You are forcing me," I said, "you are forcing me to take away your freedom and send you to some other job."

"No, no," he said. He dropped on his knees in the office and began to pray silently. It was a strange thing to be there. When he was finished, he rose and said to me earnestly, "I do not want to smoke *dagga*."

"How many more chances do you want?" I said.

"One, father."

"You can have it," I said.

Yet of all reformatory enemies, *dagga* is the most insidious. It tempts free boys to break bounds, and to go seeking it in Pimville, Kliptown, and Orlando. It tempts them to steal goods, especially clothes, which they trade for the terrible weed. And Jacky's next offence was to steal a jacket from one of the hostels, and to sell it in Orlando. So he was brought to me again. But this time it was a Special Court, which we used when we wished to bring home to a boy the gravity of an offence. The Principal and the Vice-Principal were there, and the Chief Supervisor, the African Head Teacher, and the Tailoring Instructor. When Jacky came in, he was shocked to see us all.

He pleaded guilty to the offences of theft and buying *dagga,* so that there was nothing to do but to decide how to deal with him. After the long discussion I said to him, "The Court does not say you cannot be a priest. But it says you must go back to the Main Building, and lose your freedom, and that you must go back to your tailoring. Yet if you are after some time still determined to be a priest, you will be allowed to return to the hostels and the school."

Jacky looked at us as though he could not believe it, as though he could not believe in such a punishment. He could not speak, and it was uncomfortable to look at him.

"The football," said Jacky, hoarsely.

"What about the football, Jacky?"

"Couldn't you take away the football?" he said. "Couldn't you take the freedom? But not the school, not the school."

It was painful to listen to him, so I looked at my fellow judges, but like judges, they were impassive. Left to ourselves, we might have done something; left to myself, I might have done something. But I had asked them to judge, and I could not speak first; and I was the Principal, so perhaps they felt they could not speak first either. So society and the law were not moved. Jacky was taken away, the thief recompensed, the priest defeated.

Shortly afterwards Jacky attacked the head-boy of the Tailor's Shop with a pair of scissors, and escaped into the trees. He was arrested in Pretoria for housebreaking, but this time he was sent to prison for six months. I had a letter from him there, repenting of all past follies, and saying that he was still determined to be a priest. The letter was earnest and penitent, and I had no doubt that the struggle was still being waged; therefore I answered with words of encouragement, telling him that he could come back to us if he wished. Yet I knew that the boy who wrote the letter would, so far as men knew, always be defeated, till one day he would give up both hope and ghost, and leave to his enemy the sole tenancy of the divided house.

THE UNIVERSAL FEARS

John Hawkes

Monday morning, bright as the birds, and there he stood for the first time among the twenty-seven girls who, if he had only known, were already playing the silence game. He looked at them, they looked at him, he never thought of getting a good grip on the pointer laid out lengthwise on that bare desk. Twenty-seven teen-age girls—homeless, bad-off, unloved, semi-literate, and each one of their poor unattractive faces was a condemnation of him, of all such schools for delinquent girls, of the dockyards lying round them like a seacoast of iron cranes, of the sunlight knifing through the grilles on the windows. They weren't faces to make you smile. Their sexual definition was vague and bleak. Hostile. But even then, in their first institutional moment together, he knew he didn't offer them any better from their point of view—only another fat man in the mid-fifties whose maleness meant nothing more than pants and jacket and belted belly and thin hair blacked with a cheap dye and brushed flat to the skull. Nothing in the new teacher to sigh about. So it was tit for tat, for them the desolation of more of the same, for him the deflation of the first glance that destroyed the possibility of finding just one keen lovely face to make the whole dreary thing worthwhile. Or a body promising a good shape to come. Or one set of sensual lips. Or one sign of adult responsiveness in any of those small eyes. But there was nothing, except the thought that perhaps their very sullenness might actually provide the most provocative landscape for the discovery of the special chemistry of pain that belongs to girls. Still he was already sweating in the armpits and going dry in the mouth.

"Right, girls," he said, "let's come to order."

In a shabby display of friendliness, accessibility, confidence, he slid from behind the desk and stood leaning the back of his upper thighs against the front edge of it. Through the south window came the sounds of whistles and windlasses, from closer came the sounds of unloading coal. It made him think of a prison within a prison. No doubt the docks were considered the most suitable context for a school, so-called, for girls like these. Yes, the smells of brine and tar and buckets of oil that rode faintly in on the knifing light were only complementary to the stench of the room, to the soap, the thick shellac, the breath of the girls, the smell of their hair. It was a man's world for an apparently sexless lot of girls, and there was only one exotic aroma to be caught on that tide: the flowery wash of the sweet bay rum that clung to the thick embarrassed person of their old teacher new on the job.

"Right, girls," he said, returning warm glance for hostile stare, tic-like winks for the smoky and steady appraisal of small eyes, "right now, let's start with a few names. . . ."

And there they sat, unmoving, silent, ranked at three wooden benches of nine girls each, and all of their faces, whether large or small, thin or broad, dark or light, were blank as paper. Apparently they had made a pact before he entered the room to breathe in unison, so that now wherever he looked—first row on the left, first on the right—he was only too aware of the deliberate and ugly harmony of flat chests or full that were rising and falling slowly, casually, but always together.

Challenging the prof? Had they really agreed among themselves to be uncooperative? To give him a few bad minutes on the first day? Poor things, he thought, and crossed his fatty ankles, rested one flat hand on the uphill side of the belly, and then once more he looked them over at random, bearing down on a pair of shoulders like broken sticks, two thin lips bruised from chewing, a head of loose brown hair and another with a thin mane snarled in elastic bands, and some eyes without lashes, the closed books, claw marks evident on a sallow cheek.

"Girl on the end, there," he said all at once, stopping and swinging his attention back to the long black hair, the boy's shirt buttoned to the throat, the slanted eyes that never moved, "what's your name? Or you," he said, nodding at one of the younger ones, "what's yours?" He smiled, he waited, he shifted his glance from girl to girl, he began to make small but comforting gestures with the hand already resting on what he called his middle mound.

And then they attacked. The nearest bench was going over and coming his way like the side of a house undergoing demolition, and then the entire room was erupting not in noise but in the massed and silent motion of girls determined to drive their teacher out of the door, out of the school, and away, away, if they did not destroy him first right there on the floor. They leaped, they swung round the ends, tight-lipped they toppled against each other and rushed at him. He managed to raise his two hands to the defensive position, fingers fanned out in sheer disbelief and terror, but the cry with which he had thought to stop them merely stuck in his throat, while for an instant longer he stood there pushing air with his trembling outthrust hands. The girls tripped, charged from both sides of the room, swarmed over the fallen benches in the middle, dove with undeniable intent to seize and incapacitate his person.

The pointer, yes, the pointer, it flashed to his mind, invisibly it hovered within his reach, burned like a long thin weapon with which he might have struck them, stabbed them, beaten them, fended them off. But of course the pointer was behind him and he dared not turn, dared not drop the guard of his now frenzied hands. In an instant he saw it all—the moving girls between himself and the door, the impenetrable web of iron battened to each one of the dusty windows, and he knew there was no way out, no help. A shoe flew past his ear, a full-fifty tin of cigarettes hit the high ceiling above his head and exploded, rained down on him in his paralysis and the girls in their charge. No pointer, no handy instrument for self-defense, no assistance coming from anywhere.

And then the sound came on, adding to that turbulent pantomime the shrieks of their anger, so that what until this instant had been impending violence brimming in a bowl of unnatural silence, now became imminent brutality in a conventional context of the audionics of wrath. His own cry was stifled, his head was filled with the fury of that small mob.

"Annette . . . !"

"Deborah . . . !"

"Fuck off . . ."

"Now . . . now . . ."

"Kill him . . . !"

Despite their superior numbers they were not able to smother him in the first rush, and despite his own disbelief and fear he did not go down beneath them without a fight. Quite the contrary, because the first to reach him was of medium height, about fourteen, with her ribs showing through her jersey and a cheap bracelet twirling on her ankle. And before she could strike a blow he caught her in the crook of his left arm and locked her against his trembling belly and squeezed the life from her eyes, the breath from her lungs, the hate from her undersized constricted heart. He felt her warmth, her limpness, her terror. Then he relaxed the pressure of his arm and as the slight girl sank to his feet, he drove a doubled fist into the pimpled face of a young thick-lipped assailant whose auburn hair had been milked of its fire in long days and nights of dockyard rain. The nose broke, the mouth dissolved, his fist was ringed with blood and faded hair.

"You fucking old bastard," said a voice off his left shoulder, and then down he went with a knee in his ribs, arms around his neck and belly, a shod foot in the small of his back. For one more moment, while black seas washed over the deck and the clouds burst, the pit yawned, the molten light of the sun drained down as from a pink collapsing sack in the sky, he managed to keep to his all-fours. And it was exactly in this position that he opened his eyes, looked up, but only in time to receive full in the mouth the mighty downward blow of the small sharp fist of the slant-eyed girl whose name he had first requested. The black hair, the boy's gray workshirt buttoned tight around the neck, a look of steady intensity in the brown eyes, and the legs apart, the body bent slightly down, the elbow cocked, and then the aim, the frown, the little fist landing with unexpected force on the loose torn vulnerable mouth—yes, it was the same girl, no doubt of it.

Blood on the floor. Mouth full of broken china. A loud kick driven squarely between the buttocks. And still through the forests of pain he noted the little brassy zipper of someone's fly, a sock like striped candy, a flat bare stomach gouged by an old scar, bright red droplets making a random pattern on the open pages of an outmoded Form One Math. He tried to shake a straddling bony tormentor off his bruised back, bore another shock to the head, another punch in the side, and then he went soft, dropped, rolled over, tried to shield his face with his shoulder, cupped both hurt hands over the last of the male features hiding down there between his legs.

They piled on. He saw the sudden blade of a knife. They dragged each other off, they screamed. He groaned. He tried to worm his heavy beaten way toward the door. He tried to defend himself with hip, with elbow. And beneath that struggling mass of girls he began to feel his fat and wounded body slowing down, stopping, becoming only a still wet shadow on the rough and splintered wood of the classroom floor. And now and then through the shrieking he heard the distant voices.

"Cathy . . ."

"Eleanora . . ."

"Get his fucking globes . . ."

"Get the globes . . ."

They pushed, they pulled, they tugged, and then with his eyes squeezed shut he knew suddenly that they were beginning to work together in some terrible accord that depended on childish unspoken intelligence, cruel cooperation. He heard the hissing of the birds, he felt their hands. They turned him over—face up, belly up—and sat on his still-breathing carcass. One of them tore loose his necktie of cream-colored and magenta silk while simultaneously his only white shirt, fabric bleached and weakened by the innumerable Sunday washings he had given it in his small lavatory sink, split in a long clean easy tear from his neck to navel. They flung his already mangled spectacles against the blackboard. They removed one shoe, one sock, and yanked the shabby jacket off his right shoulder and bounced up and down on his sagging knees, dug fingernails into the exposed white bareness of his right breast. Momentarily his left eye came unstuck and through the film of his tears he noted that the ringleader was the girl with the auburn hair and broken nose. She was riding his thighs, her sleeves were rolled, her thick lower lip was caught between her teeth in a parody of schoolgirl concentration, despite her injury and the blood on her face. It occurred to him that her pale hair deserved the sun. But then he felt a jolt in the middle, a jolt at the hips, and of course he had known all along that it was his pants they were after, pants and underpants. Then she had them halfway down, and he smelled her cheap scent, heard their gasping laughter, and felt the point of the clasp knife pierce his groin.

"He's fucking fat, he is . . ."

"The old suck . . ."

In his welter of pain and humiliation he writhed but did not cry out, writhed but made no final effort to heave them off, to stop the knife. What was the use? And wasn't he aware at last that all his poor street girls were actually bent to an operation of love not murder? Mutilated, demeaned, room a shambles and teacher overcome, still he knew in his fluid and sinking consciousness that all his young maenads were trying only to feast on love.

"Off him! Off him! came the loud and menacing voice fom the doorway while he, who no longer wanted saving, commenced a long low moan.

"Get away from him at once, you little bitches . . . !"

There he was, lying precisely as the victim lies, helplessly inseparable from the sprawled and bloodied shape the victim makes in the middle of the avenue at the foot of the trembling omnibus. He was blind. He could not move, could not speak. But in customary fashion he had the distinct impression of his mangled self as noted, say, from the doorway where the director stood. Yes, it was all perfectly clear. He was quite capable of surveying what the director surveyed—the naked foot, the abandoned knife, the blood like a pattern spread beneath the body, the soft dismembered carcass fouling the torn shirt and crumpled pants. The remnants of significant male anatomy were still in hiding, dazed, anesthetized, but the pinched white hairy groin, still bleeding, was calling itself to his passive consciousness while beckoning the director to a long proud glance of disapproval, scorn, distaste.

Gongs rang, the ambulance came and went, he lay alone on the floor. Had the girls fled? Or were they simply backed against those dusty walls with legs crossed and thumbs hooked in leather belts, casually defying the man in the doorway? Or silent, sullen, knowing the worst was yet to come for them, perhaps they were simply trying to right the benches, repair the room. In any case he was too bruised to regret the hands that did not reach for him, the white ambulance that would forever pass him by.

"Sovrowsky, Coletta, Rivers, Fiume," said the director from his point of authority at the door. "Pick him up. Fix his pants. Follow me. You bitches."

In the otherwise empty room off the director's office was an old leather couch, there not merely for the girls' cramps but, more important, for the director's rest, a fact which he knew intuitively and immediately the moment he came awake and felt beneath him the pinched and puffy leather surface of the listing couch. And now the couch was bearing him down

the dirty tide and he was conscious enough of adding new blood to fad-
ing stains.

Somebody was matter-of-factly brushing the cut above his eye with the
flaming tip of a long and treacherous needle. And this same person, he
discovered in the next moment, was pouring a hot and humiliating syrup
into the wounds in his groin.

"Look at him," murmured the thin young woman, and made another
stroke, another daub at the eye, "look at him, he's coming around."

Seeing the old emergency kit opened and breathing off ammonia on
the young woman's knees pressed close together, and furthermore,
seeing the tape and scissors in the young woman's bony hands and hearing the tape, seeing the long bite of the scissors, it was then that he did
indeed come round, as his helpful young colleague had said, and rolled
one gelatinous quarter-turn to the edge of the couch and vomited fully
and heavily into the sluggish tide down which he still felt himself sailing,
awake or not. His vomit missed the thin black-stockinged legs and narrow flat-heeled shoes of the young teacher seated beside him.

"I warned you," the director was saying, "I told you they were dangerous. I told you they beat your predecessor nearly to death. How do
you think we had your opening? And now it's not at all clear you can
handle the job. You might have been killed. . . ."

"Next time they'll kill him, rightly enough," said the young woman,
raising her brows and speaking through the cheap tin nasal funnel of her
narrow mouth and laying on another foot-long strip of tape.

Slowly, lying half on his belly, sinking in the vast hurt of his depthless
belly, he managed to lift his head and raise his eyes for one long dismal
stare at the impassive face of the director.

"I can handle the job," he whispered, just as vomiting started up again
from the pit of his life. From somewhere in the depths of the building he
heard the rising screams of the girl with the thick lips, auburn hair, and
broken nose.

He was most seriously injured, as it turned out, not in the groin or
flanks or belly, but in the head. And the amateurish and careless ministra-
tions of the cadaverous young female teacher were insufficient, as even
the director recognized. So they recovered his cream and magenta tie
which he stuffed into his jacket pocket, helped to replace the missing
shoe and sock, draped his shoulders in an old and hairy blanket, and
together steadied him down to his own small ancient automobile in which
the young female teacher drove him to the hospital. There he submitted
himself to something under two hours of waiting and three at least of
professional care, noting in the midst of fresh pain and the smells of
antiseptic how the young teacher stood by to see the handiwork of her
own first aid destroyed, the long strips of tape pulled off brusquely with

the help of cotton swabs and a bottle of cold alcohol, and the head rather than chest or groin wrapped in endless footage of soft gauze and new strips of official tape. He felt the muffling of the ears, the thickening sensation of the gauze going round the top of his head and down his swollen cheeks, was aware of the care taken to leave stark minimal openings for the eyes, the nose, the battered mouth.

"Well," muttered the medical student entrusted with this operation of sculpting and binding the head in its helmet and face-mask of white bandages, "somebody did a job on you, all right."

No sooner had he entered the flat than his little dog Murphy, or Murph for short, glanced at the enormous white hive of antiseptic bandages and then scampered behind the conveniently open downstairs door of the china cabinet, making a thin and steady cry of uncommonly high pitch. He had frightened his own poor little dog, he with his great white head, and now he heard Murph clawing at the lower inside rear wall of the china cabinet and, leaning just inside his own doorway, became freshly nauseous, freshly weak.

"Come out, Murph," he tried to say, "it's me." But within its portable padded cell of bandage, his muffled voice was as wordless as Murphy's. From within the cabinet came the slow circular sounds of Murphy's claws, still accompanied by the steady shrill music of the little animal's panic, so that within the yet larger context of his own personal shock, he knew at once that he must devote himself to convincing the little dog that the man inside the bandages was familiar and unchanged. It could take days.

"Murphy," he meant to say, "shut your eyes, smell my hands, trust me, Murph." But even to his own steady ear the appeal sounded only like a faint wind trapped in the mouth of a mute.

It was dusk, his insulated and mummified head was floating, throbbing, while the rest of him, the masses of beaten and lacerated flesh beneath the disheveled clothes, cried out for sleep and small soft hands to press against him and slowly eliminate, by tender touch, these unfamiliar aches, these heavy pains. He wanted to lie forever on his iron bed, to sit swathed and protected in his broken-down padded chair with Murph on his lap. But the night was inimical, approaching, descending, filling space everywhere, and the flat no longer felt his own. The chair would be as hard as the bed, as unfamiliar, and even Murphy's latest hectic guilt-ridden trail of constraint and relief appeared to have been laid down by somebody else's uncontrollable household pet. Why did the window of his flat give onto the same dockyard scene, though further away and at a different angle, as the window of the schoolroom in which he had all but died? Why didn't he switch on a light, prepare his usual tea, put water in

Murphy's bowl? A few minutes later, on hands and knees and with his heavy white head ready to sink to the floor, he suddenly realized that injury attacks identity, which was why, he now knew, that assault was a crime.

He did his clean-up job on hands and knees, he made no further effort to entice his dog from the china cabinet, he found himself wondering why the young teacher had allowed him to climb to the waiting and faintly kennelish-smelling flat alone. When he had dropped the last of poor little bewhiskered Murphy's fallen fruit into a paper sack now puffy with air and unavoidable waste, and in pain and darkness had sealed the sack and disposed of it in the tin pail beneath the sink, he slowly dragged himself to the side of the iron bed and then, more slowly still, hauled himself up and over. Shoes and all. Jacket and torn shirt and pants and all. Nausea and all. And lay on his side. And for the first time allowed the fingers of one hand to settle gently on the bandages that bound his head, and slowly and gently to touch, poke, caress, explore. Then at last, and with the same hand, he groped and drew to his chin the old yellow comforter that still exhaled the delicate scent of his dead mother.

Teacher Assaulted at Training School for Girls

Mr. Walter Jones, newly appointed to the staff of St. Dunster's Training School for Girls, received emergency treatment today at St. Dunster's Hospital for multiple bruises which, as Mr. Jones admitted and Dr. Smyth-Jones, director of the school, confirmed, were inflicted by the young female students in Mr. Jones's first class at the school. Mr. Jones's predecessor, Mr. William Smyth, was so severely injured by these same students November last that he has been forced into early and permanent retirement. Dr. Smyth-Jones expressed regret for both incidents, but indicated that Mr. Jones's place on the staff would be awaiting him upon his full and, it is to be hoped, early recovery. "The public," he commented, "little appreciates the obstacles faced by educators at a school such as St. Dunster's. After all, within the system for the rehabilitation of criminally inclined female minors, St. Dunster's has been singled out to receive only the most intractable of girls. Occasional injury to our staff and to the girls themselves is clearly unavoidable."

With both hands on the wheel and Murph on his lap and a large soft-brimmed felt hat covering a good half of the offending white head, in this condition and full into the sun he slowly and cautiously drove the tortuous cobbled route toward Rose And Thyme, that brutally distended low-pitted slab of tenements into which his father, Old Jack, as he was

known by all, had long since cut his filthy niche. The sun on the roof of
the small old coffin of a car was warm, the narrow and dusty interior was
filled with the hovering aroma of fresh petrol, and Murph, with his nose
raised just to the level of the glass on the driver's side, was bobbing and
squirming gently to the rhythm first of the footbrake and then the clutch.
As for himself, and aside from the welcome heat of the little dog and the
ice and glitter of the new day, it gave him special pleasure to be driving
cautiously along with a lighted cigarette protruding from the mouth-slit in
the bandages and, now and again, his entire head turning to give some
timorous old woman the whole shock full in the face. He was only too
conscious that he could move, that he could drive the car, that he filled
the roaring but slowly moving vehicle with his bulk and age, that Murph's
tiny pointed salt-and-pepper ears rose just above the edge of the window, and then was only too conscious, suddenly, of the forgotten girls.

Why, he asked himself, had he forgotten the girls? Why had he forced
from his mind so simply, so unintentionally, the very girls whose entry
into his life had been so briefly welcome, so briefly violent? Would he
give up? Would he see them again? But why had he applied for that job
in the first place? Surely he had not been going his own way, finally, after
what his nimble old Dad called the juicy rough. All this pain and confusion for easy sex? Not a bit of it.

And then, making a difficult turn and drawing up behind a narrow
flat-bedded lorry loaded down with stone and chugging, crawling, suddenly he saw it all, saw himself standing in Old Jack's doorway with
Murph in his arms, saw his nimble Dad spring back, small and sallow face
already contorted into the familiar look of alarm, and duck and turn, and
from somewhere in the unchartered litter of that filthy room whip out his
trench knife and standing there against the peeling wall with his knees
knocking and weapon high and face contorted into that expression of
fear and grievous pride common to most of those who lived in the ruin
and desolation of Rose and Thyme. Then he heard the silent voices as
the little old man threw down the trench knife and wiped his little beak
and small square toothless mouth down the length of his bare arm.

It's you, is it?

Just me, Dad. Come to visit.

*You might know better than to be stalking up here like some telly
monster with that head of yours and that dead dog in your arms.*

Murph's all right, Jack. Aren't you, Murph?

*It's that school, that fucking school. My own son beaten near to death
by a bunch of girls and written up in the papers. I read it, the whole sad
story. And then stalking up here like a murderous monster.*

*They're very strong girls. And there were a lot of them. Twenty-seven
actually.*

Why were you there? Tell me why, eh? Oh, the Good Samaritan. . . .
Yes, the Good Samaritan.
Or were you really after a little juicy rough?
Mere sex? Not a bit of it. Of course I wouldn't rule out possibilities, but
there's more than that.
Juicy rough. Walter, juicy rough. Don't lie.
I believe I want to know how those girls exist without romance. Or do
they?
Use the glove, Walter! Let me give you the old fur glove. It does a
lovely job. You can borrow it. . . .

"Yes," he heard himself musing aloud from within the bundle of antiseptic stuffing that was his head, and pressing first the brake and then
the accelerator, "yes, I want to be at the bottom where those girls are.
Without romance."

At a faster pace now and passing the lorry, he headed the little dark
blue car once more in the direction from which he and Murphy had
started out in the first place. Occasionally it was preferable to meet Old
Jack not in the flesh but in the mind, he told himself, and this very moment was a case in point.

"No," said the young female teacher in the otherwise empty corridor,
"it's you! And still in bandages."

"On the stroke of eight," he heard himself saying through the mouth-
slit, which he had enlarged progressively with his fingers. "I'm always
punctual."

"But you're not ready to come back. Just look at you."

"Ready enough. They couldn't keep me away."

"Wait," she said then, her voice jumping at him and her face full of
alarm, "don't go in there . . . !"

"Must," he said, and shook her off, reached out, opened the door.

The same room. The same grilled and dusty windows. The same
machinery in spidery operation in the vista beyond. Yes, it might have
been his first day, his first morning, except that he recognized them and
picked them out one by one from the silent rows—the narrow slant-eyed
face, the girl with tuberculosis of the bone, the auburn-haired ringleader
who had held the knife. Yes, all the same, except that the ringleader was
wearing a large piece of sticking plaster across her nose. Even a name or
two came back to him and for an instant these names evoked the
shadowy partial poem of the forgotten rest. But named or unnamed their
eyes were on him, as before, and though they could not know it, he was
smiling in the same old suit and flaming tie and dusty pointed shoes. Yes,
they knew who he was, and he in turn knew all about their silence game
and actually was counting on the ugliness, the surprise, of the fully

bandaged head to put them off, to serve as a measure of what they had done and all he had forgiven even before they had struck, to serve them as the first sign of courage and trust.

"Now, girls," he said in a voice they could not hear, "if you'll take out pencils and paper and listen attentively, we'll just begin." Across the room the pointer was lying on the old familiar desk like a sword in the light.

HERO'S RETURN

Kristin Hunter

I tell you, I was about to explode, I was so excited when I heard my big brother Junior was coming home.

Junior spent eighteen months in the House. He took out a long stretch, cause somebody shot off a gun the day Junior and his corner boys held up the Kravitz's ice-cream store. Nobody got hurt, but Mrs. Kravitz hollered like somebody had killed her. The others got away, and Junior caught the whole blame. It was enough to put him away for a long, long time.

My corner boys were real impressed when I told them. Course they acted like it wasn't nothing, like any one of them could do eighteen months standing on his head. But they were impressed right on, and jealous besides, not having a brother like Junior nor anybody else famous in the family.

I remember the headline—*Aging Couple Robbed*—and Junior's picture in the paper. I cut it out and saved it. It's still in my snapshot album that I never did put any other pictures in cause I never got the camera. My brother was big stuff. Front-page stuff. And now he was coming home.

Josh he acted like it weren't nothing. "Eighteen months?" he said. "What's that? I hear you get your own TV in the House, and your own room."

No ghetto kid has his own room, except me after Junior went away. And now he was coming home, and me glad to share it with him again.

"Yeah," says Marquis, "I hear tell they have ice cream every night up there. Double scoops on Sundays. And people come around and give them cigarettes, things like that."

We only used to get ice cream when we found enough soda bottles to return to the store. And now they got those No Deposit No Return bottles, we don't hardly ever get none unless somebody's Mom gives him a dime. If she does, you got to run all the way home to eat it by yourself, else fight some bigger kids for it. And even if you get past the big guys, there's your boys, Josh and Duke and Leroy and Marquis, all wanting to take turns licking off your ice-cream cone.

"Man, I ain't studying no ice cream," said Leroy. He acts like he's the baddest thing on McCarter Street just cause he's thirteen and the rest of us is only twelve. "I could use some cigarettes, though."

This was one time I was with Leroy. I don't think about ice cream much no more cause I don't like to go in Kravitz's store since it hap-

267

pened. I favor my brother in the face, and old Mrs. Kravitz might start yelling her head off again. You can get cigarettes anywhere.

But we don't never have enough money, unless King or one of the other big-time hustlers on the corner gives us some to run an errand. The other hustlers only give us fifty cents, but sometimes King gives a whole dollar. I seen him take a roll of money thick as my fist out of his pocket plenty of times.

We were standing around that July morning, waiting for King to show up, hoping he would give one of us something to do. We all want to be hustlers when we grow up. A hustler is somebody who lives by his wits, you might say, and King was the king of them all.

It was hot enough to boil water on the sidewalk that morning, and my foot was blistered from a hole in my sneaks. I was thinking, Maybe when Junior gets home he'll pull off another job and get me a new pair, when King glides up to the curb in his white air-conditioned Hog.

The Cadillac was about half a block long, and a sharp fox in a blonde wig was sitting beside King. He looked cool as an ice cube in there, his wavy hair shining and diamonds flashing on his hands.

"Hey, you boy. Come here!" He flicked a little button in the Hog, and the window slid down easy as greased silk. Josh and Duke and Leroy and Marquis all hit the sidewalk, but I had a head start in my sneakers, hole and all. I got to the car a full three feet ahead of them.

Then—man!—King shoved the girl out of the car and held open the door for *me*. I hopped in and closed the door, and we eased away from the curb. Leroy and Josh and Duke and Marquis were left standin' there with their mouths hangin' open.

"Have a cigarette, kid," King said, and handed me a pack of Marlboros with the top flipped up. But what was inside didn't look like no Marlboros. The paper was pink and it had been rolled by hand.

King handed me the dashboard lighter. I lit up and held the smoke in.

King lit a real Marlboro and leaned back, steering the Hog through tight traffic with one hand. "Kid," he said, "you got to the car first, so you must be the most ambitious one on the corner. You want to get ahead in this world?"

I nodded. I couldn't speak cause the smoke had me all choked up inside.

"Well," King said, "how'd you like to be my right-hand man?"

"Yes!" I cried.

"All you got to do," King said, "is pass this stuff out among the kids." And he pulls a plastic bag out from under the seat. "When they want more, you come back to me. I'll tell you what to charge 'em."

And then King pulled that big old wad out of his pocket and plucked off a crisp new five and handed it to me. My eyes popped. But I didn't lose my cool. Just sat back and inhaled that pink cigarette like a man.

It was making me feel like a man too. Like I could do anything. I put the five in the pocket of my jeans and sucked in the smoke and held it in like I seen Leroy do one time. I felt ten feet tall, higher than high. Way above the funky scuffling people we were cruising by on Madison.

"Man," I said to King, "this is some good stuff."

"Oughta be. It came all the way from Panama," King said. "Listen, kid. The cops don't exactly dig this action, you understand?"

"I'm hip," I said.

"Don't let any of 'em catch you with it. And don't smoke it all yourself, neither."

"Don't worry, King. I'll take care of business," I told him.

"Good," King said and grinned. The wrinkles in his handsome face sank in and made it look like a skull. "You were the one I wanted, kid, you know that? I just didn't know your name."

That made me feel good, but at the same time I got a funny feeling in the stomach. Like when I've had some corn chips and a cherry soda and Mom puts a big platter on the table and I can't eat.

King was waving at people and honking his horn. Everybody stopped what they were doing and waved back. King's the biggest man in town. Everybody wants to know him. And there I was, riding right beside him.

Then he turned sharp into McCarter, and there on the corner was Junior. Thinner than when I saw him last, and with dark smudges under his eyes. But he was *home.*

"I got to get out now, King," I said. "That's my brother over there." Junior looked up and saw me.

"Jody!" he cried and took a step toward me. I had meant to shake hands, the way men do, but instead I flew at him and we hugged right there on the street. My head used to just hit the middle of his chest, but now it touched his chin.

We stepped back, kind of embarrassed, and shook hands like I had meant to do in the first place.

"Boy," he said, "you must've grown a foot. Keep it up, you be tall as me."

And he laughed and rubbed my head. But his eyes were all squinched up like he was trying to keep tears back. I didn't like to see him looking like that, so I started talking fast.

"Did they treat you all right at the House, Junior? I bet you made 'em respect you. I bet they knew you weren't no one to mess with. Didn't they, Junior?"

"I don't want to talk about it," he said. "What were you doing in that car?"

The big Hog with the special-made front license plate, *KING,* was still parked at the corner.

"Tell you later," I said, though I was busting to tell him then. "I want to hear how you made out in the slammer."

"Let's get home," he said. But before we could, Duke and Leroy and Josh and Marquis came running up. They surrounded us and pelted Junior with questions.

"Did they give you a TV, man?"

"How was the food? Good?"

"Who'd you meet in there? Any of the big cats?"

"Yeah, I bet you got connections now. I bet you ready for the big time."

Them guys. Sometimes I wish they would leave a guy alone. But they my boys, and they was as excited to see him as I was.

Junior just kept steady walkin', his mouth set in a tight line, saying nothing to the guys until they gave up and fell back. We got to our building. And there over the door was a big cardboard sign Mom had lettered in crayon: WELCOME HOME SON. Just like they do for the heroes that come back from Vietnam.

Junior stood and stared at the sign for a minute. Then he stepped over the kids that are always hanging around out front and yanked the sign down. He ripped it in four pieces and dropped it in the gutter.

"Junior!" I hollered. "What you want to do that for? You'll make Mom feel bad."

"I already made her feel bad," he said. "Come on." He pushed me ahead of him into the hallway.

"You didn't even speak to nobody," I complained. "Josh and Leroy and them, and your old ace Tom Cat, and old Mr. Baltimore. And Mrs. Walters. She was sittin' in the front window like always. You didn't even speak to *her.* They all want to see you, Junior. They been askin' about you while you been away."

"I spoke to *you,* didn't I?" he said. "Which door is it?"

Our building has so many apartments in it I lost count. Still, it was kind of a shock that Junior didn't remember his own apartment door. Made me realize how long he'd been away. And how far, even though you can reach the House by the number 14 bus.

"One more flight up," I told him. When we got there I didn't have to give him any more directions.

Mom was standing in the door with her arms held out in welcome. Junior tried to push past her and get inside, but she had to give him a hug and have her a cry right there. People from the other apartments were watching. I was embarrassed, so I pushed between Mom and Junior and got through the door. That separated them.

Mom stepped back into the apartment. Junior followed her and shut the door real quick behind him. He locked all the locks, the bolt and the chain lock and the police lock that goes right down into the floor. Like he didn't want to ever let anybody in again.

"Lord, child, let me look at you," Mom said when she had dried her eyes on her apron. "Looks like you didn't hardly get enough to eat in that place."

That bothered me some, to tell you the truth. It wasn't at all like what Leroy and them had been saying. But maybe it was just that Junior had lost all his baby fat and was getting lean and hard.

He stood there in the middle of the floor like he hadn't really come to stay and was planning to leave any second. It kept Mom from fussing over him anymore. She started fussing over the stove instead, measuring rice and stirring the chicken and okra. Man! It sure smelled delicious. Suddenly I was real hungry.

"Stewed chicken and okra tonight, honey," she said to Junior. "Your favorite supper. And later I got some people coming in who want to see my son."

"I don't want to see any people," Junior said. "I'm kind of tired. I'm going to take me a little rest."

And without another word he went into our room and shut the door.

"Anything you say, son," Mom said. But he didn't hear her. He had already slammed the bedroom door.

Pretty soon she started crying again. I couldn't stand that, so I took a beer out of the ice box and went to the room and knocked.

"Is that you, Jody?"

"Yes."

"Come in."

"I thought you might like a beer," I said, shutting the door behind me.

"Thanks," he said and took it. He didn't say any more, just lay on his back on his bed, staring at the ceiling. I sat on the edge of my bed and watched him for a while. The room was getting tenser by the minute.

"Planning a job, huh?" I finally said.

"I can't get a job. I've got a record."

"I mean a *big-time* job," I said. "Like you pulled off at Kravitz's, only bigger."

He rolled over and looked at me for the first time. "You think I'm a hero, don't you?" he said. "A big-shot crook. Like in the movies."

"Sure, Junior," I said eagerly. "All the guys do. They expect you to do

great things. You got the connections and the smarts now. You must
know a lot more than when you went in the House. You was only seventeen then. Now you're a man."

"Yeah, I'm a man," Junior said disgustedly, "and ain't a thing in this
town I can do. Nobody's going to hire a jailbird."

"It's all right," I said. "I can take care of us for a while, till you get
yourself together."

I pulled out the five and showed it to him.

He was up on his feet, standing over me. "Where'd you get that?"

Something in his manner scared me, but I went on. "King gave it to
me. And I'm going to make a lot more. Selling this." I pulled the plastic
bag out of my pocket. "It's—"

"I know what it is," Junior said and took off his belt. "Go flush it down
the toilet."

"But, Junior—"

He gave me a whack with the back of his hand. It caught me by surprise and sent me sprawling on the floor.

"Flush it, I said. And come right back here when you finished."

I trembled, cause I knew what was coming. He had the belt in his
hand, folded over double. My face was stinging from the whack, and I
was beginning to cry, more from surprise than anything else. But on my
way to the bathroom and back I didn't let Mom see me.

Junior was waiting for me when I got back. "So you want to go to jail,
huh? All right, I'll show you what jail is like."

He locked the door from the inside and gave me the worst whipping I
ever had in my life. The only one, in fact. Pop left home before I was
born, and Mom was always too kindhearted to beat us.

She had heard me yelling and was at the door, banging on it to be let
in. "Junior, what's going on in there? What you doing to my baby?"

"Saving him, that's what," Junior yelled back through the door. "If he
ain't already ruint."

He didn't open the door, either. He went right on whipping me. When
he was through, he said, "You going to stay away from that slick hustler,
huh? You going to stay off that corner and leave those pint-size hoods
alone?"

I didn't answer, I was so mad.

"All right. You got a week to think about it." He shut the door behind
him and locked me in.

"What you doing to my baby?" Mom cried again.

Junior said, "He wants to go to jail. So let him try it for a few days. Let
him live on bread and water and stay in solitary and get knocked around
every time he opens his mouth."

Mom let out a wail that sounded like a police siren, but it didn't change

Junior's mind. He brought me bread and water for supper and took out the mattresses so he could sleep on them in the front room. *I* would sleep on the springs and get a taste of what a prison bed was like.

He explained it all to me patiently, like he wasn't angry anymore. "The small-time crooks, they get to talk to each other. But the real big-time criminals like you get solitary. And if they *real* bad actors, the guards take the springs out of the cell too. Then they sleep on the floor. I'm your guard. And if you a bad actor, I get to knock you around. Understand?"

But that was all he would say. Once or twice he knocked me around a little, just to show me it wasn't a game. The rest of the time, he didn't say or do nothing. Just brought the bread and water and took me to the bathroom.

I got so lonesome in there I wished he would come in, even to beat me. The old bedsprings stuck me no matter which way I turned, so I lay on the floor, thinking about stewed chicken and okra and having cramps in my belly. All I had to listen to was their arguments.

"You gonna kill him," Mom said.

"No," Junior told her. "He might get killed in jail. That happens to lots of guys. But this way he's gonna live."

"He's only a baby," she wailed.

"He's big enough to get in big trouble. I got home just in time."

The first night wasn't so bad. I expected Mom to come to my rescue any minute. But he wouldn't let her. In the morning I heard her going off to work. They would fire her if she took off two days in a row, so she had to go.

The second and third days, I lay there trying to remember boss things I'd done with the guys, like chasing girls in the park and stealing fruit and sneaking rides on the back of trucks. But pretty soon those things bored me too.

On the fourth day, I got some of my school books down from the closet and began reading. I even got interested in history.

Junior came in while I was lying on my stomach with the books open on the floor in front of me. For a scary moment I thought he was going to take it away. But he just looked at me. And then he smiled.

"Gonna be a big-time criminal like me?"

"No."

"Gonna drop out of school like I did?"

"No." I paused and thought very carefully, then surprised myself by what I said. "I think I might go to that tutoring place at Mom's church and make up math. I think I could pass it this time."

"What I think," Junior said, "is you ready to come out now. I'm gonna parole you. But you got to watch your step, you hear? No associating with known criminals. No messing up. A single slip, and back you go."

Then he fixed me a big breakfast. He explained that since we didn't have a father anymore, he had to be the man of the house. It made him feel good, he said, knowing at least part of what he had to do.

Then he let me go out on the street.

It looked different, like a place I hadn't seen in years and years. With all the slick people and crooks and hustlers, it looked like a place where I didn't want to stay very long.

"Hey, man," Leroy hollered at me, "where you been?"

I was still weak and wobbly in spite of the breakfast. But I felt stronger and older than Leroy and the others. I knew things they still had to learn. One thing I knew was if I ever made it off that corner, I would have to make it alone.

"I been," I said, "in jail."

Then I left them and went on my way, knowing where I was going and walking like a man.

Bibliography

Short Stories of Delinquency

ALGREN, NELSON. "A Bottle of Milk for Mother" (originally "Biceps"). In Nelson Algren, *The Neon Wilderness*. New York: Doubleday, 1947.

_____. "The Children." In Nelson Algren, *The Neon Wilderness*. New York: Doubleday, 1947.

_____. "A Lot You Got to Holler." In Nelson Algren, *The Neon Wilderness*. New York: Doubleday, 1947.

_____. "So Help Me." In Harold Ribalow, ed., *These Are Your Children*. New York: Beechhurst Press, 1952.

ANDERSON, SHERWOOD. "A Criminal's Christmas: The Confessions of a Youthful Offender Who, in Later Life, Became an Author." In Editors of Vanity Fair, *Short Stories from Vanity Fair, 1926–1927*. New York: Liveright, 1928.

_____. "I Want to Know Why." In A. Walton Litz, ed., *Major American Short Stories*. New York: Oxford University Press, 1975.

ARMSTRONG, CHARLOTTE. "And Already Lost." In Ellery Queen, ed., *Ellery Queen's Awards: Twelfth Series*. New York: Simon & Schuster, 1957.

BAKER, DOROTHY. "One Fine Day." In Helen Lamont, ed., *A Diamond of Years: The Best of the Woman's Home Companion*. New York: Doubleday, 1961.

BAR-YOSEF, YEHOSHUA. "The Lateborn." In Sholom J. Kahn, ed., *A Whole Loaf: Stories from Israel*. New York: Vanguard, 1957.

BELL, JOSEPHINE. "Murder Delayed." In John Creasey, ed., *Crimes Across the Sea: The 19th Annual Anthology of the Mystery Writers of America*. New York: Harper & Row, 1964.

BIGGLE, LLOYD, JR. "Who's on First?" In Lloyd Biggle, Jr., *A Galaxy of Strangers*. New York: Doubleday, 1976.

BLOCH, ROBERT. "Catnip." In Robert Bloch, *The Best of Robert Bloch*. New York: Ballantine, 1977.

_____. "Spawn of the Dark One" (originally "Sweet Sixteen"). In Peter Haining, ed., *The Satanists*. New York: Taplinger, 1969.

BLOCK, LAWRENCE. "The Gentle Way." In Allen J. Hubin, ed., *Best Detective Stories of the Year 1975: 29th Annual Collection*. New York: Dutton, 1975.

BOVA, BEN. "Blood of Tyrants." In Ben Bova, ed., *Forward in Time: A Science Fiction Story Collection*. New York: Walker, 1973.

BOWLES, PAUL FREDERICK. "Under the Sky." In Paul Frederick Bowles, *The Delicate Prey, and Other Stories*. New York: Random House, 1950.

BRENNAN, PETER. "The Criminal Type." In Whit and Hallie Burnett, eds., *The Stone Soldier: Prize College Stories, 1964*. New York: Fleet Press, 1964.

BRISKIN, MAE SEIDMAN. "The Boy Who Was Astrid's Mother." In Martha Foley, ed., *The Best American Short Stories, 1976*. Boston: Houghton Mifflin, 1976.

BROWN, FREDERIC. "Little Boy Lost." In Frederic Brown, ed., *The Shaggy Dog and Other Murders*. New York: Dutton, 1963.

CALLAGHAN, MORLEY EDWARD. "All the Years of Her Life." In Simon Certner and George H. Henry, eds., *Short Stories for Our Times*. Boston: Houghton Mifflin, 1950.

―――――. "Big Jules." In Edward J. O'Brien, ed., *Best Short Stories of 1941*. Boston: Houghton Mifflin, 1941.

CARLETON, MARJORIE. "Monday Is a Quiet Place." In Ellery Queen, ed., *Ellery Queen's Mystery Mix . . . #18: 20 Stories from Ellery Queen's Mystery Magazine*. New York: Random House, 1963.

CARVER, RAYMOND. "Bicycles, Muscles, Cigarets." In Raymond Carver, *Will You Please Be Quiet, Please?* New York: McGraw-Hill, 1976.

―――――. "Why, Honey?" In Raymond Carver, *Will You Please Be Quiet, Please?* New York: McGraw-Hill, 1976.

CASSILL, R. V. "War in the Air." In Paul Engle and Martin Hansford, eds., *Prize Stories, 1954: The O. Henry Awards*. New York: Doubleday, 1954.

CATHER, WILLA. "Paul's Case." In Willa Cather, *Five Stories*. New York: Vintage, 1956.

CHEEVER, JOHN. "The Pleasures of Solitude." In John Cheever, *The Way Some People Live*. New York: Random House, 1943.

CHESBRO, GEORGE. "Broken Pattern." In Allen J. Hubin, ed., *Best Detective Stories of the Year 1973: 27th Annual Collection*. New York: Dutton, 1973.

CHESSON, RAY. "You Can't Run Away." In Ellery Queen, ed., *Ellery Queen's Awards: 12th Series*. New York: Simon & Schuster, 1957.

CHUTE, MARY GRACE. "The Sheriff Sits One Out." In Mary Grace Chute, *Sheriff Olson*. New York: Appleton-Century-Crofts, 1942.

CLAYTON, JOHN BELL. "The White Circle." In John Bell Clayton, *The Strangers Were There: Selected Stories*. New York: Macmillian, 1957.

CLEAVER ELDRIDGE. "The Flashlight." In William Abrahams, ed., *Prize Stories, 1971: The O. Henry Awards*. New York: Doubleday, 1971.

COATES, ROBERT M. "Encounter in Illinois." In Robert M. Coates, *The Man Just Ahead of You.* New York: William Sloan, 1964.

COLTER, CYRUS. "Mary's Convert." In Cyrus Colter, *The Beach Umbrella.* Iowa City: University of Iowa Press, 1970.

CONNOLLY, MYLES. "The Big Red House on Hope Street." In Myles Connolly, *The Reason for Ann, and Other Stories.* Garden City, N.Y.: McMullen, 1953.

CRAWFORD, CONSTANCE. "The Boats." In Wallace Stegner and Richard Scowcroft, eds., *Twenty Years of Short Stories.* Stanford, Calif.: Stanford University Press, 1966.

DI SILVESTRO, JOHN. "Big Shots." In Ellery Queen, *Queen's Awards, 1949.* Boston: Little, Brown, 1949.

DOTY, WILLIAM LODEWICK. "Greatest of These." In William Lodewick Doty, *Stories for Discussion.* New York: Joseph F. Wagner, 1951.

ENRIGHT, ELIZABETH. "A Gift of Light." In Elizabeth Enright, *The Riddle of the Fly & Other Stories.* New York: Harcourt Brace Jovanovich, 1959.

FARRELL, JAMES T. "Boys and Girls." In James T. Farrell, *A Dangerous Woman, and Other Stories.* New York: Vanguard, 1957.

————. "Little Johnny: A Fable." In James T. Farrell, *A Dangerous Woman, and Other Stories.* New York: Vanguard, 1957.

————. "The Merry Clouters." In James T. Farrell, *Guillotine Party, and Other Stories.* New York: Vanguard, 1935.

————. "Tournament Star." In James T. Farrell, *When Boyhood Dreams Come True.* New York: Vanguard, 1946.

————. "Young Convicts." In James T. Farrell, *Omnibus of Short Stories.* New York: Vanguard, 1956.

FARSON, NEGLEY. "Expelled from Andover." In Robert J. Cadigan, ed., *September to June: Stories of School and College Life.* New York: Appleton-Century-Crofts, 1942.

FRANKLIN, MAX. "The Geniuses." In David C. Cooke, ed., *Best Detective Stories of the Year* (13th annual collection). New York: Dutton, 1958.

FRAZER, CHRIS. "Zydeco." In Whit Burnett, ed., *Black Hands on a White Face; a Timepiece of Experiences in a Black and White America.* New York: Dodd, Mead, 1971.

FRIEDMAN, PAUL. "Never Lose Your Cool." In Paul Friedman, *And If Defeated Allege Fraud.* Urbana: University of Illinois Press, 1971.

FULLER, CHARLES H. "A Love Song for Wing." In Woodie King, ed., *Black Short Story Anthology.* New York: Columbia University Press, 1972.

GARRETT, GEORGE. "The Last of the Spanish Blood." In George Garrett, *In the Briar Patch.* Austin: University of Texas Press, 1961.

GELLHORN, MARTHA ELLIS. "Ruby." In Martha Ellis Gellhorn, *The Trouble I've Seen.* New York: Morrow, 1936.

GHOSE, ZULFIKAR. "The Absences." In Kevin Crossley-Holland, ed., *Winter's Tales 14*. New York: St. Martin's, 1960.

GLANVILLE, BRIAN. "A Bad Streak." In A. D. Maclean, ed., *Winter's Tales 6*. New York: St. Martin's, 1960.

GLASS, ERIC. "Linus." In Peter Nevramont, ed., *The Great Lakes Anthology #2: A Collection of Undergraduate Creative Writing*. Yellow Springs, Ohio: Antioch Press, 1965.

GOLDBERG, LEWIS J. "Frank." In Charles I. Glicksberg, ed., *New Voices 4: American Writing Today*. New York: Hendricks House, 1960.

GREENBERG, JOANNE. "Rites of Passage." In Joanne Greenberg, *Rites of Passage*. New York: Holt, Rinehart & Winston, 1972.

GREENE, GRAHAM. "The Destructors." In Graham Greene, *21 Stories*. New York: Viking, 1962.

————. "A Marriage Proposal." In Graham Greene, *The Portable Graham Greene*. New York: Viking, 1973.

GREENWOOD, WALTER. "Any Bread, Cake or Pie?" In Walter Greenwood, *The Cleft Stick; or "It's the Same the World Over."* Palo Alto, Calif.: Stokes, 1938.

GROSSBERG, ELMER. "Black Boy's Good Time." In Herschell Brickell and Muriel Fuller, eds., *O. Henry Memorial Award Prize Stories of 1943*. New York: Doubleday, 1943.

HANER, R. "The Fix." In Robert Oberfirst, ed., *Anthology of Best Short-Short Stories*, vol. 6. New York: Frederick Fell, 1958.

HAWKES, JOHN. "The Universal Fears." In Joe David Bellamy, ed., *Superfiction, or The American Story Transformed*. New York: Vintage, 1975.

HELWIG, DAVID. "Something for Olivia's Scrapbook I Guess." In Donald Stephens, ed., *Contemporary Voices: The Short Story in Canada*. Englewood Cliffs, N.J.: Prentice-Hall, 1972.

HEMINGWAY, ERNEST. "The Last Good Country." In Ernest Hemingway, *The Nick Adams Stories*. New York: Scribner's, 1972.

HENDERSON, DION. "The Turning Point." In William H. Larson, ed., *Stand by for Adventure: Six Stories of Adventure*. Racine, Wisc.: Whitman, 1967.

HEYERT, MURRAY. "The New Kid." In Herschel Brickell, ed., *O. Henry Memorial Award Prize Stories of 1945*. New York: Doubleday, 1945.

HOWARD, CLARK. "Spook House." In Alfred Hitchcock, ed., *Alfred Hitchcock's Tales to Keep You Spellbound*, vol. 1. New York: Dial, 1976.

HUGHES, LANGSTON. "Junkies." In Langston Hughes, *Simple's Uncle Sam*. New York: Hill & Wang, 1965.

————. "Thank You, M'am." In Langston Hughes, *Something in Common, and Other Stories*. New York: Hill & Wang, 1963.

HUNT, HUGH ALLYN. "Acme Rooms and Sweet Marjorie Russell." In

Martha Foley, and David Burnett, eds., *The Best American Short Stories, 1967.* Boston: Houghton Mifflin, 1967.

HUNT, H. M. "Leila." In Kylie Tennant, ed., *Summer's Tales 2.* New York: St. Martin's, 1965.

HUNTER, EVAN. "First Offense." In David C. Cooke, ed., *Best Detective Stories of the Year—1965.* New York: Dutton, 1956.

―――――. "On the Sidewalk, Bleeding." In Evan Hunter, *Happy New Year, Herbie, and Other Stories.* New York: Simon & Schuster, 1963.

HUNTER, KRISTIN. "Hero's Return." In Kristin Hunter, *Guests in the Promised Land.* New York: Scribner's, 1973.

―――――. "The Pool Table Caper." In Kristin Hunter, *Guests in the Promised Land.* New York: Scribner's, 1973.

JOHNSON, HAROLD. "Rocky." In Ruth May Strang, and Ralph Myron Roberts, eds., *Teen-age Tales.* Boston: Heath, 1954.

JONES, LeROI (IMAMU AMIRI BARAKA). "The Death of Horatio Alger." In LeRoi Jones, *Tales.* New York: Grove, 1967.

KANTOR, MacKINLAY. "Unseen Witness." In Editors of Saturday Evening Post. *Saturday Evening Post Stories, 1954.* New York: Random House, 1954.

KELLY, MYRA. "A Bent Twig." In Myra Kelly, *Little Aliens.* New York: Scribner's, 1910.

KLIMEK, LESTER D. "Mood Music Rumble." In Robert Oberfirst, ed., *Anthology of Best Short-Short Stories,* vol. 6. New York: Frederick Fell, 1958.

LARNER, JEREMY. "Hector Rodriguez." In Tom and Susan Cahill, eds., *Big City Stories from Modern American Writers.* New York: Bantam, 1971.

LORD, JAMES. "The Boy Who Wrote No." In Cyril Connolly, ed., *Golden Horizon.* New York: British Book Centre, 1953.

LOWRY, ROBERT. "A Cruel Day." In Robert Lowry, *Party of Dreamers.* New York: Fleet Press, 1962.

LUCATELLI, LUIGI. "Law and the Malefactor." In Luigi Lucatelli, *Teodora the Sage.* Translated by Morris Bishop. New York: Boni & Liveright, 1923.

LYON, DANA. "Silence!" In Dean Dickensheet, ed., *Men and Malice: An Anthology of Mystery and Suspense by West Coast Writers.* New York: Doubleday, 1973.

MABRY, THOMAS DABNEY. "The Vault." In Martha Foley, ed., *The Best American Short Stories, 1949.* Boston: Houghton Mifflin, 1949.

MACKEN, WALTER. "The Young Turk." In Walter Macken, *Green Hills, and Other Stories.* London: Macmillan, 1956.

MALAMUD, BERNARD. "A Summer's Reading." In Bernard Malamud, *The Magic Barrel.* New York: Farrar, Straus & Giroux, 1958.

MALTZ, ALBERT. "Afternoon in the Jungle." In Bennett Cerf, ed., *Modern American Short Stories.* New York: World, 1945.

————. "The Game." In Albert Maltz, *The Way Things Are, and Other Stories.* New York: International, 1938.

MARSH, WILLARD N. "Last Tag." In Paul Engle, ed., *Prize Stories, 1957: The O. Henry Awards.* New York: Doubleday, 1957.

MAYER, TOM. "Bubble Gum and Kipling." In Tom Mayer, *Bubble Gum and Kipling.* New York: Viking, 1964.

McEWAN, IAN. "Conversation with a Cupboard Man." In Ian McEwan, *First Love, Last Rites.* New York: Random House, 1975.

McPHERSON, JAMES ALAN. "The Silver Bullet." In Martha Foley, ed., *The Best American Short Stories, 1973.* Boston: Houghton Mifflin, 1973.

MILBURN, GEORGE. "Revenge." In George Milburn, *No More Trumpets, and Other Stories.* New York: Harcourt Brace Jovanovich, 1933.

MITCHELL, DON. "Diesel." In Martha Foley and David Burnett, eds., *The Best American Short Stories, 1971.* Boston: Houghton Mifflin, 1971.

MODELL, JACK. "A Day in the Sun." In Charles I. Glicksberg, ed., *American Vanguard, 1950.* New York: Cambridge, 1950.

MORAVIA, ALBERTO. "Anguish." In Alberto Moravia, *The Fetish and Other Stories.* Translated by Angus Davidson. New York: Farrar, Straus & Giroux, 1965.

NEUGEBOREN, JAY. "Luther." In Jay Neugeboren, *Corky's Brother.* New York: Farrar, Straus & Giroux, 1969.

NEWHOUSE, EDWARD. "The Mentocrats" (originally "Benny Frankel"). In Edward Newhouse, *Many Are Called; Forty-two Short Stories.* New York: William Sloan Associates, 1951.

NICHOLSON, MARGARET. "The Outcast." In Robert Oberfirst, ed., *1955 Anthology of Best Original Short-Short Stories.* Ocean City, N.J.: Oberfirst, 1955.

NORRIS, KATHLEEN T. "Greater Love." In Kathleen T. Norris, *Over at the Crowleys'.* New York: Doubleday, 1946.

OATES, JOYCE CAROL. "Boys at a Picnic." In Joyce Carol Oates, *By the North Gate.* New York: Vanguard, 1963.

————. "How I Contemplated the World from the Detroit House of Correction and Began My Life Over Again." In Paul C. Holmes and Anita J. Lehman, eds., *The Challenge of Conflict.* New York: Harper & Row, 1976.

————. "Norman and the Killer." In Joyce Carol Oates, *Upon the Sweeping Flood.* New York: Vanguard, 1966.

————. "Parricide." In Joyce Carol Oates, *The Poisoned Kiss and Other Stories from the Portuguese.* New York: Vanguard, 1975.

O'CONNOR, FLANNERY. "A Circle in the Fire." In Martha Foley, ed., *Fifty*

Best American Short Stories, 1915–1965. Boston: Houghton Mifflin, 1965.

————. "The Comforts of Home." In Flannery O'Connor, *Everything That Rises Must Converge*. New York: Farrar, Straus & Giroux, 1965.

————. "The Lame Shall Enter First." In Flannery O'Connor, *Everything That Rises Must Converge*. New York: Farrar, Straus & Giroux, 1965.

O'CONNOR, PHILIP F. "American Gothic." In Philip F. O'Connor, *Old Morals, Small Continents, Darker Times*. Iowa City: University of Iowa Press, 1971.

————. "Matter of Ages." In Philip F. O'Connor, *Old Morals, Small Continents, Darker Times*. Iowa City: University of Iowa Press, 1971.

O'HARA, JOHN. "Do You Like It Here?" In (John) Angus Burrel and Bennett Cerf, eds., *An Anthology of Famous Stories*. New York: Random House, 1953.

OLSEN, SONDRA SPATT. "Hoods I Have Known." In Cyrilly Abels and Margarita G. Smith, eds., *40 Best Stories from Mademoiselle 1935–1960*. New York: Harper & Row, 1960.

PACKER, VIN. "Only the Guilty Run." In Joan Kahn, ed., *Some Things Weird and Wicked; Twelve Stories to Chill Your Bones*. New York: Pantheon, 1976.

PALEY, GRACE. "Gloomy Tune." In Grace Paley, *Enormous Changes at the Last Minute*. New York: Farrar, Straus & Giroux, 1974.

————. "An Irrevocable Diameter." In Grace Paley, *The Little Disturbances of Man*. New York: Viking, 1959.

————. "The Little Girl." In Grace Paley, *Enormous Changes at the Last Minute*. New York: Farrar, Straus & Giroux, 1974.

PATON, ALAN. "Death of a Tsotsi." In Alan Paton, *Tales from a Troubled Land*. New York: Scribner's, 1961.

————. "The Divided House." In Alan Paton, *Tales from a Troubled Land*. New York: Scribner's, 1961.

————. "Ha'penny." In Alan Paton, *Tales from a Troubled Land*. New York: Scribner's, 1961.

————. "Sponono." In Alan Paton, *Tales from a Troubled Land*. New York: Scribner's, 1961.

PETRY, ANN. "The Witness." In Ann Petry, *Miss Muriel, and Other Stories*. Boston: Houghton Mifflin, 1971.

PHILLIPS, JOHN (JOHN P. MARQUAND, JR.). "Bleat Blodgette." In Martha Foley and David Burnett, eds., *The Best American Short Stories, 1968*. Boston: Houghton Mifflin, 1968.

PURDOM, TOM. "Toys." In Hans Stefan Santesson, ed., *Crime Prevention in the 30th Century*. New York: Walker, 1969.

PURDY, JAMES. "Everything Under the Sun." In James Purdy, *Children Is All.* New York: New Directions, 1961.

QUEEN, ELLERY. "Kid Stuff." In Dorothy Gardiner, ed., *Mystery Writers of America, Inc., for Love or Money.* New York: Doubleday, 1957.

————. "Object Lesson." In Hans Stefan Santesson, ed., *Mirror, Mirror, Fatal Mirror; an Anthology of Mystery Stories.* New York: Doubleday, 1923.

QUENTIN, PATRICK. "Portrait of a Murder." In Patrick Quentin (pseud.), *The Ordeal of Mrs. Snow and Other Stories.* London: Victor Gollancz, 1961.

ROOK, CLARENCE. "Billy the Snide." In P. J. Keating, ed., *Working-class Stories of the 1890s.* New York: Barnes & Noble, 1971.

————. "Concerning Hooligans." In P. J. Keating, ed., *Working-class Stories of the 1890s.* New York: Barnes & Noble, 1971.

————. "Young Alf." In P. J. Keating, ed., *Working-class Stories of the 1890s.* New York: Barnes & Noble, 1971.

ROONEY, FRANK. "Cyclists' Raid." In John Chesley Taylor, ed., *The Short Story: Fiction in Transition.* 2nd ed. New York: Scribner's, 1973.

ROTH, PHILIP. "You Can't Tell a Man by the Song He Sings." In Philip Roth, *Goodbye Columbus, and Five Short Stories.* Boston: Houghton Mifflin, 1976.

RUMAKER, MICHAEL. "The Truck." In Michael Rumaker, *Gringos and Other Stories.* New York: Grove, 1967.

SANTIGO, DANNY. "The Somebody." In Katherine D. Newman, ed., *Ethnic American Short Stories.* New York: Simon & Schuster, 1975.

SAROYAN, WILLIAM. "The Parsley Garden." In William Saroyan, *The Assyrian and Other Stories.* New York: Harcourt Brace Jovanovich, 1950.

SHADBOLT, MAURICE. "Love Story." In Maurice Shadbolt, *The New Zealanders; a Sequence of Stories.* New York: Atheneum, 1959.

SHAPIRO, MADELON. "The Monstrous Summer." In Cyrilly Abels and Margarita G. Smith, eds., *40 Best Stories from Mademoiselle, 1935–1960.* New York: Harper & Row, 1960.

SILLITOE, ALAN. "The Decline and Fall of Frankie Buller." In Alan Sillitoe, *The Loneliness of the Long-distance Runner.* New York: Knopf, 1959.

————. "The Loneliness of the Long-distance Runner." In Alan Sillitoe, *The Loneliness of the Long-distance Runner.* New York: Knopf, 1959.

SIMENON, GEORGES. "The Watchmaker of Everton." In Georges Simenon, *An American Omnibus.* New York: Harcourt Brace Jovanovich, 1967.

SLESAR, HENRY. "Thicker Than Water." In Lawrence Treat, ed., *Murder in Mind: An Anthology of Mystery Stories by the Mystery Writers of America.* New York: Dutton, 1967.

SOUTHERN, TERRY. "Red-Dirt Marijuana." In Barney Rosset, ed., *Evergreen Review Reader, 1957–1967.* New York: Grove, 1968.

————. "A South Summer Idyll" (originally "South's Summer Idyll"). In Nelson Algren, ed., *Nelson Algren's Own Book of Lonesome Monsters.* New York: Bernard Geis Associates, 1963.

ST. JOHNS, ADELA R. "Walking on Air." In Adela R. St. Johns, *Never Again, and Other Stories.* New York: Doubleday, 1949.

STADLEY, PAT. "The Doe and the Gantlet." In Ellery Queen, ed., *Ellery Queen's Awards: Twelfth Series.* New York: Simon & Schuster, 1957.

STEGNER, WALLACE EARLE. "Pop Goes the Alley Cat." In Wallace Earle Stegner, *City of the Living, and Other Stories.* Boston: Houghton Mifflin, 1956.

STEWART, ORA PATE. "Citizens' Committee." In Ora Pate Stewart, *Buttermilk and Bran.* San Antonio: Naylor, 1964.

STILES, GEORGE. "Lines from the Quick." In Cyril M. Gulassa, ed., *The Fact of Fiction: Social Relevance in the Short Story.* San Francisco: Canfield, 1972.

STREET, PENELOPE. "The Magic Apple." In Martha Foley, ed., *The Best American Short Stories, 1972.* Boston: Houghton Mifflin, 1972.

STUART, JESSE. "As Ye Sow, So Shall Ye Reap." In Jesse Stuart, *A Jesse Stuart Reader.* New York: McGraw-Hill, 1963.

STURGEON, THEODORE. "Jorry's Gap." In Theodore Sturgeon, *Sturgeon Is Alive and Well.* New York: Putnam's, 1971.

SUTER, JOHN. "Just a Minor Offense." In Alfred Hitchcock, ed., *Alfred Hitchcock's Tales to Keep You Spellbound.* New York: Dial, 1976.

SYMONS, JULIAN. "The Tiger's Stripe." In Ellery Queen, ed., *Ellery Queen's Crime Carousel: 21 Stories from Ellery Queen's Mystery Magazine.* New York: New American Library, 1966.

TAYLOR, EDITH L. "I'll Be Judge, I'll Be Jury." In Allen Hubin, ed., *Best Detective Stories of the Year 1975: 29th Annual Collection.* New York: Dutton, 1975.

TEYCHENNE, M. MAREE. "The Wisdom of Getting." In Brian Buckley and Jim Hamilton, eds., *Festival and Other Stories.* Melbourne: Wren Publishing, 1974.

THOMAS, PIRI. "If You Ain't Got Heart, You Ain't Got Nada." In Rose M. Somerville, ed., *Intimate Relationships: Marriage, Family, and Lifestyles* through *Literature.* Englewood Cliffs, N.J.: Prentice-Hall, 1975.

THOMPSON, JAMES W. "See What Tomorrow Brings." In Woodie King, ed., *Black Short Story Anthology.* New York: Columbia University Press, 1972.

TOFTE, ARTHUR. "The Speeders." In Roger Elwood, ed., *The Other Side of Tomorrow: Original Science Fiction Stories about Young People of the Future.* New York: Random House, 1973.

TREAT, LAWRENCE. "C as in Cop." In Ellery Queen, ed., *Ellery Queen's 20th Anniversary Annual: 20 Stories from Ellery Queen's Mystery Magazine*. New York: Random House, 1965.

TREVOR, WILLIAM. "Going Home." In William Trevor, *The Ballroom of Romance, and Other Stories*. New York: Viking, 1972.

UPDIKE, JOHN. "The Hillies." In John Updike, *Museums and Women*. New York: Knopf, 1972.

VEZHINOV, PAVEL. "The Boy with the Violin." In Kilolai Kirilov and Frank Kirk, eds., *Introduction to Modern Bulgarian Literature: An Anthology of Short Stories*. Boston: Twayne, 1969.

VIDAL, GORE. "The Zenner Trophy." In Gore Vidal, *A Thirsty Evil: Seven Short Stories*. New York: Zero, 1956.

WAGONER, DAVID. "The Escape Artist." In Idelle Sullins et al., *The Inquiring Reader*. 2nd ed. Lexington, Mass.: Heath, 1976.

WATMOUGH, DAVID. "Seduction." In David Watmough, *Love & The Waiting Game*. Canada: An Oberon Book, 1975.

WEESNER, THEODORE. "Stealing Cars." In Martha Foley, ed., *The Best American Short Stories, 1972*. Boston: Houghton Mifflin, 1972.

WILNER, HERBERT. "Almost Brothers." In Herbert Wilner, *Dovish in the Wilderness and Other Stories*. Indianapolis, Ind.: Bobbs-Merrill, 1968.

WHITE, EDGAR. "Sursum Corda (Lift Up Your Hearts)." In Orde Coombs, ed., *What We Must See: Young Black Storytellers*. New York: Dodd, Mead, 1971.

WHITEHILL, JOSEPH. "The Day of the Last Rock Fight." In Joseph Whitehill, *Able Baker, and Others*. Boston: Little, Brown, 1957.

WHITFIELD, JERRY H. "The Hitchhiker." In Editors of Story Magazine. *The Best College Writing, 1961: An Anthology of University Writing*. New York: Random House, 1961.

WOLFSON, ROSE. "The Lesson." In Don Marion Wolfe, ed., *American Scene: New Voices*. New York: Lyle Stuart, 1963.

WRIGHT, RICHARD. "Almos' a Man." In Bennett Cerf, ed., *Modern American Short Stories*. New York: World, 1945.

YOUNG, AL. "Chicken Hawk's Dream." In Wallace Stegner and Richard Scowcroft, eds., *Stanford Short Stories, 1968*. Stanford, Calif.: Stanford University Press, 1968.

ZEBROWSKI, GEORGE. "Assassins of Air." In Roger Elwood, ed., *Future City*. New York: Trident, 1973.

ZILLER, EUGENE. "The Season's Dying." In Eugene Ziller, *In This World, and Other Stories*. New York: George Braziller, 1960.

Novels of Delinquency

(These deal in part or wholly with delinquency.)

ALBERT, MIMI. *The Second Story Man*. New York: George Braziller, 1975.

ALGREN, NELSON. *Never Come Morning.* New York: Harper & Row, 1942.

————. *Somebody in Boots.* New York: Vanguard, 1935.

————. *A Walk on the Wild Side.* New York: Farrar, Straus & Giroux, 1956.

ANDERSON, SHERWOOD. *Kit Brandon.* New York: Scribner's, 1936.

ATHAS, DAPHNE. *The Weather of the Heart.* New York: Appleton-Century-Crofts, 1947.

BAUMER, MARIE. *The Seeker and the Sought.* New York: Scribner's, 1949.

BEHAN, BRENDAN. *Borstal Boy.* New York: Knopf, 1959.

BELLOW, SAUL. *The Adventures of Augie March.* New York: Viking, 1953.

BONHAM, FRANK. *Durango Street.* New York: Dutton, 1965.

BOURJAILY, VANCE. *Confessions of a Spent Youth.* New York: Dial, 1960.

BRECHT, HAROLD W. *Downfall.* New York: Harper & Row, 1929.

BROWN, CLAUDE. *The Children of Ham.* Briarcliff Manor, N.Y.: Stein & Day, 1976

————. *Manchild in the Promised Land.* New York: Macmillan, 1965.

BROWN, KENNETH. *The Narrows.* New York: Dial, 1976.

CAIN, GEORGE. *Blueschild Baby.* New York: McGraw-Hill, 1972.

CALITRI, CHARLES. *Strike Heaven in the Face.* New York: Crown, 1958.

CARR, ROBERT S. *The Rampant Age.* New York: Doubleday, 1928.

CHAPPELL, FRED. *The Gaudy Place.* New York: Harcourt Brace Jovanovich, 1973.

CLAYTON, JOHN BELL. *Six Angles at My Back.* New York: Macmillan, 1952.

CROY, HOMER. *West of the Water Tower.* New York: Harper & Row, 1923.

DAVIS, HAROLD LENOIR. *Honey in the Horn.* New York: Harper & Row, 1935.

DEMBY, WILLIAM. *Beetlecreek.* New York: Rinehart, 1950.

DE SELINCOURT, HUGH. *One Little Boy.* New York: Albert & Charles Boni, 1924.

DICKENS, CHARLES. *The Adventures of Oliver Twist.* Oxford: Clarendon, 1966. First published 1837–39.

DIZENZO, PATRICIA. *Phoebe.* New York: McGraw-Hill, 1970.

DOS PASSOS, JOHN. *The Forty-Second Parallel.* New York: Harper & Row, 1930.

DOUGLAS, MICHAEL. *Dealing; or, The Berkeley-to-Boston Forty-Brick Lost-Bag Blues.* New York, Knopf, 1971.

DREISER, THEODORE. *An American Tragedy.* New York: Boni & Liveright, 1925.

ELLSON, HAL. *Duke.* New York: Scribner's, 1949.

————. *The Golden Spike.* New York: Ballantine, 1952.

————. *Summer Street.* New York: Ballantine, 1953.

————. *Tomboy*. New York: Scribner's, 1950.

FAIR, RONALD L. *We Can't Breathe*. New York: Harper & Row, 1972.

FARRELL, JAMES T. *Young Lonigan*. New York: Vanguard, 1932.

————. *The Young Manhood of Studs Lonigan*. New York: Vanguard, 1934.

FARRIS, JOHN. *Harrison High*. New York: Rinehart, 1959.

FAULKNER, WILLIAM. *The Hamlet*. New York: Random House, 1940.

————. *The Reivers*. New York: Random House, 1962.

FOX, WILLIAM PRICE. *Moonshine Light, Moonshine Bright*. Philadelphia: Lippincott, 1967.

FRAENKEL, MICHAEL. *Werther's Younger Brother: The Story of an Attitude*. New York: Carrefour Editions, 1931.

GALE, WILLIAM. *The Compound*. New York: Ranson Associates, 1978.

GARDNER, MAC. *Mom Counted Six*. New York: Harper & Row, 1944.

GOVER, ROBERT. *One Hundred Dollar Misunderstanding*. New York: Grove, 1962.

GRAVES, WALLACE. *Trixie*. New York: Knopf, 1969.

GREENAN, RUSSELL H. *The Queen of America*. New York: Random House, 1972

HARRIS, MARILYN. *Hatter Fox*. New York: Random House, 1973.

HARRIS, SARA. *The Wayward Ones*. New York: Crown, 1952.

HENNING, WILLIAM E. *The Heller*. New York: Scribner's, 1947.

HERLIHY, JAMES LEO. *All Fall Down*. New York: Dutton, 1960.

HORGAN, PAUL. *Whitewater*. New York: Farrar, Straus & Giroux, 1970.

HOUGH, JOHN. *A Two-Car Funeral*. Boston: Little, Brown, 1973.

HUNTER, EVAN. *Blackboard Jungle*. New York: Simon & Schuster, 1954.

————. *Last Summer*. New York: Doubleday, 1968.

————. *A Matter of Conviction*. New York: Simon & Schuster, 1959.

JACKSON, SHIRLEY. *Hangsaman*. New York: Farrar, Straus & Giroux, 1951.

KARIG, WALTER. *Lower than Angels*. New York: Farrar & Rinehart, 1945.

KENNEDY, MARK. *The Pecking Order*. New York: Appleton-Century-Crofts, 1953.

KEROUAC, JACK. *On the Road*. New York: Viking, 1957.

KIRKWOOD, JAMES. *Good Times/Bad Times*. New York: Simon & Schuster, 1968.

KLINE, NANCY E. *The Faithful*. New York: Morrow, 1968.

KNOWLES, JOHN. *A Separate Peace*. New York: Macmillan, 1960.

LARNER, JEREMY. *The Answer*. New York: Macmillan, 1968.

LEVIN, MEYER. *Compulsion*. New York: Simon & Schuster, 1956.

MacDONALD, ROSS. *The Instant Enemy*. New York: Knopf, 1968.

McAFFEE, THOMAS. *Rover Youngblood: An American Fable*. New York: Baron, 1969.

McGIVERN, WILLIAM PETER. *Savage Streets*. New York: Dodd, Mead, 1959.

MANDEL, GEORGE. *Flee the Angry Strangers*. Indianapolis, Ind.: Bobbs-Merrill, 1952.

MILLER, WARREN. *The Cool World*. Boston: Little, Brown, 1959.

MITCHELL, DON. *Thumb Tripping*. Boston: Little, Brown, 1970.

MORRIS, WRIGHT. *In Orbit*. New York: New American Library, 1967.

MOTLEY, WILLARD. *Knock on Any Door*. New York: Appleton-Century-Crofts, 1947.

NABOKOV, VLADIMIR. *Lolita*. New York: Putnam's, 1958.

NORMAN, GURNEY. *Divine Right's Trip*. New York: Dial, 1972.

OATES, JOYCE CAROL. *Expensive People*. New York: Vanguard, 1968.

————. *With Shuddering Fall*. New York: Vanguard, 1964.

PEASE, HOWARD. *The Dark Adventure*. New York: Doubleday, 1950.

PILCER, SONIA. *Teen Angel*. New York: Coward, McCann & Geohegan, 1979.

PORTER, MONICA E. *Mercy of the Court*. New York: Norton, 1955.

PRICE, EMERSON. *Inn of That Journey*. Caldwell, Idaho: Caxton Printers, 1939.

PROKOSCH, FREDERIC. *Night of the Poor*. New York: Harper & Row, 1939.

PURDY, JAMES. *Malcolm*. New York: Farrar, Straus & Giroux, 1959.

RICHERT, WILLIAM. *Aren't You Even Gonna Kiss Me Good-By?* New York: McKay, 1966.

ROSS, SAM. *Hang-Up*. New York: Coward, McCann & Geoghegan, 1967.

SALAS, FLOYD. *Tattoo the Wicked Cross*. New York: Grove, 1967.

SALINGER, JEROME DAVID. *The Catcher in the Rye*. Boston: Little, Brown, 1951.

SCOTT, VIRGIL. *The Dead Tree Gives No Shelter*. New York: Morrow, 1947.

SHAW, CLIFFORD ROBE. *The Jackroller; A Delinquent Boy's Own Story*. Chicago: University of Chicago Press, 1930.

SHULMAN, IRVING. *The Amboy Dukes*. New York: Doubleday, 1947.

————. *Children of the Dark*. New York: Holt, 1956.

SILLITOE, ALAN. *The Loneliness of the Long-distance Runner*. New York: New American Library, 1961.

SIMMONS, HERBERT. *Corner Boy*. Boston: Houghton Mifflin, 1957.

STEIN, SOL. *The Childkeeper*. New York: Harcourt Brace Jovanovich, 1975.

————. *The Magician*. New York: Delacorte, 1972.

STEINBECK, JOHN. *East of Eden*. New York: Viking, 1952.

STUART, JESSE. *Hie to the Hunters*. New York: Whittlesey House, 1950.

TAYLOR, ROSS McLAURY. *Brazos*. Indianapolis, Ind.: Bobbs-Merrill, 1938.

THOMPSON, EARL. *A Garden of Sand*. New York: Putnam's, 1971.

TREYNOR, BLAIR. *She Ate Her Cake.* New York: Morrow, 1946.

TWAIN, MARK (SAMUEL LANGHORNE CLEMENS). *The Adventures of Huckleberry Finn.* Berkeley: University of California Press, 1962. First published 1884.

—————. *The Adventures of Tom Sawyer.* New York and London: Harper & Brothers, 1903. First published 1876.

VIERTEL, PETER. *The Canyon.* New York: Harcourt Brace Jovanovich, 1940.

WALLOP, DOUGLAS. *Night Light.* New York: Norton, 1953.

WEESNER, THEODORE. *The Car Thief.* New York: Random House, 1972.

WINDHAM, DONALD. *The Dog Star.* New York: Doubleday, 1950.

WRIGHT, RICHARD. *Native Son.* New York: Harper & Row, 1940.

YAFFE, JAMES. *Nothing but the Night.* Boston: Little, Brown, 1957.

YOSELOFF, MARTIN. *The Girl in the Spike-Heeled Shoes.* New York: Dutton, 1949.

YOUNG, ISADOR S. *Jadie Greenway.* New York: Crown, 1947.

ZINDEL, PAUL. *The Pigman.* New York: Harper & Row, 1968.

ZUGSMITH, LEANE. *The Reckoning.* New York: Smith & Haas, 1934.

Textbooks on Delinquency

ABBOTT, GRACE. *The Child and the State.* Chicago: University of Chicago Press, 1938.

ABRAHAMSEN, DAVID. *The Psychology of Crime.* New York: Columbia University Press, 1960.

ADAMS, GARY B., et al. *Juvenile Justice Management.* Springfield, Ill.: Charles C Thomas, 1973.

ADDAMS, JANE, et al. *The Child, the Clinic, and the Court.* Norwood, N.J.: Walter J. Johnson, 1971.

AHLSTROM, WINTON M., and HAVIGHURST, ROBERT J. *Four Hundred Losers: Delinquent Boys in High School.* San Francisco: Jossey-Bass, 1971.

AICHHORN, AUGUST. *Delinquency and Child Guidance.* New York: International Universities Press, 1969.

—————. *Wayward Youth.* New York: Viking, 1963.

ALEXANDER, FRANZ, and STAUB, HUGO. *The Criminal, the Judges and the Public.* New York: Free Press, 1956.

ALISSI, ALBERT S. *Boys in Little Italy: A Comparision of Their Individual Value Orientations, Family Patterns, and Peer Group Associations.* San Francisco: R and E Research Associates, 1978.

ALTMAN, MICHAEL L. *Standards Relating to Juvenile Records and Information Systems.* Juvenile Justice Standards Project Series. Cambridge, Mass.: Ballinger, 1977.

AMOS, WILLIAM E., and MANELLA, RAYMOND L., eds. *Delinquent Children in Juvenile Correctional Institutions: State Administered Reception and Diagnostic Centers.* Springfield, Ill.: Charles C Thomas, 1973.

_____, and WELFORD, CHARLES. *Delinquency Prevention: Theory and Practice.* Englewood Cliffs, N.J.: Prentice-Hall, 1967.

ANDERSON, RICHARD. *Representation in the Juvenile Court.* Boston: Routledge & Kegan Paul, 1978.

ARNOLD, WILLIAM R. *Juveniles on Parole: A Sociological Perspective.* Philadelphia: Philadelphia Book, 1970.

AUDRY, R. G. *Delinquency and Parental Pathology.* London: Methuen, 1960.

BAKER, HARRY J., and TRAPHAGEN, VIRGINIA. *The Diagnosis of Behavior-Problem Children.* New York: Macmillan, 1935.

BANDURA, ALBERT, and WALTERS, RICHARD H. *Adolescent Aggression: A Study of the Influence of Child-Training Practices and Family Inter-Relationships.* New York: Ronald, 1959.

BARNES, HARRY ELMER, and TEETERS, NEGLEY K. *New Horizons in Criminology.* 3rd ed. Englewood Cliffs, N.J.: Prentice-Hall, 1959.

BARRON, MILTON L. *The Juvenile in Delinquent Society.* New York: Knopf, 1956.

BARTOLLAS, CLEMENS, and MILLER, STUART J. *The Juvenile Offender: Control, Correction and Treatment.* Boston: Allyn & Bacon, 1978.

_____, et al. *Juvenile Victimization: The Institutional Paradox.* New York: Halsted, 1976.

BECKER, HOWARD. *Outsiders.* New York: Free Press, 1963.

BELDEN, EVALINE. *Courts in the United States Hearing Children's Cases.* Washington, D.C.: Department of Labor, Children's Bureau, 1920.

BELKIN, ALLISON. *The Criminal Child.* Dubuque, Iowa: Kendal/Hunt, 1978.

BERMAN, ERIC. *Scapegoat.* Ann Arbor: University of Michigan Press, 1973.

BESHAROV, DOUGLAS J. *Juvenile Justice Advocacy: Practice in a Unique Court.* New York: Philosophical Library, 1974.

BING, STEPHEN, and BROWN, LARRY. *Standards Relating to Monitoring.* Juvenile Justice Standards Project Series. Cambridge, Mass.: Ballinger, 1977.

BITTNER, EGON, and KRANTZ, SHELDON. *Standards Relating to Police Handling of Juvenile Problems.* Cambridge, Mass.: Ballinger, 1977.

BLALOCK, HUBERT M. *Social Statistics.* New York: McGraw-Hill, 1972.

_____. *Theory Construction.* Englewood Cliffs, N.J.: Prentice-Hall, 1969.

BLISS, DENNIS C. *The Effects of the Juvenile Justice System on Self-Concept.* San Francisco: R and E Research Associates, 1977.

BLOCH, HERBERT A., and NIEDERHOFFER, ARTHUR. *The Gang: A Study in Adolescent Behavior.* New York: Philosophical Library, 1958.

BLOMBERG, THOMAS G. *Social Control and the Proliferation of Juvenile Court Services.* San Francisco: R and E Research Associates, 1978.

BONGER, W. A. *Criminology and Economic Conditions.* Boston: Little, Brown, 1916.

BORDUA, DAVID J. *Sociological Theories and Their Implications for Juvenile Delinquency.* Washington, D.C.: U.S. Government Printing Office, 1960.

BOSS, PETER. *Social Policy and the Young Delinquent.* Atlantic Highlands, N.J.: Humanities, 1967.

BOVET, LUCIEN. *Psychiatric Aspects of Juvenile Delinquency, a Study.* Westport, Conn.: Greenwood, 1979.

BOYLE, HUGH. *Delinquency and Crime.* Urban America Series. West Haven, Conn.: Pendulum, 1967.

BRECKENRIDGE, SOPHONISKA P., and ABBOTT, EDITH. *The Delinquent Child and the Home.* New York: Random House, 1912.

BREMNER, ROBERT H. *The Juvenile Court: An Original Anthology.* Children & Youth Series, vol. 8. New York: Arno, 1974.

BUCKLE, LEONARD, and BUCKLE, SUSAN. *Standards Relating to Planning for Juvenile Justice.* Cambridge Mass.: Ballinger, 1977.

BURGESS, ERNEST W. *On Community, Family and Delinquency.* Chicago: University of Chicago Press, 1974.

BURT, CYRIL. *The Young Delinquent.* London: University of London Press, 1938.

CABOT, PHILIPPE S., ed. *Juvenile Delinquency: A Critical Bibliography.* Westport, Conn.: Greenwood, 1971.

CALDWELL, ROBERT G. *Criminology.* New York: Ronald, 1956.

————, and BLACK, JAMES A. *Juvenile Delinquency.* New York: Wiley, 1971.

CARTER, ROBERT M. *Middle Class Delinquency: An Experiment in Community Control.* Berkeley: University of California Press, 1968.

————, and KLEIN, MALCOLM. *Back on the Street: The Diversion of Juvenile Offenders.* Englewood Cliffs, N.J.: Prentice-Hall, 1976.

CARTWRIGHT, DESMOND S., et al. *Gang Delinquency.* Monterey, Calif.: Brooks/Cole, 1975.

CAVAN, RUTH SHONLE. *Juvenile Delinquency.* Philadelphia: Lippincott, 1962.

————, ed. *Readings in Juvenile Delinquency.* 3rd ed. Philadelphia: Lippincott, 1975.

————, and CAVAN, JORDAN T. *Delinquency and Crime: Crosscultural Perspectives.* Philadelphia: Lippincott, 1968.

_____, and FERDINAND, THEODORE N. *Juvenile Delinquency*. 3rd ed. Philadelphia: Lippincott, 1975.

CHAMELIN, NEIL C., et al. *Introduction to Criminal Justice*. 2nd ed. Englewood Cliffs, N.J.: Prentice-Hall, 1979.

CICOUREL, AARON. *The Social Organization of Juvenile Justice*. New York: Wiley, 1968.

CLINARD, MARSHALL. *Sociology of Deviant Behavior*. 2nd ed. New York: Holt, Rinehart and Winston, 1963.

_____, ed. *Anomie and Deviant Behavior*. New York: Free Press, 1964.

CLOWARD, RICHARD A., and OHLIN, LLOYD E. *Delinquency and Opportunity*. New York: Free Press, 1960.

COFFEY, ALAN R. *Juvenile Corrections: Treatment and Rehabilitation*. Criminal Justice Series. Englewood Cliffs, N.J.: Prentice-Hall, 1975.

_____. *Juvenile Justice as a System: Law Enforcement to Rehabilitation*. Englewood Cliffs, N.J.: Prentice-Hall, 1974.

_____. *The Prevention of Crime and Delinquency*. Englewood Cliffs, N.J.: Prentice-Hall, 1975.

COHEN, ALBERT K. *Delinquent Boys: The Culture of the Gang*. New York: Free Press, 1955.

COHEN, FRED. *Standards Relating to Dispositional Procedures*. Juvenile Justice Standards Project Series. Cambridge, Mass.: Ballinger, 1977.

COLEMAN, JAMES S., et al. *Equality of Educational Opportunity*. Washington, D.C.: U.S. Government Printing Office, 1966.

CONGER, JOHN JANEWAY, and MILLER, WILBUR C. *Personality, Social Class and Delinquency*. New York: Wiley, 1966.

COTTLE, THOMAS J. *Children in Jail*. Boston: Beacon, 1977.

COX, STEVEN M., and CONRAD, JOHN J. *Juvenile Justice: A Guide to Practice and Theory*. Dubuque, Iowa: William C. Brown, 1978.

CROMWELL, PAUL F., JR. *Introduction to Juvenile Delinquency: Text and Readings*. St. Paul, Minn.: West, 1978.

CROW, LESTER D., and CROW, ALICE. *Our Teen-Age Boys and Girls*. New York: Arno, 1945.

DAVIS, F. JAMES, et al. *Society and the Law*. New York: Free Press, 1968.

DAWSON, ROBERT O. *Standards Relating to Adjudication*. Juvenile Justice Standards Project Series. Cambridge, Mass.: Ballinger, 1977.

DEPARTMENT OF HEALTH, EDUCATION, AND WELFARE. *Annual Report of Federal Activities in Juvenile Delinquency, Youth Development and Related Fields*. Washington, D.C.: U.S. Government Printing Office, 1971.

_____. *Delinquency Today: A Guide for Community Action*. Washington, D.C.: U.S. Government Printing Office, 1971.

————. *Halfway House Programs for Delinquent Youth*. Washington, D.C.: U.S. Government Printing Office, 1965.

————. *Institutions Serving Delinquent Children*. Washington, D.C.: U.S. Government Printing Office, 1957.

————. *Juvenile Court Statistics, 1964*. Washington, D.C.: U.S. Government Printing Office, 1965.

————. *Juvenile Court Statistics, 1968*. Washington, D.C.: U.S. Government Printing Office, 1974.

————. *Juvenile Court Statistics, 1970*. Washington, D.C.: U.S. Government Printing Office, 1971.

————. *Juvenile Court Statistics, 1973*. Washington, D.C.: U.S. Government Printing Office, 1974.

————. *Juvenile Delinquency Planning*. Washington, D.C.: U.S. Government Printing Office, 1971.

————. *Juvenile Delinquency Prevention in the United States*. Washington, D.C.: U.S. Government Printing Office, 1966.

————. *LSD: Some Questions and Answers*. Public Health Service Publication No. 1828. Washington, D.C.: U.S. Government Printing Office, 1970.

————. *Marihuana: Some Questions and Answers*. Public Health Service Publication No. 1829. Washington, D.C.: U.S. Government Printing Office, 1970.

————. *The Neighborhood Youth Corps: Hope and Help for Youth*. Washington, D.C.: U.S. Government Printing Office, 1969.

————. *Police Services for Juveniles*. Washington, D.C.: U.S. Government Printing Office, 1954.

————. *Stimulants: Some Questions and Answers*. Public Health Service Publication No. 2097. Washington, D.C.: U.S. Government Printing Office, 1970.

————. *Strategy to Prevent Delinquency*. Washington, D.C.: U.S. Government Printing Office, 1972.

DEUTSCH, ALBERT. *Our Rejected Children*. New York: Arno, 1974.

DONOHUE, JOHN K. *Baffling Eyes of Youth*. Westport, Conn.: Greenwood, 1957.

DRUCKER, SAUL, and HEXTER, MAURICE-BECK. *Children Astray*. New York: Arno, 1974.

DUBIN, ROBERT. *Theory Building*. New York: Free Press, 1969.

DUGDALE, RICHARD L. *The Jukes: A Study in Crime, Pauperism, Disease and Heredity*. New York: Putnam's, 1910.

DURKHEIM, EMILE. *The Division of Labor in Society*. New York: Free Press, 1933.

————. *The Rules of Sociological Method*. New York: Free Press, 1938.

————. *Suicide*. Translated by John A. Spaulding and George Simpson. New York: Free Press, 1951.

DUXBURY, ELAINE. *Youth Service Bureau in California*. Sacramento: Department of Youth Authority, 1971.

EATON, JOSEPH W., and POLK, KENNETH. *Measuring Delinquency*. Pittsburgh: University of Pittsburgh Press, 1961.

EISNER, VICTOR. *Delinquency Label: The Epidemiology of Juvenile Delinquency*. Philadelphia: Philadelphia Book, 1969.

ELDEFONSO, EDWARD. *Law Enforcement and the Youthful Offender*. 3rd ed. New York: Wiley, 1978.

————, and COFFEY, ALAN. *Process and Impact of the Juvenile Justice System*. Beverly Hills, Calif.: Glencoe, 1976.

————, and HARTINGER, W. *Control, Treatment and Rehabilitation of Juvenile Offenders*. Beverly Hills, Calif.: Glencoe, 1976

ELLIOTT, DESMOND. *Delinquency and Dropout*. Lexington, Mass.: Lexington Books, 1974.

EMERSON, ROBERT M. *Judging Delinquents: Context and Process in the Juvenile Court*. Law in Action Series. Chicago: Aldine, 1969.

EMPEY, LaMAR T., and ERICSON, MAYNARD L. *Hidden Delinquency: Evidence on Old Issues*. Provo: Brigham Young University Press, 1965.

————, and LUBECK, STEPHEN G. *Explaining Delinquency: Construction, Test, and Reformulation of Sociological Theory*. Lexington, Mass.: Lexington Books, 1971.

————. *The Silverlake Experiment*. Chicago: Aldine, 1971.

ERICSON, RICHARD V. *Young Offenders and Their Social Work*. Lexington, Mass.: Lexington Books, 1976.

ERICKSON, KAI T. *Wayward Puritans*. New York: Wiley, 1966.

FAUST, FREDERIC L., and BRANTINGHAM, PAUL J. *Juvenile Justice Philosophy: Readings, Cases, and Comments*. 2nd ed. Criminal Justice Series. St. Paul, Minn.: West, 1978.

FEDERAL BUREAU OF INVESTIGATION. *Uniform Crime Reports, 1971*. Washington, D.C.: U.S. Government Printing Office, 1972.

————. *Uniform Crime Reports, 1972*. Washington, D.C.: U.S. Government Printing Office, 1973.

————. *Uniform Crime Reports, 1973*. Washington, D.C.: U.S. Government Printing Office, 1974.

————. *Uniform Crime Reports, 1975*. Washington, D.C.: U.S. Government Printing Office, 1976.

FELD, BARRY C. *Neutralizing Inmate Violence: Juvenile Offenders in Institutions*. Cambridge, Mass.: Ballinger, 1977.

FERDINAND, THEODORE N., ed. *Juvenile Delinquency: Little Brother Grows Up*. Beverly Hills, Calif.: Sage, 1977.

————. *Typologies of Delinquency*. New York: Random House, 1966.

FERGUSON, ELIZABETH. *Social Work*. Philadelphia: Lippincott, 1963.

FERRACUTI, FRANCO, et al. *Delinquents and Nondelinquents in the Puerto Rican Slum Culture*. Columbus: Ohio State University Press, 1975.

FERRI, ENRICO. *Criminal Sociology*. Translated by J. I. Kelley and John Lisle. Boston: Little, Brown, 1917.

FILSTEAD, W. J., ed. *An Introduction to Deviance*. Chicago: Markham, 1972.

FINESTONE, HAROLD. *Victims of Change: Juvenile Delinquents in American Society*. Westport, Conn.: Greenwood, 1976.

FLAMMANG, C. J. *Police Juvenile Enforcement*. Springfield, Ill.: Charles C Thomas, 1972.

FLEISCHER, BELTON M. *The Economics of Delinquency*. New York: Quadrangle, 1968.

FLICHER, BARBARA. *Standards for Juvenile Justice: A Summary and Analysis*. Juvenile Justice Standards Project Series. Cambridge, Mass.: Ballinger, 1977.

FOX, LIONEL. *The English Prison and Borstal Systems*. London: Routledge & Kegan Paul, 1952.

FOX, SANFORD J. *The Law of Juvenile Courts in a Nutshell*. 2nd ed. Nutshell Series. St. Paul, Minn.: West, 1977.

FREED, DANIEL J., and TERRELL, TIMOTHY P. *Standards Relating to Interim Status*. Juvenile Justice Standards Project Series. Cambridge, Mass.: Ballinger, 1977.

FRIDAY, PAUL C., and STEWART, V. LORNE, eds. *Youth Crime and Juvenile Justice: International Perspectives*. Praeger Special Studies. New York: Praeger, 1977.

FRIEDLANDER, KATE. *The Psycho-Analytic Approach to Juvenile Delinquency*. London: Routledge & Kegan Paul, 1947.

FYVEL, T. R. *Troublemakers: Rebellious Youth in an Affluent Society*. New York: Schocken, 1964.

GARABEDIAN, PETER G., and GIBBONS, DON. *Becoming Delinquent*. Chicago: Aldine, 1970.

GARDINER, MURIEL. *The Deadly Innocents: Portraits of Children Who Kill*. New York: Basic, 1976.

GAROFALO, RAFFAELO. *Criminology*. Boston: Little, Brown, 1914.

GATH, DENNIS, et al. *Child Guidance and Delinquency in a London Borough*. New York: Oxford University Press, 1977.

GAZDA, GEORGE. *Approaches to Group Psychotherapy and Group Counseling*. Springfield, Ill.: Charles C Thomas, 1968.

GIALLOMBARDO, ROSE. *Delinquency Rehabilitation in Juvenile Delinquency: A Book of Readings*. New York: Wiley, 1966.

————, ed. *Juvenile Delinquency: A Book of Readings*. 3rd ed. New York: Wiley, 1976.

GIBBONS, DON C. *Changing the Lawbreaker.* Englewood Cliffs, N.J.: Prentice-Hall, 1965.

————. *Delinquent Behavior.* 2nd ed. Englewood Cliffs, N.J.: Prentice-Hall, 1976.

————. *Society Crime and Criminal Careers.* 2nd ed. Englewood Cliffs, N.J.: Prentice-Hall, 1973.

GIBBONS, T. C. N., and AHRENFELDT, R. H. *Cultural Factors in Delinquency.* Philadelphia: Lippincott, 1966.

————, and PRINCE, J. *The Results of Borstal Training.* Sociological Review Monograph No. 9 (1965).

GIBBS, JACK. *Sociological Theory Construction.* New York: Dryden, 1972.

GITTLER, JOSEPHINE. *Standards Relating to Juvenile Probation Function: Intake and Predisposition Investigation Services.* Juvenile Justice Standards Project Series. Cambridge, Mass.: Ballinger, 1977.

GLUECK, ELEANOR T. *Family Environment and Delinquency.* Boston: Houghton Mifflin, 1962.

————. *Unraveling Juvenile Delinquency.* Cambridge, Mass.: Harvard University Press, 1957.

GLUECK, SHELDON S., and GLUECK, ELEANOR T. *Delinquents and Nondelinquents in Perspective.* Cambridge, Mass.: Harvard University Press, 1968.

————. *Delinquents in the Making.* New York: Harper & Row, 1952.

————. *Juvenile Delinquents Grown Up.* Millwood, N.Y.: Kraus Reprint, 1940.

————. *One Thousand Juvenile Delinquents.* Millwood, N.Y.: Kraus Reprint, 1934.

————. *Physique and Delinquency.* New York: Harper & Row, 1956.

————. *Toward a Typology of Juvenile Offenders: Implications for Therapy and Prevention.* New York: Grune & Stratton, 1970.

GODDARD, HENRY H. *Feeblemindedness: Its Causes and Consequences.* New York: Macmillan, 1923.

————. *Human Efficiency and Levels of Intelligence.* Princeton, N.J.: Princeton University Press, 1920.

————. *The Kallikak Family: A Study of the Heredity of Feeblemindedness.* New York: Macmillan, 1919.

GOLD, HARRY, and SCARPITTI, FRANK R., eds. *Combatting Social Problems: Techniques of Intervention.* New York: Holt, Rinehart and Winston, 1967.

GOLDBERG, JACOB A., and GOLDBERG, ROSAMOND W. *Girls on the Streets: A Study of 1400 Cases of Rape.* Women in America Series. New York: Arno, 1974.

GOLDMAN, NATHAN. *The Differential Selection of Juvenile Offenders for Court Appearances.* New York: National Council on Crime and Delinquency, 1963.

GORDON, I. J. *Human Development: Birth to Adolescence.* New York: Harper & Row, 1962.

GOSHEN, CHARLES E. *Society and the Youthful Offender.* Springfield, Ill.: Charles C Thomas, 1974.

GOUGH, AIDAN. *Standards Relating to Non-Criminal Misbehavior.* Juvenile Justice Standards Project Series. Cambridge, Mass.: Ballinger, 1977.

GREENBERG, ALLAN M. *Standards Relating to Architecture of Facilities.* Juvenile Justice Standards Project Series. Cambridge, Mass.: Ballinger, 1977.

GRIFFIN, BRENDA S., and GRIFFIN, CHARLES T. *Juvenile Delinquency in Perspective.* New York: Harper & Row, 1978.

GRUNHUT, MAX. *Juvenile Offenders Before the Courts.* Westport, Conn.: Greenwood, 1978.

GRUPP, STANLEY. *The Marihuana Muddle.* Lexington, Mass.: Heath, 1973.

HAHN, PAUL H. *The Offender and the Law.* 2nd ed. Criminal Justice Text Series. Cincinnati, Ohio: Anderson, 1978.

HALLORAN, J. D., et al. *Television and Delinquency.* Atlantic Highlands, N.J.: Humanities, 1970.

HARDY, RICHARD E., and CULL, JOHN G., eds. *Climbing Ghetto Walls: Disadvantagement, Delinquency and Rehabilitation.* Springfield, Ill.: Charles C Thomas, 1973.

————. *Fundamentals of Juvenile Criminal Behavior.* Springfield, Ill.: Charles C Thomas, 1975.

————. *Psychological and Vocational Rehabilitation of the Youthful Delinquent.* Springfield, Ill.: Charles C Thomas, 1974.

HARRIS, LOUIS, et al. *Corrections, 1968: A Climate for Change.* Washington, D.C.: Joint Commission on Correctional Manpower and Training, 1968.

HART, HASTINGS H. *Juvenile Court Laws in the United States.* Russell Sage Foundation Reprint Series. New York: Irvington, 1969.

HARTJEN, CLAYTON A. *Crime and Criminalization.* New York: Praeger, 1974.

HASKELL, MARTIN R., and YABLONSKY, LEWIS. *Crime and Delinquency.* 2nd ed. Skokie, Ill.: Rand McNally, 1977.

————. *Juvenile Delinquency.* Skokie, Ill.: Rand McNally, 1974.

HATHAWAY, STARKE, and MONACHESI, ELIO D., eds. *Analyzing and Predicting Juvenile Delinquency with the Minnesota Multiphasic Personality Inventory.* Minneapolis: University of Minnesota Press, 1953.

HAWES, JOSEPH M. *Children in Urban Society: Juvenile Delinquency in Nineteenth Century America.* New York: Oxford University Press, 1971.

HEALY, WILLIAM, and BRONNER, AUGUSTA. *Delinquents and Criminals.* New York: Macmillan, 1926.

_____. *The Individual Delinquent, A Textbook of Diagnosis and Prognosis for All Concerned in Understanding Offenders.* Boston: Little, Brown, 1915.

_____. *New Light on Delinquency and Its Treatment.* New Haven, Conn.: Yale University Press, 1936.

_____. *Treatment and What Happened Afterward.* Boston: Judge Baker Guidance Center, 1939.

HEAPS, WILLARD A. *Juvenile Justice.* New York: Seabury, 1974.

HILLIARD, MOZELLE. *Please Rise: Delinquent and Dependent Children, A Community Responsibility.* Milford, Mich.: Mott Media, 1977.

HIRSCHI, TRAVIS. *Causes of Delinquency.* Berkeley: University of California Press, 1969.

HOENIG, GARY. *Reaper: The Inside Story of A Gang Leader.* Indianapolis, Ind.: Bobbs-Merrill, 1975.

HOFFMAN, LOIS, and HOFFMAN, MARTIN, eds. *Review of Child Development Research,* vol. 2. New York: Russell Sage Foundation, 1966.

HOLMES, DONALD. *The Adolescent in Psychotherapy.* Boston: Little Brown, 1964.

HOOTON, ERNEST A. *Crime and Man.* Cambridge, Mass.: Harvard University Press, 1939.

HOPSON, D., JR., et al. *Juvenile Offender and the Law: A Symposium.* Symposia on Law and Society Series. New York: Da Capo, 1979.

HURLEY, TIMOTHY D., (comp.). *Origin of the Illinois Juvenile Court Law: Juvenile Courts and What They Have Accomplished.* 3rd ed. New York: AMS Press, 1979.

HYDE, MARGARET O. *Juvenile Justice and Injustice.* New York: Franklin Watts, 1977.

INTERNATIONAL PENAL AND PRISON COMMISSION. *Children's Courts in the United States.* New York: AMS Press, 1979.

JAMES, HOWARD. *Children in Trouble.* New York: McKay, 1969.

JESNESS, CARL F. *The Jesness Inventory: Development and Validation.* Report No. 29. Sacramento: California Youth Authority, 1962.

JOHNSON, ELMER H. *Crime, Correction and Society.* 3rd ed. Homewood, Ill.: Dorsey, 1968.

JOHNSON R. E. *Juvenile Delinquency and Its Origins.* New York: Cambridge University Press, 1979.

JONES, ERNEST. *Sex in Psychoanalysis.* New York: Basic, 1950.

KAHN, ALFRED J. *A Court for Children: A Study of the New York Children's Court.* New York: Columbia University Press, 1952.

KAMM, ERNEST, et al. *Juvenile Law and Procedure in California.* 2nd ed. Beverly Hills, Calif.: Glencoe, 1971.

KASSEBAUM, GENE. *Delinquency and Social Policy.* Social Policy Series. Englewood Cliffs, N.J.: Prentice-Hall, 1974.

KATKIN, DANIEL, et al. *Delinquency and the Juvenile Justice System.* North Scituate, Mass.: Duxbury, 1976.

KEISER, R. LINCOLN. *The Vice Lords.* New York: Holt, Rinehart and Winston, 1969.

KELLER, OLIVER J., JR., and ALPER, BENEDICT S. *Halfway Houses: Community-Centered Corrections and Treatment.* Lexington, Mass.: Lexington Books, 1970.

KELLY, DELOS H. *Delinquent Behavior: Interactional and Motivational Aspects.* New York: Dekker, 1978.

KLEIN, MALCOLM W., ed. *Juvenile Gang in Context: Theory, Research and Action.* Englewood Cliffs, N.J.: Prentice-Hall, 1967.

————. *The Juvenile Justice System.* Criminal Justice Systems Annuals, vol. 5. Beverly Hills, Calif.: Sage, 1976.

KNIGHT, JAMES M. *The Juvenile Courts Functions and Relevant Theory.* San Francisco: R and E Research Associates, 1978.

KOLB, LAWRENCE C. *Noyes' Modern Clinical Psychiatry.* Philadelphia: Saunders, 1968.

KONOPKA, GISELA. *The Adolescent Girl in Conflict.* Englewood Cliffs, N.J.: Prentice-Hall, 1966.

————. *Young Girls: A Portrait of Adolescence.* Englewood Cliffs, N.J.: Prentice-Hall, 1976.

KORNHAUSER, RUTH R. *Social Sources of Delinquency: An Appraisal of Analytic Models.* Chicago: University of Chicago Press, 1978.

KRISBERG, BARRY, and AUSTIN, JAMES, eds. *The Children of Ishmael: Critical Perspectives on Juvenile Delinquency.* Palo Alto, Calif.: Mayfield, 1978.

KVARACEUS, WILLIAM C. *Juvenile Delinquency and the Schools.* New York: Harcourt Brace Jovanovich, 1945.

————, and MILLER, WALTER B. *Delinquent Behavior.* Westport, Conn.: Greenwood, 1959.

LANDER, BERNARD. *Towards an Understanding of Juvenile Delinquency.* New York: Columbia University Press, 1954.

LAW ENFORCEMENT ASSISTANCE ADMINISTRATION. *Children in Custody: Advance Report on the Juvenile and Correctional Facility Census of 1972–73.* Washington, D.C.: U.S. Government Printing Office, 1975.

————. *Children in Custody: A Report on the Juvenile Detention and Correctional Facility Census of 1971.* Washington, D.C.: U.S. Government Printing Office, 1974.

————. *Crimes and Victims: A Report on the Dayton–San Jose Pilot Survey of Victimization.* Washington, D.C.: U.S. Government Printing Office, 1974.

————. *Criminal Victimization in Five Major Cities.* Washington, D.C.: U.S. Government Printing Office, 1975.

_____. *Criminal Victimization in Thirteen American Cities.* Washington, D.C.: U.S. Government Printing Office, 1975.

_____. *National Jail Census.* Washington, D.C.: U.S. Government Printing Office, 1971.

_____. *Sourcebook of Criminal Justice Statistics, 1974.* Washington, D.C.: U.S. Government Printing Office, 1975.

LEMERT, EDWIN M. *Human Deviance, Social Problems and Social Control.* Englewood Cliffs, N.J.: Prentice-Hall, 1967.

_____. *Instead of the Court.* Rockville, Md.: National Institute of Mental Health, 1971.

_____. *Social Action and Legal Change: Revolution in the Juvenile Court.* Chicago: Aldine, 1970.

_____. *Social Pathology.* New York: McGraw-Hill, 1951.

LERMAN, PAUL. *Community Treatment and Social Control: A Critical Analysis of Juvenile Correctional Policy.* Studies in Crime and Justice. Chicago: University of Chicago Press, 1977.

_____, ed. *Delinquency and Social Policy.* New York: Praeger, 1970.

LEVIN, MARK M., and SARRI, ROSEMARY C. *Juvenile Delinquency: A Comparative Analysis of Legal Codes in the United States.* Ann Arbor, Mich.: National Assessment of Juvenile Corrections, 1974.

LEVINE, PHYLLIS. *Delinquency Proneness: A Comparison of Delinquent Tendencies in Minors Under Court Supervision.* San Francisco: R and E Research Associates, 1978.

LEWIN, KURT. *Field Theory in Social Science.* New York: Harper & Row, 1951.

LEWIS, DOROTHY O., and BALLA, DAVID A. *Delinquency and Psychopathology.* New York: Grune & Stratton, 1976.

LINDSEY, BEN B., and BOROUGH, RUBE. *The Dangerous Life.* Metropolitan America Series. New York: Arno, 1974.

_____, and O'HIGGINS, HARVEY J. *The Beast.* Americana Library Series. Seattle: University of Washington Press, 1970.

LOTH, DAVID. *Crime in the Suburbs.* New York: Morrow, 1967.

LUDWIG, FREDERICK J. *Youth and the Law: Handbook on Law Affecting Youth.* New York: Foundation Press, 1955.

MAESTRO, MARCELLO. *Voltaire and Beccaria as Reformers of Criminal Law.* New York: Columbia University Press, 1942.

MALEWSKI, HANNA, and PEYRE, VINCENT. *Juvenile Delinquency and Development: A Cross-National Survey.* Research Papers in the Social Sciences. Beverly Hills, Calif.: Sage, 1976.

MANNHEIM, HERMANN, ed. *Pioneers in Criminology.* London: Routledge & Kegan Paul, 1960.

MARTIN, JOHN M. *Toward a Political Definition of Delinquency.* Youth

Development and Delinquency Prevention Administration. Washington, D.C.: U.S Government Printing Office, 1970.

————, and FITZPATRICK, JOSEPH P. *Delinquent Behavior: A Redefinition of the Problem.* Philadelphia: Philadelphia Book, 1965.

MARX, KARL. *Das Kapital.* New York: Modern Library, 1936.

MATZA, DAVID. *Delinquency and Drift.* New York: Wiley, 1964.

MAYHEW, HENRY. *London Labor and the London Poor.* London: Routledge & Kegan Paul, 1951.

MAYS, JOHN B. *Growing up in the City: A Study of Juvenile Delinquency in an Urban Neighborhood.* Liverpool: Liverpool University Press, 1964.

McCAGHY, CHARLES H. *Deviant Behavior: Crime, Conflict and Interest Groups.* New York: Macmillan, 1976.

McCORD, WILLIAM, et al. *Origins of Crime.* New York: Columbia University Press, 1959.

McCREEDY, KENNETH R. *Juvenile Justice: System and Procedures.* Albany, N.Y.: Delmar, 1975.

McDONALD, LYNN. *Social Class and Delinquency.* Hamden, Conn.: Shoe String, 1969.

McEWEN, CARIG A. *Designing Correctional Organizations for Youth: Dilemmas of Subcultural Development.* Cambridge, Mass.: Ballinger, 1978.

McPARTLAND, JAMES M., and McDILL, EDWARD L., eds. *Violence in Schools: Perspectives, Programs and Positions.* Lexington, Mass.: Lexington Books, 1977.

MENNEL, ROBERT M. *Thorns and Thistles: Juvenile Delinquents in the United States, 1825–1940.* Hanover, N.H.: University Press of New England, 1973.

MERRILL, MAUDE A. *Problems of Child Delinquency.* Boston: Houghton Mifflin, 1947.

MERTON, ROBERT. *Social Theory and Social Structure.* 2nd ed. New York: Free Press, 1968.

MORAN, MICHAEL. *Standards Relating to Appeals and Collateral Review.* Juvenile Justice Standards Project Series. Cambridge, Mass.: Ballinger, 1977.

MORRIS, TERENCE. *The Criminal Area.* London: Routledge & Kegan Paul, 1958.

MUELLER, GERHARD O., et al. *Delinquency and Puberty: Examination of a Juvenile Delinquency Fad.* New York University Criminal Law Education and Research Center Monograph No 5. South Hackensack, N.J.: Fred B. Rothman, 1971.

MUELLER, JOHN H., et al. *Statistical Reasoning in Sociology.* 2nd ed. Boston: Houghton Mifflin, 1970.

NATIONAL ADVISORY COMMISSION ON CRIMINAL JUSTICE STANDARDS AND

GOALS. *Corrections*. Washington, D.C.: U.S. Government Printing Office, 1973.

NATIONAL COMMISSION ON MARIHUANA AND DRUG ABUSE. *Directory of Detention Centers in the United States*. New York, 1968.

————. *Guides for Juvenile Court Judges on News Media Relations*. New York, 1957.

————. *Marihuana: A Signal of Misunderstanding*. Technical Papers of the First Report of the National Commission, Appendix, vol. 2. New York, 1972.

————. *Model Rules for Juvenile Courts*. New York, 1969.

————. *Standard Family Court Act*. New York, 1959.

————. *Standard Juvenile Court Act*. 6th ed. New York, 1959.

————. *Standards and Guides for Detention of Children and Youth*. 2nd ed. New York, 1961.

NATIONAL PROBATION AND PAROLE ASSOCIATION. *Guides for Juvenile Court Judges*. New York, 1957.

————. *Detention Practice: Significant Developments in the Detention of Children and Youth*. Reprinted by the National Council on Crime and Delinquency. New York, 1967.

NYE, F. IVAN. *Family Relationships and Delinquent Behavior*. New York: Wiley, 1958.

NYQUIST, OLA. *Juvenile Justice*. Cambridge Studies in Criminology, vol. 12. Westport, Conn.: Greenwood, 1975.

OFFER, DANIEL, et al. *The Psychological World of the Juvenile Delinquent*. New York: Basic, 1978.

PARK, ROBERT E., et al. *The City*. Chicago: University of Chicago Press, 1925.

PARKER, HOWARD J. *View from the Boys: A Sociology of Downtown Adolescents*. People, Plans and Problems Series. North Pomfret, Vt.: David & Charles, 1974.

PARKER, T., and ALLERTON, R. *The Courage of His Convictions*. London: Hutchinson, 1962.

PARSLOE, PHYLLIDA. *Juvenile Justice in Britain and the United States: The Balance of Need and Rights*. Library of Social Work. Boston: Routledge & Kegan Paul, 1978.

PEREZ, JOSEPH F. *Family Roots of Adolescent Delinquency*. New York: Van Nostrand Reinhold, 1978.

PHELPS, THOMAS R. *Juvenile Delinquency: A Contemporary View*. Pacific Palisades, Calif.: Goodyear, 1976.

PHILLIPSON, MICHAEL. *Sociological Aspects of Crime and Delinquency*. London: Routledge & Kegan Paul, 1971.

————. *Undertanding Crime and Delinquency: A Sociological Introduction*. Chicago: Aldine, 1974.

PICKETT, ROBERT S. *House of Refuge: Origins of Juvenile Reform in New York State*. Syracuse: Syracuse University Press, 1969.

PLATT, ANTHONY M. *The Child Savers: The Invention of Delinquency.* Chicago: University of Chicago Press, 1969.

POLIER, JUSTINE W. *Everyone's Children, Nobody's Child: A Judge Looks at Underprivileged Children in the United States*. Children and Youth Series. New York: Arno, 1974.

POLK, KENNETH, and SCHAFER, WALTER, eds. *Schools and Delinquency.* Englewood Cliffs, N.J.: Prentice-Hall, 1972.

POLSKY, HOWARD W. *Cottage Six: Social System of Delinquent Boys in Residential Treatment*. Huntington, N.Y.: R. E. Krieger, 1977.

————, et al. *Dynamics of Residential Treatment: A Social System Analysis*. Chapel Hill: University of North Carolina Press, 1968.

POLSKY, NED. *Hustlers, Beats and Others*. Chicago: Aldine, 1967.

PRESIDENT'S COMMISSION ON LAW ENFORCEMENT AND ADMINISTRATION OF JUSTICE. *The Challenge of Crime in a Free Society*. Washington, D.C.: U.S. Government Printing Office, 1967.

————. *Task Force Report: Juvenile Delinquency and Youth Crime.* Washington, D.C.: U.S. Government Printing Office, 1967.

PRIESTLY, PHILIP, et al. *Justice for Juveniles: The Nineteen Hundred Sixty-nine Children and Young Persons Act—A Case for Reform?* London: Routledge & Kegan Paul, 1978.

PUBLIC HEALTH SERVICE; SURGEON GENERAL'S SCIENTIFIC ADVISORY COMMITTEE ON TELEVISION AND SOCIAL BEHAVIOR. *Television and Growing Up: The Impact of Televised Violence*. Washington, D.C.: U.S. Government Printing Office, 1972.

————. *Television and Social Behavior*. 5 vols. Washington, D.C.: U.S. Government Printing Office, 1972.

QUAY, HEBERT C., ed. *Juvenile Delinquency*. New York: Van Nostrand, 1965.

QUINNEY, RICHARD. *Criminal Justice in America*. Boston: Little, Brown, 1974.

————. *The Social Reality of Crime*. Boston: Little, Brown, 1970.

RECKLESS, WALTER. *The Crime Problem*. 4th ed. Englewood Cliffs, N.J.: Prentice-Hall, 1967.

————, and DINITZ, SIMON. *The Prevention of Juvenile Delinquency: An Experiment*. Columbus, Ohio: Ohio State University Press, 1972.

REDL, FRIZ, and WINEMAN, DAVID. *Aggressive Child*. New York: Free Press, 1957.

————. *Children Who Hate: The Disorganization and Breakdown of Behavior Controls*. New York: Free Press, 1965.

REED, JOHN P., and BAALI, FAUD. *Faces of Delinquency*. Englewood Cliffs, N.J.: Prentice-Hall, 1972.

REID, SUE TITUS. *Crime and Criminology.* New York: Holt, Rinehart and Winston, 1976.

REIFEN, DAVID. *The Juvenile Court in a Changing Society: Young Offenders in Israel.* Philadelphia: University of Pennsylvania Press, 1973.

RICHARDS, PAMELA, and BERK, RICHARD A. *Crime as Play: Delinquency in a Middle Class Suburb.* Cambridge. Mass.: Ballinger, 1978.

RIEKES, LINDA, and ACKERLY, SALLY M. *Juvenile Problems and Law.* Law in Action Series. St. Paul, Minn.: West, 1975.

RIGGS, JOHN E., et al. *Interpersonal Maturity Level Classification: Juvenile.* C. T. P. Research Report, No. 4, Sacramento: California Youth Authority, 1964.

RILEY, MATILDA WHITE. *Sociological Research.* New York: Harcourt Brace Jovanovich, 1963

ROBISON, SOPHIA. *Can Delinquency Be Measured?* Millwood, N.Y.: Kraus Reprint, 1973.

ROSENBERG, BERNARD, et al. *Mass Society in Crisis.* New York: Macmillan, 1964.

————, and SILVERSTEIN, HARRY. *Varieties of Delinquent Experience.* New York: Wiley, 1969.

ROSENHEIM, MARGARET K., ed. *Justice for the Child: The Juvenile Court in Transition.* Midway Reprint Series. Chicago: University of Chicago Press, 1977.

————. *Pursuing Justice for the Child.* Studies in Crime and Justice. Chicago: University of Chicago Press, 1978.

ROSENQUIST, CARL M., and MEGARGEE, EDWIN I. *Delinquency in Three Cultures.* Hogg Foundation Research Series. Austin: University of Texas Press, 1969.

ROUCEK, JOSEPH, ed. *Juvenile Delinquency.* New York: Philosophical Library, 1958.

RUBENFELD, SEYMOUR. *Family of Outcasts.* New York: Free Press, 1965.

RUBIN, SOL. *Crime and Juvenile Delinquency.* 3rd ed. Dobbs Ferry, N.Y.: Oceana, 1970.

————. *Law of Juvenile Justice: With a New Model Juvenile Court Act.* Legal Almanac Series No. 22. Dobbs Ferry, N.Y.: Oceana, 1976.

RUBIN, H. TED. *Juvenile Justice Policy, Practice and Law.* Pacific Palisades, Calif.: Goodyear, 1979.

————. *Standards Relating to Court Organization and Administration.* Juvenile Justice Standards Project Series. Cambridge, Mass.: Ballinger, 1977.

RUTHERFORD, ANDREW, and COHEN, FRED. *Standards Relating to Corrections Administration.* Cambridge, Mass.: Ballinger, 1977.

RYERSON, ELLEN. *The Best-Laid Plans: America's Juvenile Court Experiment.* New York: Hill & Wang, 1978.

SAGARIN, EDWARD. *Deviants and Deviance.* New York: Praeger, 1975.

SALISBURY, HARRISON E. *Reaching the Fighting Gang.* New York: Youth Board, 1960.

—————. *The Shook-up Generation.* Greenwich, Conn.: Fawcett World Library, 1958.

SANDER, WILLIAM. *Juvenile Delinquency.* New York: Praeger, 1976.

SANDERS, WILEY B. *Juvenile Offenders for a Thousand Years.* Chapel Hill: University of North Carolina Press, 1970.

SANDHU, HARJIT. *Juvenile Delinquency—Causes, Control and Prevention.* New York: McGraw-Hill, 1977.

SCHAFER, STEPHEN. *Theories in Criminology.* New York: Random House, 1969.

—————, and KNUDTEN, RICHARD D. *Juvenile Delinquency: An Introduction.* New York: Random House, 1970.

SCHASRE, ROBERT, and WALLACH, JO. *Readings in Delinquency and Treatment.* Los Angeles: University of Southern California, Youth Studies Center, 1965.

SCHLOSSMAN, STEVEN L. *Love and the American Delinquent: Theory and Practice of "Progressive" Juvenile Justice.* Chicago: University of Chicago Press, 1977.

SCHMITT, RAYMOND L. *The Reference Other Orientation: An Extension of the Reference Group Concept.* Carbondale, Ill.: Southern Illinois University Press, 1972.

SCHULMAN, HARRY M. *Juvenile Delinquency in American Society.* New York: Harper & Row, 1961.

—————. *A Study of Problem Boys and Their Brothers.* Albany, N.Y.: State Crime Commission, 1929.

SCHUR, EDWIN. *Crime Without Victims.* Englewood Cliffs, N.J.: Prentice-Hall, 1965.

—————. *Labeling Deviant Behavior.* New York: Harper & Row, 1971.

—————. *Radical Non-Intervention: Re-Thinking the Delinquency Problem.* Englewood Cliffs, N.J.: Prentice-Hall, 1973.

SCHWITZGEBEL, RALPH. *Streetcorner Research.* Cambridge, Mass.: Harvard University Press, 1965.

SELLIN, THORSTEN, and WOLFGANG, MARVIN E., eds. *Delinquency: Selected Studies.* New York: Wiley, 1969.

—————. *The Measurement of Delinquency.* New York: Wiley, 1964.

SELLTIZ, CLAIRE, et al. *Research Methods in Social Relations.* New York: Holt, Rinehart and Winston, 1959.

SHAW, CLIFFORD R. *The Jackroller: A Delinquent Boy's Own Story.* Chicago: University of Chicago Press, 1930.

—————. *Natural History of a Delinquent Career.* Westport, Conn.: Greenwood, 1968.

————, et al. *Brothers in Crime*. Chicago: University of Chicago Press, 1967.

————, and McKAY, HENRY. *Juvenile Delinquency and Urban Areas*. Chicago: University of Chicago Press, 1942.

————. *Report on the Causes of Crime*, vol. 2, no. 13. Washington, D.C.: U.S. Government Printing Office, 1931.

SHELDON, WILLIAM H. *Varieties of Delinquent Youth*. New York: Harper & Row, 1949.

————. *Varieties of Temperament*. New York: Harper & Row, 1942.

————, et al. *Varieties of Human Physique*. New York: Harper & Row, 1940.

SHORT, JAMES F., JR., ed. *Delinquency, Crime, and Society*. Chicago: University of Chicago Press, 1978.

————. *Gang Delinquency and Delinquent Subcultures*. New York: Harper & Row, 1968.

————, and STRODBECK, FRED L. *Group Process and Gang Delinquency*. Chicago: University of Chicago Press, 1965.

SIMON, JULIAN L. *Basic Research Methods in Social Science*. New York: Random House, 1969.

SIMONSEN, CLIFFORD E., and GORDON, MARSHALL S. *Juvenile Justice in America*. Beverly Hills, Calif.: Glencoe, 1979.

SIMPSON, GEORGE. *Emile Durkheim: Selections from His Work*. New York: Crowell, 1963.

SINGER, LINDA R. *Standards Relating to Dispositions*. Juvenile Justice Standards Project Series. Cambridge, Mass.: Ballinger, 1977.

SJOBERG, GIDEON, ed. *Politics and Social Research*. Cambridge, Mass.: Schenkman, 1967.

————, and NETT, ROGER. *A Methodology for Social Research*. New York: Harper & Row, 1968

SLAVSON, S. R. *Reclaiming the Delinquent*. New York: Free Press, 1965.

SNEDECOR, GEORGE W., and COCHRAN, WILLIAM G. *Statistical Methods*. 6th ed. Ames: Iowa State University Press, 1967.

SOCIAL, SCIENCE AND SOCIOLOGICAL RESOURCES. *Delinquency, Deviancy and Youthood Conflicts*. New York: Social Science and Sociological Resources, 1976.

SORRENTINO, ANTHONY. *Organizing Against Crime: Redeveloping the Neighborhood*. New York: Human Sciences, 1977.

SOWER, CHRISTOPHER, et al. *Community Involvement*. New York: Free Press, 1957.

SPERGEL, IRVING. *Racketville, Slumtown and Haulberg*. Chicago: University of Chicago Press, 1964.

STAPLETON, W. VAUGHAN, and TEITELBAUM, LEE E. *In Defense of Youth: A*

Study of the Role of Counsel in American Juvenile Courts. New York: Russell Sage Foundation, 1972.

STERNE, RICHARD S. *Delinquent Conduct and Broken Homes.* New Haven, Conn.: College and University Press, 1964.

STEWART, V. LORNE, ed. *The Changing Faces of Juvenile Justice.* New York: New York University Press, 1978.

STINCHCOMBE, ARTHUR L. *Constructing Social Theories.* New York: Harcourt Brace Jovanovich, 1968.

STOTT, D. H. *Saving Children from Delinquency.* New York: Philosophical Library, 1954.

STRANG, RUTH. *Juvenile Delinquency and the Schools.* Chicago: University of Chicago Press, 1948.

STRASBURG, PAUL A. *Violent Delinquents.* New York: Monarch, 1978.

STRATTON, JOHN R., and TERRY, ROBERT M. *Prevention of Delinquency: Problems.* New York: Macmillan, 1968.

STREET, DAVID, et al. *Organization for Treatment.* New York: Free Press, 1966.

STREIB, VICTOR L. *Juvenile Justice in America.* National University Publications Multi-Disciplinary Studies in Law. Port Washington, N.Y.: Kennikat, 1978.

SUSSMAN, FREDERICK B., and BAUM, FREDERICK S. *Law of Juvenile Delinquency.* Dobbs Ferry, N.Y.: Oceana, 1968.

SUTHERLAND, EDWIN. *Principles of Criminology.* 4th ed. Philadelphia: Lippincott, 1947.

————, and CRESSEY, DONALD. *Criminology.* 8th ed. Philadelphia: Lippincott, 1970.

SZUREK, S. A. *The Antisocial Child.* Palo Alto, Calif.: Behavior Books, 1969.

TAFT, DONALD. *Criminology.* 3rd ed. New York: Macmillan, 1956.

————, and ENGLAND, RALPH, JR. *Criminology.* 4th ed. New York: Macmillan, 1964.

TANNENBAUM, FRANK. *Crime and the Community.* New York: McGraw-Hill, 1951.

TAPPAN, PAUL W. *Comparative Survey of Juvenile Delinquency, Part I: North America.* New York: United Nations, 1958.

————. *Crime, Justice and Correction.* New York: McGraw-Hill, 1960.

————. *Juvenile Delinquency.* New York: McGraw-Hill, 1949.

TARDE, GABRIEL. *The Laws of Imitation.* New York: Holt, Rinehart and Winston, 1903.

————. *On Communication and Social Influence.* Chicago: University of Chicago Press, 1969.

————. *Penal Philosophy.* Boston: Little, Brown, 1912.

TEITELBAUM, LEE E., and GOUGH, AIDAN, eds. *Beyond Control: Status Offenders in the Juvenile Court.* Cambridge, Mass.: Ballinger, 1977.

THOMAS, WILLIAM I., and THOMAS, DOROTHY S. *Child in America, Behavior Problems & Programs.* Social Welfare Series. Norwood, N.J.: Walter J. Johnson, 1979.

THORP, RONALD, and WETZEL, RALPH. *Behavior Modification in the Natural Environment.* New York: Academic, 1969.

THRASHER, FREDERIC M. *The Gang.* Chicago: University of Chicago Press, 1963.

TRASLER, GORDON. *The Explanation of Criminality.* London: Routledge & Kegan Paul, 1962.

TROJANOWICZ, ROBERT C. *Juvenile Delinquency: Concepts and Control.* Englewood Cliffs, N.J.: Prentice-Hall, 1973.

TURNER, KENNETH A. *Juvenile Justice: Juvenile Court Problems, Procedures and Practices in Tennessee.* Charlottesville, Va.: Michie, 1969.

TUTT, NORMAN. *Care or Custody: Community Homes and the Treatment of Delinquency.* New York: Agathon, 1975.

TWENTIETH CENTURY FUND. *Confronting Youth Crime: Report of the Twentieth Century Fund Task Force of Sentencing Policy Toward Young Offenders.* New York: Holmes and Meier, 1978.

TYLER, GUS, ed. *Organized Crime in America: A Book of Readings.* Ann Arbor: University of Michigan Press, 1962.

UNITED NATIONS, BUREAU OF SOCIAL AFFAIRS, DEPARTMENT OF ECONOMIC AND SOCIAL AFFAIRS. *The Prevention of Juvenile Delinquency in Selected European Countries.* New York: Columbia University Press, 1955.

UNITED NATIONS, DIVISION OF SOCIAL WELFARE, DEPARTMENT OF SOCIAL AFFAIRS. *Comparative Survey on Juvenile Delinquency: Asia and the Far East.* New York: Columbia University Press, 1953.

UNITED NATIONS, INTERNATIONAL LABOR ORGANIZATION, THIRD UNITED NATIONS CONGRESS ON THE PREVENTION OF CRIME AND THE TREATMENT OF OFFENDERS. *The Role of Vocational Guidance, Training, Employment Opportunity and Work in Youth Adjustment and the Prevention of Juvenile Delinquency.* New York, 1965.

―――. *Special Prevention and Treatment Measures for Young Adults.* New York, 1965.

UNITED STATES CHILDREN'S BUREAU. *Standards for Specialized Courts Dealing with Children.* Westport, Conn.: Greenwood, 1978.

U.S. CONGRESS—SENATE COMMITTEE ON THE JUDICIARY. *Juvenile Delinquency: National, Federal and Youth-Serving Agencies.* Westport, Conn.: Greenwood, 1968.

―――. *Juvenile Delinquency, Youth Employment.* Westport, Conn.: Greenwood, 1968.

VAN WATERS, MIRIAM. *Youth in Conflict.* New York: AMS Press, 1970.

VAZ, EDMUND. *Middle Class Juvenile Delinquency.* New York: Harper & Row, 1967.

VEDDER, CLYDE B. *Juvenile Offenders.* Springfield, Ill.: Charles C Thomas, 1979.

VIRTUE, MAXINE B. *Family Cases in Court: Four Case Studies Dealing with Judicial Administration.* Durham, N.C.: Duke University Press, 1956.

VOLD, GEORGE. *Theoretical Criminology.* New York: Oxford University Press, 1958.

WADSWORTH, MICHAEL. *The Roots of Delinquency: Infancy, Adolescence and Crime.* New York: Barnes & Noble, 1979.

WALLENSTEIN, NEHEMIAH. *Character and Personality of Children from Broken Homes.* New York: AMS Press, 1979.

WATTENBERG, WILLIAM W., ed. *Social Deviancy Among Youth.* Chicago: University of Chicago Press, 1966.

WENK, ERNST A., ed. *Delinquency Prevention and the Schools: Emerging Perspectives.* Beverly Hills, Calif.: Sage, 1976.

WEST, DONALD J. *Present Conduct and Future Delinquency: An Inquiry into Behavior Problems of Primary Schoolboys.* New York: International Universities Press, 1969.

————. *Young Offenders.* New York: International Universities Press, 1967.

WHEELER, GERALD R. *Counterdeterrence: A Report on Juvenile Sentencing and Effects of Prisonization.* Chicago: Nelson-Hall, 1978.

WHEELER, STANTON, and COTTRELL, LEONARD, JR. *Juvenile Delinquency: Its Prevention and Control.* New York: Russell Sage Foundation, 1966.

WHINERY, LEO H., et al. *Predictive Sentencing: An Empirical Evaluation.* Lexington, Mass.: Lexington Books, 1976.

WHITE, MORTON, and WHITE, LUCIA. *The Intellectual Versus the City.* Cambridge, Mass.: Harvard University Press, 1962.

WHITEBREAD, CHARLES. *Standards Relating to Transfer Between Courts.* Juvenile Justice Standards Project Series. Cambridge, Mass.: Ballinger, 1977.

WHYTE, WILLIAM F. *Street Corner Society.* Chicago: University of Chicago Press, 1955.

WICKMAN, PAUL M., and WHITTEN, PHILIP. *Readings in Criminology.* Lexington, Mass.: Heath, 1978.

WIERS, PAUL. *Economic Factors in Michigan Delinquency.* New York: Columbia University Press, 1944.

WILENSKY, HAROLD L., and LEBEAUX, CHARLES N. *Industrial Society and Social Welfare.* New York: Russell Sage Foundation, 1958.

WILLIAMS, L. WEINBERG. *Our Runaway.* Valley Forge, Pa.: Judson, 1979.

WINES, E. C. *The State Prisons and Child-saving Institutions in the Civilized World.* Montclair, N.J.: Patterson Smith, 1968.

WINSLOW, ROBERT W. *Juvenile Delinquency in a Free Society.* 3rd ed. Belmont, Calif.: Dickenson, 1976.

WOLFGANG, MARVIN E., et al. *The Sociology of Crime and Delinquency*. 2nd ed. New York: Wiley, 1970.

WOODEN, KENNETH. *Weeping in the Playtime of Others: The Plight of Incarcerated Children*. New York: McGraw-Hill, 1976.

WRIGHT, J., and JAMES, R. *A Behavioral Approach to Preventing Delinquency*. Springfield, Ill.: Charles C Thomas, 1974.

YABLONSKI, LEWIS. *The Tunnel Back*. Synanon, N.Y.: Macmillan, 1965.

————. *The Violent Gang*. Baltimore: Penguin, 1966.

ZETTERBERG, HANS. *On Theory and Verification in Sociology*. Totowa, N.J.: Bedminster, 1965.